UNDER *the* Banyan TREE

ABDALLAH M. ISA

ISBN: 978-1-09830-008-1 (print)

ISBN: 978-1-09830-009-8 (ebook)

DEDICATION

This biography is dedicated to the love of my life, my granddaughter Lilli Ryann Reep, who was born with Down syndrome, to her sister Halle Isabella Reep and cousins Deena Summer Hodzic, Amar Harrison Hodzic, Kaden Nicolas Krishna and Cameron Lucas Krishna who have given me the pleasure, satisfaction and appreciation of a fulfilled life dream.

To the memory of my parents who died before I attained my second birthday and to my late sisters: Nazha, Fatima and Amina who raised me to become the man I am.

1940-1948
MY BIRTHPLACE

I WAS BORN IN AL-BASSA (A VILLAGE IN MIDDLE EASTERN TERMINOL-ogy and a town in American classification) in northern Galilee, Palestine with no more than 4000 inhabitants at the time of the 1948 catastrophe. It was under the administrative jurisdiction of the Sub-district of the city of Acre. The town had a unique location: mountains on the north separating Lebanon from Palestine, hills on the east, home to three Jewish settlements, sprawling groves of olive trees on the south and arable lands planted with different types of vegetables and grains on the west. The town is one mile east of the Mediterranean Sea. Citrus groves, primarily oranges, lemons and tangerines covered vast areas on the shores of the Mediterranean Sea, where friends and I used to walk to the Mediterranean Sea to have a good swim. In addition, we used to swim in *al-Sadd* (a dam of naturally occurring collection of fresh water springs). *Al-Sadd* waters used to provide irrigation to the citrus groves in its vicinity as well as swimming.

Al-Bassa is also described as the 'Bride of Galilee' for many good reasons: It was the educational center for the villages and towns of Galilee with several educational institutions, including one that had boarding facilities. Students from neighboring villages and towns came to have an education at al-Bassa schools. Another reason is its location and its proximity to the Mediterranean Sea. In Spring, its fields show their beauty with the blooms of almond trees, citrus trees and of different wild flowers. Poppies exhibited their beauty in an array of colors, red, white, blue, yellow and purple.

The town had neither electricity nor running water. Kerosene lanterns were the only means of lighting. Cooking and heating of water for bathing and washing clothes done on the "Primus", a little appliance that runs on kerosene. Should the primus or kerosene be unavailable, heat for cooking, boiling water for bathing and washing clothes was on makeshift wood burning stoves.

The Primus head has a tiny pinpoint hole in its center of the head through which the kerosene passes to fill the top of the head. The kerosene-soaked head is, lit with matches or other means. When the kerosene-filled head gets hot, the kerosene in the head, as well as the pumped-in kerosene coming through the pinpoint hole vaporizes to form a mist that burns and produces the heat required for cooking and heating of water.

(This is the Primus, the little kerosene gadget that was the only means used for cooking and heating water in the absence of electricity, coal or wood)

The source of water for drinking, washing clothes and bathing, was from a well that is about five hundred yards from our house. Young women went to the well to fill their five-gallon containers and carrying the containers, filled with water on their heads and head home. Depending on the amount of water needed, these young women may make more than one daily trip to the well! My sister, Fatima, went to the well to fill the containers with water several times a day. She carried the 5-gallon can or pottery jar, full of water, on her head to bring it for use by the master, uncle Mohamad's second wife and her family. As there was no electricity and no washing machines in existence, washing of clothes was always done by hand. Because of the scarcity of water, washing of clothes was done once a month. For the same reason people used to bathe once a week!

A water distribution network was, installed in al-Bassa in 1946. Water dispensing centers, were installed at several neighborhoods at strategic locations to serve as a source of water for drinking and other purposes in the town. The source of water came from a well that was, dug and pumps were installed to feed the distribution centers. The well's location was less than a mile west of the town. Water was piped into each of the distribution centers through a pipeline that connected the well to the distribution centers. People brought their jars and cans to these centers, filled them up and brought them back home. This was a reprieve for my sister Fatima, instead of her going to the well that was five hundred yards away, to fill up the cans and jars as ordered by uncle Mohamad's wife, the distribution center was only ten yards away from uncle Mohamad's house.

The weather in al-Bassa is subtropical in nature. It is very warm and humid during the summer months because of the physical location of the town. It is surrounded by mountains and hills on the north and east sides, olive groves on the south side, the Mediterranean Sea and citrus groves on the west side. Since there was no electricity or refrigeration in the town, meals were cooked daily in amounts enough to feed the whole family for that day. Cooking meals for several days was not an option, as the food will spoil due to the absence of any means of its preservation. Leftovers were, kept in a hanging flat rimless basket attached to a hook in the ceiling to avoid having mice, rats or cockroaches from reaching it. Of course, that did not prevent flies or other flying insects to use the food for their dinner.

Drinking water was, kept in pottery pitchers and placed on the lower window frame. The porosity of pottery allows water to saturate the body of the pitcher by the process of osmosis. Because of the heat in the area surrounding the pitcher, evaporation of water from its outer walls occurs, thus rendering the water in the pitcher to become a little cooler to drink. The fact that pottery absorbs little or no heat from the surrounding environment makes the pottery pitcher ideal to keep the water a little cooler to drink. When glass pitchers, were introduced as an alternative to pottery pitchers, and because heat waves are transmitted through glass and no osmotic effect taking place, as opposed to the pottery pitcher, water in the glass pitcher does not cool off at all but may get a little warmer. Pottery pitchers were, placed by the window so that the humidity on the walls of the pitcher evaporates, thus enhancing the osmotic effect, which in turn renders the water in the pitcher a little cooler.

Pottery pitchers were still in use all over the Middle East until the late 1950s and early 1960s after refrigerators and freezers became available. Glass pitchers replaced the pottery ones and glass bottles filled with water were placed in the refrigerator to provide cold drinking water. The introduction of refrigeration had a great impact on the ability of having cold drinking water, and to keep food from spoiling for at least a week under refrigeration conditions. Instead of cooking meals for every day consumption, cooking for a week at a time, was done and the food saved in the refrigerator.

The luxury of having refrigerators, however, was not universal as only the very well- to-do were able to own such appliances. The bulk of the country, especially in south Lebanon where people, with limited means had no access to these luxuries. Even for those who were able to purchase these electrical appliances could not use them, as there was no electricity to run them. Well, my sisters and I, living in Beirut did not have the financial means to purchase a refrigerator, let alone a freezer. We still had to rely on the pottery pitcher for drinking water. Food was cooked every day. Of course, that was time consuming, but time was the only commodity we had available.

(Pottery pitcher was, used as a ready-to-use drinking water container)

The streets in al-Bassa, were laid with beautiful smooth rectangular stone tiles. For transportation purposes in the town, donkeys and mules were the main source of transporting people to and from the fields.

There were no privately owned, cars in the town except for one that was used as a taxicab by its owner. However, there was a bus service between the town and the city of Acre, a fifteen-mile journey. Buses were, scheduled to leave every thirty minutes. Since uncle Mohamad was a shareholder in the bus company, his family members were, allowed to ride in the buses any time and as many times as they chose at no charge!

Because there were no other means to transport goods from the field for storage or for processing in the town, the only means of carriage to and from the fields was on the backs of donkeys, mules or camels.

(The streets of al-Bassa were paved with rectangular and irregular shaped smooth stones, but after so many years of neglect and non-existent maintenance that occurred after occupation of the town by the Israelis, the beautiful stones, crumbled and grass grew between these beautiful stones).

The only means of recreation for men in town was through socialization with each other in the coffee houses. There were three such coffee houses in the Moslem and four in the Christian areas of the town. Many a time, Moslem men would go to the Christian coffee houses to have an alcoholic drink, as it was not available in the Moslem part of the town. Occasionally, I have seen Christians come to socialize in the Moslem coffee houses, but heavier traffic in the opposite direction was always the case. Since I had no money to spend, I used to dip into my sister Fatima's piggy bank, get few coins and head to the Christian part of town to have a soft drink. At the soft-drinks joint, in the Christian area, I used to sit crossed-legged on the chair, to give the impression that I am an important person and place my order of the soft drink. It so happened, one day, a fly fell into my soft drink and the owner of the joint offered a replacement at no charge. I said to him, please do not worry about it, discard the drink that has the fly in it and get me a new one. I will pay for the replacement soft drink. I wanted to let the man know that I am 'important', have the financial means and willing to pay for the replacement drink! Of course, that was not my money, but was easy money that I got from my sister's piggy bank without her permission or approval, of course!

Two other recreational events took place in the Moslem part of town that attracted my attention were: camel racing, with participating camels from neighboring villages, participate in the event. The winner of the camel races is, bestowed with the title of the best "Cameleer". The other event was to identify the strongest among the men and who has the most powerful muscle. The competition among young men, was instituted and planned during the fall and winter months when the sugarcane is ripe and available. In that game, the most powerful man is the one who has the muscular power to cut through a large bundle of sugarcanes. That competition involved the use of bundles of long sugarcane sticks that were, held at both ends by two men. The competitors will strike the stack with big knives hoping to cut through all the sticks in the bundle in one hit. The number of sugarcane long sticks was increased gradually, and the previous winners will compete again. Those who fail to cut all the sticks in the bundle with one stroke, were eliminated while the semi-finalists who had succeeded in earlier competitions will now compete against each other with larger numbers of sugarcane sticks in the bundle. The winner who can completely cut through the whole bundle with the largest number of sugar cane sticks is recognized as the winner is, awarded the title of the most powerful man in town. He will also take home his bounty, all the sugar cane sticks he had cut.

Since fruits and vegetables, are seasonal in nature, they were, consumed fresh as there was no means available to store them in a manner that maintained their integrity and freshness. Some vegetables such eggplants, turnips and cauliflower, however, were pickled for use in off-season times.

Items with a longer shelf life, such as wheat products are kept for longer periods without spoiling. *Burgul* (cracked wheat) is one of these items that were prepared and kept for longer periods. To prepare *Burgul* for later use in cooking, the wheat is first boiled, drained and then spread on the roof of houses to dry under the heat of the sun. The boiled and dried wheat is, crushed by the *jaroushi (*crusher*)*, a hand operated crusher. The *jaroushi* consisted of two heavy round stones with holes in the middle. The lower stone immobilized while the upper one is movable. In the middle of the upper wheel sits a hole through which the boiled and dried wheat is introduced. On the side of the upper stone is a handle by which the rotary operation is done. The *jaroushi* could be, operated by one or by two persons. If operated by one person the wheat is, introduced by one hand while the other hand is used to work the rotary motion of the *jaroushi.*

Should two persons perform the operation of the *jaroushi*, one person runs the operation by moving the upper stone in a clockwise motion, while the other person introduces the boiled and dried wheat through the hole in the upper stone.

Different grades of *Burgul* are prepared depending on the kind of dish they are to be used for. The products are then stored, for later use, in jars or in cloth bags as there were no plastic bags in existence at the time.

After finishing crushing the boiled and dried wheat, the upper wheel of the *jaroushi* is removed to clean the lower wheel from any leftovers. After cleaning, the upper wheel put in place by aligning it with the lower wheel.

(This photo depicts husband and wife operating the *jaroushi*.)

Should a need for a finer grade of the *Burgul* (cracked wheat) be needed the crushed wheat is run repeatedly until the desired grade is achieved. To clean the *jaroushi* after use, the upper wheel is removed and any leftover wheat or burgul is removed and the wheel is put back in place.

Al-Bassa was a bastion of religious harmony. Two thirds of the inhabitants belonged to the Christian faith, both catholic and orthodox. There was only one Protestant family in the town. There was one Catholic Church that was in the southeastern part of town and one Orthodox Church in the southwestern part of the town. The Orthodox Church was no more than 100 yards from our house while the Catholic Church was about 300 yards away. The other religious groups in the town, in addition to the Catholic and Orthodox Christians, belonged to the Moslem faith, both Sunni and Shia. The Shi'a were the minority Moslem group that originated from southern Lebanon. They have come to Palestine in search of work and a better life. Many of them had decided to establish residence in the town after they have legally met the immigration requirements set forth by the British mandated government of Palestine.

The labor force in the town, especially during the Olives harvest season consisted primarily of Lebanese employees who came down south to Palestine. On one day during the olive harvest season, I counted 73 Lebanese men and women in uncle Mohamad's house. They were, hired to harvest the olives from uncle Mohamad's property as well as from our own property that was under uncle Mohamad's control. Their job was to harvest the olives, bag them in large canvas bags and load them on the back of donkeys to head to the press or for storage in designated storage places.

Uncle Mohamad owned, a press, which was used to extract the oil from the crushed olives. The olive crusher consisted of two large circular stone wheels with an inch clearance between the two wheels. While the lower wheel is stationary, the upper one is moved by rotary motion. The olive kernels are introduced through a cone-shaped structure sitting on top of the upper grinding wheel. To avoid overheating of the wheels, water is, added along with the olive kernels. The Olives and water introduced through the cone-shaped structure in the middle of the upper wheel and the olives kernels are crushed into a paste without over heating of the wheels. The wheels, measure about one and a half foot in thickness and three yards in diameter. The lower wheel being stationary, the upper wheel is the one that does the moving. The clockwise rotary movement of the upper wheel causes the crushing of the olive kernels. The rotary movement, of the upper wheel is, driven by a mule with the operator sitting on top of the upper wheel. The crushed olives are, pushed out by the centrifugal force caused by the rotary movement of the upper wheel, into a built-in twenty-inch wide and forty-inch deep circular trench erected around the grinding wheels.

The Lebanese workers had their job description well defined. The jobs of male and female workers were, designated based on the difficulty of the chore they do. Men's job was to climb up the tree and beat the branches with long sticks to affect the dislodging of the olive kernels. Women's job was to collect the olive kernels, bag them in large canvas sacks and wait for the men to load the filled-up sacs on the back of donkeys for delivery to a store room or to the press. In case there was no room to store the olives in the press area prior to crushing, the sacs were, emptied and the olives stored in large heaps at home. A huge pile of olives was stored at our house prior to transport to the press to be processed, to extract the oil.

After crushing the olive kernels the paste is shoveled out from the retaining trough and packed into the round double-layered canvas outfits through a hole in the middle. The filled pocket-canvas circular structures are stacked on the press and pressed with a manually operated handle. Olive oil and water coming out of the crushed and pressed olives are drained into a big concrete receptacle dug in the ground with concrete floor and walls. Olive oil being lighter than water floats on top is decanted and stored in large pottery jars. Five-gallon tin cans are also filled with olive oil and readied for shipment to customers worldwide. Nothing was, wasted in the process of oil extraction. The leftover coarse particles of the crushed olives, after extraction of the oil are sent to bakeries for use as a source of fuel.

The workers were, compensated at the following rate: Men received one Palestinian pound (equivalent to 3 dollars at the time) per day. Women on the other hand, were paid one half pound per day each. Men's job being more involved and more dangerous as they had to climb up the tree or use ladders to beat the branches with long sticks so that the olive kernels drop to the ground and then loading the heavy canvas bags filled with olives on the back of donkeys. Women's jobs are less strenuous and less labor intensive than those of the men. Picking the olive kernels and bagging them was not that big of a deal, hence justifying the in inequality of pay between men and women.

In addition to their pay, the workers were provided with housing, three meals and an afternoon snack every day. When the olive harvest season is over the workers pack up and go back home to Lebanon. Additionally, each of these workers received a five-gallon can of olive oil to take home when they leave.

Several of the Lebanese workers opted to stay in Palestine and ultimately became citizens of the country. Many of them have settled in al-Bassa and established roots by purchasing property and building their homes.

Because of the religious harmony among different religious faiths and sects in town, everyone knew everybody else and accepted every person as a 'Bassawi' (a member of al-Bassa community). Although the different religious, groups, lived in separate parts of the town, there were continuous interaction and integration of both the Christian and Moslem communities. There were three butcher shops in town: One Christian, one Sunni and one Shi'a. According to Moslem beliefs that prior to slaughtering of an animal a religious ritual is recited to claim it as *halal* meat. It is not the case with Christian butchers. Meats purchased from Christian butchers, therefore, are not *halal* meats! As a child and every Sunday, I was asked to go to the Christian butcher to purchase meat as instructed by one of the family elders. To me, it was ironic to go to the Christian butcher, with no *halal* meat and who was much farther than the Moslem butcher shops with supposedly *halal* meats that were only few yards away!

As children we were, brought up in a way that did not and should not distinguish a Moslem from a Christian, a Catholic from an Orthodox nor a Sunni from a Shi'a. We Moslems used to celebrate Christian holidays and Christians used to celebrate Moslem holidays. I and other Moslem kids used to go to church to celebrate Christmas and Easter holidays. Christian kids used to come to the mosque to celebrate *Al-Fitr and Al-Adha Eids* Moslem holidays. It was indeed a well-integrated secular community. The only one Mosque in the town that was about fifty yards from our house. The Mosque served the needs of both the Sunni and Shia Moslem communities. There were two churches in town: One that served the Catholic community and the other served the Orthodox community.

As a confirmation of the religious harmony in town, I as a Moslem born to Moslem parents was, baptized in the Orthodox Church. The reason for my baptism was due to a vow my parents had taken upon themselves. They were desperate to have a son to carry the name. They had three daughters and were worried that having no sons, the Isa name will go down with them to the grave. Being a patriarchal male-dominated and controlled society, every father wanted to have a son so that he, not only will carry the family name and keep it alive, but also to take over and care for the property after the father passes on. My parents prayed and turned to God for help through a vow. They pleaded with God by, asking Him through a pledge, to please grant us a son God. When You our God grant us our wish, and we have our son we WILL implement our vow by having him baptized in the Orthodox Church! The reason Baptism was performed at the Orthodox Church and not at the Catholic Church is not known to me. It could have been due to the Orthodox Church was closer to our house than the Catholic Church is and because of the proximity of Orthodox to our house. Because Orthodox Christians lived closer to us than Catholics and having more interaction between the two communities. may explain the choice of the Orthodox Church for my Baptism.

It appeared, as though God had answered my parents' prayers and vow by granting them their son. They had me baptized, in the Orthodox Church as they promised. My baptism took place within few weeks of my arrival to this world. It was performed by Father Wakim, the priest of the Orthodox Church. My godmother at the church was Mrs. Marie Mariyanni who I kept in touch with until she passed on. May God bless her soul as she was, not only a wonderful godmother but was also a great person.

In addition. Al-Bassa, to being secular with complete tolerance between the different religious faiths and between different sects within the same faith, Christians and Moslems looked at each other as brothers and sisters. They would share in the use of the land they owned to plant trees or crops in each other's land. It was not uncommon to have olive trees or other crops owned by Moslems or Christians planted in each other's land. I remember, we had two olive trees, which my parents planted in a land that belonged to a Christian neighbor.

Socially, men and women in the town danced together during weddings and other festivities with no inhibitions whatsoever. One of the most elaborate ceremonies was of weddings in the Moslem part of town. Men and women would hold hands in long rows dancing and chanting, while other women danced while carrying large trays of candy and other sweets on their heads. The dancing and chanting continued until the groom comes out riding his horse and the bride coming out from the opposite direction riding her horse, with her face covered with a white transparent veil. When both horses carrying the bride and the groom come close to each other, the groom lifts the bride's veil and kisses her forehead. This tradition signaled the beginning of the subsequent celebrations that followed. The singing and dancing celebrations lasted until the wee hours of the night. Celebrations normally, depending on the social status of the newlyweds in the town, may last up to one week at a time.

Prior to wedding ceremonies and the preparation of food for the guests, young unmarried girls in the town, would assemble in the groom's family house to make 'angel hair' for use in cooking of rice to feed guests and celebrants during the wedding celebrations. I remember, cousin Adel, uncle Mohamad son's wedding ceremonies. For Adel's wedding to his first cousin, guests were invited from across Palestine and from Lebanon to come and join in the celebrations of the wedding of the two cousins who are members of an elite family in the town. It was the tradition for the guests to bring gifts for the occasion. One of the guests brought ten, 220-pound. bags of rice and another guest brought in sixty heads of sheep. The groom's family is expected to house the out of town guests and feed all the guests that attend the wedding ceremonies.

Weddings and traditions, in the villages and small towns, contrasted with those traditions observed and practiced in the cities. Folks in the city tended to be more conservative where intermingling between the sexes is considered a taboo. Small town and village people, on the other hand, are very liberal in their way of thinking. Social interaction between the sexes in rural and urban societies in the Middle East contrasts with that of the United States, as rural folks tend to be more conservative than city dwellers compared to those in the Middle East. Both men and women in rural Palestine worked together in the field and danced together during weddings and other ceremonies, without any inhibitions as both sexes looked at each other as equals in anything they did. There was one difference, however, between Christians and Moslems in the conservative cities. Christian boys and girls could date in the open while Moslems would date only in secret. This was not the case in the villages and little towns where dating, regardless of religious affiliation was all in the open, but with some restrictions in the Moslem community.

Al-Bassa was an agrarian community whose major products were olives, olive oil, citrus fruits, almonds, wheat, barley, lentils, tobacco and seasonal vegetables such as onions, zucchini, peppers, okra, green beans and eggplants.

Despite being an agrarian community, the al-Bassa people had an open mind especially when it comes to education. Learning and getting an education was, highly revered and sought after by the people of the town. Parents wanted their children to have an education so that they may have a more prosperous future than theirs.

The children were provided with the opportunity to branch out and seek other careers that are different from those of their parents who had no education, otherwise they will be destined to be agricultural workers. It is important to note that al-Bassa, a small town with a population of four thousand was home to several schools. In addition to the government co-ed school, there was a girls' school sponsored and supported by German missionaries. Girls, at that school were, taught the usual courses like science, math, history, geography and of course, bible studies with emphasis on the Protestant version of Christianity. The German Mission occupied a vast area on the southern edge of the town that was close to the main highway connecting the town to other parts of the country.

In addition to the government co-ed elementary school, school for girls only, yet there was another school for boys only. These elementary schools prepared pupils from first grade to the seventh grade. Some of the parents, who could afford sending their children to the city where some schools offered programs leading to the High School diplomas. Others were content with their grammar school graduation and opted to follow their careers in Agriculture.

(This was, the building that housed the girls' school where the German Missionaries were headquartered in al-Bassa)

In addition to the elementary schools in the town, was a*l-Kullia al-Watania* (the National College). The student body consisted of local students as *Al-Kullia al-Watania,* a High school, with boarding facilities. well as others who came from different parts of Palestine. *Al Kullia al Watania* offered the British Matriculation (a high school) diploma that prepared the students to go to Jerusalem and enroll in the elite a*l-Kullia al- Arabia* (the Arab College) or to go to Lebanon to attend college at the *American University of Beirut.*

The curriculum of the German school was based on the German system of education while those of the government and other elementary schools and that of a*l-Kullia al-Watania*, were tailored on the British system of education, as Palestine was under the British mandate since the first World War.

English, a requirement was imposed by the Brits to be the spoken and written second language of the land. English, as a foreign language was, taught in all schools beginning with the fourth grade.

None of the schools at al-Bassa, except that of *al-Kullia Al-Watania,* had a sports program. *Al-Kullia al-Watania* had quite an impressive sports program that included

Soccer, Basketball and Track and Field. At the end of the school year competition in these sports events were, held at the school's vast field. Everybody was, invited to attend the events at no charge. At the end of the school year, pupils in the government schools in al-Bassa and in other villages and towns went to Acre, the sub-district under whose jurisdiction these villages and towns belonged. They used to take part in the competition of the annual sports events.

All villages and towns that were under the jurisdiction of the city of Acre, held their annual sports event in the city's sports field. Competition among different teams from different villages and towns included all organized sports such as soccer, basketball and track and field. There were two competitions testing the coordination and balance of the individual:

1. Standing in a canvas sac and holding the open end of the sac by both hands, the competitor runs while in the bag to reach the finish line. Competitors, who fall while competing and before reaching the finish line are, disqualified and eliminated from the competition.

2. The other competition was, designed to assess the coordination ability of the competitor. This competition involved placing a small potato in a tablespoon, holding the spoon with the potato at its handle between the teeth while running towards the finish line. Should the potato fall off the spoon, the competitor is, disqualified and eliminated from the competition. The winner is the one who reaches the finish line with the potato still is in the spoon.

Al-Bassa community, as a staunch believer in education, it also encouraged exposure of children to cultural activities such as, Boys Scouts, acting and poetry clubs. I was involved in two of such acting activities in the town. Fees for attending any the cultural activities were not in the form of money, as it was not available, but rather were in the form of an egg or a loaf of Arabic bread!

EARLY CHILDHOOD

MY PARENTS WERE ILLITERATE, YET THEY WERE ECONOMICALLY ON a solid footing. They owned land with olive trees, almond trees, grains and vegetables. In addition to olive and almond trees, they cultivated the land with wheat, lentils, zucchini, cucumbers and other vegetables. Their major products however, were olives, olive oil and almonds intended and set for export.

Palestinians, in general, did not hold cash as such, but whatever cash they may have, they used it to purchase more property!

As there was no electricity in the town or other means to cool our home during the hot and humid summer months, my parents packed their four children, including myself, and headed to camp in the field. They used to build makeshift living quarters constructed from shrubs and weeds. This was their summer retreat. Families who did not own property to camp in, would build their makeshift quarters on the roofs of their homes.

I was not supposed to have lived beyond few months after birth! While the family spent the summers in their makeshift summer headquarters they had erected in the field and in the early evening hours, a hyena paid a visit to our living quarters. The predator snatched me and ran away with me dangling from between its jaws. My parents and sisters were screaming and wailing for the loss of their only son and brother who was supposed to ultimately become the heir-apparent, is now lost to the hyena. In a frantic desperation, my father chased the hyena off and retrieved his son unharmed! Thanks dad for giving me a new lease on life.

My father, I am told, was a hard-working man. He was a family man who had devoted all his life to provide for his wife and for his four children. He had no brothers but had only one sister who died before I was born. My mother, on the other hand, had no sisters but one twin-brother who died in Lebanon at the age of eighty-five. My mother was my father's second wife. He divorced the first one because he determined, she was not fit to be part of the family and did not honor the values his family holds, as she did not get along with his only sister!

I have no idea as to the identity of the midwife who had delivered my sisters. Identity of the midwife that delivered me and where I was delivered is now, known. I am, told I was delivered at home by Miss Hilani, an illiterate Christian woman was referred to as midwife Hilani. At birth, I was given the name Wasif (describer), but because I was a crybaby, crying all the time, my parents thought, perhaps the name Wasif was not fitting for their son. They had to find out what the real cause due to my continuous crying. Since there was no doctor or medical facility in the town to take their son to for diagnosis or possible treatment, their only option was the outlandish belief that evil spirits may have taken over their son's behavior that caused him to cry all the time. Because of their belief of the influence of evil spirits on peoples' daily lives, they sought out and went to a superstition 'specialist' for the diagnosis and possible treatment. They were told the reason the boy is crying all the time is due to his name. It does not appear that the name Wasif agrees with him. To fix his continuous crying syndrome, he must have his name changed with another one. The superstition 'specialist' suggested the name, Abdallah, as he could determine from his readings, to be a good and appears to be appropriate for me. My parents welcomed his suggestion to give me the name Abdallah as this name was, also the name of my great grandfather. They took the superstitions 'specialist's' advice and dropped the name 'Wasif' and adopted the new name, Abdallah. They took his advice to heart and proceeded to have my name legally changed. Indeed, his diagnosis and suggestion of the name change making the boy overcome the crying syndrome came to be true. The fact that I stopped crying after my name was changed made my parents become firm believers in the devil's influence that affects the behavior of people. They also believed that the original name, Wasif, the one they gave me at birth, was a curse that kept me crying all the time. The replacement name, Abdallah did have the effect on the removal of the curse that caused my continuous crying to cease! That name change did its job by making me stop crying and live like any normal non-cry baby! It also re-affirmed, in my parents' minds, that evil spirits are all over the place and the superstition 'experts' can ward off these evil spirits once and for all.

I have no idea of how my parents looked like. I cannot recall their faces or their figures. They died within six months of each other while I was a little baby. I was eighteen months old when my mother died and twenty-four months old when my father died

As circumcision is, a tradition acquired from the days when *Ibrahim (Abraham) was, ordered by God to undergo circumcision* as required in Islam, to be performed on all male children. I, and other boys my age, were condemned to the painful procedure. The person who performed the operation on us was an illiterate man whose main job was to install shoes on horses. He was the only 'expert' on performing circumcision in the area. Abu Saleh was quick and professional. After the operation, all of us boys who had undergone circumcision, were, sequestered into one room. We wore white dresses (seamless robes) that we kept on all day and night. Absence of bandages or other means to shield the wound forced us to keep holding the dress at the front to avoid it rubbing against the genital area.

It was quite surprising that the operation worked out safely with only a little post circumcision inflammation. It was also amazing that no infection ever developed after the procedure. Antibiotics were not in existence in the town and even, if they were available there were no doctors or medical personnel to treat infections should they occur and in case other complications may develop. One cannot imagine the pain we would encounter should the dress we wore rubbed against the wound. We were, kept in that room for at least a week or until the wound had completely healed.

Upon growing up and after graduating from high school, I realized that after all I have gone through I may have wanted to believe that I am a holy person relating to what my full name stands for. Abdallah Mohamad Isa al-Shaikh may suggest my holiness. Additional thoughts that gave me the feeling of being a holy person came later through my schooling and employment experiences:

Abdallah is a compound name combining God and man:

Abd, (servant or slave). Allah (the Almighty God)

Mohamad, my middle name, which is my father's name, is the name of the Prophet of Islam

Isa is the name of Jesus Christ (Jesus in Arabic) and is the name of my paternal grandfather name, which I have adopted as my last name

Shaikh, my original, but later deleted family name, (Moslem cleric or title of important people). However, in our case Shaikh was the title bestowed upon our great grandfather by the Ottoman Sultan for the services he had rendered to the empire.

My schooling and work experiences added to my 'holiness':

Khoury, the principal of my high school and first employer's name (Christian priest)

Shammas, my second employer's name meaning (Bishop)

I have combined the Servant, God, Prophet Mohamad, Jesus Christ, Moslem cleric, Christian priest and Christian Bishop, all in one name. What could be more holy than that?

My mother died when she was thirty-five years old. The cause of her death is unknown to me. At the time of her death, I was a year and half old. Her last words before she died were, as I was told, "take care of Abdallah" and then she ascended to Heaven. My mother was my father's second wife who he married after divorcing his first wife. Because our family was closely knit, my father believed in love and harmony among family members. He demanded his wife and his only sister get along well with each other. His reasoning in justifying divorcing his first wife was, while it was impossible to have another sister, yet it is always possible to have another wife! Upon finding out the mutual disliking and arguing between his sister and his wife, he felt that arguing and fighting, between the two were not only against his family structure and tradition but were detrimental to the family as a solid unit. He then decided to divorce his wife because she did not fit in and conform to his family values!

My mother was born to a family of limited means where she, her twin brother and their parents struggled to survive in the aftermath of World War I. My father, on the other hand, was born to a well-to-do family with lots of property and a good social standing in the town. He inherited property from his parents, which he had to take care of, as he had no brothers to share in the burden of the work. He never went to school as he was, busy taking care of his property, as a young kid after the death of his parents. My father who was thirty older than my mother, died at the age of sixty-five, six months after my mother's death. Both died after being married for five years. They had, three daughters and me: My oldest sister Nazha (Picnic) was thirteen years old when she died in 1944, in Palestine. My second sister, Fatima, who raised me and was like a mother, died on January 8, 2002 in the United States. My third sister, Amina, died in Lebanon on December 2, 2016, I am the only one left from the Isa clan.

The reality of having no parents or grandparents to enjoy set in and a feeling of emptiness, in my life, has become engraved in my psyche as it was and still is felt by me, that the only family I could claim as my own were my two surviving sisters, Fatima and Amina as I could barely remember my oldest sister, Nazha. They were, more than sisters to me as they filled the roles of parents and grandparents too. Both of my sisters had a tremendous impact on my mental and physical development. May God bless their souls!

The only means of transportation and carriage of agricultural products in the town were camels, mules, horses and donkeys. My father had the celebrated and the so-called, the 'Cypriot' donkey that he used as a means of transportation and to carry crops from the field. The "Cypriot" donkey differs from the common donkey in that its size lies between the horse and of the common donkey. It is generally taller than the common donkey but shorter than the horse.

Uncle Mohamad owned a mule he used for transportation and carriage. The mule disappeared for few days and uncle Mohamad was worried the hyenas may have ambushed it and put it on their dinner table. He, like others and my parents before, believed in the power of superstition. That belief led uncle Mohamad to go to a man in the town, who claimed to be able to protect domestic animals from hyenas and other carnivores, by having an invisible barrier between the hunter and the hunted! Whether that mystic barrier would shield, the mule from the hyenas or not is only a matter of speculation. People, however, with their simplistic way of thinking believed in the supernatural abilities of this man. They believed the invisible shield this man placed between the mule and hyenas is real. 'Confirmation' of this magical shield came when I found the mule alive and well. I found it grazing in one of our properties. I was a little scared of it at first, as I was afraid it could kick or bite me, should I come any closer. I picked a bunch of grass and walked slowly towards the mule. When the mule started eating grass from my hand, without any aggressive signs on its part, I felt it may have recognized me and I was not a threat. I jumped on its back and brought it home to uncle Mohamad's house.

As there were no childcare facilities, kinder gardens or family members he could trust available in the town and after my mother's passing, my father used to load his four children on the back of his donkey and carry them to the field where he had to tend to his properties. He would cry all the time. When asked as to why he was crying, he would say, I miss my wife and I am afraid of dying. Should I die while my children are still very small, I worry my children will suffer from the abuse and mistreatment by the rest of the family. Indeed, his fears came to fruition after he died and the abuse and mistreatment of his children by family members were the norm of the day.

Upon the death of both of my parents, a squabble erupted among family members as to who will take care of these orphans. One of my father's distant cousins, named Mustapha refused outright to take care of us. He said, 'I fear God, because if one of their olive kernels gets mixed with mine, God will never forgive me for committing such a sin for taking orphans' property and claiming it to be mine'. The winner, of course, was his brother Mohamad, the other distant cousin of my father's.

Uncle Mohamad, like his brother Mustapha, was very well to do as they inherited lots of property from their parents. He was, well respected in the town as it relates to the lineage of 'our' family. Because of the high social status of 'our' family, people in the town always looked up to the elders of the family, especially to uncle Mohamad seeking advice and guidance.

Uncle Mohamad was married to a woman from a very well-to-do family in the town. They both had two sons and two daughters together. He then decided to marry another woman. His new wife came from the city of Acre. Instead of divorcing his first wife, he kept her under his name, but abandoned her completely. The two wives lived in different houses that were fifteen feet away from each other. To appease the new wife, he had completely neglected, ignored and would not even talk to his first wife. To me, that was an act of absurd inhumanity.

Polygamy was legal under the law, 'sanctioned' by the government and favored by men. Of course, this is due to their ignorance and to their intent of empowerment to maintain their powers over women. Men claim their religion of Islam permits them to marry more one woman at a time. This claim of Islam's permission of having more than one wife is farthest from the truth as they believed and wrongly so, that the Holy Qur'an allows them to have more than one wife and to have up to four wives in their household. This is a farce! It is either due to their misinterpretation of the Qur'anic verses organizing family life or due to their wanting to satisfy their sexual urges regardless of what their religion states. For all practical purposes, they were practically illiterate and could not read and comprehend what the Qur'an says.

Regardless of the reasons they allege, polygamy is indeed anti-Islamic. The Qur'an clearly states, "You can have two, three or four women (wives) at a time, if you are fair and just to all of them, otherwise only one". The Qur'an, Women 3, 3. The men knowingly and willingly ignore the last part of the Qur'anic verse that does not permit multiple wives but having only one wife at a time. Further, the next verse in the same chapter in the Qur'an explicitly states, "But if you are not fair and just to them, women that is, and you will never be fair and just, therefore only one". Of course, being fair and just, to more than one wife is beyond the realm of human capability. Fairness and justice, to more than one wife, as mentioned in the Qur'an, does not refer to material things only, but more importantly, it includes the emotional aspect, respect and treatment of all wives in the man's household, equally, with no favoritism towards one of them over the other(s).

The inability of the man to be fair and just to two or more wives is, further affirmed in the same chapter, Qur'an, Women 3, 129. In this verse, the Qur'an states, "You will never be fair and just to women, meaning wives, if they are more than one". Of course, having more than one wife at a time, dictates preference and favoritism, by the husband towards one of the wives at the expense of the other wives. This unfairness will have stressful impacts on the other wives who do not happen to be the ones chosen to be his favorite. This is what a patriarchal male-dominated society promotes.

The situation becomes murky and complicated when there are children in the picture. Children of the favorite wife are always well treated and are well taken-care of. In fact, this was the case in uncle Mohamad's situation. He favored children from the new wife more than favoring his children from the first wife. He gave more attention to the children of the new wife than to those children from the first wife. I have always wondered whether this was the reason that had an impact on the mental development of his son, Darwish, from the first wife. It was unfortunate that Darwish did not have an education past grammar school, but worse of it all he turned to drinking and ultimately became an alcoholic. I do not know the cause of his death in 1994, but my suspicion points to the possibility of cirrhosis of his liver, perhaps a heart attack or a combination of both.

Although uncle Mohamad now, has two wives, but for all practical purposes, he had only one, that is the new wife from the city! Having had two daughters and two sons from the first wife, and three sons and two daughters from this new wife, he treated his children from both wives differently. The children from the new wife, as opposed to those from the first wife were, very well taken care of. They were, sent to schools in Acre, the city where their mother came from, while children from the first wife attended the local government school in the town. Financially and economically, children from the new wife were, very well taken care of, whereas children from the first wife did not receive the same degree of attention being emotional or financial from their father as their half brothers and sisters did.

Uncle Mohamad's oldest son Adel, from the first wife, finished grammar school in the town and wanted to go to Jerusalem to attend al-*Kullia al-Arabia* (the Arab College), but because his father did not provide him with the application fee, five Palestinian Pounds (15 US $) to *al-Kullia al-Arabia* in Jerusalem, he never got an education past grammar school. He then found a job as a storekeeper at the British RE (Royal Engineers) camp located at the outskirts of the town. He took over the burden of supporting his mother and siblings financially. He was very kind to me too, as he would give me few pennies when he received his monthly salary from the Royal Engineer outfit.

MISTREATMENT OF MY SISTERS AND ME BY UNCLE MOHAMAD AND HIS NEW WIFE

IT WAS LATER REALIZED THAT UNCLE MOHAMAD WAS MORE INTER-ested in our property than in the wellbeing of us orphans. It made me convinced of uncle Mohamad's motives, when he used my sisters as maids in the service of his new wife and of her sister. He used my sister Fatima, in the service of his new wife and had my other sister Amina, employed as a servant to his new wife's sister who lived in another town. While he sent his daughters from both wives to school, he never sent my sisters to school knowing well enough that public schooling was available and free of charge! Uncle Mohamad wanted me to quit school too, saying I should start taking care of my properties! Of course, I was elated and happy to hear what he said as it was music to my ears. I did not like going to school in the first place and would rather spend the time playing around with other kids. Well, who does like going to school?

As children, my sister Amina, before he sent her off to his wife sister's home to work as a maid, and I carried our little baskets and headed to one of our properties to pick green almonds to eat. One of the town's people spotted us and went straight to uncle Mohamad telling him that Abdallah did not go to school today and he is right here. Uncle Mohamad held me in the hand and took me to school. He was smacking me, on the face, all the way to school. I do not understand how he had changed his mind about wanting me to go to school, when a year earlier he wanted me to quit school altogether.

My older sister, Fatima, stepped in and threatened me by saying that should I quit school, as uncle Mohamad wanted, she will disown me and will never have anything to do with me. Fearing my sister's ultimatum and because of my fondness and love for her, I disobeyed uncle Mohamad's wish and decided to stay in school!

My sister Fatima, at the time, suspected uncle Mohamad's motive to have me quit school, so that I be as illiterate as she was, and I would never be as educated as his children are.

To give a speck of fairness to Uncle Mohamad he was not all that bad as he had some good qualities. He did protect us, orphans from any possible intimidation, abuse or harm by others outside his family, but left our mistreatment to him and to his new wife. He was a strict disciplinarian. Should any of us be disrespectful to others or use cuss words, we would get his wrath that usually ended with severe punishment. I was, whipped hard by him because someone alleged that I threw a cuss word at him. These good qualities of his were unfortunately completely blocked by me, as they were overtaken by the bad ones that were instilled in him by his new wife.

Surprisingly and amazingly enough, as this had never happened before, uncle Mohamad purchased a blue jumpsuit for me! This jumpsuit proved to be a bad omen for me, as every time I wore that jumpsuit to school, I would receive severe beatings from the teachers. That suit was the only decent daywear I had and liked to wear it because I felt it looked good on me. That blue jumpsuit must have had a curse or perhaps it could possibly, have been jinxed!

Although my sisters and I were supposed to have been well-to-do and have a normal childhood, as we have inherited sizeable chunks of land with olive groves and almond trees, neither my sisters nor I did have access to the needs and requirements of basic human living and dignity. We were denied the sense of belonging to a family that we could claim as our own. If uncle Mohamad were ever asked, by any person, as to who this boy (me) is, his response always was "he belongs to us". The term "belongs to us" is of course, reserved for servants, slaves, domestic animals or material things! He never said this boy is our son or he is my late cousin's son. That hurt me so bad and destroyed my psyche to the point that I started to feel as though I did not exist. I always felt like I am a boy with no heritage, no past to speak of, a miserable present and probably a dismal future.

This sense of non-belonging had a devastating impact on me as it hit me hard during my formative years. It left a huge scar in my psyche for years to come. As a result, of this psychological trauma, I have developed a severe anxiety syndrome and always thought of the negatives before I would even pause to have a chance to consider the positives. My glass was always never full, it always was half empty! I was always striving to have others recognize me as a real and legitimate human being to be accepted by anyone. It was not a good feeling to be 'unaccepted' in, ignored or unrecognized, although I tried my best to give a good impression of myself. Admittedly, I was in denial all the time.

My sisters and I inherited a house from our deceased parents. To get into the house we had to climb the three steps behind the door. We had a very large wall-to-wall, built-in wooden closet that was used as storage area for our clothes and mattresses. The lower compartment of the closet was the resident hall of mice. We could hear the mice fighting and chasing each other all the time. I had become an expert on catching mice by holding them by the tail and disposing of them. Of course, I had the displeasure of mice bites inflicted on my fingers. One afternoon, I decided to go to our house and upon entering, I heard a little noise emanating from a large pan that is normally used to wash clothes. I thought it to be a mouse that fell into the pan and could not get out. I decided to check it out and try to catch the mouse by the tail. Looking into the pan, there was no mouse, but a large snake with beautiful colored markings that looked like those of the rainbow. I ran away screaming, snake in our pan. The snake jumped out of the pan and went through a hole outside the house.

Sadness set in, when uncle Mohamad sent my sister Amina off to work as a servant to his wife's sister in a different town while my sister Fatima is working as a servant to his wife. Now my only sister Fatima was left behind to stay with me, in our house, in the evenings after finishing service work in his new wife's house. Going to our house, in the evening, was at different times, depending when my sister is let go by Mohammad's wife, as there was no set time to quit. Sometimes we would go, to our house, in the early hours of the evening, yet at other times we would go at later hours.

During the day when I was not at school, I spent most of the day in Mohamad's first wife's house. My older sister, Fatima, while spending her days serving uncle Mohammad's new wife will meet me only in the evening.

Adjoining our house were two apartments: one was rented out for a monthly fee of one Palestinian schilling (15 US pennies) and the other one was destroyed by rain-water and was never repaired. It remained in ruins. On one wintery day, a big storm passed through and rained so heavily that the torrential rains soaked the roof of our house. Half of the roof collapsed, and rainwater was gushing down like a waterfall. We had no bed frames to lay our mattresses on, as we slept on mattresses that my sisters laid down on the floor. My sisters and I moved the mattresses to the dry area of the floor as we tried to avoid the gushing rainwater coming down. Of course, we did not have a single wink of sleep, as we were anxious and frightened the rainwater may lead to the collapse of the other part of the roof and kill us or the water would creep in and ruin our mattresses. We had to keep our eyes fixated to the ceiling hoping the other half of the roof would not fall off over our heads. Fortunately, the rain stopped and couple of days later, uncle Mohamad contracted a person to fix the roof. He paid the contractor and a day later, demanded my sister Fatima reimburse him for the money he had paid the contractor! Is this action a sensible one of a caretaker who is supposed to be compassionate towards his orphan relatives? I do not think so.

At the same time, uncle Mohamad who had no legal authority to dispose of any part, small or large, of our properties, had sold few acres of land that belonged to us. Of course, he had no right to sell any of our properties, as these properties did not belong to him, but belonged to under-age orphans. They belonged to the under-age orphans. He pretended, in front of others, as Islam dictates, that the money he received for the property he had sold, belongs to us orphans and should be given to us in the presence of witnesses. He did so by giving the money, in the presence of some witnesses, to my sister Fatima. However, a day later he demanded she pay him back the money he had given her for the sale of a chunk of land of our property the day before!

There was no electricity, running water, not to mention hot water in our house and, for that matter in the entire town. The only means of lighting that was available, at the time, was a kerosene lamp. Many a day we did not even have any money to purchase the kerosene fuel for the lamp! Extreme poverty was the name of the game as far as my sisters and I were concerned. Because we had no money even to purchase kerosene, many a night we were, left in complete darkness.

(The kerosene lamp was the only source of light in the house at night when we could afford purchasing kerosene)

Burning of kerosene emits clouds of thick black smoke. The emitted black smoke is full of the odor of kerosene. Many a night food was not available, to me or to my sisters, except dry old bread. We looked at the black smoke, although has the strong smell of kerosene, that is emitted from the kerosene lamp as being a "good" smoke and a blessing, as it helped give a little dark tinge to the bread crumps when passed over the black smoke. Although it gave it a different look, an unpleasant aroma, yet the bread did not have a bad taste after all!

During the spring and summer months as children, my sisters, when not serving Mohamad's wife and her sister, and I would spend a lot of time in our properties. One of these properties close to the borders with Lebanon had a *Carob* tree. The *Carob* fruit is in the form of long and slightly curved (like a banana) pods. Mature and dry *Carob* fruit is used in the preparation of *Carob* molasses.

One summer day, I was asked by uncle Mohamad's wife, to go to our tree to harvest the mature pods and bring them home form processing to *Carob* make *Carob* molasses, I loaded two big canvas sacs of *Carob* pods onto the back of the donkey. The donkey lost its balance coming down the steep terrain and rolled over several times, before it could stand on its feet.

The green, immature *Carob* pods, in contrast to the dark brown mature ones, have a very bitter taste. Mature pods acquire a different color and a sweet taste compared to the immature green ones. The color changes, upon maturity, from green to dark brown.

As a treat for dinner, my sisters and I used to pick the immature green *Carob* pods and bring them home for 'processing'! The green pods were broken to smaller pieces and made into a paste by pounding with a rock. The paste is squeezed to extract the juice which when added to raw goat or sheep milk and continuous stirring causes the milk to become viscous and formed. My sisters and I would then huddle together and 'cook' this new recipe made of raw milk and juice from green *Carob* pods. The dish referred to as "*Mieaʾa*" did not taste bad at all. The *Carob* juice contains enzymes that cause the protein, casein in the milk to curd thus giving it a viscous consistency. The dish is, easily scooped with the dry pieces of bread or with a spoon, if available. It did not taste bad at all!

Goat or any kind of meat was a great luxury, if we could get it. We rarely did! Butchers slaughtered their goats or sheep every Sunday morning and whenever I asked uncle Mohamad to buy us 200 grams (6 ounces) of meat on Sundays, he would always say 'I do not have any money'. He did have money, however, to buy meat for his new wife and their children. Of course, he had no money for us as he was always short of it. The reason he confessed to having no money, as he always claimed he has is, because he had to support his new wife with five children, as well as her six sisters and their widowed mother who lived in the city of Acre. So why should he have any money for me or for my sisters? I was always afraid of reminding him that we have the right to be supported, as he was using revenues from our properties to cover for the short fall in his finances. My sisters and I are more deserving of financial support than his new wife's mother and her six daughters! People in the town looked with disgust and negativity at uncle Mohamad for his mistreatment and abuse of us orphans. They felt that we were supposed to have had a decent life as our deceased parents left us lots of property to live on.

A gentleman in the town, whose family was close friends of my parents and whose wife was particularly close to my mother, felt very sad and sorry for me as he thought I was malnourished. He offered me a piece of goat meat to cook and eat. That piece of meat was loaded with maggots. He told me, it is o.k. to go ahead cook it and eat it. The look of wiggling maggot on that piece of meat made me nauseated and was about to throw up. Of course, I took the piece of meat, out of respect and appreciation of him, but could not stand looking at it. I went to a nearby field and placed the meat under a big rock. This person had good intentions and felt good trying to help an orphan eat some meat. Neither he nor I, at the time, knew that that meat was dangerous to eat because of the maggots and other parasites that are lurking in that piece of meat!

I have always craved for food and for fruit. Many a time, when I find a rotten orange or a piece of an orange in the street, I would kick it around pretending I was playing football (soccer) and kick it as if it were a ball and direct it to a corner where nobody can see me. I would then pick it up and start munching on it.

Uncle Mohamad owned an orchard that had several apple trees. This kind of apple trees bears delicious small apples. Dead apples, like any dead fruit, fall off the tree. There were several of them scattered under the trees. While walking with him in that orchard, I craved for and picked an apple from the tree to eat. He got upset and told me not pick apples from the tree any more, I should eat those apples that have fallen off to the ground!

Money was very scarce, and we had none of it. One day, when uncle Mohamad was socializing with his friends at the coffee house, I came and whispered in his ears asking him for a *ta'arifi*, a Palestinian coin that was equivalent to one and a half US pennies. He answered by asking me, what for? I was very intimidated and outraged and yelled loudly, making sure everybody heard me, I want to spend the *ta'arifi* what else do you think I will do with it?

I did not have any "good" clothes. New clothes were never bought for me except that infamous blue jumpsuit. The clothes I had were, primarily donated by a neighbor, who had a son my age. That neighbor was very close to my mother and every time she puts her eyes on me or on any of my sisters, she would start crying. This neighbor donated shorts and shirts to me to wear. I never had any underwear and pajamas were a fantasy I have always dreamt about having. I would sleep in the shorts and shirts that I would be wearing the following day. I did not know the difference between nightwear and daywear.

To add insult to injury, every summer, I was the only member in the family to succumb to Malaria. A devastating infection caused by the bite of the mosquito *Anopheles aegyptis,* inflicted me. This mosquito harbors either *Plasmodium falciparum* or *Plasmodium vivax* or both strains of the parasite that cause malaria. When the mosquito bites, it pierces the skin with its proboscis to suck blood. In the process of biting to suck blood for its meal, it introduces the parasites from its gut into the victim's blood stream. The parasites infect and destroy the red blood cells of the victim thus leading to Malaria.

Symptoms of Malaria I had exhibited included anemia, severe headache, vomiting, bi-phasic temperature chart (alternating between fever with high temperature and chills), general malaise and of course lack of appetite and loss of weight. Since there was no doctor in the town and no medications available, survival from the disease depended only on prayers and on good luck! Since I was the only one in the family who contracted Malaria, I was curious to find out why the *Anopheles aegyptis* mosquito was so choosy and selective of having me on its dinner table. I tried to ask the mosquito as to why it selected me for its bite, is it because of my looks, my name or the color of my skin? The mosquitos never answered my questions.

Although we do not have the *Anopheles aegyptis* mosquito in the United States to be worried about Malaria, yet we have other mosquitos that carry dangerous viruses. In addition, we have other bugs that roam the land especially during the spring and summer months. I assumed that American bugs are more understanding and more compassionate towards me in sparing me from their bites, like the mosquitos and bugs in the Middle East did, but my assumption was proven to be wrong especially when I found that I am not spared the bites of these bugs. When I asked the American bugs, as to why did you, selectively bite me as the *Anopheles aegyptis* mosquitos did? A chigger jumped out and said, it is your blood type stupid. We love to have your blood type on our dinner table.

I found out later, that the reason for the mosquitos that harbor the Malaria-causing parasites, to have me as their choice to bite was, related to my blood type. Mosquitos and for that matter, other insects bite people who happen to have type O+ blood. Since I have that same blood type, I was the victim of choice for these mosquitoes and other insects to have my blood for a snack. These mosquitos, in addition to the *Plasmodia* that cause malaria may also carry other dangerous bacteria and viruses. Notable among those is the Encephalitis virus.

I have always had blisters on my feet because of the poor fitting shoes. I never was, taken to a shoe store to fit me with the right size shoe. The shoes that uncle Mohamad bought for me were always of, cheap quality. They were either of small or of large sizes, but never the right size to fit my small feet. I had to wear those shoes, as the other alternative was to bare footed. Because of the painful blisters in my feet, and to avoid limping because of the pain, many a time I opted to go bare footed.

Although going bare footed relieved the pain caused by the blisters, other infections appeared on my toes and on my feet. These infections were pussy and very painful to the touch. In either case, I did not fare well by either wearing the out-of-size shoes or going shoeless.

In addition, to the Malaria infection and the blisters on my feet, pus was oozing out from both of my ears for months without abatement.

It was the custom for children get new clothes during the Moslem religious holidays. I was hoping that uncle Mohamad would buy me a good woolen suit or at least a woolen pair of pants similar, to those he always bought for his sons. Instead of the woolen clothes, he purchased me a two-piece outfit made of cheap material with different color (yellow, red, black and green) stripes on a white background). That outfit looked more like pajama material than outerwear. After ordering me to wear the suit, I refused and ran away to our house. He chased me, beat the hell out of me and forced me to wear that ugly suit. He wanted others to see how good he is to me and how well he took care of my needs by showing that I am wearing the new suit he bought for me for the holidays!

Uncle Mustapha, like his brother Mohamad, inherited lots of property from their father. Unlike his brother Mohamad, he was always compassionate towards me. He had one daughter, Deeba and one son, Suleiman. He was attentive to me and many a time, asked me to read some verses of the Qur'an. He always looked at me as his own son. In contrast to uncle Mohamad who can read and write, and because uncle Mustapha was illiterate, he wanted his son to get an education that he never had. One day, and in my presence, he told his son Suleiman, "I will keep you in school until you are twenty-five years old". That meant the son, will have to finish grammar school, prep school, high school and then college. When I heard what uncle Mustapha told his son, my heart started dancing with happiness and joy. I said to myself, thank God, I do not have a father to push me to go to and stay in school as uncle Mustapha did his son!

Uncle Mustapha was very determined to have Suleiman get an education so that he will be educated and unlike his illiterate father. He sent him to the Gerard Institute, a Christian Missionary boarding school in Sidon, Lebanon. After a month or so at the boarding school, Suleiman ran away from the school and came back to the town complaining of loneliness and of missing his parents! He then, enrolled in the local government grammar school. Unfortunately, he never got a formal education past grammar school. He later enrolled in a vocational school in Lebanon that was sponsored and supported by the United Nations, where he became a certified electrician.

Uncle Mohamad had a weak personality. He was married to a new wife who was quite controlling. He had no choice but to let her run the show in any manner she saw fit. Her use of my sister Fatima as her servant not only was met with his blessings, but also because he had to comply with her orders. She used to send my sister or me, separately and on different occasions, to the fields late in the day or early evening to get her a bunch of the *Cilantro* herb, to use in her cooking. The herb grows wild in the fields. We were scared to death from wild *Cilantro* animals especially hyenas that roamed the area after the Sun sets.

My sister Amina did not fare better either. She was, sent to another town to work as a servant for one of his new wife's sisters. Having my sister been sent away was devastating to me. I would go to our house, during the day, and start crying and chanting '**we were three but now we are only two**', a hymn I composed to describe the loneliness and the psychological devastation I felt caused by the missing of my sister. I would see my other sister Fatima, only in the evening, after she finishes her servant work to uncle Mohamad's wife's.

At the time of the holidays, it was customary that women prepare pastries and cookies that fit the occasion. Uncle Mohammad's new wife prepared large quantities of such holiday cookies filled with dates or walnuts. She placed the cookies on a large brass tray that is about a yard and half in diameter. Although she had two daughters, three sons, two-step daughters and two-step sons, she never bothered to ask any one of her children or her step- children to carry the tray to the bakery. I always was, the easy target she picked to carry such a large and heavy tray on my head, to the bakery. I had to wait my turn, at the bakery for the cookies to be baked and after they were baked, I had to wait longer until the brass tray cooled down to load on my head to bring it back to her. The wait time, at the bakery, prior to baking the cookies was a little over three hours. After baking, I had to wait for another hour or so until the tray cools down so that I could carry it on my head back to her house. She never gave me a cookie, nor even thanked me as a reward for my service to her! That confirmed, at least, in my own mind that my sisters and I were neither related to uncle Mohamad nor to his new wife, but servants who were born and destined to serve them!

One of uncle Mohamad's new wife's six sisters living with their widowed mother in the city of Acre, was visiting her in the town. When it was time for the sister to go home, she wanted to take my sister Fatima, to whom I was, attached with her to Acre to do servant work for them. I wanted very badly to ride the bus and go with them to the city. She was very adamant in refusing to let me accompany them as both, she and my sister left without me. I cried for hours as I did miss my sister, missed riding the bus and missed going to the city.

Few months later that same sister of uncle Mohamad's wife came to visit her again and wanted to take my sister Fatima with her. This time, my sister insisted that I go with them to the city. I was not allowed to come into their house but was kept outside for three hours until my sister picked me up and we rode the bus back home.

Uncle Mohamad's first wife was very much like a mother to me. She treated me like one of her own children. She had two sons and two daughters. One of the sons, her youngest, Darwish was my age. He was never nice to me. We did not talk to each other directly, but always communicated in a third person singular language. This cousin contrasts, very sharply, with cousin Suleiman, uncle Mustapha's son. Suleiman was always nice to me, not only as a cousin, but also as a friend.

Again, I was striving, to be recognized and accepted as a real person, especially by 'my own' relatives. Our school, in one of the cultural events, meant to expose the kids to attend a show by a magician who came to school to show us his tricks. Tickets were one and a half Palestinian piasters (less than 5 cents) a person. I wanted, very badly to go and see the magician, but did not have any money. It was amazing and perhaps a strike of luck or a miracle may have been in the making where God felt sorry for me. While walking by a little tributary with running water, I spotted three piasters on the bottom under the running water. That was a God-given gift to me. Now I can go see the magician's show. The three piasters I found were enough to pay for two persons to go and see the magician. In addition to my ticket, I still had one and a half piasters left in my possession. Now, trying to appease him and gain acceptance by, and possible friendship with, cousin Darwish, I gave him the money so that he can also go to see the show! Of course, he was happy for that, but I know he would have never grant me that favor and will never do the same thing for me.

BRITISH "DEMOCRACY" AND BRITISH ENFORCEMENT OF "INHUMAN RIGHTS" AT THEIR BEST

THE INFAMOUS SYKES-PICOT PACT WAS WRITTEN BY THE BRITISH Sykes and the French Picot after World War I as Britain and France were victors in the War. In the Sykes-Picot pact, the victors of the war decided to pursue the policy of divide and rule. They decided to divide the one country at the time, Greater Syria, into five mini states: Present day Syria, Iraq, Palestine, Trans Jordan and Lebanon. Palestine was, placed under the British mandate, in addition to ruling Iraq and Trans Jordan and Egypt, while France mandated Syria and Lebanon.

Uncle Mohamad spent time behind bars because the Brits accused him of taking part in the 1936 and the 1939 uprisings against British rule. The Brits were brutal in treating the suspected Palestinian 'terrorists' of whom uncle Mohamad was alleged of being. The British army's quest in search for arms or political documents supporting the rebellion, they ransacked the homes of these suspected rebels and destroyed the furniture and all the contents of their homes.

As a very young child in the early 1940's I, like every other child, was scared to death from the sight of the British soldiers. We would hide anywhere we could to avoid being seen by the soldiers.

Uncle Mohamad's new wife occupied the second floor of a two-story building. The first floor was used a guesthouse to provide sleeping quarters, at no charge, for outsiders who would visit the town but had no relative and no place to sleep. When the British soldiers came to the second floor where uncle Mohamad's wife resides, we all hid under the bed. The soldiers smashed everything in the house and broke the antique glass works that uncle Mohamad's wife had gathered over the years. I was bare-footed, wearing a dress and no underwear and wanted to go down the staircase to uncle Mohamad's first wife's house. I was crying because the staircase was, littered with broken glass, and I was afraid to step on the broken glass and cut my feet. A black African soldier, a member of the British army, felt sad and sorry for me. He went up the stairs and carried me down to safety from the broken glass. That was a great compassionate gesture from an 'enemy' soldier.

I have no recollection as to how I had acquired a machinegun bullet. I was, scared to death of being caught with it. I carried it, hid it in my pocket, went to the fields looking around so that nobody could see me and threw it in a wheat field. What a relief that was after disposing of that machine gun bullet!

Palestinians were, denied the right to bear arms even for self-defense. Jews, on the other hand were carrying arms in public and under the watchful eyes of the Brits with no questions asked.

The *Hagenah*, the Jewish militia that later became the Israeli army, were riding in their military jeeps with their guns in the open and under the eyes of the British army. They did not have any worries to be seen by, the Brits as the orders from London, to the British forces to look the other way when the Jewish militia drive by with their loaded guns. There was complete complicity between the Brits and the Jewish militias as though they are both fighting the same enemy, the Palestinians.

Palestinian men whose homes were searched, and anti-British documents or guns smuggled from Lebanon were found, were stripped in the nude and laid face down on a stack of a thorny shrub called *andole* in Arabic. This shrub has long sharp pointed thorn like those of the Mesquite tree (*Prosposis pubescens*) found in the United States. Should anyone have told me this story, I would have been skeptical as to its authenticity and would not have believed it, but the fact remains that I have witnessed it myself with my two eyes, there was no way I could disbelieve my own eyes! The thorns were about three inches long.

The alleged 'Palestinian terrorists' were beaten with whips and with rifle butts, while lying face down on the thorny shrub for half hour at a time. This was the most horrific and terrifying scene I have ever witnessed in my life. This was, of course, the practice and implementation of human rights in the democratic fashion as authorized and practiced by the Brits. Resentment of British occupation of Palestine by the local Arab population was very high. The Arab majority of Palestine, felt and rightly so, thought that the Brits were paving the way to grant Palestine to the Jews as a fulfillment of the infamous Balfour declaration of November 2, 1917.

Palestinians had no arms or other means to fight the British army or to protect themselves from the encroachment of Jewish settlements. Any Palestinian Arab caught, with any kind of firearm would be taken, into custody and face torture the democratic British way!

As students, in the government school we were, ordered, to line up on the main road, in the scorching heat from the sun, to 'welcome' the British general who was coming in the direction of the town. He was not coming to visit our town. He was on his way to visit the Jewish settlements in the neighboring hills. The school was, closed for the day, as the route of the motorcade of the British general will be passing through that road across from the school! As children, we could not pronounce the word 'general' and instead we were saying the 'geninar' is coming! The 'geninar' is coming. Well the 'geninar' never showed up that day thus wasting the whole day of school. Since the 'geninar' never showed up, all pupils at the school, were, sent home as it appeared to be, to us, as a holiday. To me, cancellation of classes that day was a good omen, as I was, relived, from the potential beating by the teachers. I, was hoping the 'geninar' has a change of heart to, come another day, so that the school would be closed that other day and the pupils sent home!

(On a similar shrub (*Andole*), with its sharp and long thorns, suspected Palestinian militants, were stripped in the nude, laid face down on the shrub and beaten with whips and rifle butts by the 'civilized' British soldiers for 30 minutes of a beating session)

For those Palestinian men who could afford to purchase pistols or some outdated and antiquated French-made rifles and guns that were smuggled from Lebanon had no idea as to how to use them. They used these weapons to show off and try to impress others that they are ready to fight the Zionist enemy and defend the homeland! What a farce that was! They neither had any knowledge of, or training in, the use of these weapons nor how and where to get the ammunitions for these weapons from. They did not receive any formal training as there was no Palestinian military or authority that is capable and authorized to train them on how to use the rifles and pistols. They had to figure out how to use these weapons by themselves by trial and error.

MY ELEMENTARY EDUCATION

I ATTENDED THE PUBLIC GRAMMAR SCHOOL IN THE TOWN. AS Palestine was under the British Mandate, rules governing student behavior and personal health adopted from the British standards were, enforced at the schools in Palestine. Every morning, and before entering the classrooms, we were, lined up and the teachers inspected our hands, fingernails, ears and the length of our hair. Should any of the students have dirty hands, long fingernails, dirty ears or long hair, was sent home to clean up, or have his head shaved. To determine whether the student has long hair or not, the teachers used to pull our hair from the side right by the temple. If the teacher can grab the hair as he pulls, then the pupil is, sent home to have his head shaved. Uncle Mohamad had a contract with a Christian barber to shave our heads whenever we were, sent home from school due to our long hair. The school required that all students, male and female, must wear clean clothes, have clean hands, short fingernails and clean ears. Male students were required to have their heads shaved. There was no rule relating to the length of a girl's hair. Shaving of our heads was a requirement that was enforced to the letter by the school. Pupils who did not heed the teacher's orders to have their heads shaved will be suspended the whole term.

(This was the daily routine of us, pupils, lining up for inspection by the teachers prior to getting into the classrooms. Inspection of our fingernails, ears and the length of our hair was the daily routine practiced by the teachers!)

I hated going to school because of the teachers' attitude towards me. They were very mean and cruel to me. They humiliated me by beating me up in front of the class. Of course, it was not always the teachers' fault in bullying and beating me, but rather it was partially mine as well. I was not a good student. I had no self-confidence and no abilities to comprehend what was required of me in the classroom. However, I have always done well in the final exams scheduled at the end of each term.

Although child corporal punishment was supposed to have been illegal, yet teachers were quite creative in finding ways to punish students. Some of their innovations was the possession of hard sticks and strips of rubber cut out from automobile tires. It was very painful to be hit with the rubber strips and more so if these rubber strips, were used during the cold winter months. The palms of both of my hands were, always swollen resulting from the beating with these rubber strips. I had no parents to tell them about the abuse the teachers have taken upon me and for them to go to the school to complain about the teachers' mistreatment of me. Uncle Mohamad could not care less what happened to me and would never confront the teachers on my behalf.

One day, during the school year, an inspector from the Palestine Department of Education, in Jerusalem came to evaluate the educational program at our school. He was, caught by surprise when he asked one of the students to recite some verses of a poem by the great Arab poet, *Abu el-Tayyib el-Mutanabbi.* The student stood up, in attention, and said: he hid the stick above the blackboard. The inspector plucked the stick from the top of the blackboard and asked the student to continue reading more of the poem. The student responded by saying he hid the stick in the drawer. The inspector found the stick in the drawer and in many other places. The inspector wrote his report, but as far as is known no action was taken by the department of Education against the teachers or against the school. After the inspector left the school premises, the teachers went back to their business as usual. They took revenge, across the board against the students. They continued beating us for no obvious reasons that warrant the beatings. Perhaps they wanted to convince themselves that they are in control and have the upper hand. Most of the teachers at the school had no interest in educating the kids. To them it was a paying job. Their main interest was to pick their salary at the end of the month and nothing else. Their teaching positions were nothing more than a paying job or killing time five and a half days a week,

Another beating innovation introduced by the teachers was to inflict more pain when punishing students was, to deny them permission to go home for lunch. School hours were from 8:00-12:00 noon and 2:00-3:30 PM. The time span between 12:00 noon and 2:00 O'clock was the lunch break. We would go home for lunch and come back to school for the afternoon classes.

One of the teachers, Mr. Abdel Rahman al- Qiblawi, who originally came from the city of Acre, punished me for not doing well in his class. His way of punishment was to have me stand on one foot, facing the wall with both of my hands raised up from 12:00 noon to 2:00 PM in the afternoon, thus denying me to use the time slot 12:00 noon-2:00 PM to go home and have a bite to eat. That meant that I cannot go home for lunch nor can I stand on both of my feet and my hands to my sides for two hours. While standing, as ordered, on one foot with both of my hands raised up to the sky, I looked at the window and saw a fight breaking out between two people. Looking carefully outside the window found out who is fighting who, I spotted this same teacher and another student fighting it out. The teacher and the student were wrestling and beating each other back and forth in the schoolyard. Other students witnessing the fight were happy and were yelling loudly, 'go for it boy, go for it boy'. Their fight gave me a great window of opportunity to sneak out of the punishment room and run home to have lunch and then come back to punishment room to stand on one foot with my hands raised to the sky.

The only lunch available for me was a piece of bread that I would dip in olive oil and nothing else. When I came back to school, I went to the room where I was supposed to have been punished, continued my punishment by standing on one foot facing the wall with both of my hands raised, the way the teacher had ordered me to do. The teacher came in five minutes before the afternoon class time and told me to go to class now as my punishment is over and I must have learned my lesson!

This same teacher taught us fine art and drawing. He asked the class to draw a carnation flower. I drew the flower with different colored petals. He graded my paper and gave me a perfect score of 100. A week later, that same teacher, as lazy as he was, gave us a pop quiz by asking the class to draw a carnation flower. I felt good at the time and thought I would have a perfect score this time around. My good feeling of getting a perfect score was because I thought well, the last time I got a score of 100 why don`t I draw the carnation flower the same way this time as I did before by drawing the flower with different colored petals? I did, and when that teacher graded my test paper, I got a zero on my drawing. I asked him as to why did I get a zero this time, having drawn the carnation flower as I did last week when I got a perfect score of 100? He said, "Have you ever seen a carnation flower with different colored petals"? That shows the dedication of the teachers towards providing students with 'quality' education in the Palestine public school system.

Another teacher, Mr. Sa'ied Khoury, who happens to have come from my hometown, used to sit on the chair, in front of the class, puts his hands on his jaws and his elbows on the table and go to sleep. Suddenly, we started hearing loud snores as the teacher went into deep sleep! In retaliation, we used to chew pieces of paper to soften them with our saliva, roll the softened paper into balls, and using a rubber band as a gun to shoot the wet pieces of paper to hit him. One of the balls hit him in the face with the momentum and the speed of a rocket. He woke up mad and demanded to know who did that. Of course, nobody would admit doing it. This was the only way we could get his attention. We wanted to let him know that his job was to teach us instead of going to sleep in the classroom.

Yet another teacher, Mr. Suleiman Bishara, who originally came from the neighboring town of Tarshiha and established residence in my hometown, was one of the permanent fixtures at the school. He was the villain who would take revenge for his insecurities on the pupils. He was always very mean to me. He would beat the heck out of me in front of the class claiming that I did not know how to point different countries or different rivers on the world map in his geography class. He, however, was a very cheap person and was easily bribed. One day, he made it clear to the class that he needed little metal containers to use for his cigarettes. This was a good opening for me. I asked a relative of mine who worked for the British army, to give me a little container. I brought that container to class and proudly placed it on the table in front of this teacher. He nodded with approval and asked me to take my seat. This time it was unlike other times when he would pick on me the moment he came into the classroom by asking me to point the location of a city, a country or a river on the map, which I did not know. He would beat me with his rubber strip or other means at his disposal at the time. This time it was different as I was, saved from the beating. Thanks to the little metal container!

As always, frightened of being beaten, I have developed a complex against going to school and especially against this teacher, Mr. Bishara will have me scheduled for another beating and humiliation in front of my classmates. Having no confidence in myself, frightened of the coming and impending beating, I had become very anxious as to what is coming next. I had to find ways to appease Mr. Bishara. I would complement him on his new haircut, on a new jacket, he wore, or on a new pair of pants, he was wearing. My appeasements and complements of him did not bear any fruit all the time. He still would pick on me in the classroom and give me his usual beating treatment.

Another creative way of punishment of students was giving them a 'homework' in which they asked the students to write twenty pages of the same statement "I am not a good student…." Repetition to fill out the twenty pages.

HARVESTING AND PROCESSING OF SORGHUM AND WHEAT: A PLEASANT AND YET AN UNPLEASANT EXPERIENCE

THE SORGHUM HARVEST TIME WAS A PLEASANT EXPERIENCE. IT WAS very exciting for us children, as we used to accompany the workers to the field at 2:00 AM in the morning to start harvesting the sorghum. Going to the field that early was to avoid exposure to the heat from the hot sun and the humidity that were intolerable. We would brag that we woke up very early around 1:00 AM in the morning to accompany the workers to the field. Our interest in going with the workers was, to collect grubs of insects that infest the stems of the sorghum plant. We used these grubs as a bait to catch birds. In that process of catching birds, we used to tie the grub at one end with a string and attaching it to a hook on the bird trap. The wiggling grub attracts the birds to come to pick it up and eat it. When the bird picks on the grub, the trap closes in with the bird trapped inside. This use of such traps to catching birds was very humane, as it did not cause any harm or pain to the bird itself.

During the summer months when the wheat is ready for harvest, men with experience in harvesting were set out to manually harvest, the wheat crop using their sickles. Sickles were the only tools available for farmers to use in the harvest of wheat and other grains at the time. There were no combines or other mechanical means to do the job available for use by the farmers. The harvested wheat was, delivered to a flat area in the field designed and prepared for the crushing of the long wheat stems and for release the grain from its thistle. The primitive process resulted not only, in freeing and release the wheat kernels from the wheat thistles but also caused the braking of the dry wheat stems into smaller pieces later used as feed for the animals.

The process of crushing the wheat stems consisted of primitive tools that included, in addition to the operator and a donkey, a mule or a horse, a 3x6-foot rectangular slab of wood curved upward at its front end. Irregularly shaped flint stones are affixed and spaced evenly on the bottom of the wooden slab. The flint stones help break the wheat straws into smaller pieces and free wheat kernels from the thistles. The harvested wheat straws bearing the wheat kernels are, placed on the ground and the wooden slab laid on top of the wheat stems. The wood slab is pulled by a donkey, a horse or a mule with the operator standing or sitting on the wooden slab guiding the animal pulling the slab in a circular movement. The heavy weight of the wooden slab combined with the weight of the operator and the repeated circular trips over wheat stems, causes the crushing and breakage of the straw into smaller pieces. The crushing of the wheat stems to free the wheat kernels from the thistles is, achieved by repeated circular trips over the wheat stems until the straw is broken to about half an inch in length. At this point, the wheat kernels released from the wheat thistle are still mixed with the broken wheat stems. To separate the grain from the chaff, the crushed product is, raked to form a large heap. Using a farmer's fork, the worker will then scoop the crushed straw and wheat kernels mixture and throws it up in the air to separate the chaff from the grain. It was fun for us children, to go to the field where the process of separating the grain from the chaff takes place to ride with the operator on the wooden slab. Should the operator allow us to do the operation by ourselves, he would jump out, hand us the whip and show us how to steer the animal to go in the circular motion. I have always wondered as to why neither the operator nor the animal, get sick for going in circles for hours at a time!

(The operator sitting on a wooden slab drawn by the animal and moving in circular counter clockwise movement to break the wheat stems and thistles into smaller pieces and in the process release the wheat kernels from the wheat thistles.)

The separation of grain from chaff relies heavily on the presence of the wind. Because of the combination of wind and gravity, two heaps, one for grain and the other for the chaff are formed.

The process of separating the grain from the chaff, by throwing the mixture into the air, is quite a bothersome and a time consuming, activity. Throwing the mixture into the air several times to achieve the separation. The heat from the sun is high, the humidity is close to saturation and wearing such a heavy garb and absence of a shade lends the worker to have a bath in his own sweat. A little help to the farmer and a reprieve comes when there is a little breeze. The chaff and the grain land nearby forming two heaps, one for grain and the other for the chaff. Farmers, however, avoid doing this chore on days with high wind, as the chaff would spread over large areas without forming a heap, thus becoming difficult to collect and carry home for storage to feed the animals during the winter months. Another worry is the wind might land the chaff over the grain heap, which may require additional time and effort to re-separate the grain from the chaff

Uncle Mohamad employed a young man who suffered from mental disability, to work the wooden board and donkey to crush the wheat straw and to separate the grain from the chaff. For lunch, he found this mother sent him a tomato and a loaf of Arabic bread for lunch. He got so mad and threw the bread and the tomato up in the air and said, God please take this tomato and have it for your lunch.

(This photo depicts a farmer using a farmer's fork to throw the crushed wheat straw up in the air to separate the wheat kernels from the chaff)

The grain being heavier than the chaff and because of gravity, it falls off and forms a large heap. The chaff flies up in the air and falls at an area farther away forming another heap. Should there still be some chaff mixed with the grain, the process of throwing it up in the air is repeated several times until the grain is completely free of any remnants of the chaff. The grain is, bagged using large canvas bags and carried home on the back of donkeys for storage or sent directly to the mill to be ground into flour.

Should donkeys be unavailable for carriage the choice between mules and camels is, made to carry the crops. Most of the people in the town owned donkeys, but few people owned mules and only one person owned a camel.

Of all animals, the donkey carried the brunt of carriage of all crops and for transportation of people to and from the field.

Donkeys have never complained about abuse or of use as carriers of all the chores the farmers needed, yet people have never given the donkey the credit it deserves. People have always had the assumption that donkeys are stupid and dumb, an assumption that is farther from the truth. Donkeys are smart animals that obey orders of their masters.

(This photo shows the sacs full of wheat mounted on the back of the donkey for transport to the desired destination either for storage or directly to the mill. Chaff, being lighter than the grain is also bagged and sent home for storage for later use as feed for the animals)

The chaff is, carried home and stored in the t*abban,* (silo*)* for use as feed for the animals. The *tabban,* a windowless room that has only a door on one side and an opening in its roof.

The chaff is, introduced to the *tabban,* through the opening in the roof and when needed it is collected through the door to use it as feed for the animals.

Boys will always be boys, as we all know it. We, as boys used to climb up to the roof of the *tabban* and jump ten feet down onto a pile of dirt. One day I decided to go down through the opening in the roof of the *tabban.* I sank into the chaff and could not breathe, as there was no other opening or exit to use. The door to the *tabban* was too far down with no possible way for me to reach it as the whole area was full of chaff and no outlet other than the hole in the roof was available. Luckily, the *tabban* was almost full of chaff and I was close to the opening in the roof. In a frantic manner, I grabbed the edge of the opening and pulled myself out. Had the *tabban,* not been that full to about ten inches from the rim and the opening in the roof not that close to where I was, I would not have made it and may have died from asphyxiation! This incident was my second brush with death with the first being when the hyena grabbed me while I was few weeks old. Luckily, I have survived both of, these two ordeals.

Ignorance never pays. As a child and a vehement lover, of animals and birds, and while in the field I spotted a fox running by. I thought I could catch the fox and use it as a pet. When the fox saw me and figured out that I am getting too close, it ran away. Chasing the fox was a scary ordeal as the fox stopped and looked me in the face with open jaws and a threatening posture. I then realized that this fox was serious and is ready to attack. I retreated, and the fox and I went our separate ways.

After school, we used to take our shoes off and start running around playing hide and seek or other games. One of the favorite recreational games we used to play was the use of wheels such as bicycle metal wheel rims. We used to push these wheels using a long handle of curved-wire to direct the wheel in the direction we were intending to go. Other kids had the fancy bicycle wheel metal rims, but mine was always the rim cut off from the 44-gallon drums!

Uncle Mohamad bought me a cheap pair of tennis shoes (sneakers) that made me feel very proud and happy. I was so proud of these new shoes not only because they fit my feet, this time and causing no blisters, but also because I wanted everybody see me wearing them. I was, fascinated by the imprints of the pattern on the bottom of the soles of the shoes that forms upon stepping over dusty and loose dirt.

The summer months were the best times for me, as there was no school to go to and of course, no more beatings by the teachers. During the early summer season, all fruit trees, including Fig, Almond and Pomegranate trees start showing their early fruit. My best childhood friend, Mohamad al-Anouti who we used to call him by his baby name, Hammoudi and I would spend the whole day in the fields look-ing for bird nests, killing snakes and of course, trespassing other peoples' property to sample the seasonal fruits. Unlike me, Hammoudi was a very good shooter, as he always had a direct hit on a bird with his rubber sling. I rarely had that pleasure, as I never succeeded in hitting a bird or any other object with my rubber slingshot due to my lacking coordination.

I was obsessed with the mourning dove. Hammoudi and I were keen on finding any mourning dove nests. We roamed and checked the trees in the fields for nests, especially the olive trees where the mourning dove nests. Once we spot a nest, we would climb up the tree and check the nest out to see if the eggs have hatched. Should we find no hatching of the eggs has occurred, we would make daily trips to check on the nest to see if the eggs have already hatched with hatchlings in the nest. We would pick the hatchlings up and bring them home to raise as pets. I had one of these mourn-ing doves used as a pet. This pet bird was never caged but was free to roam around the

house. Unfortunately, and with deep sadness that engulfed me when the mourning
dove was caught by a stray cat who had it on its dinner table.

Al-Bassa organized a Boy Scout team where boys 6-8 years of age enrolled in
to form the backbone of a viable Boy Scout troupe. I am not sure whether uncle
Mohamad or his oldest son, Adel bought me the Boy Scout garb consisting of woolen
dark blue shorts, a Kaki shirt, a hat, a scarf and a rope. Now I have become all set to
be a boy scout with all its trimmings.

**(Photo of the four cousins, three of which in Boy Scout garb and standing in
attention. From left: cousin Darwish, cousin Suleiman,
me and cousin Adnan standing in attention and giving the
Boy Scout salute)**

Every evening cousin Adel asked us, to line up by the window and recite a poem
he had taught us before. Cousin Darwish, the one on the left of the picture was asked
to first recite the poem, then followed by cousin Suleiman, myself and then by Adnan.
It was unfortunate that neither Darwish nor Suleiman could recite the poem and only
me who was successful in the recitation. Of course, Adnan was a little kid and was
not expected to know the poem.

1948
THE CATASTROPHE

I HAVE NOT FINISHED GRAMMAR SCHOOL IN PALESTINE. OUR EDUCA-
tion was, interrupted by the war of 1948. On the very early hours of May 14, 1948,
troops wearing the Arab Legion (Jordanian army) uniforms attacked our town. For
a moment, people thought they have come to protect us against the Jewish militias,
but as they came closer, they started shooting at us. We realized then that they were
indeed Jewish militia impersonating the Jordanian army! We started screaming and
crying fearing for our lives. My sister Fatima, uncle Mohamad's first wife, her children and myself, headed north and climbed the mountain separating Palestine from
Lebanon. My sister Amina was sent to a different town to, work as a servant for uncle
Mohamad's second wife's sister and her family. My sister Fatima, myself and other
members of the family, hid behind boulders, for cover and as a shield from bullets
fired by Jewish rifle and machine guns as the firing kept going on until the late hours
of the night. We ran away with nothing to carry. I, for one was wearing a short sleeve
shirt, shorts and sandals without socks. That was all I had, and the rest of the family
had nothing except the clothes they had on their bodies. Uncle Mohamad, his new
wife and their children, headed for Lebanon a month earlier and settled in the town
of al-Ghaziyeh east of the southern city of Sidon.

The Arab governments assured us that our stay outside Palestine was only temporary, and we will be back home within a couple of weeks! We were brainwashed by
the Arab governments that the 'glorious Arab Armies' will liberate Palestine from the
Jewish thugs within two weeks. Wow what a farce that was.

Many of the Arab countries, in the Middle East were under occupation, after
World War I. They were, occupied and colonized by the British and by the French.
The Arab governments had no say in, or perhaps no understanding of foreign policy
or how the games nations play. They did understand neither the colonial western
mentality nor did they understand the games nations play in achieving their goals
and promoting their own interests. Well, the Brits controlled Palestine, Egypt, Iraq
and Trans Jordan while the French controlled Syria and Lebanon. Trans Jordan had
a titular ruler who as the new king who was crowned by the Brits, of course. This
titular king, named Abdallah was one of the remnants of the Hashemite dynasty
that that once they lived in, but were ultimately driven out of the Arabian Peninsula.
They were, promised a foothold in Trans Jordan by the Brits. The real ruler of Trans

Jordan was not king Abdallah, but a British general named John Bagot Glubb. He was, placed in that position, because of his Masonic affiliation and under pressure of the International Masonic organization. His role in that position was to promote and protect the British 'Empire's' interests and policies in the Middle East. Of course, British interests were to make sure that the infamous Balfour declaration of November 2nd, 1917, is implemented and enforced with the fulfillment of establishing a Jewish homeland in my country that was once called Palestine.

In that infamous Balfour declaration, foreign Minister Arthur Balfour granted Palestine to the Jews, for the establishment of a Jewish homeland. Did Balfour or the government of 'His Majesty' ever own an inch of Palestine so that they can give the country away as a gift to the Jews? Of course, not. They did not own a single inch of Palestine. Victors of wars are always the ones who dictate the terms and conditions as to how to rule the defeated and conquered people and their countries. That was the decision, based on appeasing the Jews and conforming to their demands. Britain, as one of the victors in World War I, was determined to offer the Jews a homeland in Palestine. The infamous Balfour declaration was the reward to the lobbying efforts and to the monies, paid by these Jewish lobbyists to British politicians by the Zionists. Theodore Herzl declared in the Zionist congress in Basel, Switzerland in 1889 that Palestine belongs to the Jews and that it will be the Jewish homeland. Support to his claim was forthcoming when on November 2nd of 1917, the British Foreign Secretary, Arthur Balfour spit out his infamous declaration. Herzl's predictions came to fruition in 1948, resulting in the establishment of Israel as the homeland for the Jews at the expense of the majority, Palestinian Arab population.

Knowing well enough that the Arab population in Palestine vastly outnumbered the Jewish population, by at least threefold in 1947, the Brits, while mandating Palestine, allowed Jews to immigrate into Palestine with no restrictions imposed on the number of immigrants or on the country from which they were coming from. It could be argued that the Christian West represented by, the Brits at the time felt the guilt of what Hitler and the Nazis have done to the Jews in Germany prior to and during World War II. Does that feeling of guilt justify the uprooting of a population of a whole country and supplant it with another group of people who are foreign to the land? Does that feeling of guilt and sympathy to the Jews, as exhibited by the Christian West towards the Jews, justify the uprooting of the Palestinians (Christians and Moslems) to create a new diaspora? Is not this Palestinian Arab diaspora identical, in form, to the diaspora the Jews had suffered through the centuries? Well, history not only is a great teacher, but it also repeats itself.

Well, never forget the saying 'what goes around comes around'! It is ironic that victims of atrocities perpetrated against them, do themselves become the perpetrators of the same or more vicious kind of atrocities against their perceived enemies.

This is the case, in which we have witnessed for the past seventy plus years, where the Israeli Jews mistreated and many a time tortured, killed and expelled the Palestinian Arabs from their homes and from their land just like what the Nazis did to the Jews!

The Nazis treatment and torture and the use of gas chambers to eliminate the Jews from Germany and neighboring countries as their final solution, was an absolute war crime. It was savagery and inhumane for a human being to treat his fellow human being the way the Nazis did to the Jews. It should never, be condoned nor should it ever be allowed to be practiced against any people. It should not have any room in any civilized society.

I have several Jewish friends in the United States. Many of them feel sympathy with the Palestinian people, yet they are vehement supporters of Israel. Sympathy is one thing and many a time it conflicts with reality.

Sympathy is an expression of emotions. It does neither buy, groceries nor does it lead to the resolution of the subject matter. It does not address the root causes of the problem nor does it offer any plausible remedies to the damages that have already taken place. How could sympathy to the Palestinian cause help the Palestinians regain their rights? It could only happen when sympathy is, combined with a clear road map and plan of action to achieve the intended goal of the liberation of Palestine.

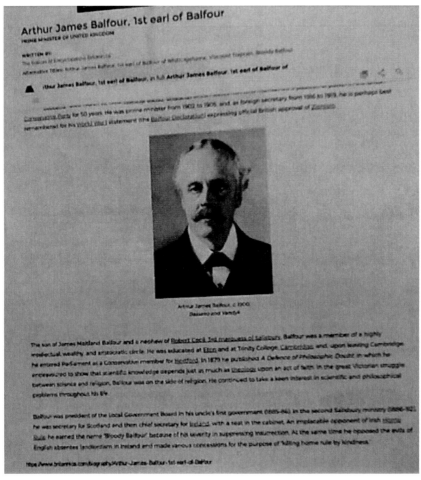

(This is the photo of the infamous Arthur Balfour, the British Foreign Secretary, who gave Palestine on November 2nd, 1917 to the Jews so that they establish their homeland in Palestine. Herzl's dream of a Jewish home in Palestine was, achieved and the country now called Israel)

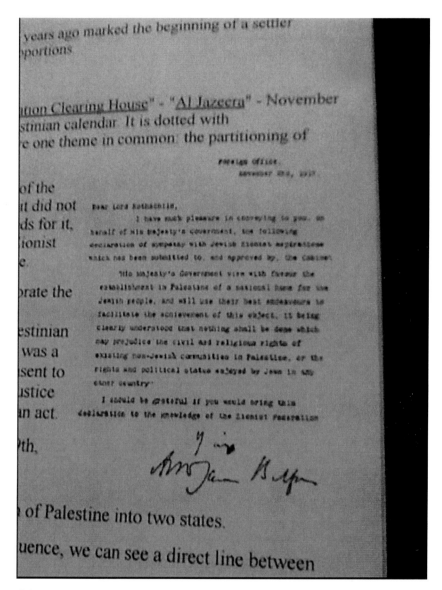

(Photocopy of the text of the infamous Balfour declaration obtained from the archives related to Palestine)

To have a joint Arab action to liberate Palestine from Jewish thugs, the Arab League appointed King Abdallah of Trans Jordan to lead the combined Arab Forces in their effort to liberate Palestine from the Zionist thugs. Abdallah was neither qualified nor was he a military person to lead a military expedition. It should be noted that the

Arab League offices were in Cairo, Egypt and Egypt was under the British occupation, thus the Arab League could not and would not go against the dictates of the occupier but rather will obey the directs and wishes of the occupier. Although King Abdallah of Transjordan was the titular head of the Arab forces, the real commander of the Arab Legion (Jordanian army) from 1939 to 1956, was John Bagot Glubb, the British general who later was, bestowed with the Ottoman title of 'Pasha'. Pasha Glubb and knighted by the British monarch with a 'Sir' title, not Abdallah, was the real commander-in-chief of these combined Arab forces. When the Iraqi troops crossed into Transjordan from Iraq to enter the fighting for the liberation of Palestine, they were told, by Glubb's mouthpiece, king Abdallah said NO. That showed the naivety of and the misplaced trust in king Abdallah by the other Arab states. More than likely king Abdallah had a close relationship with the Jewish enemy. It was rumored that he had a romantic relationship with Golda Meir, who later became the Prime Minister of the Zionist entity. The cozy relationship between the Hashemite dynasty and the Jewish leadership again confirmed in 1967 and again in 1973 when Abdallah's successor to the throne, his grandson Hussain, who inherited the throne from his grandfather, after passing over Abdallah's son, prince Talal, to become king of Jordan. He flew to Tel Aviv to warn Golda Meir of the impending Syrian and Egyptian attack against Israel! Being a member of the Joint Arab Defense Committee of the Arab League, Jordan's Hussain had access to all the military plans and secrets drawn up, by the Syrian and Egyptian armies to attack Israel. Treachery and obeying orders of their western handlers are in their character and runs in the blood of the Jordanian rulers.

One needs not ignore the fact that king Hussain of Jordan was an agent of the CIA with a monthly stipend of one million US dollars. It leaves no doubt, in my mind, that he may have been ordered, by the CIA to fly to Tel Aviv and alert the Israelis of the impending Syrian and Egyptian attack. As an agent of the United States Central Intelligence Agency (CIA), a leader of an Arab country, he had access to information and intelligence about all Arab countries, their armies and armaments, their leaders and politicians. All intelligence and details of each of the Arab countries and their armies were, transmitted to Israel directly by Hussain or indirectly through the CIA.

The question remains as to how could the Brits grant the country of Palestine which they did not even own as a freebee to the Jews to establish their homeland? It was, realized that the Jewish lobby in Britain was very vocal and powerful to influence the British government to obey its orders. It was Jewish bribe money used to bribe the British members of parliament to force Balfour to issue his infamous declaration.

As it may be difficult to read the declaration as depicted by Aljazeera, the full text is, thus presented in a clearer format of the declaration:

Following is the full text of the Infamous Balfour declaration that was issued by Arthur Balfour, the foreign Secretary of Britain on November 2nd, 1917

"The Balfour declaration:

Foreign Office

November 2nd, 1917

Dear Lord Rothschild,

I have much pleasure in conveying to you on behalf of His Majesty's government the following declaration of sympathy, with Jewish Zionist aspirations which has been submitted to and approved by, the cabinet.

The declaration addressed to Lord Rothschild by Arthur Balfour clearly stipulates

His Majesty's government view with favour the establishment in Palestine of a national home for the Jewish people and will use their best endeavour to facilitate the achievement of this object. It is being clearly understood that nothing shall be done which may prejudice the civil and religious rights of the existing non-Jewish communities in Palestine, or the rights and political status enjoyed by Jews in any other country'

I should be grateful if you would bring this declaration to the knowledge of the Zionist Federation.

Arthur Balfour"

Although the Balfour declaration did not specifically stipulate the partition of the land of Palestine between Palestinian Arabs and Palestinian Jews. This declaration was the beginning that eventually allowed the Zionists to take over the whole country of Palestine, delete its legal name and replace it with the name of the newly established state of Israel!

The United Nations General Assembly, on November 29, 1947 passed Resolution 181 recommended the partition of Palestine into two States: One Palestinian Arab and the other Palestinian Jewish.

The seeds for establishing a Jewish homeland in Palestine were sown by the Balfour Declaration on November 2nd, 1917, germinated throughout the years and reached fruition and became ready to harvest in 1947. Although the United Nations

Partition plan was accepted, by the Zionists they later trashed it. The Arab States spent their time and energies lamenting and complaining.

Although the Arab states rejected the Partition Plan for Palestine, yet they were, out-maneuvered by the Zionists who accepted it outright. The partition plan, although endorsed by the Zionists, it was later dumped in the waste basket as David Ben Gurion, the first Israeli prime minister said in his memoirs, that we accepted the plan as a tactical move to take over all of Palestine.

Atrocities committed by Jewish militias, including the Stern gang of Yitzhak Shamir, the Irgun gang of Menachem Begin, the Lehi militants and the Hagenah against armless Palestinians, caused mass exodus into neighboring countries. The massacre of Deri Yasin, perpetrated by the Lehi Zionist terrorist group against the inhabitants of this Palestinian village, was enough to scare people off and force them to run for safety and shelter wherever they can find one. Men, women and children were, murdered left and right in cold blood. Pregnant Palestinian women bellies were, cut open to get the fetuses out and throw the fetuses to the dogs. Young and old women were, raped in the open. These atrocities were, well publicized in newspapers and on radio to frighten the Palestinian Arabs to flee the country! Of course, these atrocities and fear of rapes of women and children did the job. That forced the Palestinians to flee the country into neighboring states.

There were prominent Jewish voices who condemned these atrocities. Notable among these was Albert Einstein who on April 10, 1948, just one month before the establishment of State of Israel, wrote a letter to Shepard Rifkin, Executive Director of American Friends of the Fighters for the Freedom of Israel, denouncing these atrocities perpetrated by the Jewish militias against the Palestinian people.

The plan as designed by the Zionist movement of having ethnic cleansing of Palestine of its Arab population was implemented regardless of what albert Einstein or other pacifists' protests were.

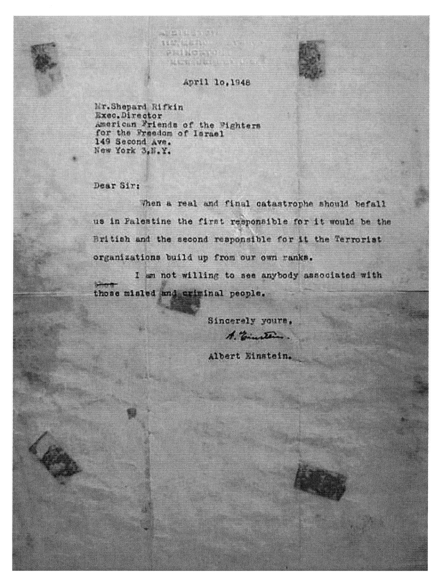

April 1o,1948

Mr.Shepard Rifkin
Exec.Director
American Friends of the Fighters
for the Freedom of Israel
149 Second Ave.
New York 3,N.Y.

Dear Sir:

When a real and final catastrophe should befall
us in Palestine the first responsible for it would be the
British and the second responsible for it the Terrorist
organizations build up from our own ranks.

I am not willing to see anybody associated with
those misled and criminal people.

Sincerely yours,

A. Einstein.

Albert Einstein.

(Photocopy of the April 10, 1948 letter that Albert Einstein wrote to Shepard Rifkin, Executive Director of the American Friends of the fighters for the Freedom of Israel blaming the atrocities against Palestinians blamed on the Brits first and on the Jewish terrorist organizations second.

Einstein's letter was sent thirty-five days before the declaration of the existence of the State of Israel)

Text of the letter from Albert Einstein to Shepard Rifkin adds, then a real and final catastrophe should befall us in Palestine the first responsible for it would be the British and the second responsible for it the terrorist organizations build up from our ranks. I am not willing to see anybody associated with these misled and criminal people.

Albert Einstein denounced the atrocities that were committed by the Zionist Jewish terrorists against Palestinians. He blamed the Jewish terrorists, in his letter to Shepard Rifkin, 'the terrorist organizations build up from our own ranks' implying that such atrocities are not compatible with Jewish values.

Based on his human and Jewish cherished values, Einstein declined the offer to be the first president of the newly established State of Israel. Albert Einstein could not in good conscious, accept an offer that he felt was in direct contradiction with his own values and his commitments to humanity.

As can be noted in the Balfour declaration, the non-Jewish communities, in Palestine, 'should not be prosecuted or discriminated against by Jews and Jews in other (Arab) countries should not be discriminated against either'. Of course, contrary to the stipulations mentioned in the Balfour declaration, the opposite has and still is taking place nowadays. Palestinians, including myself were, forced out of their homes and land under the force of arms. Israel, being a staunch ally of the United States can do anything it so desires with impunity. The United States umbrella to protect Israel, gave the latter the green light to commit any atrocities, not only against Palestinians but also against its neighbors as well. All United Nations Resolutions regarding the Palestinian question and of the Palestinian refugees were trashed by Israel as it is under the protection of the American political umbrella. Because of the United State government protection of Israel, it could neither be touched nor criticized by any other country for what it does otherwise that country will pay the price! Israel, like the United States, belongs to the untouchables club. Is this, the democracy we are trying to promote worldwide? I do not think so. The loss of Palestine due to the establishment of a Jewish homeland is, a western conspiracy in which foreign lands occupied and claimed to belong to the occupier with no regard to the local population or for the international law.

Western countries are leaders in the occupation and colonization of other countries and peoples. The occupying and colonizing countries, in addition to the Brits include Holland, Portugal, France, Belgium, Italy and of course, our country, the United States.

One cannot deny the fact that the French, not only occupied Algeria for 132 years, but they went as far as to claim Algeria, as a territory, that was part of France. They named it *Algerie Francaise*. The same goes for the Belgians. They occupied the Congo and claimed it to be one of their own, naming it the Belgian Congo! The Portuguese occupied present day Brazil, the Dutch occupied parts of Indonesia, the Italians occupied Libya and the Brits occupied Australia by using it as a dump of British criminals. Our country of the United States occupied North America and the list, goes on and on. In no instance, was there any ethnic cleansing of the local population of these occupied countries and none were, pushed out of their homes or their land, as the Israelis did to the Palestinian population.

I have a Jewish neighbor who I consider as a 'good' neighbor said, Israel was established in Palestine because Jews were, in Palestine two thousand years ago, hence the Jews are not occupiers, but liberators of their own occupied country! They came back to their own country, the Promised Land! Wow! I laughed at his logic and reminded my 'good' neighbor that he and I are living in an occupied land. Are we not? You know, my 'good' neighbor, our country was established by European occupiers who defeated the native population and our republic was declared in 1776, barely 241 years ago. Are you saying the Native Americans have the right to liberate the country you and I live in, should they become powerful? I remind you my 'good' neighbor that your reasoning is not only ridiculous, it does not hold. I advise you to read and acquaint yourself with events in history. I may also recommend that you read and comprehend the historical events pertaining to American history, especially as they relate to the establishment of the republic. Further, when the republic was established, not a single person of the defeated Native Americans was thrown out of the country. Your argument that the Jews were in Palestine two thousand years ago, is not only futile, but it has no merit and does not even hold! It is therefore, in my opinion, null and void. It is based on ignorance, lies, deceit and on fabricated facts.

Some Arab rulers were part of the conspiracy that led to the loss of Palestine to the Jews. The Arab countries were, occupied and colonized by two western powers, the Brits and the French. Western leaders were bribed and pressured by the powerful Zionist lobby, to abandon their prestige, their principles and their honor by not only favoring, but also by paving the way for Jewish immigration into Palestine to create facts on the ground, that will help in the establishment of a Jewish homeland in the country.

Some Arab supporters of the British Balfour declaration was the founding monarch of present day, Saudi Arabia, Abdul Aziz Al-Saud was bribed by Chaim Weizmann with thirty million pounds sterling when he requested his help in facilitating Jewish immigration and accepting the establishment of a Jewish homeland in Palestine. King Abdul Aziz saw the money and could not resist the offer. He then declared that he had no objection to having Palestine given to the 'poor Jews" as can be seen in the following document, bearing his photograph and his signature. Arab leaders and business people owning or controlling property, in Palestine, also sold their properties to the Jewish Agency. It is also reported that the Lebanese al-Salam family who owned large swaths if land in Palestine also bowed out and sold the properties they controlled to the Jewish Agency.:

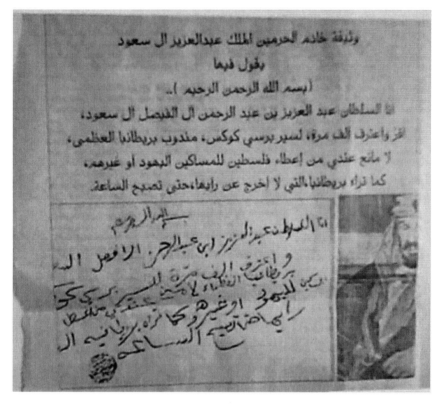

(The founder of the kingdom of Saudi Arabia, Abdul Aziz Al-Saud conspired with the Brits to offer Palestine to the "poor Jews" or others as Great Britain may see fit)

Of course, that was after he was, bribed by Chaim Weizmann with thirty million British pounds. Well, everything has a price, and the price of Palestine, according to Abdul Aziz al-Saud was thirty million pounds Sterling!)

Following is the translation, from the Arabic of the document bearing Abdul Aziz al-Saud's signature granting Palestine to the 'poor Jews' or any others as Britain sees fit:

Document of the Protector of the two Holy places states that:

"In the Name of God, the most kind, and the Merciful.

I, the Sultan, Abdul Aziz son of Abdel Rahman al-Faisal Al-Saud, confirm and admit one thousand times to Sir Percy Cooks,

**representative of Great Britain, that I have no objection to offer
Palestine to the poor Jews or others, as Britain sees fit and I will not
deviate from her opinion until the end of the world".**

This admission and assertion, that Abdul Aziz Al-Saud had no problem giving
Palestine to the poor Jews or to others stems from the need of Abdul Aziz for the Brits
to keep him in power and to maintain his grip on the Arabian Peninsula. The thirty
million-pound sterling, Chaim Weizmann had offered to Ibn Saud was enough of an
enticement to lead him to his infamous declaration. As usual and as always, the end
justifies the means.

To add to the conspiratorial portfolio of the Saudi dynasty, Faisal Ibn Saud, son of
Abdul Aziz, who inherited the throne after deposing his own brother, Saud followed
his father's footsteps in paving the way for the establishment of a Jewish home for the
Jews in Palestine. He wrote a letter, in 1966, to President Lyndon Johnson asking him
to encourage and urge Israel to attack Egypt, Syria and the West bank of the Jordan,
which was under the control of the Jordanians.

Faisal's rationale, a defeat of the Egyptian and Syrian armies and the occupation of the West Bank of the Jordan River was two-fold: A defeat of the Egyptian and
Syrian armies will lend more protection of the kingdom and its interests for a long
time to come. Occupation of the West bank will deny the Palestinians any right of
return to historic Palestine. The text of the attached letter from Faisal to President
Lyndon Johnson:

The text of the letter, in Arabic was, published by the official proceedings of
the Yemen Congress Party depicting Faisal's appeal to President Johnson for help
in destroying the Egyptian and Syrian armies as well as the occupation of the West
Bank. Faisal's wish was, achieved less than a year later by the June 5, 1967 six-day war
in which Israel attacked both Egypt and Syria. Such an attack resulted in the neutral-
ization of the Egyptian, the Syrian and the Jordanian armies and the occupation of
Egyptian, Syrian and Jordanian controlled territories. As a result, this war fulfilled
king Faisal's wishes and aspirations leading to the Israeli occupation, of the Sinai from
Egypt, the Golan heights from Syria and the West bank of Palestine which was under
the Jordanian jurisdiction

(Photo of King Faisal, King of Saudi Arabia with United States President Lyndon Johnson upon the visit of the former to the United States in 1966)

King Faisal, in his letter to Lyndon Johnson indicated Egypt, will not withdraw from Yemen unless Israel moves to occupy Gaza, the Sinai and the West Bank of the Jordan. Such an Israeli move will force Gamal Abdel Nasser to withdraw from Yemen, thus relieving Saudi Arabia of the pressures caused by the Egyptian troops in neighboring Yemen.

Referring to the Egyptian role in Yemen as a danger, not only for the region and to Saudi Arabia, but also to the United States. King Faisal offered suggestions as to how deal with Egypt, to protect the common interests of both the United States and of Saudi Arabia: Firstly: The United States should encourage and support Israel to attack Egypt and occupy all important areas. This will not only force it (Egypt) to withdraw its forces from Yemen, but also will make Egypt pre-occupied with Israel for a long time to come.

King Faisal's letter to Lyndon Johnson also described Egypt as the great enemy not only for Saudi Arabia, but also for the United States.

Faisal further stated that Syria, should also be attacked by Israel and a part of its territory occupied, so that after the defeat of Egypt, Syria will not be able to fill the Egyptian void in promoting Arab nationalism.

Israel should also be encouraged to occupy Gaza and the West Bank, so that any hope Palestinians may have for return to Palestine or for the establishment of an Arab state next to Israel will be, quashed forever.

Following is the translation of King Faisal's letter to president Lyndon Johnson:

In the name of God, the Merciful

Kingdom of Saudi Arabia

King of Saudi Arabia

Your Excellency the great President Lyndon Johnson

President of the United States Washington DC

The Great Mr. President:

During my visit to the United States in May 1966, I was honored to meet with you and was extremely pleased with the extreme interest you have shown at what I explained to you about the dangerous role Egypt was playing in Yemen, the area in general in supporting, by its broadcasts, our enemies in the area. I am pleased to know of your interest in what I explained to you about Egypt's dangerous role in Yemen and in the region in general, with the support of the revolutionaries and their broadcasts promoting the negative feelings of the people against us all, against the United States of America and against the Kingdom of Saudi Arabia. Saudi Arabia has always been a constant and historic target of the Egyptian plan to overthrow our rule, but your Excellency, you saw that the best way to confront the evil is to continue to exert pressure and to increase efforts for possible mediation to draw closer to Egypt itself. Perhaps through this convergence, it may ensure the silencing of its (Egyptian) negative broadcasts about the Kingdom of Saudi Arabia, which is our great nation in the region due to the sanctity of its territory. The United States may not, be interested in what Egypt and others say, and through the agreement of the Kingdom of Saudi Arabia with Egypt, we may solve many problems in the region, including the problem of (Yemen). This is what you have said Mr. President and you should not ignore. Mr. President, what the mediators such as the Sudanese President Mohamed Mahgoub and other personalities have done along, with the efforts I have made, in this regard since I took over governing the country.

On August 9, 1964, I met Egyptian President Abdel Nasser at the Summit in Alexandria. We also met at the Conference of

Non-Aligned Countries in Cairo in October 1964. At that time, the two sides agreed on the following points:

1. To stop the defamation campaigns emanating from Cairo against us.

2. Resolving the differences between the various parties in Yemen as we see fit as follows:

   (a) The withdrawal of the Egyptian army from Yemen;

   (b) The radical elements that overthrew King Mohammed Al-Badr and his family such as al-Sallal, al-Jazilan and others are to be, and must be, exiled away out of Yemen

   (c) The involvement of the monarchists in governance with people of moderate views in running the country.

   (d) At that time, the Kingdom undertook the decision of suspending any external Aid and Supplies to the monarchists

However, what we have agreed upon with Abdel Nasser fell through, because he ignored all of what we have agreed upon and his radio broadcasts continued against us and accusing us of being agents of America and of Israel. Knowing well enough that we never denied our friendship with America, which bestows upon us the great honor. Knowing well enough, Egypt did not comply with her promises, but the agreements fell through, as the other party did not abide with what we had agreed to with Abdel Nasser. Knowing well enough we did not deny our friendship, with America, a friendship which bestowed upon us that great honor, and since Egypt did not honor its obligations, we have extended our patience and we told Abdel Nasser to stop the flow of blood in Yemen, we both must work together, to find the appropriate solution. We proposed the following:

1. Establishment of a Presidential council consisting of 5 monarchist members and others who promote and respect the interests of Yemen only

2. Establishment of a Ministerial council the numbers of which to be agreed upon

3. Establishment of a Consultative body to help in overseeing progress and governance. These councils will serve for a period of six months or a year:

   (a) The withdrawal of the Egyptian forces from Yemen

   (b) As soon as the withdrawal of the Egyptian forces from Yemen begins, the kingdom of Saudi Arabia will stop providing any war or military help to the monarchists

   (c) A referendum on the kind of government (monarchist of republican) which the tribes and other Yeminis will approve

   (d) The Kingdom of Saudi Arabia will commit to guarantee that no military or non-military aid will be provided to any Yemini government unless that government formally requests such aid from us

This is one of the proposals we presented to Egypt. Although Egypt accepted and agreed with the proposal, yet Egypt did not stop meddling in the affairs of Yemen.

The Egyptians did not honor any agreement. On the contrary, they increased their involvement until they became the only source of supply to our enemies. In addition, they have doubled the number of their forces after fifteen thousand Egyptian soldiers and hundred thousand monarchists and republican Yemenis were, killed.

This has led to a general discontent, against Egyptians, among the Yemenis, which prompted a large number, of Yemeni leaders to ask us for help to put an end to the Egyptian colonizers. Another group, of Yemeni tribe leaders held a conference at the beginning of August 1965. At that conference which they named the "Taif Agreement". They asked us to work with them, for kicking the Egyptians out, and work in such a way to make the Egyptians stay away from Yemen. The sustained Yemeni Jihad against the Egyptians and against the republicans continued until Abdel Nasser came to us in Jeddah where he kissed my forehead and my nose, according to Arab tradition. At that meeting, he asked our help to end the Yemeni catastrophe.

The meeting referred to the "Jeddah Agreement" ended with the broadcasting of the terms of the agreement that lasted from August 22nd to August 24, 1965:

1. Establishing a conference consisting of fifty members representing all Yemeni groups, to be held in the Yemini town of al-Hard on November 23, 1965 to decide on the following terms:

   (a) Determination of the manner which the Yemeni people are to be ruled

   (b) Establishment of an interim ministry

   (c) Establishment of a popular referendum no later than November 23, 1966

   (d) The Saudi kingdom will promptly stop providing the monarchists with any military aid

   (e) Egypt will have to withdraw, all its military forces, from Yemen within ten months beginning on November 23, 1965

   (f) One Saudi committee and one Egyptian committee will oversee the implementation of these decisions. Indeed, the conference in the presence of both the Saudi and Egyptian committees was held on time however, the meetings that lasted from November 23, 1965 until January 6, 1966 have ended without any progress and without even the least tangible result favoring the monarchists.

The letter addressed to me, by the head of the monarchist team in this conference, Mr. Ahmad el-Shami, clearly illustrates:

1. Members of the other team consist of criminals who have massacred innocent people, stole the funds and committed atrocities in the name of the republic that is to be imposed upon us under the force of the arms of the occupying Egyptians

2. The arrogance exhibited by the members of the so-called Republican team in denial of the Jeddah accords cannot be, but is the result of the strong Egyptian support

3. According to our confirmed reports, the Egyptian army will not withdraw from Yemen, but a ploy to gain time for the Egyptians and for the republican thugs

4. We understood the Jeddah accords to be the half way proposal to rule Yemen, that is, not republican and not monarchist. However, the so-called republicans told us that they are not willing to a single step to meet the monarchists. The republicans insist the legal regime be, recognized by, the United Nations as well as by the Arab League. We understand that America, Britain. Saudi Arab kingdom and all other monarchies did not recognize this implied republican regime.

Based on Mr. Ahmad al-Shami's report and of others, the following has become clear to us:

1. It is obviously clear that even if the revolutionary rulers of Yemen did go away even with the current Yemeni regime and should the Egyptian army not withdraw or even any Egyptian presence remaining in Yemen is dangerous.

2. It will result with a very unpleasant outcome not only for us alone but also for our friends, the Americans, the British and other western countries. This is especially significant, as Nasser has declared in his speech in Yemen. In that speech, he reiterated that he will support the revolutionaries in the South in an effort to kick out the British and force them to leave this Arab land which they have, all along, referred to it as their protectorate.

This, Mr. President, is how Abdel Nasser reaffirmed in his speech by saying that the Egyptian army will stay in Yemen and will not withdraw unless Saudi Arabia stops supplying the monarchist thugs. He will not withdraw his troops not only until Saudi Arabia stops supplying the monarchist thugs, but also until the withdrawal of the last British soldier from the southern part of the Arabian Peninsula. Abdel Nasser also said, the Egyptian army did not come to occupy Yemen, it is, neither a mercenary army nor did it come to gain from Yemen. The Egyptian army came in to shed blood and bear the cost for the defense of the Yemeni revolution and the Yemini soil from the dangers of Saudi Arabia. This danger to Saudi Arabia is not different from the dangers inflicted by both America and Britain. For these reasons, the Egyptian army came to Yemen, as it did, to support the revolutionaries of the South and the revolutionaries of the Arabian Peninsula. Abdel Nasser ended his speech by saying that "the boots of the smallest and youngest (Egyptian) soldier that fights the Saudi reactionaries in Yemen and their cohorts is more honorable, to us, than the crown with golden-thistles and double looped on Faisal's head".

Frankly, this is Egypt's opinion, Mr. President. It is the new Egyptian opinion under the leadership of Abdel Nasser and his gang. This opinion reminds us of the old opinion of Egypt under the leadership of Mohammad Ali Pasha and Ibrahim Pasha in the year 1818 when they annihilated members of our early Saudi dynasty as well as the religious clerics. They killed some of our ancestors and chained others were sent to Egypt. They placed some of them in large pots and boiled them while others were, kept as captives in Egypt until they died.

Mohammad Ali justified these actions by saying "my intention is to get rid of the Saudi and Wahabi dynasties, in an effort to stop the sectorial division (*fitna*) among the people". The division that the Arabic Profit said, when he was, asked about this (*fitna*) division, he responded by saying it three times: The division originates from Najd (Saudi Arabia) and will return to it. Now we have destroyed the Saudi and the Wahabi *fitna* so that it will not return to the Moslem Arab Najd once again. This is what Mohammad Ali said, however, the survivors from our dynasty gave the free world this strong and great fighter (Saudi Arabia) against the promotors of destructive principles.

For this reason, the rulers of the new Egypt will do anything they can to restore their history with the intention of annihilating us.

The reason they succeeded the first time around because there was no big, compassionate and friendly great America and because of our great friend, they will not succeed now.

In addition, Mr. President we will be frank with you as we were with your predecessors. The destiny of the Saudi dynasty and the strong bond with America do not get their power from any other source, but from the same common aspirations and goals that bind America with our dynasty and the dependence on us, to protect western interests, in both the Arab and the Islamic worlds as a great power to be reckoned with.

The bonding between us America will, protect the common interests and will continue the fight against communism and other destructive principles. Whether these principles come out in the name of "revolutionary" or "Republican" or "fighting imperialism" in the name of Arab Nationalism, Freedom, Socialism, and unity or in the name of Freedom and Socialism. The Saudi family confronts these evil principles because they are the bulletin boards and the propaganda machines for communism, the enemy of all of us.

In the name, of the same common destiny and the shared interests we ask you Mr. President, as to what would the opinion of the United States be regarding protecting our throne from the danger of these evil principles. This contagion was, brought to our kingdom by the Egyptian sympathizers and by the presence of the army on our borders, and the broadcasts by Egyptian radio, in our environment.

From all of what we have briefly explained, Mr. President, it is clear to you that Egypt is the big enemy to all of us. This enemy, if allowed to continue supporting our enemies, whether through the media or through military means, the year 1970, as the American experts have said, our throne and our common interests will not be in existence. For this reason, I honor and respect what the American experts have said to bring forth to you the following suggestions:

1. The United States should encourage and support Israel in launching a lightning strike against Egypt and take over all the essential places in Egypt that it will be forced not only to withdraw its forces from Yemen. It will also have Egypt become preoccupied with Israel. That will keep Egypt away from us for a long time to come. This will have the effect of having no Egyptian, to ever raise his head with the intention of fighting us, thus reinvigorating Mohammad Ali's and Gamal Abdel Nasser's ambitions in the name of Arab Unity. In this way, we will have granted ourselves a long pause to rid the destructive principles from our environs, not only from

our kingdom, but also from the Arab countries. Thus, we have no objection of providing Egypt and the like countries with aid so that we can silence the voices of their media.

2. Syria the second country should not, be spared from the Israeli attack. The occupation of parts of its territory will make it preoccupied so that it will not step in and fill the vacuum left by the defeat of Egypt seeking Arab nationalism

3. The Gaza Strip, currently under Egyptian control as well as the West bank from Jordan, by Israel. Occupation of the Gaza Strip and the West Bank of the Jordan River is extremely important, as it will control the Palestinians, so that they will have no claim for any land ruled by an Arab country. That will not permit the Palestinians, to be exploited by, the Arab country with the excuse of the liberation of Palestine. At this point, any hope of return will sublime. It also becomes easy to hit any of those Palestinian opposition groups in any Arab country neighboring Israel, as no country will be able to endure the outcome of their opposing Palestinian actions. This will also facilitate their forced assimilation and citizenship in the Arab countries where they reside.

4. We should strengthen Mustapha al-Barazani by supporting him to establish a Kurdish state in Northern Iraq. The main function of the Kurdish government will be to have any Arab leadership seeking Arab unity north of our kingdom, in the land of Iraq, at present or in the future to be futile, as the central government of Iraq will be preoccupied with the new Kurdish entity. Knowing well enough, we have been supplying Mustapha al-Barazani with funds and with arms from, within Iraq and through other channels in Turkey and Iran. Mr. President, you and us being united in our goals, our common interests, our destiny and survival will depend, to a large extent, on whether, we implement these suggestions or not.

Lastly, I cease this opportunity to renew my best wishes for you and for the United States for a bright future and for a stronger bond and relationship between our two countries in the future.

Sincerely,

Faisal Ibn Abdel Aziz

King, Kingdom of Saudi Arabia   27 December 1966

15 Ramadan 1386H

All of Faisal's suggestions and requests to Lyndon Johnson bore fruit six months later when Israel attacked Egypt, Syria, Gaza and the West Bank in on June 5, 1967. Israel occupied the Sinai Peninsula from Egypt, the Gaza Strip which was under Egyptian control, the Golan Heights from Syria and the West Bank from Jordan. Lyndon Johnson complied with Faisal's suggestions and indeed Faisal had a great strategic intuition by depending on the United States to achieve his goals of maintaining the survival of the Saudi dynasty.

There was an erroneous document circulated on the internet that alleges the Saudi dynasty goes back to its Jewish origin! Should that be the case, why would anyone suspect then that the Israelis and the Saudis have the same agenda in regards to the Arabs in general and to the Palestinian cause in particular?

It does appear that the Jewish ingenuity of using money to bribe Arab leaders like the Saudi king Abdul Aziz and others as intended bore fruit and with time all their plans and ambitions were achieved. Some Arab leaders were hungry for, and willing to, do anything to secure a source of income regardless of the outcome of such bribes.

THE ZIONIST OCCUPATION OF PALESTINE COMPARED TO THE OCCUPATION OF OTHER LANDS BY THE CHRISTIAN WEST

UNLIKE THE BRITS, THE FRENCH, THE BELGIANS, THE DUTCH, THE Portuguese, the Italians and the Americans conquering and occupying foreign lands, the native population of the countries they conquered and occupied were, never expelled from their homes or from their properties. Neither the homes nor the properties were, confiscated, like what the Zionists have done to the Palestinian people. The Zionists occupied the country expelled the local Arab population including myself, under the force of arms and confiscated our property. We have become 'stateless' overnight with no government or country to claim us as its citizens.

The western mind works in one and only one direction. It preys on the weak, fights them, occupies their land, rubs them of their resources and dictate how the occupied lands should be governed. It was, brought to my attention upon discussing this issue with others, that Moslems and Arabs are not different from the westerns as far as occupation and colonization are concerned. They, the Moslems and Arabs, occupied Spain for seven centuries and their conquests reached China and Western Europe, so how different is the occupation and colonization of Spain, by Moslems and Arabs from those of western occupations and colonization? Did they, Moslems and Arabs, not name Spain, the country they occupied as Andalusia? Very true and history confirms these facts, however, it should be pointed out, the Moslems and Arabs did not expel the local population out of the country. Further, when the re-occupation of the country of Andalusia in 1492 by the Christians, they expelled, not only occupying Moslems and Arabs, but also all the Jews who have lived there for centuries as well! Expelling the Moslems and Arab occupiers may have been legitimate, to regain sovereignty of the country. Why were, the Jews also expelled?

The occupation of Palestine by the Jews did not only change the name of the country to eliminate any reference to Palestine or to the Palestinians, *but in addition, changed the species of the fungus, Actinomyces palestinensis,* from *palestinensis* to *israelii.* The *'Wandering Jew'segment'* in Mussorgsky's 'Pictures at an Exhibition' classical piece was, also deleted under pressure from Jewish and Zionist quarters! They committed atrocities against the native Palestinian population and forced the expulsion of over 650,000 Palestinians in a plan to change the demographics of the country! Neither the Christian Western countries nor the Moslems and Arabs did ever expel a single native from the countries they occupied and colonized.

LIFE IN LEBANON AS PALESTINIAN REFUGEES

HAVING NO MONEY, NO CLOTHING OR ANYTHING ELSE TO SUPPORT us after being forced out of Palestine, it was a nightmare to say the least. Uncle Mohamad's first wife and her children, my sister Fatima and I ran away across the mountain to Lebanon, hiding behind boulders to avoid being hit by, Jewish machinegun fire. I was wearing sandals with no socks, a half-sleeved shirt and a pair of shorts. That was all I had at the time!

We settled in a Shi'ite village, *Tair Harfa*, in South Lebanon. A Shi'ite family was very gracious to offer us a studio apartment at no rental charge. The owner of the apartment refused to charge any rent for the apartment he allowed us to use because we offered them jobs back in Palestine.

A very funny incident happened to uncle Mohamad when he came to visit his children from his first wife in *Tair Harfa*. A shoe-polish man from al-Bassa, kissed the ground when he saw uncle Mohamad and said to him: thank God, we both are now in the same boat and of equal status, meaning uncle Mohamad, a well to do and one of the leaders of the town, is in the same boat as the shoe-polish man as both are refugees! This incident, caused by the expulsion of the Palestinians, by the Jewish militias was very humiliating to uncle Mohamad. He lamented that life is not fair. A shoe-polish man now has, the same social status as mine! It is absurd, he said! Well history repeats itself in different forms and fashions.

The owner of the studio apartment in *Tair Harfa*, where we lived said, "**You Palestinians were very kind to us South Lebanese and now we are paying you back in kind**". That was a great help, as we did not have to pay rent. The savings of rent helped in our sustenance.

To provide food for the family we went to the wheat fields and pick the leftovers after the harvest. Since there were only two boys in our family that fled Palestine, cousin Darwish and me were the ones who were supposed to do the work in support of the family. I remember loading the bags of wheat on the back of the donkey to deliver to the mill that was about five miles away, to have it ground into flour for us to use in making bread, our basic staple for survival. I also used to go to the vegetable fields of tomatoes, cucumbers, beans, okra, cauliflower and eggplant to pick leftovers after the vegetable harvest was over. This was the only source of food we could have. Cousin Darwish, by choice, would not do any of these chores. The burden of provider for the family, was laid upon me as the sole provider for these services.

Water was scarce in the village. Many villagers had wells they used as a source of water. Cousin Darwish would do nothing to help and I, again was the only one who will carry on the burden and do all the chores required to meet the needs of the family. Luckily, we had access to a donkey, which I used to fetch water from an underground aquifer in the valley. The donkey and I headed down the valley to have two five-gallon cans filled with water. After the filled-up cans were loaded on the back of the donkey, he and I headed home to provide water for use by members of the family. This routine was repeated daily. It was a scary trip down the valley particularly after sunset. I was always afraid of wild animals, especially hyenas that roamed the area after dark.

Having no prospects to find work in the village and our survival was at stake, the elders of the family decided to leave Tair Harfa and move to the city of Tyre, the biggest city in south Lebanon. It was, thought that after spending six months in the village, the move to the largest city in South Lebanon could help us find work that may perhaps improve our economic condition. The move from the village to the city was a good omen especially for me, as I did not have to fear wild animals when going down the valley to fill the 5-gallon cans with water seven times a week.

THE MIGHTY DONKEY AND THE HEALING POWERS OF ITS DUNG

THE ONLY MEANS OF TRANSPORTATION FROM ONE PLACE TO another, in the village, was the donkey. While living in the village of Tair Harfa and prior to moving to the city, I picked a terrible eye infection. Both of my eyes were, affected and made it very difficult to see. It was not possible to open my lids and because of the swelling made it impossible to see. There was no medical facility, drug store or doctors in the village to try to diagnose the infection and possibly to prescribe a treatment. The lids of my eyes were, completely shut and bulged out in such a way that both of my eyes had the look of a beer-belly.

One of the old villagers, upon seeing the situation I am in and the misery I was in, felt very sorry for me and could not believe what he saw. He was quite astonished as to what had happened to my eyes. He scratched his head and paused for few minutes to see what he could do to help. He said, I know what you should do to alleviate the swelling of your eyes and perhaps solve your problem. He said, years ago I had essentially the same kind of problem when I was a teen ager. An older man told me the story as to how to have my eyes open again as they were completely closed due to an infection. He had a recipe that was, passed on to him, through many generations that still works. It worked for me too, he said, and I believe it will work for you too. He prescribed the old remedy that has proven its safety and effectiveness in the past and still works very well. His prescription consisted of dry donkey dung, which upon burning will emit thick clouds of smoke. He suggested t I should burn the dry donkey dung and direct the thick smoke towards my eyes, wait for few minutes and your eyes will open. Of course, I was desperate to try anything to find a solution to my misery and was a little skeptical of his prescription whether it will work for me without damaging my eyes or my eyesight. After churning the thought in my mind, I then decided to take a chance and try the recipe this man prescribed.

After burning the dry donkey dung, I exposed my eyes to the thick smoke coming from the burning dung. To my very pleasant surprise and relief, the smoke did the job. My eyelids opened and the tears that were held back under my closed eyelids came out gushing like a waterfall! No antibiotics or eye drops could have done the trick that the donkey dung did! Thank you donkey, for the great therapeutic effect your dung has done for me!

As Palestinian refugees in Lebanon, we were required to register with the *United Nations Relief and Works Agency (UNRWA)* for Palestine refugees. My cousin Adel, uncle Mohamad's son, the oldest in the group, registered all members of the family including myself with the *United Nations Refugee and Works Agency for Palestinian refugees (UNRWA)*. The birthdates of many of us, as he could remember, were 2-3 years older than the actual birthdates. The birth dates were a guesstimate on his part. We all were, issued ration cards that confirmed us as Palestinian refugees. The ration card entitled the holder to receive monthly rations of 10 kilograms (22 pounds) of flour, one kilogram of sugar and five kilograms of rice. In addition, we also qualified to receive free medical and dental care in *UNRWA* medical and dental facilities in designated areas in the country. These facilities were out of reach for us as they were in Beirut, fifty miles away. We also were entitled to enroll in elementary schools sponsored by *UNRWA* at no charge. Having lived fifty miles away and the schools as well as medical and dental facilities, were in Beirut, we could neither take advantage of enrollment in the schools nor receive any medical or dental care benefits. Medical and dental services, even to the Lebanese was not in existence in the city of

Tyre. The only available medical facility for the Lebanese was in the city of Sidon that is twenty-five miles north of the city of Tyre. Being a Lebanese Ministry of Health facility, however, it was not open for Palestinians.

1949

MOVING TO BEIRUT TO LIVE WITH THE AL-HAJJ FAMILY

A FEW WEEKS AFTER THE FAMILY MOVED TO THE CITY OF TYRE, IN south Lebanon, a lady, I had never met before, came to the city of Tyre looking for my sisters and for me. Mrs. Miri al-Hajj was a distant relative of my father, which I later learned she was the daughter of my father's paternal aunt. She was born and raised in al-Bassa but moved to Beirut after marrying Mr. Mohamad Al-Hajj, a Lebanese gentleman who lived in Beirut.

She said, she spent a long time searching for us all over Lebanon without any success, but now she was very happy to have found us safe and sound in Tyre. She insisted that we, my sisters and I move in and live with her family in Beirut. She said, you eat what my children eat and sleep where my children sleep. What a great savior this woman was. Mrs. al-Hajj, who was widowed recently, had two daughters, Fatima who was married and Kawthar who was still in school. She also had four sons: Ahmad owned and operated a bakery, Mahmoud was an employee of the Lebanese Ministry of Finance, Mustapha worked at the Lebanese Ministry of Defense and the youngest, Ali, was still in school.

They considered and treated my sisters and I as members of their family. The three older sons always gave me pocket money and bought me clothes and always treated me with compassion. Because of this God-sent family, I started to have a sense of belonging to a family that I was, denied of, by the action of uncle Mohamad, his new wife and their family. Now, I said to myself, "this is the break I have always been looking for, and now, I have a family to belong to". From now on, I will completely detach myself from uncle Mohamad and his family, and as of now. I will belong to al-Hajj family. This is my newly adopted family. The bitterness I grew up with, due in a large part to the mistreatment and abuse of my sisters and me by uncle Mohamad's family members. This bitterness made me realize that 'our' family is, fake and I must have nothing to do with it. The al-Hajj family has transformed me into a different person and made me realize that not all people are evil as I used to think. There still are some good, compassionate and caring people in the world we live in.

The scars in my psyche had a great influence on my demeanor and on my behavior. I had no self-confidence. Many a time I felt as if I am a hopeless, helpless and a worthless fellow. I was always trying to project an image of myself that I am a real person to be recognized and to be what I really am not! Of course, I was always in denial as to what I really am. The way I tried to project myself to others was, the mirage I was chasing did not have a speck of the reality I am in.

As a way of convincing myself, before I could convince others, I had an old box camera that never worked, but used carry it around to give the impression that I am not loaded with ignorance, but rather I am quite a 'sophisticated' fellow who owns and can operate a modern gadget!

We had no income other than the help we got from al-Hajj family. Luckily, within a month of moving to Beirut, my sister Fatima found a job close to the al-Hajj family house where we lived. Her job description was to mend the tears in used socks imported from Europe and from the United States. My sister Amina on the other hand was, still working, as a servant for uncle Mohamad's new wife's sister in a town about twenty miles south of Beirut.

My sisters were very concerned about my future to the point that my sister Fatima went to a psychic to get a 'prediction' as to what would the future hold for me and how will it look like. She was very happy and elated to hear what the psychic told her that his readings tell him her brother's future looks good. The psychic assured her that 'your brother's future will definitely be fine'.

As a child in Palestine, I was inflicted with Malaria in the summer months on an annual basis. I survived the deadly Malaria disease that inflicted me in Palestine. I never had that infection in Lebanon. I was, saved from its debilitating symptoms as the organism did not exist in Lebanon. The climate in Lebanon, as opposed to that in Palestine, is neither conducive nor optimal for the survival and the spread of the *Anopheles aegyptis* mosquito. This mosquito harbors the malaria-causing parasites, *Plasmodium falciparum*, *Plasmodium vivax* or both. These mosquitos paid me their annual visits during the summer months in Palestine. The mosquitos bite, by introducing their proboscis into the skin of the victim to suck blood. In the process, they introduce the malaria-causing parasites into the victim's blood stream. The parasites infect and destroy the red blood cells and cause the patient to show symptoms of anemia followed by severe headaches, vomiting and biphasic temperature chart.

The Al-Hajj family had me enrolled in a private elementary boarding school that was less than one hundred yards from the house. When I asked as to why am I being sent to a boarding school that is so close to the house? Their response was a boarding school will help you develop a strong personality and you will become more independent.

While at the boarding school, I became ill with an illness of unknown origin. I lost weight and became like a skeleton of skin and bone. The doctor that was brought in to examine me, could not diagnose the illness. The symptoms I had were severe headaches, high fever, loss of appetite and loss of weight. A second, opinion was sought by having another doctor come in to the school to examine me and diagnose the illness and hopefully prescribe a treatment. When he examined me and checked my vital signs, he said, "there is no hope of him making it, he is dying. Let him go in peace"!

A third doctor was, brought in and after examining me, he determined that my heart is very weak. It must be, taken care of immediately. Because of my weak heart and as a last resort to try to revive my heart, he prescribed an injection of Camphor in the hip area to improve the capability of my heart. Following the Camphor injection and to this day, I cannot sit on the floor with my legs crossed and hugging each other! Of course, to everybody's surprise and happiness, the second doctor's assessment that my death was around the corner did not happen. My health started to improve and gradually I regained my strength and within few weeks, I started to gain weight. This experience points to the importance of a second and perhaps a third or more opinions at reaching a sound diagnosis!

While being a student at the boarding school, one of the female teachers, Ms Wadi'a, liked me and looked at me as though I were her pet kid. She used to bring me to her room in the evening and help me with my homework. Over the weekend, she would take me home with her to visit her family. This teacher had a lot of influence on the improvement of my behavior and on regaining the self-confidence I have lost throughout the years. Her help was in the way of giving me a boost towards regaining my believing in myself and have a more positive outlook at life. Well, I found out that after all, I am fine and likable by other people. I loved Miss Wadi'a.

UNCLE MOHAMAD'S DEMANDS FOR MONEY

UNCLE MOHAMMAD WAS ASKING FOR AND DEMANDING MONEY FROM my sister Fatima and from my sister Amina. My sister Fatima while working at an outfit that mends used socks while my sister Amina working as a maid for his second wife's sister, neither had any money to spare. When money dried up and uncle Mohamad's wife's sister could not afford paying a servant, uncle Mohamad looked for another job in Beirut, for sister Amina to work as a servant with a Lebanese family. I said to myself, enough is enough. I stood up and told him that this is not going to happen and keep your hands off my sisters. We no longer are under your jurisdiction, and as of now, we will neither, obey your orders nor will we ever succumb to your demands. I said to him, have one of your daughters and not my sister, work as a servant for the Lebanese family. It is not going to be my sister Amina period! Of course, having my sister Amina work as a servant with the Lebanese family was potentially an easy source of income, for him and now I have turned off the spigot denying him any income from my sister's employment.

Having been denied of getting money from my sisters before, now he thought he still can get money from my sisters. He would practice his monthly routine visits, by coming to Beirut at the end of each month with the hope of collecting his bounty. He had changed his tactics in that, in case my sister Fatima had no money to give him, he would demand a piece of her gold jewelry such as rings, earrings or bracelets in lieu of cash.

Although he had four daughters whom he could have had them employed as servants, but never did, as he found easy money coming from those orphan girls who are under his control and who he was supposed to have taken care of them, but now he is demanding that they take care of him!

As a youngster, in Beirut, and before I told him to keep his hands off my sisters, I needed shoes and my sisters could not afford to buy me the new shoes. My sister Fatima, and wrongly so, thought that uncle Mohamad still cares for us, put me on the bus to go see him at his residence in al-Ghaziyeh, a twenty-mile drive, to ask him to buy me a new pair of shoes. This trip was a disaster for me to say the least. Spending that night at his residence was a nightmare. His wife laid the mattress on the floor, gave me a 'masnad' (a hard pillow stuffed with dry wheat straw) that was as hard as a rock, to use as a pillow. The 'masnad', normally used as a cushion usually placed behind peoples backs to act as a barrier, between their backs, and the concrete walls when they sit on the floor. The masnad, is never used as a pillow because of its hardness. Uncle Mohamad's wife also provided me with a cover that was a torn-up blanket that stunk from the smell of dried urine from her baby. I did not have a single wink of sleep that night, not only from the hard 'pillow' under my head, but also from the strong stench of urine in the blanket.

The following morning, as I was still hoping uncle Mohamad would buy me the shoes, but instead he took me to the bus station and told me: You pay your bus fare and go back to Beirut to have your sister buy you the shoes! I was very devastated as I was anticipating having a new pair of shoes, but instead went back home empty handed! This was, the straw that broke the camel's back. It made me realize, once and-for all, that uncle Mohamad was never interested in taking care of us, whether as children living in Palestine or now as refugees in Lebanon. At this point, I felt it was time for me to break away from this family and wanted to be completely detached from any relationship with uncle Mohamad and with his family. My first course of action was to delete the 'al-Shaikh' family name completely from my own name. As the family name was al-Shaikh, a title bestowed upon our great grandfather by, the Ottoman sultan for the services he rendered to the empire. I adopted my paternal grandfather's name, Isa, as my last name. It did feel good to be independent after many years of subjugation and emotional torture.

1950

ENROLLING IN *AHLIAH HIGH SCHOOL* AS A BOARDING STUDENT

AFTER FINISHING THE FOURTH GRADE IN THE BOARDING GRAMMAR school in Beirut, a rumor surfaced around that Mr. Kamel Khoury, a Christian educator from al-Bassa, had established a boarding school for Palestinian kids. The only requirements for acceptance and admission into the boarding school were identity as a Palestinian, a fee of fifteen Lebanese Pounds (five US dollars), a mattress, a pillow and a blanket. These requirements would guarantee acceptance into the school as a bona fide boarding student. My sister Fatima heard of the rumor and after investigating it further, to make sure the rumor is legitimate and to be true, she sent me there with the admission fees, a mattress, pillow and a blanket. I was, accepted right away as a boarding student.

The school was, located in al-Na'ameh, a town that is about ten miles south of Beirut. The school was housed in a run-down two-story building that had a great location. It was very close to the highway and was less than twenty yards from the shore of the Mediterranean Sea. Although it has a great location, the school had no amenities to speak of. No electricity, no running water and of course no bathrooms were available in the building. There was however, a fresh water well, within the building that we used to get water from for drinking, bathing and washing our clothes. Although we were, provided with a good education, we had a little amount of food and many a night we would go to bed hungry. We never went to bed on a full stomach!

Over the weekend, our job was to go the neighboring hills and fetch wood for use as fuel for cooking the meals by the school and to boil water for us to bathe and wash our own clothes. Mrs. Mary Shammas Khoury, the principal's wife, another al-Bassa native, used to cook the meals for the students.

The makeup of the teaching faculty at the school were, the principal of the school, Mr. Kamel Khoury and his two brothers, Sa'adallah and Zaki and their cousin Nimer Jabbour Khoury. They were the backbone of the teaching faculty. Mr. Kamel Khoury taught us Arabic, Sa'adallah, taught us English, Shorthand and Poetry. Zaki taught us History and Geography and Nimer taught us Chemistry, Physics, Math, Geometry and Algebra. The curriculum, at the school was, designed and tailored, to meet the needs of the labor markets in the Middle East.

The job market, for Palestinians in Lebanon was non-existent, as the country could not provide jobs for its own citizens. The only possibility of finding a job was in the Gulf Region such as Saudi Arabia and Kuwait, because these countries were exporters of oil. The oil boom in these countries dictated the need for employees who can communicate in English and know shorthand, thus the need for English speaking employees. The employment of Palestinians was favored over others as the Palestinians were the only group of people that can speak and write in English.

Palestinian refugees who could read and write flocked to the Gulf region in search of jobs. The government offices including the ministries and the armies of these countries were, organized and headed by Palestinians.

Since the Gulf States were ruled by the British, their governments decided to open the door to recruit teachers who are fluent in English. The choice of Palestinian teachers to teach Gulf Arab students English and other courses was set as priority by these governments. An influx of educated Palestinian teachers ceased the opportunity, went to the embassies of these governments to apply for the teaching jobs.

(This is the picture of us students at *Ahliah High School* in al Na'ahmeh, Lebanon when I was a fifth grader. I am the third, from right in the picture, standing with my hand in my pocket. We were getting ready to head to the hills to bring wood).

As other boarding schools in the country provided some services that included washing of clothes for the students, our school did have nothing of that sort. We, the students, were responsible to wash our clothes by hand, of course. We had never heard of washing machines at the time, because there were none available in the country or if they were, available they were out of reach for us. Well-to-do families used to hire poor women to wash their clothes. Whereas these laundresses, in addition to washing clothes and the ironing of clothes, the not so well-to-do families and people like us, had no other choice other than washing their clothes by their hands. The location of the school and its proximity to the beach gave us the great pleasure of swimming in the Mediterranean Sea after classes and over the weekends especially after we had been to the hills to fetch wood.

One day during the spring semester and while we were still in class, a shepherd with about four hundred fifty goats passed by the school. A couple of students and I saw the opportunity that we may have a piece of meat for dinner. We snatched one of the goats and hid it in one of the rooms on the second floor of the building. In the evening, we butchered the goat, skinned it and gave the carcass to Mrs. Shammas Khoury to cook it for the students. We dug a hole in the ground and buried the skin, the head and the interior organs of that goat so that no sign of it, will ever be detected. Indeed, it was, never detected. To our surprise, however, the shepherd came by the following day, looking for his missing goat. He asked the principal and others at the school if they had seen the goat he was missing. Of course, we all lied and told him we have never seen it! This was the only time in months we had a tiny piece of meat included in our meal.

It is still unclear to me why did the principal of the school administration trusted me to take the dough to the bakery, for baking and brought back, to the school. Wakim, another student and I, used to place the trays of dough on a cart and roll it to the bakery that was about a mile away. After baking, we would place the bread on the cart and roll it back to the school. That chore of taking the dough to the bakery was during the early evening hours. One evening, Wakim and I decided to keep some of the bread for our own personal use and decided to hide it in the grass in the neighboring field. After the darkness sets in, we would go back to the spot where we left the bread, to get the loaves of bread we hid in the field.

The school had employed, an older woman who I befriended, to manage the storeroom. The woman had poor eyesight, but she recognized our voices. After picking the bread from the field, I went to her and asked for a little *Carub* molasses. She placed the molasses on a flat plate and after carrying it to where my bed was, I invited my cousin Adnan to join me in the feast of bread and molasses. Without me knowing as it was very dark due to the absence of lighting, the molasses spilled to form a long trail right to the vicinity of my bed. The following morning, the trail was, discovered and the principal of the school never said a word to me about it. He was furious and angry at the incident, whether his anger was, directed at the loss of the molasses, at me or at the woman who gave me the molasses was not clear. To vent his anger, he ordered the student body to clean up the schoolyard from stones and other debris!

A few months later, on his way home to al-Ghaziyeh, uncle Mohammad stopped by the school. He had just come back after making a short trip to Jordan. His trip to Jordan was to collect money from a Jordanian merchant he had sold olive oil while we were still in Palestine. He gave money to his son Adnan, who also was a student at our school, but never gave me a single penny. I felt so betrayed by his action as I knew the oil he had sold to the Jordanian merchant contained oil that came from our own olive trees!

TRAINING OF STUDENTS BY OUR SCHOOL TO MEET THE NEEDS OF THE LABOR MARKETS IN THE MIDDLE EAST

KNOWING WELL ENOUGH THAT PROSPECTS OF FIND A JOB BY A Palestinian refugee in Lebanon was, an impossibility the school administration followed a strategy that will train students for job possibilities anywhere in the Middle East outside Lebanon. The oil boom in the Middle East, especially in Saudi Arabia, required a labor force that is educated and capable of speaking and writing in English.

The employers required the new recruits able to compose correspondence, in English and to know how to type and use shorthand. Mr. Sa'adAllah Khoury taught us shorthand to improve our chances to gain employment as secretaries in Saudi Arabia. We could not learn how to type, as we had no access to a typewriter at the time. One of the letters that we read, in the shorthand book while studying shorthand and which we were required to translate it from English into shorthand language, using the Pittman Shorthand system was signed by a name under which the address was Walla Walla Wash. Of course, we did not know what Walla Walla Wash stood for until later we found out it is the name of the town Walla Walla in the state of Washington. Mr. Sa'adAllah Khoury gave us a lecture about the' broken pencil'. He said, one should never give up trying to write even though his pencil was broken. He should find a way to continue writing. This was his way of instilling in us the ability to improvise and be creative.

I was curious as to why my academic standing in the class was always at the tail end, knowing well enough that I thought I was a good student. I found out later other students were paying nominal tuition fees, but I never did. I did not know why I was never, asked to pay. Should I ever been asked to pay tuition fees my answer would always be, I do not have any money! I was a rebel and complained all the time, not only about the quality of but more importantly about the amount of food served. The 'choosy beggar' title applied to me, with honors, as I was paying no tuition fees, no room and board and was getting a great education, yet I was complaining all the time! My chronic complaining left a negative impression with the school administration and with the teachers as well. The negative impressions I have left with the faculty and the school administration were indeed the cause of placing my academic performance at the tail end of the class.

My academic standing in the class was very low. There was only one person who had a lower standing than mine. I knew I was a good student, but because I was a non-paying chronic complainer, as opposed to those students who paid nominal tuition fees and who were less academically proficient than I was, were given preferential treatment and of course, better grade scores and better standing in the class.

I have always had and still have a problem of memorization of the subject matter. Poetry was one of those areas I had difficulty memorizing. A question on the final exam, in poetry, was to write down John Milton's "the Burning Babe" poem. I only knew that the poem consisted of 12 stanzas, I made up a poem of 12 stanzas hoping that will fool the teacher. To my pleasant surprise, I got the score of 100% in the final exam. The perfect score I received was not due to my abilities to write John Milton's poem, but rather it was due to the instructor's having not read what I wrote. He must have counted the number of the stanzas in the poem to give his final grade! Should the instructor have read the poem I wrote, I will receive a score of zero. Even with this score of '100%' in my poetry final exam, my ranking in the class was just a notch above the lowest one.

The government of Lebanon had, at the time, a 'National Board Examination for all the elementary Schools in the country'. Although our school was not a member of the Lebanese public elementary school system, yet it was, allowed to participate in the national elementary school exams. Our school participated with fifteen pupils who took part in that examination. Of the fifteen who participated only one passed. The one who passed was only me! Now being the only one who passed the Lebanese National Board Examination from my school, the attitude of the faculty and that of the school administration towards me has turned hundred eighty degrees. As of that moment, I have earned the title of the 'scholar of the school'!

ADDITION OF AN EXTRA PERSON TO THE ROSTER OF 'THE CHRISTIAN STUDENTS'

THE SCHOOL WAS RECEIVING AID FROM THE UNION OF CHURCHES IN Europe and the United States. The dollar amount of aid to the schools was, based on the number of Christian Palestinian students enrolled at the aid program. That meant the more Christian students registered at the school, the more funds the school will receive from the Union of Churches. Mr. Kamel Khoury, the principal of the school was a shrewd planner, but a poor business manager. He knew how to identify sources of funds he could tap into to get aid for the school. He had an opening, using me as a Christian student to be included in the list of the Christian kids at the school because of my name: Abdallah M. Isa. Both names, Abdallah and Isa (Jesus in Arabic) are common names, used by Christians and Moslems alike. There was no way to determine the religious affiliation of a person by his/her name alone should they have names that are common to both Christians and Moslems like mine. He asked me if I would agree to have him register me as a Christian student. I said, of course, I agree and please know that you have my permission to have me registered as a Christian student, so that the school gets more aid! The school received funding for one extra 'Christian' student over and above the true number of Christian students at the school. I was neither coached nor even given any orientation as to what to expect or how to respond to potential questions from the envoys that would come, from the Union of Churches, whenever they come to inspect the school.

Father Menassa, the envoy of the Union of Churches that provided aid to the school, came to our school to meet the Christian students on a Friday afternoon. We as 'Christian' boys were, sequestered into one room and waited for Father Menassa to come in. When he came in, we all stood up in attention, out of respect for him. He started by giving us a little pep talk about the good values we could acquire from going to church and in dedicating our lives to Jesus Christ. He then, from all the kids in the room, picked me and asked me to recite some verses of so and so chapter in the Bible. Of course, I stood like a fool, because I did not know what to say Father Menassa, a very kind and compassionate man, said in a very assuring voice, 'it is O.K. son'! It was very embarrassing to me not to be able to respond to Father Menassa's request.

In the summer of 1951, the Pope sanctioned a grant to the government of Lebanon to help pay for the cost of having Christian Palestinian kids to have a summer vacation. The planned vacation was for Christian Palestinian boys to spend the three summer months in a Maronite convent in the mountains of Lebanon. That was a great gesture by the Pope. Of course, because of my name, commonly used by both Christians and Moslems and now as a bona fide 'Christian' student in the school, I qualified to benefit from the Pope's grant. The Lebanese army truck came to the schools to pick the Christian Palestinian kids up and transport us to the town of Ghazeer. I was one of those 'Christian' kids that boarded the Lebanese army truck to the Maronite convent in the town of Ghazeer. At the registration desk at the Ghazeer convent, was a husky priest sitting on a desk who was registering our names. He asked me as to what my full name was: Abdallah Isa, Father. He then asked for my father's name. I said, Elias, Father, a common name used by both Moslems and Christians alike. I would not have known what his reaction be should I have told him my father's real name is Mohamad!

Ghazeer, a beautiful town located in the mountains east of Beirut. It is the seat of a Maronite convent in Lebanon. We spent the three summer months splitting the time between staying at the convent and camping at different places in Lebanon. Every morning we had to go to church and pray. I am not sure whether the priests, at the convent, knew that I am a Moslem and not a Christian. Whether they knew it or not it did not really matter. They treated me the same way they treated any other true 'Christian' kid in the group.

Our daily routines included going to church to pray every morning while at the convent or at makeshift churches at camping places. While going to church one morning and after the sermon, the priest gave us a pep talk with special emphasis on the existence of God. The way, he explained it to us, was that God is and will always be there to look after us. His talk was very impressive and convincing. I, for one was very impressed by the priest's attempt to prove God's existence. He brought an empty wine bottle, turned it upside down several times and then asked as to what was in that bottle. We responded by saying, "nothing, Father the bottle is empty". He said, the bottle is not empty it is full of air. You cannot see air, can you? Of course, we said no Father! Then he retorted by asking if we can feel air in the way of breeze or wind. We said, yes Father. He had a very big grin on his face and said, my children, you cannot see air, but you can feel it. Right? Yes Father! Well, you cannot see God, but you can feel his presence! This was a very convincing way, in which a child can start believing in the existence of God and He is all around to protect us.

Whether at the convent or at camping places, we had three meals a day and an afternoon snack. We would get the snack after a two-hour siesta. While at the convent and not on a camping trip, we would play games and enjoy swimming competition in the convent pool.

We would spend two weeks at the convent and two weeks a month camping somewhere else in Lebanon. It was a great experience for us as we discovered many different places in Lebanon because of our camping trips. We were very grateful to the Pope and the Vatican for providing us with such a beautiful and unforgettable three-month vacation. At the end of the vacation, reality set in and now we are back to the same unsettling routine.

UNCLE MOHAMAD'S PLANS TO USE ME AS A SOURCE OF INCOME WENT DOWN THE DRAIN

A WEEK AFTER COMING HOME FROM THE THREE-MONTH VACATION at the Maronite Christian convent, uncle Mohamad popped up and paid us a visit. He had planned, in his own mind, that a potential source of income for him may now be a reality. He thought he could use me as that potential source of income. He asked me to accompany him to a photographer's studio in the city of Sidon, to have my picture taken. His plan was to send the picture to a recruiter for Saudi Arabia. It was a rainy and a stormy day and I was soaking wet. Upon entering the photographer's studio, I saw a beautiful picture of him placed on top of his front desk. I asked the photographer if it were at all possible.to please have my picture look like his. He was very crude and in a very ugly and sarcastic way said, "You are not as good looking as I am"! Of course, the photographer's statement added to the list of negatives that have become part of my insecurities. Now, not only that I am inadequate and good for nothing, I have now nothing to offer to anybody and have no family to belong to, I am not good looking or at least average looking either! That was devastating.

Well, after taking my picture I was anxious to see how I looked in that picture. When I looked at my picture, I was shocked at seeing myself in that picture. For a moment though, I felt the photographer is, right that I am not as good looking as he is. I indeed, looked unattractive in the picture, looked like a wet rat that just crept out of the sewers line!

My "gorgeous" wet rat-like picture and my poor qualifications provided by uncle Mohamad to the recruiter, did not fare well either. They did not impress the recruiter who trashed my application and my picture, with the comment on the application, 'not qualified and poor background'! Of course, Uncle Mohamad was distraught and dismayed and perhaps had sleepless nights because I did not get the job. This meant a potential source of income for him has dried up before it had even started.

1952
RELOCATION OF OUR SCHOOL TO BURJ EL-BARAJNEH

IN THE MEANTIME, MY SCHOOL, THE *AHLIAH HIGH SCHOOL* HAS moved from *al-Na'ameh* and relocated in *Burj el-Barajneh*, a suburb south of Beirut. Now, a co-educational school established by a Christian Palestinian in the heart of a conservative Shi'a Moslem Lebanese community, was a very bold move. It was a new revolution in inter-religious relations, social environment and in the educational system with boys and girls sitting side by side on benches in the same classroom. This contrasted with the Lebanese public school system, where the two sexes were segregated into different schools, one for boys and one for girls.

There were two Lebanese public schools in the town: a boy's school and a girl's school. Surprisingly the Palestinian private co-ed school was, welcomed and accepted by the conservative residents of the town as they now have a new source of good education for their children. The new school had not only a superior system of education but also was an alternative to the only outdated and antiquated public schools in the town. The Palestinian school had several advantages over its Lebanese government counterparts:

1. It is co-educational

2. Its curriculum tailored on the British system of education where English, as opposed to French, which was the foreign language that is taught in the Lebanese schools. Now English has replaced French as the language of choice. Teaching English in Lebanon was, for the most part, due to American influence after World War II. Institutes and night schools that taught English sprang in the city like a Spring Garden. This, of course, is not to minimize the influence of the Palestinians who immigrated to Lebanon after the 1948 catastrophe and the loss of Palestine to the

Zionists. These Palestinians were highly educated and were fluent in English and they were the ones who introduced and promoted the teaching of the English language in Lebanon.

3. The English curriculum prepared students to enroll at *the American University of Beirut*, the only university in Lebanon that teaches in English.

Prior to our school's move to the new location, French was the foreign language taught in the Lebanese public school system. French was the spoken language throughout Lebanon as the country was under the French mandate that began after World War I. The French were, forced to evacuate the country on December 31, 1943 when Lebanon gained independence from French occupation.

The relocation of our school to the Beirut suburb was a great omen for us students. Now there was electricity, running water and bathrooms at the new school building. We could now have a hot water bath and have our clothes washed without having to build a fire to heat the water. The move of the school to the new location saved us the weekly trips to the hills to collect wood for use as a source of fuel to build the fires. Yet the move was an expensive deal, for us students and for the school administration as well. To compensate for the expenses, the school had to endure for the cost of rent and utilities as well as other expenses, the school had to find a source to pay for these expenses. As an outcome of the move, the administration mandated an increase in the tuition fees. The tuition fees were, raised for everybody including myself. My tuition fees were six hundred Lebanese pounds (equivalent to $200 and with a purchasing power of $600) per the nine-month school year. Of course, neither my sisters nor I had that kind of money.

After failing to use me as a source of potential income, uncle Mohamad tried to show his concern about my education. Telling me that he had already talked to Mr. Kamel Khoury, the principal of the school, who in turn agreed to reduce my tuition fees from six hundred to four hundred eighty Lebanese pounds, a 25% reduction in fees! What a deal? Even with that discounted tuition fees neither my sisters nor I could muster the funds to defray the annual cost of my education.

My sister Fatima was, very adamant and persistent that I must get an education, but it was problematic for her to find money to pay for my tuition fees. As it was customary for girls, in the Middle East, to spend any money they ought 18-carat gold jewelry in the way of bracelets, necklaces, rings, earrings and other jewelry. This tradition of owning golden items was, the only means of financial security for the future. Sister Fatima was a very good manager and was brilliant at problem solving. She said, since we do not have the money to pay for your tuition fees, why don't you take my jewelry and give to the principal of the school in lieu of your tuition fees. I said O.K. I will. When I took the jewelry, and presented it to Mr. Kamel Khoury, the principal of the school, he took the jewelry and told me that the jewelry will take care of my tuition fees.

My relative Mahmoud el-Hajj, as an employee of the Lebanese Ministry of Finance, was also concerned about my future and ability to land a job to support myself and my two sisters. He had access to an old manual 'Underwood' type-writer from the Ministry of Finance. He made that typewriter available for me to practice typing to improve my chances of landing a job with this kind of exper-tise. Practicing on that typewriter helped me develop a good speed in typing that sometimes exceeded eighty words per minute.

During my school years, at *Ahliah High School,* when my tuition fees were, paid off with the jewelry, I supported myself by giving private tutoring lessons in Mathematics, Chemistry, Algebra, Geometry and Physics to some students who needed help. I charged these students ten Lebanese pounds (a little over three dollars) a month, for a weekly one-on-one hour tutoring session.

In addition to my school schedule and my private tutoring I was, asked by Mr. Zaki Khoury, the principal's younger brother, to manage a concessions kiosk he had established at the school. I did that willingly. Since he did not offer me any pay for managing the kiosk, I outsmarted him by getting kickbacks from the vendors, when I went the market in Beirut to purchase supplies for the kiosk! With the tutoring funds and the money, I received from the vendors, I have become self-sufficient and told my sister that she should not worry about providing me with any pocket money as I can handle it now!

In addition to the great educational experience, *Ahliah High Scho*ol, provided us, it also gave us what it takes to become good and well-rounded citizens. Although the school had very limited resources, yet a boys scout program was, instituted at the school. I was, chosen to be the drummer boy of the team. As boy scouts, it was imperative that we do practice and perform exercises to perfect our chores especially in my case, playing the drums. I remember once, we had to march to another town, to parade in our boy scout attire at the funeral of a close friend of the principal of our school.

Over and above these scholastic offerings, an acting program was instituted at the school. I took part in two with two plays. In one of the plays, I played the role of a judge in a criminal case and in the other my role was, that of a drunken man.

To attest to the great and remarkable educational experience we had received at this school, many of us have been accepted and enrolled at the *American University of Beirut,* after graduating with a high school diplomas from *the Ahliah High School.* Several of us graduates including myself, have gone to graduate schools and medical schools and earned higher and professional degrees from the most prestigious universities in the United States and in Europe. For me, I graduated from *the University of California at Berkeley* and from *the University of California Medical Center in San Francisco*.

Other graduates opted to study Engineering and Architecture and were content to practice, with a BS degree, yet others went further to obtain their Ph.D. degrees in Engineering and Architecture from universities in the United States and in Europe.

For recreational and sports purposes, the school purchased a Volleyball net with its masts and a few balls. The school had formed two opposing teams to play against each other. Game time was always in the afternoon after classes were over, and during the weekends.

Mr. Zaki Khoury, the principal's younger brother, had a business mind and wanted to supplement his meager teaching income from the school. In addition to having me manage his concessions stand on campus, he found out that I can type. He felt he could add to his income by purchasing a typewriter to use as a teaching tool, to teach typing to those students who wished to enroll in the typing class. He now found another source of income using my expertise in typing, by having me manage the typing classes. The typing class consisted of a one-on-one weekly hour of tutoring and training session. The monthly fee he charged was ten Lebanese pounds for four one-hour sessions. The reason he put me in charge of the typing classes was because, I was the only one at the school, who could type in English. Mr. Zaki Khoury purchased an additional manually driven Olivetti typewriter to use for training students in typing. Enrolling in the typing classes required payment of fees upfront to his coffers. As there were five students in the typing classes, he used to get an additional net fifty Lebanese pounds a month from the typing classes.

The typing teaching responsibility he asked me to do was in addition to managing his concessions kiosk. I made sure that the responsibility of either managing the kiosk or the typing classes I was giving each day did not interfere with my own school responsibilities. My school schedule was from 8:00 AM until 4:00 PM with an hour lunch break. I had to schedule the tutoring and typing classes after 4:00 PM that lasted until 8:00 PM. After that, I managed to study for 3-4 hours a night.

The school requirements, the kiosk management, the typing and tutoring responsibilities were very taxing on me and had a great impact on my daily activities. Time for relaxation was becoming a mirage that I could not get to catch. The only means of relaxing my mind was to play a game or two of volleyball, after classes and before I would start my other chores.

Of course, my daily schedule was always full, and I had no time for loitering. I had to adjust to the requirements of the day. It was not easy, but as always, need supersedes the desire to have fun.

**(My photo teaching two students typing using
Mr. Zaki Khoury's Olivetti typewriters)**

These responsibilities did not leave room for time to have fun or for relaxation. Managing Zaki Khoury's kiosk did not appear to be enough for him as he asked me to oversee the typing classes. The newly added burden of the typing classes was the fault of nobody but of my own. It was because I was bragging, all the time, that nobody could beat me in typing. I could type eighty words plus a minute! Well I thought and hoped that I may be paid something in return for my services to him, but my thoughts and hope of making some money on the side went unanswered as he never paid me a single penny for the services I rendered to him, whether at his concessions stand or at his typewriter desk.

MEETING THE WOMAN, I LOVED AND WHO LATER BECAME MY WIFE

A VERY PLEASANT AND POSITIVE OUTCOME THAT CAME OUT OF THE non-paying typing responsibility was meeting Miss Laila Fadda, who later became my wife. I met Laila the first time at school and talked to her when she enrolled in the typing class.

Unlike me, Laila was always open-minded and sure of herself. She would talk to other male students with no inhibitions. I must admit I was very possessive and jealous especially when I saw her talking to other male students especially to those who I did not particularly care for. I could not dare tell Laila that I have a liking for her, as I was afraid she may be offended and react in a negative way. I was always hoping for a positive gesture from her side to indicate that the liking is mutual.

During the summer months, when the school was out, I worked for three months as a day laborer at a mirror-manufacturing outfit in East Beirut. My pay as one Lebanese pound (33 cents) for an eight-hour workday. I worked 6 days a week, Monday-Saturday with Sundays off. I was paid on a weekly basis every Saturday.

My job, as a day laborer, was to carry buckets filled with sand to the professional Mr. Husni al-Hajj, a relative who ran the glass-etching machine. This professional's job was grinding and smoothing the edges of the glass prior to addition of the chemicals required for making the mirror.

I was anxious and worried as to what would my future hold. I was quite concerned and searching, in my own mind, as to what career I may have to be able to provide support for me and for my family in the future. I thought making mirrors was potentially a good career. I wanted to learn how to make mirrors and what chemicals to use and how much and sequence of each of the chemicals to apply. Every time I asked Master Joseph to teach me how to make mirrors, he would refuse and insist I stay away from his area. I have tried, several times, to sneak in and have a peek to learn the names of the chemicals used to make mirrors. Master Joseph, the technician who applied the chemicals made very sure I stay away from his area so that I do not learn the secrets of his work. Perhaps he was worried that one day should I learn how to make mirrors, I may become one of his competitors in the future!

By the end of the summer working at the mirror factory, I told the boss, I must resign my position because I must go back to school. He was very upset and tried to entice me to stay on by raising my wages by fifty percent. I said thank you, but I must resign my position because I must go back to school.

My first weekly payment, of six Lebanese pounds (2 dollars) from, the mirrors factory felt like a bonanza for me. I went to the farmers' market and spent the whole salary of six Lebanese pounds buying different kinds of fruit. I felt very much like the responsible head of the household who takes pride in taking care of his family!

The following summer. I landed a job as manager of the bakery outlet that my relative Ahmad el-Hajj had established and owned. In the evening and after closing the outlet, he and I would head back to the bakery, where the oven is located, to have dinner and spend the night. In addition to room and board I was, paid one Lebanese pound (33cents) a day managing the bakery outlet.

While going to school at *Ahliah High School,* my sister Fatima promised to buy me a watch if I excelled in school and if I attained the rank of the first in my class. This was her way of enticing me and encouraging me to stay focused on my schoolwork. My classmates and I were very competitive. It was not easy, as I had to use my time wisely between the kiosk, typing classes and tutoring. I learned how to concentrate on my studies which I went to school for. I worked very hard to achieve the goal of being the first in my class and to please my sister so that she be proud of her brother. There was another motive, of course, to get the watch my sister had promised to buy for me should I excel and attain the top rank in my class!

My formidable competitor was Mr. Ahmad Khorsheed. Ahmad and I compared well in all subjects except Math. He always had an edge over me in this subject. When the Mathematics instructor corrected our final exam papers, Mr. Khorsheed found out that I scored better than he did and now I am guaranteed to be the first in the class, he burst with anger and rage and started throwing cuss words he directed at everybody in the class, at the school and more pointedly against the Mathematics teacher. Because of his tantrum and his use of foul language, Ahmad was suspended from the school.

Ahmad's uncle contacted his friend, my uncle Mohamad, and asked him to have me intercede with the school administration to have Ahmad re-instated. I did talk to the principal of the school and asked him to please forgive Ahmad, as what he said was a result of his outrageous behavior and please have him re-instated so that he can continue pursuing his education. The principal of the school honored my request and Ahmad was, allowed back in school to finish the school year.

Now that I have beaten the competition, in all courses including Mathematics, my weakest subject of them all, led me to achieve the rank of the first in my class. I was very proud of myself and felt assured that my sisters will also be proud of me. Now I may be getting the watch my sister Fatima had promised me before. When I told my sister that I attained the rank of first in my class, showed her the certificate, she was elated and happy that her brother is indeed a smart cookie. Sensing her happiness, I then asked her as to where is the watch she had promised to buy for me? She hugged me tight, cried and said, I am very proud of you brother, but I am very sorry I do not have any money to buy you a watch. With a sad and mumbling voice, I said, yes sister, I understand.

Well, the news got out fast that Abdallah M. Isa is the smartest student at the school as he has achieved the highest scores in all subjects and ranked the first in his class. The news spread beyond the walls of the school and into the neighborhoods. The girl whose house was on the south side of the school sent me palm dates, the girl on the west side sent me bread and the girl on the north side sent me soft drinks! I did not know how the girls who sent me dates and bread looked like as there was a high wall separating the school from their properties. My ranking as the first in my class kept pace with me until my high school graduation in June 1953.

Success, many a time leads to some unanticipated problems due to jealousy or for other reasons. Some of the schoolmates became irritated with me because of my scholastic achievements and my popularity with the girls. They started to cause problems for me as it so happened in two different occasions. They plotted, to have me humiliated by being beaten up by two different mentally deranged individuals. One of these individuals attacked me with a six-inch long shoemaker's needle that caused a scar that I, proudly still show, on the back of my left shoulder. The plots against me were, meant to humiliate me especially in front of the girls!

The other incident happened one evening when I was accompanying Laila and her sisters to their home after a late event at the school. Of course, I could not dare go with them to their house but had to depart about thirty feet from the house. At that moment and before the girls left, a young man jumped out of the bushes and started yelling and throwing foul language towards me to humiliate me in front of the girls. My immediate response was to grab him by the neck, wrestle with him and throw him to the ground with many kicks to his torso. He stood up and ran back to the bushes and never attacked me again.

On June 15, 1953, our graduation day, the school had a party for us graduates that lasted until six in the morning. I failed to notify my sisters that I might be late coming home. When I knocked at our door at seven o'clock in the morning, my sister Fatima came to the door and immediately handed me a very big smack to the face telling me she spent the whole night going from one police precinct to another trying to find any information about me. From that day on, she imposed a curfew on not allowing me to leave the house after seven o'clock in the evening!

Uncle Mohamad found out that I have graduated from High School and I am good at typing in English. He thought of that as a new opportunity for him, again to use me as a source of income. The Arabian American Oil Company (ARAMCO) was recruiting people with English typing capabilities to work as secretaries in Saudi

Arabia. He took me to the recruiter at the ARAMCO office in Beirut with the intent of having me sit for and pass the typing test. He became quite anxious while waiting to get my test results. Of course, his ambitions were that should I pass the typing test and be offered a secretarial job by ARAMCO in Saudi Arabia, that I can send him money. I did not want to go to Saudi Arabia, but since our culture dictates full respect and obedience to older members of the family, and not to be disrespectful to uncle Mohamad as I did years before, I went along with him to the recruiter's office. I had already made my mind up that I will make sure I fail the typing test. Prior to taking the typing test, the recruiter said, I am allowed no more than three mistakes in the allowed time to do the test. Should I have four or more mistakes, it means I fail the typing test, and would not be offered the job. While taking the test I counted the number of mistakes I intentionally had made making sure they are more than three. Upon handing the test paper to the recruiter who was timing me and upon counting the mistakes he said, sorry you did not make it as you had six mistakes. Failing the typing test as I intended was fortunate for me, but unfortunate for uncle Mohamad as all his ambitions and plans to make money on me went down the drain.

Another classmate of mine was, also interviewed for another secretarial job. He failed the interview, not in typing, but in the oral English language test. When the recruiter asked him as to what the term 'homesick' means. His answer was, it means 'sick at home'. Of course, he failed the interview and neither he nor I got the jobs we were interviewed for.

Since my ranking as the first in my class every year until I graduated from High School in June 1953, I discovered I may be smarter than I thought I really am. I found out I am capable of being of university quality and not just of a high school stock. The only university that was possibly available for me, in Beirut, was the *American University of Beirut* (*AUB*). *AUB* was established by American Presbyterian Missionaries in 1866, but later it shed off the religious umbrella and became secular and co-ed in the early 1900s. There were two other universities in town: the *Lebanese University* and the *St. Joseph University*. Neither of these two universities was an option. The *Lebanese University* was off-limits for me, as it was strictly for Lebanese students and is not open for Palestinians. *St. Joseph University,* on the other hand, was also off-limits school for me because it teaches in French and my training was in English. *AUB*, being a private institution that teaches in English, was my only option. *AUB* was, not only expensive, but was very difficult, to be enrolled in. The option of attending *AUB* was essentially out of question too, as I had no money to pay for my tuition fees and other required books and supplies. At that point, I had to resign myself to the fact that several obstacles relating to finances stood in my way of becoming a university student. Now I should try to find me any other job that will help in supporting myself and of my two sisters.

1953-1955

Mr. Kamel Khoury, the principal of my high school, had satisfied his passion and fulfilled his nationalistic ambitions by establishing a school intended to educate Palestinian children and to prepare them to join the labor market as well as to become good and responsible citizens. This was the *Ahliah High School,* from which I graduated with a high school diploma. Mr. Khoury expanded his horizon by establishing the *Institute of General Education* in Beirut. The Institute, was an addition to the *Ahliah High School* located in a suburb of the city, was primarily a night school that taught English as a second language for adults seeking proficiency in a foreign language and who would come to class after work. Day classes were also available at the institute for those students who had no day job obligations.

Mr. Khoury offered me the job of teaching English at the *Institute* for a salary of 75 Lebanese pounds ($25) a month. Having a job paying $25, a month for a high school graduate was great at the time. Monthly salary payments from the Institute were sporadic. Some months I was paid, yet other months went on without any payment.

Although French was, the foreign language taught and spoken in Lebanon, English became the language of choice after World War II. American influence after the war spread worldwide including countries in the Middle East. Lebanon was one of those countries that benefited from the expanded American influence.

In addition to teaching English as a second language, the *Institute* also offered training in typing. Several *Olivetti* typewriters were, purchased for that purpose. Not a single female student registered for the typing classes. The reason is because the only possible job opportunities for typists and secretaries were in Saudi Arabia and females were not allowed to enter the country to join the expatriate labor force! Additionally, culture and tradition dictate that parents of females will not permit their daughters or sisters to go to work in a foreign country.

For teaching English, the 'Reader', an English elementary school textbook, was required for the students to purchase. After learning the alphabets and construction of sentences, students were required to talk to each other, in class, in English only. The intent was to have them remember the lessons they were taught and to practice using the information by talking to each other in English. This requirement of communicating in English only which I have adopted at the *Institute,* from our high school days, as we students were required to talk to each other in English only. Clandestine 'Student cops' were installed in the schoolyard to spy and to listen on conversations between students. Should any two students, were overheard talking to each other in Arabic and not in English, meant they are caught in the act of not talking to each other in English, they were reported to the school administration.

Punishment of students who were reported for not communicating in English did not go beyond a reprimand by, the principal of the school and a demand that they should converse in English only. What was unique about this spying system was, the 'student cop' yells "signal" at the students who are talking to each other in a language that is different from English. The student cop will record the names of the non-complying students and pass them to the office of the school principal.

Looking back, I feel like it was a genuine approach that was instituted by the school for us to be able to learn the foreign language and to retain the information by talking to each other in English, of course.

The teaching faculty at the *Institute* were all Palestinian nationals. The reason for choosing Palestinian faculty members and not Lebanese was, because only Palestinians can speak and write in English. The core of the faculty at the Institute were, me, Victor Sader, Peter Sabbagh and Ali al-Jishi. Mr. al-Jishi and I were graduates of *Ahliah High School.* In addition to teaching English, I was also responsible for teaching typing. The rest of the faculty members taught English only.

I thought, it may be worthwhile to expand the offerings at the *Institute* by introducing mathematics, history, geography and perhaps French to the curriculum. After extensive discussions of the matter, it was decided the issue was not compatible with the original charter for which the *Institute* was established, to only teach English as a foreign language and nothing else.

(Photo with colleagues at the *Institute of General Education*. From Left: Victor Sader, Peter Sabbagh, me, and Ali Al-Jishi. We were the backbone of the teaching faculty at the *Institute of General Education*)

The curriculum at the *Institute* was, designed to provide working adults with the opportunity to learn English as a foreign language in the evenings.

My job description at the *Institute*, in addition to opening the doors at 8:00 in the morning and closing them at 9:00 in the evening, was also to teach English and typing students on a one on one hourly sessions. My work schedule was a grueling one as it spanned from 8:00 AM to 9:00 PM, a thirteen-hour shift, six days a week, Monday-Saturday.

After graduating from high school and having a job to teach English at the *Institute of General Education*, I rented a one-bedroom studio apartment to house my sisters and me. The monthly rent was 25 Lebanese pounds ($8.33) that covered the rent and utilities. Now, we have 50 Lebanese pounds left over after paying the rent, provided I am paid every month and paid on time. The salary of 75 Lebanese pounds is net income as no income taxes levied on low income, people like me. Now we can use the balance of the 50 Lebanese pounds to buy good food and other essential items.

The 1950s were the better decade of my life. After graduating from High School, family members, meaning uncle Mohamad's family started to look up to me and treat me with respect. The 'cousins' started to admit, for the first time, and amazingly enough as they never did before, to saying Abdallah is our cousin and we are very proud of him! Wow! What a change of heart that was? It was, also the decade that changed my life to the better. Graduating from high school and subsequent admission to the *American University of Beirut* provided me with a new horizon, with the possibility of a promising good future.

Now, as an employee at the *Institute of Higher Education* and a money earner, gave uncle Mohamad the outrageous idea of a possible source of income that he could tap into. I thought he would never come back again to visit us again and ask for money, after I snubbed him some time back. He started his monthly routine to come to Beirut and stay with us for a week at a time. He acted as if he were, the apartment manager knocking at the doors of tenants to collect the monthly rent. One morning and after we had finished our breakfast, my sister Fatima prepared my brown lunch bag to take with me to work. As I was by the door leaving the apartment, uncle Mohamad said, "You should start making something for us every month". I asked him as to what he meant by making something for them every month. He responded by saying, I mean about thirty Lebanese pounds a month! This was more than one third of my perceived monthly salary. I responded by saying: 'I will look into it and see what I can do'.

I was quite intimidated and outraged by his request. Resentment about his treatment of my sisters and of myself spanned for many years. It started when we were children in Palestine and continued throughout our teenage years as refugees in Lebanon. I thought about his request for several days and then made my mind up as to how I should respond to his request. I decided to write him a letter with details stating how I felt about his mistreatment of my sisters and of me throughout the years. I sat down, after finishing my first assignment at the *Institute of Higher Education* and before going to the second assignment and wrote him a letter of three-page legal size paper airing out our grievances against the mistreatment and abuse we endured from him and from his family. I mailed the letter to him at his residence in al-Ghaziyeh, a little town that is about twenty miles away. In my letter, I mentioned all the incidents relating to abuse, mistreatment, denying my sisters and me the basic means of survival, by him and by his new wife. I was also very clear in my letter that he took over our property and was supposed to 'have taken care' of us, orphans after the death of our parents. Instead he chose not to. His commitment to take care of his late cousin's children was not genuine. His interest in taking care of us was to grab the property that our deceased parents had left for us. He used the revenues accrued from these properties to support his family and his new wife's mother and her six daughters, but not to support us orphans who owned the property.

In my detailed letter, citing abuses and mistreatment of my sisters and me ever since we were children. In my three-page legal size letter, I posed five questions for him:

1. Why did he not send my sisters to school while he sent his daughters to school? He knew, well enough, that schools did not cost anything as they were all free of charge

2. Why did he have my two sisters, Fatima and Amina work as servants for your new wife and for her sister while we were still living in Palestine.

3. Why did he want my sister Amina work as a servant for a Lebanese family after we became refugees to Lebanon?

4. Why did he pocket most of the income my sister Amina, was paid while working as a servant to his wife's sister in Palestine?

5. Why was he demanding money from my sisters and now from me?

6. Why did he always say, when asked by anybody, as to who this boy is? His response always was, 'he belongs to us'. Do he, not know what the term 'belongs to us means? Well, I am going to tell you. It is reserved for servants, slaves, animals and material things. You never said, "This boy is my late cousin's son", or he is, our son. Am I a slave to you? Am I, a servant or a commodity to belong to you? Or perhaps you may be ashamed of me

7. Why did he abandon us after becoming refugees to Lebanon?

I ended the letter by saying 'I am sorry pal and because of your and of your family's mistreatment and abuse of us, I find it extremely difficult to give you any money. I suggest you look for another source to dip into. You ought to know all of us are accountable for what we do and for what we say as everything has a price, I hereby declare that as of this moment, I have nothing to do with you and inform you in the strongest terms possible and with no regrets on my part, that I do not have any money for you. The spigot is shut off forever. This is the well-deserved price you have earned for your misguided actions and mistreatment of us orphans.

After he received my letter, I can guess he must have been very depressed and upset about it and now he has lost hope of getting any financial aid either from me or and from my sisters in the future. He wrote back and left the letter at a little kiosk in the neighborhood and asked him to pass it to me when I stop by his shop.

In his letter, he indicated that he raised me, sent me to school and took care of my needs. While it is true that he may have had the perception that he raised me and sent me to school, but he never took care of my needs!

Again, in his letter he mentioned that back in Palestine, an out-of-town visitor (a bedouin), asked him as to who that boy (me) was. When he told him, this boy belongs to us, then the visitor said, be very careful and beware of this boy. He will not be good and helpful to you in the future! A good reading into the future relationship uncle Mohamad will have with me. That was a good and correct prediction of this man. Is it not?

After my letter, he not only was quite mad at me and probably disowned me and will never have anything to do with me in the future. The rest of his family, including his children followed suit and became very angry with me. They said, how dare I, talk to their father the way I did? I said, I understand where you are coming from and wish you would understand where I am coming from. Your father and his new wife mistreated my sisters and me and looked at us as if we are their slaves and were born to serve them and we are not your father`s blood relatives.

My sister Fatima got very upset with me too. She was crying and said, I should not have done that to him. After all, she said, he raised us after the death of our parents! My response to her was, he did not raise us, but society did. He pretended to have raised us, but he used you and our sister Amina as servants at his wife's and her sister's households. He used the revenues from our property, in Palestine, to provide for his new wife and her mother and six sisters. He denied us the most basic requirements for sub-decent living that is required by any human being! I did remind my sister of the many nights we went to bed hungry because we had no food. I also reminded her of the situation when half of the roof, in our house collapsed and he demanded her to pay him back what he had paid the contractor who fixed the roof. Therefore, my sister, I stand firm by what I did to him as I feel that my conscious is clear as far as my relationship with him is concerned.

Knowing all my income from the *Institute of General Education* was insufficient to cover all our expenses, I did try my best to find another job to supplement of meager salary from the *Institute of General Education*. I contacted my former teacher,

Mr. Zaki Khoury, who now established the *International Institute*, a night school that taught English to adults. Mr. Zaki Khoury is the one teacher who I had managed his concessions kiosk and taught typing using his typewriters for a fee he charged the typing students. Of course, since he never paid me a single penny for, either of the two services I rendered for him I thought he may reward me, by offering me a part time job at his institute. I asked him for a job to teach English in his night school. He refused to give me one giving several excuses as to why there was no job available for me.

I was, flabbergasted by his refusal to offer me a job despite all of what I had done for him when I managed his concessions stand and taught typing on his behalf with no pay for either service. I felt betrayed by him as he proved, to me, to be nothing but a cheap, grudging and a stingy person.

I did, however land another day job to teach English at one of *al-Maqassid Al-Khayriah's* schools, six days a week. That job paid me 104.50 Lebanese pounds ($35) /month. One quarter of a pound was, deducted from the monthly salary to pay for the taxicab expenses incurred by one of the teachers who was, assigned the job of going downtown to the *al-Maqassid* headquarters to pick up the salaries for all the teachers at the school. That was a good salary considering the economic situation of a Palestinian refugee in Lebanon!

Now I am making good money, I needed to buy a watch, and found a Swiss watch, Enicar, that I liked. I did not have the extra cash to pay the whole price of fifty Lebanese pounds for the watch in full. I found a jeweler who was willing to sell watches on credit. I could have the watch, the jeweler said, only if he is provided with two credible witnesses who are willing to sign the papers guaranteeing the monthly installments. I sought the help of a relative of mine and his friend, both of whom signed the agreement guaranteeing the monthly payments. Now that I got the watch I wanted to, have everybody see me wearing that Swiss watch!

I negotiated with Mr. Kamel Khoury, that since I have now a day job at *al-Maqassid,* if I could still work at the *Institute of General Education* in the evenings from 6:00 PM-9:00 PM. He agreed and offered me a salary of sixty Lebanese pounds ($20) a month for working six evenings a week. With these two jobs, I was netting 164.25 Lebanese pounds/month about $55 a month, should the night school pay me on time as promised. Wow! I am rich now making 164.25 Lebanese pounds per month! My sisters and I can now afford to buy clothes and good food! There was no contract with the *Institute of General Education* however there was a binding contract I had to sign with *al-Maqassid Al-Khayrriah.*

The *Institute of General Education* occupied half of the fifth floor of a five-story building in downtown Beirut. The other half was, occupied by a small hotel. Across the street and on the fourth floor resided a young pretty girl named Huda. She waived at me and I waived back at her. As meeting each other face to face was a taboo and socially unacceptable, I used to communicate with her by writing the notes that were, wrapped around a stone or a small apple and tossing it across the street to hit the balcony where she lived. Huda would do the same by throwing the notes hoping they land on the institute's balcony. My notes always made it to her balcony, but because of the balcony on my side is one floor higher and is much smaller than hers many of her notes did not hit the balcony but fell off to the street. In that case, I used to run down the staircase, jumping 5 stairs, at a time, to go down to pick the note before it is picked by someone else. The first question she asked me if I were Christian. I responded with the affirmative that I was, but the truth is I was not. Later, I did tell her that I was a Moslem. She felt like a huge rock fell over her head from the shock that I delivered to her for not being a Christian. A couple of days later she said, it is O.K if you are Moslem, but I still love you. At the time, in the 1950s, it was a taboo for a Christian girl to, even across the street, date a Moslem boy or for a Moslem girl to date a Christian boy. Huda's mother found out that we were communicating by sending notes to each other and I was a Palestinian and a Moslem. The mother was infuriated and very angry with her daughter and of course, with me too. She told her daughter 'a Palestinian may be O.K., but a Moslem too-NO WAY'! I want you to immediately and completely ignore this Palestinian Moslem refugee and never to communicate with him again. The mother would stand at their balcony to cuss at me and threaten me with her closed and raised fists!

Working at al-Maqassid and the Institute of General Education, from eight in the morning until nine in the evening, six days a week for two years was very taxing on me. I have decided to look for another career that may improve my prospects for a better future. My future called for something better than working for thirteen hours a day teaching English at two places and no prospects for an acceptable and durable future.

While working at the Institute of General Education I was, coached and mentored into Arab Nationalism. At that time, the Arab Nationalist Movement, in Lebanon, published a weekly magazine, Al-Rai (Opinion) and a little weekly pamphlet called al-Tha'ar (Revenge). Both publications were, geared towards informing the public of the tragedy of the loss of Palestine and keep the memory of Palestine fresh in the minds of the people.

Both publications were, intended to remind the public of the loss of Palestine to the Jews and to keep reminding the people that the liberation of Palestine is and should remain a top priority. My duty, in the movement, was to deliver both, the weekly magazine pamphlet to Mr. Ma'arouf Sa'ad, the chief of Police in Beirut. Mr. Sa`ad was not only an Arab nationalist who was sympathetic to the Palestinian cause but was also opposed to the foreign policy the government of Lebanon. I recall once I went to his office to deliver the publications and the guard at the door asked me, as to what did I want. I responded by saying, I want to see General Ma'arouf Sa'ad. The guard laughed at me and in a sarcastic way made fun of me saying this boy wants to meet with the chief of police. A teenager wanting to see the chief of Police! He stood up and shouted, "Get out of here or else I will have you arrested". I told him I want to hand deliver to General Sa'ad these two publications as I have always done. Well, after arguing for about an hour with that guard, he still would not let me in. I then asked him if he would be kind enough to inform Mr. Sa'ad that I wished to see him. He went and told Chief Sa'ad, with a sarcastic smile that a boy, at the door, wants to see you. General. Sa'ad was tall, handsome and a very humble man. He came to the door and welcomed me in. He wrapped his arms around me and said welcome brother Abdallah and escorted me to his huge office. I could see the eyes of the guard opened widely with surprise. When I came to the door to leave, this guard said, Goodbye Mr. Abdallah with a big smile on his face!

The last time I saw Mr. Ma'arouf Sa'ad was, in June 1974 when I visited Lebanon with our daughter Reem (Kim). He was very forthcoming and pleasant not only to me but towards our daughter too.

The public transportation system in Beirut was the tramway that crisscrossed the city with lines traveling from east to west and from north to south with a hub in the center of the city. At the hub passengers change trains and head in the direction of their destination.

As students in grammar school, high school and in college, the government of Lebanon offered us the option of purchasing an annual transportation "Pass" to use to ride the tramway. Nominal fees are, paid upfront and one can ride the tramway any time and as many times for the whole year at no additional charge.

Another means of help the government offered to students was reduced rates on movie tickets. That required the student to present the student ID, provided by the school, to the box office operator. Movie ticket prices that were, charged to students were, ninety percent lower than the prices the public was charged. I have always liked to watch American movies whenever they were, shown at the movie theaters. One thing that attracted my attention was Dwight Eisenhower's photo that appeared on the screen and the American national anthem played before the start of each American movie!

One day in the early 1950s, I wanted to travel to Europe and seek a better life. To leave Lebanon, Palestinians are required to have a security clearance from the department of the Interior General Security Services Office, prior to leaving the country. While at that office, applying for the clearance I saw an older Palestinian man sitting on the bench, with a sad look on his face. I introduced myself to him and asked as to what was wrong. He replied by saying, "well son, I have been waiting for four hours and they will not acknowledge my presence or talk to me. I spoke with one of the officers who was sitting behind his desk with the name of Ali Hudaib posted on top of his desk. I approached him and politely said, "Brother Ali, please help this old man as he said, he has been waiting for four hours". 'Brother' Ali jumped from his chair and yelled at me "I am not your brother I am better than you". I told him you are a disgrace to the government position you are holding. You should be fired as you are not fit to be in such a position. You are rude and have neither sense of social communications nor the willingness to do the job you are assigned to. Yelling by both of us prompted senior officers to come out to find out what the screaming and yelling was all about. I told them the story of what had happened, and I was very respectful by saying, Brother Ali please help this old man who has been waiting for four hours without any help. One of the top officers, General Ameen Ghanem, tried to cool me down and reassured me that the old man's needs will be promptly met.

Few years later, I went to purchase an LP from a music store and there was 'Brother Ali'. I asked him if he were still at the General Security office. He said no, I lost my job years ago, Then, I reminded him of the incident I had with him and perhaps I have contributed to his firing and said, what goes around comes around, my friend! I had the gut feeling that General Ghanem, a very dedicated public servant was behind the firing of 'Brother Ali'.

When a Palestinian friend of mine, had to leave Beirut to go to Damascus to see his ailing mother, needed a security clearance to leave the country asked me, if I knew any person in the Internal Security Apparatus. I responded in the affirmative and said I know General Ameen Ghanem as an honest and a professional civil servant. He is a man of principle who takes his job seriously and will do the right thing. I called General Ghanem and requested his help.

General Ghanem said, Abdallah, meet me in my office at 1:00 PM tomorrow and I will provide you with the security clearance for your friend. I said, but tomorrow is Sunday and all government offices are closed on Sunday. He said, I know tomorrow is Sunday, but I will do what I must do because you (me) were very instrumental in exposing the corruption disease in our department when you had the infamous incident with one of our employees, Mr. Ali Hodaib! My complaint and loud arguments and yelling with this government employee at the Internal Security Office apparently paid off in the end. Firing of that incompetent employee due to the incident I had with, alerted the higher ups to the existence of corruption that is rampant in these government departments and they did what is needed to clean up the department.

Well, fate has it. I have never seen or been in contact with General Ghanem again since I left Lebanon heading to the United States in 1963. To my great and very pleasant surprise, I had the great pleasure of meeting his daughter Firyal and his son Saleem. Meeting these fine people did not take place in Lebanon, not in the Middle East, not in Europe but from all places, in Nashville, Tennessee sixty years later!

1955
MY COLLEGE EDUCATION AT THE AMERICAN UNIVERSITY OF BEIRUT (AUB)

AFTER GRADUATING FROM HIGH SCHOOL IN 1953 AND WORKING FOR two years, six days a week, teaching English as a second language and after long thoughts, I decided that being an English language teacher is not the career I wanted to pursue. In 1955, I applied to study agriculture in the United States, to prepare me to take care of my properties in Palestine. To my surprise, not only was I accepted, but was offered a scholarship too! When I told my sisters of my plans to go to the United States to study, they started crying and wailing. The atmosphere in the apartment, felt and sounded very much like a funeral home. I then decided to cancel the trip to the US and opted to, if possible, pursue my college education in Beirut

At the time, there were three universities in Beirut: the *Lebanese University,* which catered for Lebanese students only, thus it was not possible for me to enroll in, as I am a Palestinian and not Lebanese. The other University, *St. Joseph University* taught in French and since my second language was English and I do not speak or read French, it meant that this university is out of question for me too. The only other option for me was, perhaps the *American University of Beirut (AUB).* The *American University of Beirut*, being a private institution, it was very expensive and was available only to people with deep pockets such as the sons and daughters of politicians and business-people. Since I belonged to neither of these two groups, my prospects to enroll at *AUB* were in the zero category.

I decided to take a chance and take a shot at it. I applied to the *American University of Beirut. (AUB),* which was and still is, thought of as being the Harvard of the Middle East, is open only to well-heeled families with deep pockets, politicians and business-people, who could send their children to that institution. It was a very big gamble on my part, but I felt it was worth the try. Most of the students were children of politicians and businesspeople from Lebanon and from other countries of the Middle East. The student body at *AUB* consisted of several nationalities as students came, not only from Lebanon, but also many came from neighboring countries in the Middle East as well as from Turkey, Greece, Cyprus, Pakistan and Afghanistan. As a Palestinian refugee with limited financial resources, it was next to impossible to even think about enrolling in and be a member of the student body at the elite *American University of Beirut.*

It was a risky and scary gamble that I was willing to take. Ultimately, that gamble proved to be a sound one that paid off later. I submitted my application with the $5.00 application fee. A month later, I received a letter advising me that I have a provisional acceptance stipulating that I must pass an entrance examination to have a formal and final acceptance. The letter specified the time and date of the examination and the room number on campus where the entrance exam to be held. The entrance exam was, scheduled three months from the date posted on the letter. Since I have been out of school for two years, I had to refresh my memory by studying and reviewing Mathematics, Physics, Chemistry, Algebra, Geometry, Arabic, History, Geography and English. I studied for at least ten hours a day for three consecutive months.

One hundred and sixty applicants from across Lebanon sat for the entrance examination. Of the one hundred sixty examinees, only fourteen passed and I was one of the lucky fourteen. Now I can register and receive the 'Handbook' a little pocket size notebook that has a calendar, the student information and confirming the holder to be a legitimately registered student at *AUB*. This 'Handbook' was not only the passport to success, but also was meant to suggest a higher social status of the holder. I was so proud of myself that I am a student at the elite *American University* and wanted everybody to see the handbook that I have always kept in my shirt pocket.

Wow! This was the time to celebrate my success for the potential of improving my social standing and of a better future. This is the break I have always been looking for. Now I have regained some of my lost confidence and envisaged my future to, perhaps, be brighter than being a teacher of English in a grammar school and in a night school. What a relief that was!

When I shared the news with Huda, she was elated at first, yet she had second thought and worried that I may meet another girl in college and forget all about her. I assured her that it is not going to happen. Now her mother, who used to stand at the balcony, with a threatening fist, and cuss at me, after hearing that I am a student at *AUB,* started to go out of her way to wave at me and say niceties across the street, of course! That was a hundred eighty-degree turn, in Huda's mother attitude towards me.

Huda and I rode the tramway without the knowledge of her family, of course. While riding the tramway we discussed our future together. She insisted that we must choose Christian names for our children. I did say it was premature to discuss these issues, as we are not married yet. I then said, to make both of us happy and have no conflicting issues, perhaps we should give our children names that are common to both Christians and Moslems, however I must insist on giving our first son the name of Mohamad, to honor the memory of my late father. She was very adamant about giving our children Christian names. I then asked her, what would happen should we be unable to have children? Her response, that takes care of the problem!

Christians and Moslems, in the Middle East, have different beliefs and traditions that have impacts not only on their behavior but also on their mannerism. Essentially that leads to two different, and sometimes opposing cultural arenas. Because of these cultural differences, it signaled, the end of a failed love affair. An affair, that saved me the agony of defeat should Huda's family, as expected, oppose my marrying their daughter!

Now that I am a member of the elites, by being accepted at the *American University of Beirut*, the question arose, as to how will I be able to, pay the hefty tuition fees and at the same time be able to pay the household expenses? What source of funds I can dip into to pay for my tuition fees and living expenses? Will I seek help from family members? Of course not. There were no prospects in the horizon, as I have no job or savings to rely on and take care of these obligations.

Well, uncle Mohamad popped up and was in the picture again. Having failed to get any money from me for several years, he has given up on the possibility of me helping him out. After hearing of my acceptance at *AUB,* and as the saying goes, hell may have broken loose with him. How could an orphan like me, be accepted at the *American University of Beirut*? He was happy, to see me struggling, yet he would come to ask me for money when I was working thirteen-hour days. Having been accepted, to *AUB* according to his tribal way of thinking was, not only a bad omen for him as it will continue to block the possibility of any potential stipend from me, but also and more importantly, he may lose complete control over me. I could become more independent and start thinking and planning on my own. He did his best to dissuade me from going to *AUB* citing financial difficulties relating to tuition fees and home expenses needed to support my sisters. Of course, he neither was concerned about me being not able to pay my tuition fees nor was he ever concerned about the expenses I will incur supporting my sisters.

He never had any concerns about me or about my sisters. He never tried to improve my sisters' situation or mine. He never offered any help to improve our well-being. He never had that even when we were children in Palestine, and why would he have any now to us as refugees in Lebanon?

The truth of the matter was that, his attempts to dissuade me from attending *AUB* was because he did have an ulterior motive. As I found out later, his efforts to dissuade me from enrolling at *AUB* were because his son, Adnan, was also going to *AUB* at the same time I was. In uncle Mohamad's limited way of thinking, an orphan like me should not be entitled to go to the elite university where his son was going to attend! He used scare tactics in trying to dissuade me from going to *AUB* by putting a huge list of obstacles in my way. These obstacles, according to him, will prove that

I am incapable of continuing my education at the *American University* of *Beirut* because of the financial burdens I will be faced with and have no means to overcome such burdens.

It appeared to me, for a moment, and contrary to my readings of him, he may be a calculating man. After considering my sisters and me as being non-belonging to his family and using my sisters to work as servants, he now wanted me to marry one of his daughters as an enticement for me not to go to college! I was very adamant and told him in a nice way, of course, that I am not ready to get married yet, because I want to go to college and improve my prospects for a better future. I tried to assure him that everything was under control. Of course, as far as I was concerned, I was in absolute denial as what I was telling him to be untrue and nothing was really under control!

To impress him that all is well, however, I borrowed money from friends and invited him to lunch in a very prestigious restaurant close to campus. He never thanked me for the lunch, but still insisted I should not go to *AUB*! Then I told him bluntly, I am sick and tired of your tribal way of thinking. I want you to know that, should I ever come to you and ask you for help, I do encourage you and expect you to please spit in my face and tell me to go to hell! That took care of that discussion and he gave up on dissuading me to abandon my quest for a college education. He must have resigned himself to the fact that I am capable of planning and pursuing my own future by myself and not by anybody else especially not by him.

Acceptance to *AUB* gave me the feeling of being an important and perhaps a brainy person as a new horizon opened for me. My future will be much better than working six days a week and thirteen hours a day teaching English to beginners at the night school and to rowdy kids in the day school.

I did not have a binding contract with *the Institute of Higher Education* but had a binding contract with *al-Maqassid* al-*khayrriah*. It was very troubling to me as I was worried I, may not be able to get out of that contract. That was, a nightmare that kept me having sleepless nights! Should that happen then I would not be able to continue my studies at *AUB*. Relief came to my rescue through my friend and al-Bassa native, Mr. Jiryis Shammas whose classmate at *AUB* was the daughter of the president of *al-Maqassid Al-khayrriah* conglomerate. I requested his help by asking him to see if Miss Kolthom Salam could help me, by talking to her father, to get out of the contract. Apparently, Mr. Shammas had spoken to Miss Kolthom Salam as she told him that she did talk to her father. I got a message, from Mr. Salam's office to go and meet with Mr. Mohamad Salam in his downtown, al-*Maqassid al-khayrriah,* office. I went to meet with Mr. Mohamad Salam, the president of al-*Maqassid al-khayrriah*, at the specified date and time. I was very anxious and apprehensive as to what his response might be when I went to meet with him. I was a little shaking when I arrived at the door of his office. He welcomed me in and pointed to a chair for me to sit down then asked as to what he can do for me. I requested his help in relieving me of the contract with al-*Maqassid* as I was accepted and am now, enrolled at the *American University of Beirut*. This is the wish and ambition, I always had to enroll at *AUB*. He was very courteous and understanding to my request.

With his face armed with a big smile, he said his daughter, Kolthom had talked to him about me and requested that I be granted a reprieve by annulling the contract, I had with his organization. He indicated that this was his daughter's request to him to honor my request to get out of the contract. He said, I am very proud of you and of your ambition for a better future by furthering your education. I wish you the best of luck in your university education. As far as your contract with *al-Maqassid* is concerned, I want you know that the contract, as of this moment is null and void and you have neither obligations nor liabilities as far as *al-Maqassid al-khayrriah* is concerned. I was elated to know that I am off the hook with al-*Maqassid* and have no worries about any liabilities to that institution. I could now devote more time with a clearer head and less worries, to my studies.

My next step was to resign from the *Institute of General Education* too. Now having resigned my positions at the *Institute* and at *al-Maqassid* school, although I will have no income, provided me with adequate time to devote to and to concentrate on my studies.

Now the excitement of the new horizon at *AUB* has subsided and reality set in. Where will I and how will I be able to secure the funds to defray the cost of my tuition fees and provide rent and support of my sisters with no income coming in. I have tried to get part time jobs on campus, but none was forthcoming. It was very hard to concentrate on my studies as new worries of financial disparity have overtaken my abilities to focus on and to retain the information of what I was studying.

One other contributing factor that had an impact on my inability to comprehend and retain the information of what I was studying, was that neighborhood kids kept on playing and making loud noises until 10:00 in the evening.

As I could not order those kids to go home and stop making noises, or ask their parents to do the same, I opted to contact the Minister of the Interior of Lebanon, by lodging my complaint, specifying the issue of the children noises directly to him.

I sent a letter to the Minister of the Interior of Lebanon complaining about the absence of police patrols that are supposed to guarantee the peacefulness and quietness of the neighborhood after 7:00 PM. I did mention that there are persons who may be ill and needed quietness to rest and there are students who want to study but cannot because of the noise. I did not provide him with my home address, but to impress him, I provided my P. O. Box number at *AUB* instead, because our neighborhood is a poor one and does have any clout. I did not hear a word from the Minister of the Interior until four weeks later when the head of police precinct overseeing our neighborhood came in with six other officers. This was the response of the Minister of the Interior for my complaint.

The officer, leading the group, asked the neighbors close to our residence as to who this fellow, Abdallah M. Isa is. Their response was unanimous that Abdallah is a good neighbor. He leaves in the morning and comes home late in the evening. He never bothered anybody. When the officers came close to our apartment and while I was sitting on the balcony having my coffee, the leader of the group asked, if I am Abdallah M. Isa? I responded with the affirmative. With a serious look and a threatening tone of voice, ordered me to come on down now. I said no sir. I will not come down. You should come up here and if you do, I may offer you a cup of coffee. He again said, you better come down now or else I will have you arrested! I asked him if he had a warrant for my arrest, if so, I would like to see it. If you come up, however, I may consider chatting with you about my complaint to the Minister of the Interior and at the same time, I will offer you a cup of coffee or a cold drink. Well, he realized that this fellow, me, is not a dummy and knows what he is talking about and cannot be bullied. He and his six other officers decided to come up and we all went inside to have our coffee.

This officer mellowed a little bit when he saw my framed national grammar school certificate of passing the national board examinations hanging on the wall. His tone of voice changed from ordering me to pleading and requesting me to sign a document indicating he has come and took care of the situation. I said, sorry sir, I will not sign any papers until I see positive changes in the neighborhood and no children playing and making noises after 7:00 PM. Then he tried to be conciliatory by asking as to why did I not come to him directly to discuss the issue before addressing the complaint to the Minister of the Interior? I said, I have never seen your face before sir, and I have no idea where your precinct is, so how could I have contacted you? He was mum at the question and never voiced an answer.

After that meeting, officers started patrolling the neighborhood every night. Any children seen playing after 7:00 PM were sent home and the parents were given a warning that they will be given a citation of disturbing the peace should their children be found playing after 7:00 PM. My letter to the Minister of the Interior did help improve the situation in our neighborhood from that time on.

It is tragic to know that people in the Middle East, in general, do not complain to the authorities about situations they see as disturbing or unlawful. Many a time the higher-ups do not really know what is going on in the neighborhoods and assume all is well and everything is under control. My complaint to the Minister of the Interior did indeed help the situation in the neighborhood.

Another incident that involved a taxicab driver who did not stop to let a pedestrian holding a child cross the street. I yelled at the cab driver and shamed him for not stopping to allow safe passage of the person holding a child. Well, the driver stopped and a traffic cop, who was a passenger in the cab, came down and started to threaten me for yelling at the cab driver!

I said to him, as an officer, one of your responsibilities is to make sure the laws are, enforced and you are responsible to protect the public. Instead of being the enforcer of the law, you give me the impression that you are above the law! Is protecting the taxicab driver who did not give a damn about the safety of a person holding a child, according to you, a lawful act? I do not think so, sir. I want you to know that your action, in this incident, will be reported to the proper authorities. A couple of days later, I saw this same cop directing traffic in an area that was close to where I used to work. I stood in front of this cop, with my eyes fixated at his badge with the intention of getting his name and his badge number. He asked me as to what did I need? I said nothing sir, I just want to get your badge number and your name. That is all I need, sir. That same evening, I discussed the issue with the chief of police in the Ministry of the Interior, Mr. Ahmed Arnaout, who happened to have been my student at the *Institute of General Education.* He said, I will take care of this complaint. As a result, of my complaint, that cop was punished by reducing his salary by, 10 per cent for that month and was handed a warning that should he behave in the same manner again, he will be terminated.

It so happened that this cop came from the town of *Barja,* the same town where my adopted Lebanese, al-Hajj Family came from. To my surprise, I found this cop at al-Hajj family house. He pleaded with me to please contact the head of the Police department and request him to re-instate the 10% deduction that he levied against my salary! I said sorry sir, but you must pay the price for your unprofessional action. Let me remind you sir that we all are accountable for what we say and more so for what we do! I hope you have learned your lesson and remember that nobody, including you and me, is and should be above the law.

ACADEMIC PRODBLEMS
AT *THE AMERICAN*
UNIVERSITY OF BEIRUT (AUB)

BECAUSE OF THE FINANCIAL BURDENS AND NO JOB TO PROVIDE ME with an income, I barely passed all the courses the first semester of the freshman class. When it came to the second semester it was, a different story altogether.

I enrolled in English 102 that was taught by a Lebanese woman, Mrs. Bader. She asked the class to write a story that had an impact on some aspects of our lives and hand it to her a week later. I wrote the story about the Christian Maronite girl, Huda, who I loved and knowing well enough it may won't work out as her parents would never allow her to marry a Moslem boy. I was hoping Mrs. Bader would be sympathetic to my situation. I knew I did well in English 102 and felt I was passing all along. This teacher gave me a score of 58 out of a hundred as my final grade in the English 102 course. This was a failing grade as the passing score was set at 60. I was two points off passing. I pleaded with her to reconsider by re-grading my final exam paper. She refused to not only to re-grade my final exam paper, but also to change the grade. She said, this is your final grade, period!

I felt her actions were unprofessional and politically motivated, as I learned later that it was known around campus, that she was an active member of the ultra-right-wing Christian Lebanese Phalange Party. That party hated anything Palestinian and more so if they happen to be Palestinian Moslems!

The other course I have failed in was, Math 102 and again the score was 58. Math 102 was taught by, an American who also was a Pastor at an evangelical church in Beirut. He was married to a Lebanese woman who, someone said, he and his wife were having serious marital problems and she may be seeking divorce. Whether he was taking his frustrations with his wife on me or not, a possibility however is as remote as it may have been. Since I failed two courses, legitimately or not, university regulations dictate dismissal of the student from the university.

At the end of the second semester, I received the letter from the Registrar informing me that because, I failed two courses in one semester, I am being dropped from the university altogether. The news was devastating to me and I felt hopeless and helpless to be able to do anything to reverse the university decision. I had a window of opportunity, however, that the registrar's letter came in June and I have more than three months to deal with the situation. I wrote a letter to the president of the university, Dr. Constantine Zuraik, the first Arab to hold the office of president of *AUB*, asking him for an appointment. Dr. Zuraik wrote back specifying the date and time he can see me. I went to his office and explained my situation to him that I am a Palestinian and I want to learn and improve my chances of survival. I could see tears coming down his cheeks when he told me, "I will instruct the Dean and the Registrar to give you another chance." A week later, I received a letter from the Registrar telling me that I can re-enroll at the university in the coming fall semester on one condition that the acceptance would be for the fall semester only and will be provisional. I will be placed on probation again and my progress will be monitored. Should I fail again, I will be dropped from the university altogether and will never be allowed to re-enroll at *AUB*. With this ultimatum, I had to prove myself by getting good grades, otherwise

I may be dropped again and never will I be re-admitted to the university. That was a frightening situation to say the least!

Now, that I have been re-admitted, I had a sigh of relief that my future though still, hanging in the balance, and there was no guarantee that I will make it and go past the probation period may be, possible. Now that my future received a shot in the arm, and it may even get better depending on how well I do at school. When I rejoined the University the following fall semester, things started to look up for me. I found three part-time jobs on campus: one was to wash dishes in the laboratory, another one in the library and a third in the cafeteria. The first two jobs paid one Lebanese pound (33 cents) an hour each, while the cafeteria job paid half a pound (16.5 cents) an hour, but with a free meal on the days I worked.

Dr. Levon Melikian, a Palestinian Professor of Psychology at *AUB* was, entrusted with funds from the university, to provide needy students with food cards to the cafeteria. He provided me with a card that allowed me to eat one meal a day for the whole month at no charge. Whenever Dr. Melikian had a research project that involved students, he always called on me to participate in the study for a nominal pay. He was a great help.

In addition to my two sisters Fatima and Amina, Mr. Kamel Khoury, his wife Mary Shammas Khoury and Dr. Levon Melikian filled the five very dear spots on the list of my idols. They all had a great impact on my personal development and to a large degree on my future. They were the example for me to follow and always think of their contributions to my being as to who and what I am today. They were my inspiration and the confirmation that there are still some kind and caring people in this world. My gratitude and love for these five idols will never wane.

In the meantime, my sister Fatima who was illiterate, because uncle Mohamad never sent her to school, was obsessed with education. She contracted with a private tutor to teach her, as an adult, how to read and write in Arabic, of course. She instilled her obsession with education into me first and later into her children. She had five sons and one daughter. Three of the sons became doctors, the other two became engineers and the daughter became a dentist. Who can beat that? May God bless your soul my sister Fatima.

I still owed the university tuition fees that I was not able to pay. When asked to pay, I always said, the check is in the mail. My cousin (Adnan's half-brother) works in Saudi Arabia and he promised to send me the money. When I receive the money, I will pay my tuition fees. Of course, that was a big lie. Cousin Adel had never sent me and never promised that he will send me money even if I asked him to. He was always short of money as he was supporting his brother Adnan's education and two other households in addition to his own: His mother and his three siblings, his father with his new wife and their five children and his wife with six children.

Receiving my monthly pay for my three jobs on campus was very uncertain. The accounts payable and the accounts receivable departments were, housed in the same office. To pick my check from accounts payable I had to find a new way to avoid being seen by, Mr. Albert Madani as he oversaw accounts receivable at the university and would demand payment of my tuition fees every time he sets his eyes on me.

Luckily, Accounts Receivable and Accounts Payable departments did not share information about funds paid out to any vendor including me. Once Mr. Madani saw me coming in to pick my check, he immediately instructed the accounts payable department to stop paying me and divert the money to his department. I had to find ways to block Mr. Madani's view of me coming into the accounts, payable office.

During the summer months and with clear blue skies, and no sign of any clouds in the horizon, I would go in with an open black umbrella tilted to the right of my head upon entering the accounting department. The umbrella use was intended to block the view of my head and face from Mr. Madani who was sitting on the right-hand side facing the door through which I had to use to get in. After picking the check and before leaving the accounts payable desk, I would tilt the umbrella, to my left side to block Mr. Madani's view of me leaving the room. On other occasions, I would raise the collar flaps of my heavy winter coat to cover the sides of my face or to wear a hat or a scarf that covered my head and part of my face! Those tricks did not work all the time, but at least I could get some money from the jobs I held on campus.

In addition to the three jobs I held on campus I had a fourth job helping the children of *Time* Magazine's correspondent in Beirut, Mr. Abu-Said Abu al-Reesh, with their homework. I inherited this job from my friend and al-Bassa native, Mr. Jiryis Shammas who held it for some time. I kept this job until I graduated from *AUB* in June 1960.

Now that I am making good money with no worries about economic survival, I could spend productive time focusing on my studies. Because of my improved performance during the fall semester after I was re-admitted to the university and excelling in my studies, I was elated to see my name advertised on the Dean's Honor list at the end of the semester. The names of students, including mine, on the Dean's Honor list were posted on all bulletin board across campus.

In the meantime, I had to find a source of funds to pay my tuition fees that I owe the university and to pay for other accessories. I contacted Mr. Ahmad Toukan, a Palestinian executive at the *United Nations Relief and works Agency (UNRWA) for Palestine Refugees* for his help. He was full of promises which I later found out were empty promises. He was no help and I got nowhere with him. Then I decided to go to the British Council, in Beirut, and request a meeting with Mr. Williams who was, in charge of the Council. I introduced myself and told Mr. Williams, I am a Palestinian refugee and his government was the cause of all my troubles. His government granted my country of Palestine, which it did not own, to the Jews to establish their homeland. As a result, of your government's action I have become a refugee. I hold the British government responsible for all the difficulties I am facing. Mr. Williams did not agree with my assertions, yet he was a very gracious and understanding man. He asked as to what can he do to help me out? I said I, would be grateful and appreciative of your efforts, if you would be kind enough to request Miss Farah, his secretary, to put a good word for me with her brother Fouad who is, in charge of the Education department at the *United Nations Relief and works Agency (UNRWA) for Palestine refugees* to possibly grant me a scholarship. I am on the Dean's Honor list at the *American University of Beirut* and I have satisfied all the requirements for the scholarship. Mr. Williams promised to honor my request by asking Miss Farah to talk to her brother about me.

Two weeks later, I received a communication from Mr. Fouad Farah asking me to come over to his office for an interview. When I met with him, he indicated that his sister had talked to him about me and requested him to help me. I explained to him my situation in detail that I am a Palestinian student at the *American University of Beirut*. I excelled in my studies as evidenced by having my name placed on the Dean's Honor list. I have no source of support to defray the cost of my education and now I am requesting his help to provide me with a scholarship. He promised to, investigate my request and will let me know in due time.

While studying Agriculture at *AUB,* we had to spend at least one semester at the *AUB* farm in the Bika'a Valley in East Lebanon. At the farm, we were, trained in driving tractors draw different attachments to the tractors, how to use the tractors with the attachments in tilling the land. The school of Agriculture at *AUB* introduced the American pickling cucumber to the Lebanese market. The Arab markets and the Lebanese markets favored, the small cucumbers that are common in the Middle East over the American ones, thus the American pickling cucumbers were, trashed.

Additional training was, in seeding, weeding and harvesting crops especially wheat by the combine. We were, trained in raising chickens beginning with fertile eggs, to incubation and finally to hatching was part of our training. Egg production, as well as, grading of the eggs into small, medium and large sizes were, also taught at the farm. Raising cattle and sheep for and meat production were high on the list. Maintenance of trees with emphasis, especially on pruning the deciduous trees were required.

Fruit trees such as apple trees and grape vines are an important part of the Lebanese economy. Apples were the source of foreign currency as a large part of the crop was destined for export to Europe and to other Arab countries. Grapes on the other hand, in addition to some exports, the bulk of the grapes crop was used locally in the manufacture of wine, *Arak*, the Lebanese national drink and other products. In an effort, on my part, to impress our horticulture instructor, I climbed the apple tree to show him and my classmates, how to properly prune the apple trees. In the accompanying photo, Dr. Kamal Da'ouk, our horticulture instructor and with one of my classmates, watching me pruning an apple tree

(Me sitting on the apple tree showing the instructor and a classmate the proper way of pruning an apple tree)

Two weeks have passed and had not heard a word from Mr. Farah. By the end of the third week however, I received an urgent message from Dr. Frank O. Smith, vice-dean of the School of Agriculture at *AUB*, to come to his office as soon as possible. I became very apprehensive and was scared to death, as I was stung before by having been dropped from the university, what now? I became very anxious and worried as to what does the vice-dean want to see me for. What does he have in mind! I was afraid that the same thing might happen to me again and my ambition to have a good future may go down the drain. Should this happen then I am guaranteed I will have a dismal and bleak future. When I went to see Dr. Smith, I was very worried as to what he was about to tell me. I was shaking as I stood by the door. He looked at me with a big frown on his face and yelled at me with a raised voice asking, "Why did you do it?" With a shaking voice I responded by saying I did not do anything sir! What do you think I did? Do you know something that I do not know? He smiled and pointed to a chair for me to sit down. I was still shaking from fear of the unknown and then he had a very big smile on his face and said, Isa, because of your outstanding scholastic achievements at *AUB,* you have been awarded scholarships from three different sources and they are:

1. AUB university scholarship that pays all your tuition fees

2. Ford Foundation scholarship that pays all your tuition fees

3. United Nations scholarship that pays your tuition fees, books other supplies and in addition, a monthly stipend of forty Lebanese pounds a month while in Beirut and one hundred sixty Lebanese pounds a month when you are on assignment outside Beirut. Now you know what these scholarships are, which scholarship would you like to have? I said I, would like to have the three scholarships sir. He said, you have only one and you must choose which scholarship you want. That settled the choice and I chose the United Nations scholarship. That scholarship stayed with me until I graduated from *AUB* in June 1960. At that time, I have become a firm believer in the saying "When it rains it pours!" That was a confirmation that Mr. Williams of the British Council and Mr. Fouad Farah were men of their words. They promised to investigate my request and now Mr. Farah honored it by granting me the United Nations scholarship. Big thanks go to Mr. Williams of the British council and to Mr. Farah of the Education Department of *UNRWA.*

Success may sometimes lead to some unwanted results such as jealousy and some unpleasant situations. Because I was a student AUB and I received a United Nations scholarship, my name was, deleted from the United Nations Registry of Palestine refugees, and was no longer qualified to receive rations or medical care provided by the *UNRWA.* I suspected a former classmate at *Ahliah High School* and who also, happened to have come from my hometown in Palestine, may have had a hand in deleting my name from the Registry. She was working as a secretary at the United Nations Office in Beirut and never showed a liking for me! On my part and as far as I was concerned, the feeling was quite mutual.

My cousin Adnan, uncle Mohamad's son also enrolled at *AUB* at the same time I did. Although he was a couple of years younger, he was not only my cousin, but also a very close friend too. He and I had a serious discussion in which I reminded him about the problems I have had all along with his father. He has the choice of being my cousin and my friend or follow his father's side and outlook towards me. I said to him, please think about it and let me know within a week's time. I told him there would not be any hard feelings regardless of the decision he may arrive at. Few days later Adnan said, I have nothing to do with my father's treatment of you, nor do I condone what he did, you are not only my cousin but above all, you are my very close friend and confidante. I love you and I would associate with you as a cousin and a friend. You and I should be above all these trivialities and rise to the occasion that we are both adults.

We have a good future ahead of us and we should always look at the positive aspects in life. We should avoid dwelling on the negatives especially those of the past,

**(Cousin Adnan and I discussing our future relationship
as cousins and friends)**

Our senior class in the school of Agriculture had only eight students. Although we were competitive, yet we were very close friends. On several occasions we would study together to prepare for a test and always lent a hand to each other in trying to explain scientific concepts relating to Agriculture.

On one occasion, we all sat on the steps of West Hall, on campus, when I was asked by the goup to read the notes I had taken in the course of dairy production, As can be seen in the accompanying photo, I am reading my notes to my clasmates while sitting on the steps of West Hall.

(From left, John Yousef. Me in the middle with a suit and tie,
George Ma'alouf , Shawki al-Masri. Behind us were Ali Shahroudi, George
Battikha and M. Ghandour on the lower steps.
I was reading to my classmates on the steps of West Hall
on campus at *AUB*)

I graduated, with a BS degree and an Agricultural Engineering degree from *AUB*
in June 1960. It was unfortunate though that cousin Adnan did not graduate at the
same time I did but had to spend extra semester before he could graduate. Adnan was
worried and afraid to meet his family upon telling them that he did not graduate on
time. He asked me to accompany him to his family in Ghaziyeh. He was afraid of a
possible confrontation by members of his family for not graduating on time. Indeed,
his fears came to be true when we entered their house, his sister 'spit on his face and
told him: I am very ashamed of you. Abdallah M. Isa graduated, and you did not? You

are a failure and should be ashamed of yourself'. I tried to calm her down, but she was still very furious and would not quit.

The whole family of uncle Mohamad got very jealous too as that orphan, Abdallah M. Isa, who did not belong to their family, is now a university graduate with an Agricultural Engineering degree. They have resigned themselves to the fact that no other member of the family except for this orphan to graduate with a university degree and none of them had attained the privilege and honor of enrolling in and graduating from the elite *American University of Beirut!*

It so happened that when I was studying at the library and sitting in one of the carrels with my feet placed on the table, *AUB* president Zuraik walked by. I guess he did not appreciate seeing me, an Arab boy sitting with my feet raised on the table in front of me, as American students do. This was not an acceptable behavior in our Arab culture. He walked by, back and forth several times never said a word, but looking at me with disgust. I was embarrassed and got the message, put my feet down and sat down properly.

After seeing me sitting down properly with my feet down, he walked by and never came back again. Dr. Zuraik was a great Arab nationalist who practiced and applied our cultural norms to the letter.

I have graduated with a degree in agricultural engineering and with a BS degree in Agriculture. I chose that field because I felt it would prepare me and help me to, take care of my property when Palestine is liberated! Of course, that was a dream that was not supposed to be realized as Palestine was not and still is not liberated and would unlikely be liberated in my lifetime.

I know I was the first and the only person in my family and for that matter, perhaps from my hometown in Palestine, to graduate from high school and later from the university, especially from the elite *American University of Beirut!*

As always, things happen for a reason. Had the catastrophe in which we lost Palestine not taken place and I was still living in Palestine taking care of my properties, would I have gone to college in Lebanon? Unlikely, as I would have been engaged in farming and spend my time tending to my properties. Now fate has it, as a refugee with no property to care for, I had no other choice but to seek a college education with the hope that it may help provide me with the means of improving my future and my way of life. One should not hate anything as it may be to his advantage, or love anything as it may be to his disadvantage or detriment.

RECONNECTING WITH MY HIGH SCHOOL SWEETHEART

AFTER CLASSES AT *AUB*, IT WAS CUSTOMARY THAT WE STUDENTS HEAD to the Milk Bar to have a cup of coffee and a snack. While heading to the Milk Bar, I spotted a beautiful young woman sitting on a bench, under the Banyan Tree. Her face was, vaguely familiar and I was not too sure who she really was. I approached her slowly and reluctantly asked if she were so and so. She did not answer my question, but responded by asking, if I were so and so. I said yes, I am Abdallah and then she said yes, I am Laila. Well, we both were in high school at the same time, but she was two grades lower than me. I taught her typing and developed a liking for her but could not dare tell her that I liked her as I was afraid she might be offended and respond in a nasty way. I later found out that the feelings were, somehow mutual.

Going back to high school days and while my class was having our final examination in Chemistry and Laila's class was having her final exam in Algebra. She was stuck with an algebraic problem that she could not solve because she did not know the solution. Although she was a couple grades lower than me, her class and mine were having the final examinations in the same room. She wrote the question she was having problems with on a piece of paper and threw it to me. I wrote the answer on a piece of paper, rolled it into a ball and threw it back at her hoping the proctor would not see it. Unfortunately, however, Mr. Saleh Akki, our Chemistry teacher, who was proctoring the exams, saw the note, picked it up and read it. He looked at me with disgust and with a frown on his face asked me as to why did I do that? I said, because I love her and want to help her, sir. He smiled at me, gave her the piece of paper with the solution to the problem and told me not to do it again. I said, yes sir I promise you I will never do it again!

Few months after I graduated from high school in June 1953 and landing a job at the *Institute of General Education* teaching English as a second language, Laila and her neighbor friend came by to say goodbye to me as Laila was on her way to London to further her studies. I have not heard from Laila for five years. Her sister, Najwa, who also attended *Ahliah High School* with Laila and me, now is a student at *AUB* too. It so happened that I asked Najwa, in passing, as to how is her sister Laila doing? She said, Laila is still in London and she asked about you and asked me to say hello to you. I said well, please say hello to her for me. That was in February of 1958.

'FULFILLMENT' OF MY DREAM
OF ARAB UNITY

THAT SAME YEAR, 1958, WAS A GREAT YEAR FOR ME AS I FELT MY DREAM of Arab unity was around the corner. I was honored to have witnessed the birth of the *United Arab Republic (UAR)* and to see president Gamal Abdel Nasser and Mr. Shukry al-Quwatly, president of Syria only few yards away from where I was standing. I attended the announcement and the ceremony that followed in the great city of Damascus when Mr. Shukri al-Quwatly, the president of the Republic of Syria at the time, abdicated his position as President of the Republic of Syria to President Gamal Abdel Nasser, President of Egypt and now the president of the newly born *United Arab Republic*. It was such a moving ceremony when the *United Arab Republic (UAR)* came into existence. I have had the great pleasure and honor to have seen, in person, both Presidents al-Quwatly and Nasser on the balcony declaring the union between Egypt and Syria. This union of establishing the *United Arab Republic* was the wish and aspiration of every Arab nationalist to have the Arabs united into one state. It was a sweet dream that came to fruition.

The *Arab Nationalist Movement* co-founded and headed by Dr. George Habash had $100 in its coffers at the time. Dr. Habash, met with President Gamal Abdel Nasser, offered him the $100 and said, my president, our movement was established with the intention of promoting Arab unity and the liberation of Palestine. Since Arab unity is now a reality under your leadership, please accept this tiny amount of money we have as a token of the support of our movement to the coffers of the *United Arab Republic*. Our mission is, now over and we know that Arab unity in the person of the *United Arab Republic* is in your safe hands. We fully understand and firmly believe that the *UAR,* under your leadership will ultimately liberate and free Palestine from its occupation by the Zionists

The *UAR* was, envisioned as the nucleus of the newly unified Arab countries with a population of over three hundred million people at the time, and massive amounts of oil and other natural resources reserves. The *UAR* was the first brick in building a united Middle East under one roof. Syria, prior to the establishment of the *UAR,* was continuously harassed by Turkey and of course by Israel. Such harassment by Turkey ceased completely after the union between Syria and Egypt came into being.

THE 1958 CIVIL WAR IN LEBANON

CONSPIRACIES AND PLOTS AGAINST THE *UAR* WERE NOW IN FULL swing. Camille Cham`oun, the president of Lebanon, spread false allegations that not only the *UAR* was a communist regime, but also the communists from Syria are invading Lebanon! That was a ploy Cham`oun used to use as he wanted to go against the constitution and run for the presidency for a second six-year term. Corruption during his presidency was the rule of the day. It is, alleged that his Attorney General had ties to a prostitution ring headed by *Afaf,* a 'madam' who ran the prostitution ring in one of the elite areas of Beirut. *Afaf,* as rumored would send her pimps to meet teenage girls after school is out to offer them good paying part time jobs in sales. Instead, these teenaged girls were used to, forced to perform sex acts with very important clients. *Afaf* had access to sophisticated means of surveillance. She had hidden cameras installed in the ceilings of bedrooms in her condominium. Politicians and business-people coming in for sex were, photographed and before leaving the premises were, blackmailed by showing them their photographs while engaging in the sexual act. That was enough to warn them of exposure should they report the illegal brothel to the authorities. These checks and balances employed by this 'Madam' were at work in protecting her prostitution business.

Recently an operation, which appears to be an exact replica of *Afaf's* prostitution ring in Lebanon, appeared in the United States. Jeffrey Epstein's human trafficking operation using underage girls for sex with important and powerful people with the intention of controlling them and possibly blackmailing them should they deviate from and act on their intended agenda. Jeffrey Epstein's operation was, discovered and he was arrested and sent to jail. While in prison, an investigation of Mr. Epstein and his operation was underway. Unfortunately, Mr. Epstein, allegedly, committed suicide while serving time in prison before the closure of the investigation. There were serious questions as to whether his death was indeed a suicide or a murder to protect his male clients and the tentacles of his operation There is an increasing number of voices questioning the validity of the suicide theory and claiming it to be a murder to cover up!

It was also reported that Mr. Epstein had a strong connection to, and still was, an agent of the *Mosad*, the Israeli foreign intelligence service. Epstein, as an agent of the *Mosad*, was confirmed by a former Israeli *Mosad* spy, Mr. Ben-Menashe, who admitted that Epstein was entrusted by the *Mosad* to blackmailing American and other political and important figures, When I read this information, I immediately thought of *Afaf's* prostitution operation in Beirut in the *1950s* struck me that both the Epstein's operation and that of Afaf's show the same pattern and suggest the possibility of being related and connected to the *Mosad,* the Israeli Intelligence Service!

Cham'oun's insistence on amending the constitution, to succeed himself, led to the start of the 1958 civil war that unfortunately carried religious overtones that led to a Moslem/Christian divide. Moslems from West Beirut were, slaughtered when they crossed into Christian East Beirut and Christians were, slaughtered should they cross into West Beirut. The fate of a person's life was, determined by his/her name. Persons with Moslem names were, murdered by Christians and persons with Christian names were, murdered in the Moslem areas! Having lost control of the situation, Cham`oun appealed to Dwight D. Eisenhower, president of the United States, by asking his help citing his allegation that *The United Arab Republic* is a communist country and communists from Syria, are moving into Lebanon and these communists were fomenting trouble that led to the civil war!

These were the reasons Cham'oun cited behind his request for Eisenhower's help. On his part, Eisenhower sent the marines into Lebanon, not only as a show of force, but also to pretend they were sent in support of Camille Cham`oun and his government. The Marines presence was very evident in parts of the city that were controlled by the Christian militia. Marine's planes were flying all over Beirut, in a show of force in support of the 'legitimate' government, but ploy did not work and Cham`oun was forced to resign the presidency with the end of his hopes for a second term were now out of the question.

Having found no evidence of communists invading from neighboring *United Arab Republic (UAR)* by, Eisenhower and the resignation of Cham'oun as president of Lebanon, convinced Eisenhower to withdraw the marines from Lebanon.

**(My sister Fatima, center, with me and her friend,
Miss al-Husseini in Damascus to witness the creation
of the *United Arab Republic*)**

At the height of the Civil war, going to *AUB* for me, was a very dangerous ordeal. We lived in the Moslem area of West Beirut and I had to go through the Christian area to catch the tramway to go to the university that is located at the other end of West Beirut. To catch the tramway to go to the university we had to cross, areas controlled by Christian militias.

There were several checkpoints scattered all over the area connecting Moslem West Beirut and Christian East Beirut. I was, stopped by a former grammar school classmate, who was holding a machinegun and several hand grenades. He ordered me to stop or else he will shoot. I tried to reason with him by reminding him as to who I was and told him that he should remember me, as both of us were grammar school classmates years ago. He refused to heed to my explanation and still insisted I must stop, be searched, or else he will shoot. Stupidity, on my part, ruled and seized the moment. I told him to go to hell and dared him to shoot! Well, luckily, he came to his senses and remembered me, and decided not to shoot.

Having passed the first checkpoint with no problem then I was, stopped by yet another checkpoint that was thirty yards away. At that time, *AUB* issued us a little card indicating that we are students at the university. The card had our names and university affiliation in English with no Arabic writings. Knowing well enough, the militias manning the checkpoints, may be illiterate and may not be able to comprehend the English writings on the card, I wrote the information in Arabic on the back of the card and said the information in Arabic is on the backside of the card. He became agitated and furious by saying, not only can he read Arabic but also can read Egyptian!

At that second checkpoint I was, asked about my destination. The American University, I said. The man said, you are a spy and escorted me for questioning at the "headquarters". The headquarters consisted of a pile of sandbags, a machine gun emplacement and few recruits. The 'chief' at the "headquarters" questioned me for about an hour and then let me go without recrimination as he could not determine that I was a spy for either the Americans or for the Lebanese government!

During that infamous civil war, the Lebanese army split into two factions based on religious lines. Now we have a Christian Lebanese army opposed to a Moslem Lebanese army. Because the situation was so chaotic, dangerous and unpredictable, *AUB* realized the dangers we might face trying to cross the checkpoints on our way home. The university offered us the option to spend the nights on campus by providing us with inflatable air mattresses, which we were grateful for university for its understanding of our situation.

Splitting of the army, the killing of hundreds of innocent civilians and the deteriorating security situation in the country forced, Camille Cham'oun to resign the presidency of the republic and forced him to abandon his quest to amend the constitution to be president for a second term.

To add insult to injury the year of 1958 was also a year of disasters to the country. In addition to the devastation of the civil war, a high magnitude earthquake hit the country. The intensity of the quake was so high that it split the mountain, southeast of Beirut, into two halves. Witnessing the high- rise buildings swaying left and right during the earthquake was a very frightening scene. Although the damage to property in Beirut was minimal with no loss of life, the situation in the mountains was a different story. Several villages were, wiped out off the map and hundreds of casualties have fallen dead. A family of seven was, buried under the roof of their destroyed home. It was so ironic that the earthquake hit two hours after I left the theatre that was showing the movie *Earthquake* in one of the movie theatres in Beirut. The scare of the earthquake was so intense that people in our neighborhood were terrified and were, forced to flee the carnage in a hurry to spend the night in open areas to avoid the collapse of their homes over their heads!

While working at the *Institute of General Education,* I joined the *Arab Nationalist Movement* and as a student at *AUB*, I participated in all activities the *Arab Nationalist Movement* had. The *Movement* had a strong showing on campus. Dr. George Habash, the Palestinian doctor who had graduated with honors from the *AUB* School of Medicine, refined the ideology of the *Arab Nationalist Movement* on campus and beyond as it now has a great appeal by the population, especially the Moslems in Lebanon. Because of his excellent scholastic achievements, Dr. Habash was, recruited by the university and appointed as an Assistant Professor at the *AUB* school of Medicine. As a staunch Arab nationalist who despised and opposed all forms of foreign control, he led an anti-American demonstration on campus, for the American support of the Baghdad Pact in the early nineteen fifties. He resigned or perhaps was forced to resign his position at the university because of the anti-American demonstration. He then devoted his energies, full time, organizing and refining the ideology of the *Arab Nationalist Movement*. Every one of us, in the movement, was supposed to be 'married to the cause', meaning that all our energies and resources were to be dedicated and devoted to the cause of the Liberation of Palestine and nothing else.

Although there were several female members in the movement, yet it was a taboo and forbidden for any one of us to ever express our male to female or female to male feelings to each other. I must admit that we all were in a state of denial. I for one was, reprimanded by my handler, in the movement, when someone reported me to the higher hierarchy in the movement that I was sitting on a bench, on campus, with a female student! We were, not allowed to love anything or a person, except the love of Palestine and its liberation.

HAVING COFFEE WITH MY SWEETHEART OF YESTERYEARS

SIX MONTHS AFTER MY LAST CONVERSATION WITH LAILA'S SISTER Najwa when I asked her as to how Laila is doing. She said Laila is back home in Beirut now. I said in passing, maybe she and I will cross paths and I will be able see her if she ever comes to the campus.

Few days later and while walking by West Hall, on campus, in my way to the Milk Bar I, saw a very young lady, sitting on a bench under the Banyan tree. A feeling of happiness and curiosity touched my heart and suggested to me that this young woman may be Laila. That feeling led me to reluctantly, approach her and ask her if she were Laila. She responded by the affirmative and asked if I were Abdallah? I said yes, I am Abdallah. Of course, both of us have changed physically and emotionally as we are now five years older and I now have become a young man with a Douglas moustache sprung under my nose.

We chatted for few minutes and then I asked her if she would like to join me for a cup of coffee at the Milk Bar few yards away. She agreed. We started to exchange notes and memories for the past five years. She gave me all the details about her studying in London, but she was not sure she was happy leaving London and coming back to Beirut. She then asked me to relate to her about my life for the past five years. I said, well where do I start? I am married to an uneducated woman and we have three children. I am struggling, emotionally and financially, worrying all the time as to how I can support a wife and the three kids and still be able to fulfil my university obligations. She was very upset and sad about my situation and asked as to why did I not tell her about all these things before? I did not know what she really meant by "tell her". I asked her as to what she meant and said, I did not even have any idea as to where you were other than that you are in London. I could see tears coming down from her beautiful brown eyes running down to her innocent cheeks. The scene of her tears broke my heart and I immediately said, what I just told you that I am married with three kids was nothing but a 'white' lie. I am still single and am waiting for you! This brightened the atmosphere and both of us were smiling with happiness that we have crossed paths again and were able to see each other after five years of separation.

Graduating from *AUB* was a mixed bag. As students, we were sheltered by the university, and the only thing on our minds was the hope of graduating and finding good jobs. I for one, deferred thinking about the future job until I graduate. Yet, after graduating, we lost that university shelter and are now on our own, ready to join the labor market. Anxiety set in and in my case as a Palestinian, I had no idea or clue about landing a job in Lebanon or anywhere else in the Middle East.

Prior to graduation, my classmates and I got together at a beer joint close to campus to figure out and share with each other as to what our plans would be after graduation. Everyone except for me, voiced his ambitious plans by saying, he plans to go to the United States to further his education and ultimately obtain the Ph.D. degree in his field of interest. I said good luck to all of you and wish you success in your endeavor. I am not going anywhere, I plan to get married and settle down in Beirut. It so happened that I was the only one from the whole group who came to the United States to further his education!

It was a great feeling to have graduated from *AUB* after many years of struggle. The feeling of elation was, marred by a deep-seated feeling of insecurity and anxiety.

Now I am on my own, and have unwillingly, shed the university protection, I asked myself as to what does the future hold for me. I kept thinking about it and asking myself, as to what am I going to do? Will I be able to find a job? If so, when and where? No plausible answer came to mind to, alleviate my anxiety.

I have joined the long lines of the unemployed in Lebanon. I have knocked all doors to find a job, but to no avail. There was, an advertisement by Lebanese company dealing with sales of agricultural products. The ad. specified the need of an agricultural engineer to fill the position of sales of their agricultural products in Lebanon and possibly in neighboring countries. After sending my resume to the company for consideration, I was, surprised to be asked to come for interview. At the interview, I was, asked about my qualifications, my nationality and of course my religion. At the end of the interview, the interviewer told me I am not the kind of employee the company is looking for!

(Graduating from *AUB* with a BS degree in Agriculture and with an Agricultural Engineering degree. I am flanked by, my two sisters: Fatima on my left and Amina on my right. Next to my sister, Fatima is my relative, Mr. Mahmoud al-Hajj. On his left is Mr. Mohammad Saleem al-Arna'out and his wife. Laila, my high school sweetheart, who became my future wife pictured first from left next to my sister Amina)

Laila and I dated, in secret of course, for a while then broke up. We dated on again off again for almost two years and then decided to be engaged. The engagement ceremonies took place on October 20, 1960, few months after graduation from college.

Tribal thinking still was the norm of the day in the Middle East. Several traditional protocols, requirements and formalities that must be adhered to prior to the consummation of marriage, were in existence at the time.

The girl's parents prefer their daughter to be married to a relative so that the properties of both spouses remain within the family. It is a common tradition to have first cousins marry each other. The tradition is, practiced by both Moslems and Christians alike in the Middle East. Should that not be possible where a first or distant cousin be available to marry the girl, then preference would be for somebody from her parents' hometown who they would know his background and family lineage.

Parents of the girl insist on finding out as much as information about the boy's past, his behavior and his standing in society, before they consider him as a potential son-in-law. They need to know his background, and family lineage. They need to know whether he is an addict who drinks alcohol, uses illicit drugs or if he is a gambler. Is he going to be a good husband to their daughter? Will he be a good protector of her and will he be a good provider for her? The girl's parents are preoccupied with these questions and are anxious to find answers with the hope that the answers are positive and satisfactory. Based on the information the parents of the girl get determines whether they will accept or reject the potential husband for their daughter.

Laila's father asked the people who he thought knew me as to what kind of a person I was. An acquaintance of Laila's father who he thought may be able to provide the information and full details about Abdallah. This person happened to have come originally from my hometown in Palestine. Laila's father asked him many questions, in an effort, to have as much information about Abdallah as possible before he can arrive at a plausible decision. The man told him that Abdallah comes from a very well to do family that holds a very high social standing in our town, and he is a property owner in Palestine. He is the most educated and is the first person from our town to ever graduate from the *American University of Beirut*. He has no family obligations other than himself, as both of his parents are, deceased and his two sisters are married and have their own families.

Laila's father wanted to find out if Abdallah uses drugs (*Hasheesh*), is he a gambler, an alcoholic or is he fit to be good husband for his daughter.

The man from my hometown was, complementary about Abdallah, told

Laila's father as far as he knew, Abdallah does not use drugs, drink alcohol or gamble. I believe, he will be a good husband to any woman he marries.

The man then asked Laila's father, as to why he was so interested in finding all these details and information about Abdallah by asking him so many personal questions about him?

Laila's father responded by saying, Abdallah is, interested in marrying my daughter, Laila, and is planning to formally ask for her hand. I need to find out as much information as I possibly can about him and about his past before I arrive at a decision. The man from my hometown was shocked and said, but 'it has been my understanding that Abdallah is, planning on marrying my sister'! Well, this ended the inquiries about Abdallah and his past as Laila's father got the message.

TRADITIONS, PROTOCOLS AND PROCEDURES TO BE FOLLOWED PRIOR TO CONSUMMATION OF MARRIAGE

1. Getting married according to Islamic tradition dictates, and as demanded by Laila's father that before the engagement, that women from the groom's family, must come to the future bride's home to meet the women of her family and to ask for her hand on behalf of the groom.

   After that, men from the groom's family must come to the bride's home to meet the men, of her family and officially ask for her hand.

2. After all these traditions and acceptance of the groom by the bride and her family are complied with, a date for the exchange of rings are set.

   Prior to the official engagement which must be sanctioned by the religious authorities and approval by the religious court and later by the government, the names of the bride and that of the groom are to be posted at the religious court bulletin boards.

   The announcement states the following: Mr. so and so (the groom) is intending to, marry Miss so and so (the bride). Should anyone wish to challenge this union, to please come forward within ten days of the date of this posting. The posting is directed at other men primarily relatives of the bride. Worried that one of Leila's relatives might challenge my request to marry her, I went to the religious court every day and sometimes more than once a day to see if any challenges had taken place. The fact that after ten days of posting no challenges were ever made gave me a sigh of relief the anxiety that engulfed me is over after the ten days of posting not, a single challenge was recorded.

   Should any of the relatives, object to having his female relative, marrying someone outside the family, he will then have the first right to marry her and the other non-family man's request will be abrogated! Marriage among relatives, is always the preferred union between husband and wife. The tradition of relatives marrying each other was, practiced by Moslems and Christians alike in Middle Eastern societies. Both Christians and Moslems apply this tradition where cousins, first or distant are encouraged, to marry and are given preference to marry each other, because:

1. They know all the details and background of the potential husband.

2. The properties, if any owned by the bride stays within the family

The official engagement is to be formalized by the religious court. On the set date the religious official, authorized by the religious court, comes to the bride's home with the groom present and with other witnesses to formalize the union between the two. Signatories to the document is the groom, the bride, the bride's father or guardian and the other witnesses in attendance. This document is then presented to the religious court to have its final approval. The formal document is, sent to the government authorities to issue the legal marriage certificate as the binding marriage certificate of the union between the groom and the bride.

The preliminary engagement is when the rings, are exchanged between the bride and the groom. Even after the preliminary engagement and the exchange of rings, take place, the bride's family does not allow her to go out with the groom without a chaperone.

The last and final official and legal engagement could be combined with the preliminary engagement, if desired, and consummated at the same time if both parties wish to do, otherwise they are performed separately. After the final and official engagement being approved by the religious court and by the government declaring groom and the bride as husband and wife. The bride can go out with her fiancé without a chaperone.

In the formal document drawn by the religious court, the financial obligations, referred to as the dowry are, clearly specified: The dowry consists of two components:

a.   Advance payment, by the groom, to the future wife, to purchase what she needs in the way of a wedding dress, jewelry and other items of interest. Should the financial capability of the groom be not up to the challenge, as it was in my case, a nominal or symbolic amount may be appropriate and acceptable.

b.   Deferred payment commitment, in local currency, by the groom to the wife as a guarantee she will receive in case of divorce. This indeed is a system of checks and balances. This is not only for the financial help of the divorced woman but also it is a means of discouraging divorce as much as possible, especially if the deferred payment is beyond the financial capability of the husband.

In our situation and after the official engagement was finalized, we were explicitly told that our marriage is a 'Catholic Marriage' meaning no divorce under any circumstances. Divorce between Catholic couples in the Middle East is nether condoned nor is ever sanctioned by the church.

When the 'Deferred' payment was, announced uncle Mohamad jumped and said the amount is too high. I responded by saying Laila is worth more than that. He then angrily asked is, she worth more than his daughter? I said yes Laila is!

Laila's father was still not yet convinced that I am the right person to marry his first daughter. He used delaying tactics after the first part of the engagement formalities have taken place, when I wanted to have the exchanging of rings ceremony. Since I was working at a farm that was fifty miles away and would be available only over the weekend. Every time I asked him, to have me come over and exchange the rings, he always had an excuse that he will be out of town during that weekend. I wanted that done as soon as possible. He was hoping, by his delaying tactics I may give up and refrain from consummation of the marriage obligations. Laila's mother, on the other hand, was more accommodating. She had always said, things will, work out to the best of both parties.

Looking back, at these Islamic traditions may sound complicated and tribal in nature, which may appear ridiculous in a way, have their great merits. Knowing the details about the groom's background as to his lineage, social standing and not having any of the unacceptable habits and social ills such as drinking of alcohol, using illicit drugs or gambling. Having any of these evils on the part of the groom raises a red flag that he may not be a good husband for the girl. Having the groom pass all the queries of these potentially harmful habits may lead to a good and solid relationship, not only between the newlyweds, but also between their respective families. Indeed, these traditions help reduce the incidence of a divorce later in life. These are the Islamic traditions that follow the dictates of the Qur'an.

Although Islam was the first and only religion to have introduced divorce as a means of dissolving the union between incompatible couples, in an amicable manner, it places many restrictions and obstacles to make it extremely difficult to have a divorce.

Woman's rights are well preserved and protected in such a way that should a divorce ever take place the woman will not suffer from the consequences of the divorce especially finances. Only men, then could ask for divorce, but now the rules have been relaxed to allow women to seek divorce. With the relaxation of the divorce terms, it is no longer the husband's weapon to use to threaten the wife. She can now use the same weapon to threaten him if she decides to break up the union.

It should be, mentioned that marriage and divorce, at the time, were only formalized and recognized by the religious courts, as there were no recognized provisions for civil marriage. Should there be children in the picture and the religious court determines the fault to be that of the woman custody of the children is granted to the father. Conversely, should the fault be determined to be the man's, then custody of the children is granted to the mother and the father will be responsible for alimony and child support. Is there any woman willing to lose custody of her children or is there a man with limited financial resources able to pay alimony and child support after divorce? Unlikely. This is where checks and balances play a major role in keeping married couples under the same roof. Both will strive to make the marriage work, at least for the sake of the children, if not for anything else. Unfortunately, things have changed with time and now the divorce rate is about 50% among married couples. It may be said; some people marry for the wrong reason and the union heads for a breakup within few years of marriage. Again, the ultimate victims of divorce are the children of those incompatible couples.

While open dating among Moslems was a taboo and socially unacceptable, yet it went on in secret, making sure however, that the girl's family does not know anything about it.

Christians, on the other hand, were free to date with no restrictions imposed on either party. Unlike western societies, where it is socially acceptable for boys and girls to live together and premarital sex may be tolerated as a given, it is an absolute taboo of the highest degree in the Middle Eastern culture. 'Boyfriends and girlfriends' are expected to live together only and only after they get married and never before. The girl must maintain her virginity until she gets married otherwise a scandal may erupt with the girl and her family stigmatized and become the talk of the town. Tragically, however, in some instances the girl may lose her life due to the so-called honor killing. This may sound discriminatory against girls as loss of virginity may result from means other than sexual interactions, but rather it could occur due to other causes that may lead to breakage of the hymen. Loss of virginity, among boys, cannot be proven yet it is tolerated as a given as we live in a male dominated society.

Contrary to the Islamic tradition in which the groom is supposed to pay all wedding expenses, the Christian tradition, in the Middle East and in the West, dictates that the girl was the one who pays all the expenses in the form of a 'dotta'. In case the woman and her family do not have the financial means to provide for the 'dotta', may lead her to end up as a not ever get married. To circumvent this tradition of financial inability, especially where the woman's family is incapable of providing the financial obligations to get their daughter married, the woman and her future husband may decide to elope.

In our situation, the advance payment that I, being the groom was supposed to pay for the wedding expenses were waived in favor of a very nominal one. It was 'five silver dirhams', and frankly I still do not, know its nature or its value is! However, the deferred payment, in case of divorce, is much more important than the advance payment. The deferred commitment of payment to the woman is intended to provide her with financial security should a divorce ever take place.

The Arab gulf region, including Saudi Arabia, has a high number of unmarried women because their parents demand large sums of money as advance payments from the future groom. It appears these parents are using their daughters as a sales commodity! I remember hearing King Fahd of Saudi Arabia addressing the issue, as it has become a social crisis in that country.

When I decided to come to the United States to further my education, Laila's father was very opposed to having his daughter accompany me to America. He was worried and afraid for the safety of his daughter as a war might break out between the United States and the Soviet Union during the Cuban Missiles crisis of 1962. His fears were well founded and justified. I was able to convince him that the perceived war is never going to happen. We were married on December 15, 1962 and planned on leaving for the United States soon thereafter. That was the time when the cold war was at its peak and the world was holding its breadth with the hope that no shooting war will ensue between the Soviet Union and the United States over the Cuban Missile crisis.

DISCRIMINATION BY THE SUNNI LEBANESE MOSLEMS AGAINST THEIR PALESTINIAN SUNNI 'BROTHERS IN ISLAM'

AFTER RECEIVING THE UNIVERSITY DEGREE IN AGRICULTURAL ENGI-neering from *AUB*, it was now time for me to look for a job in my field of 'expertise'. Palestinians were, denied the right to work for the government of Lebanon, join the army because the door was, shut tight with a very big and heavy lock. There was an opening with an American company in Beirut, *American Cyanamid*. The company's office in Beirut was the hub that served the whole Middle East. The company adver-tisement for the position of an agricultural engineer was, to be located, in Beirut. Because, as a Palestinian and being denied the opportunity to work for the govern-ment I thought it may be possible for me to be able to get the job with the American company. The manager of the company, Mr. Tabbara, a Lebanese Sunni Moslem and after reviewing my resume, requested me to come for interview.

The interview between Mr. Tabbara and myself lasted about two hours. He was explicit in questioning me about my credentials, my outlook to the future with the American company and, of course, about my nationality. At the end of the interview, Mr. Tabbara said, all looks good and your qualifications fit well with the requirements of the position at *American Cyanamid*. Please come in tomorrow to sign the contract. I was elated that I have a job with an American company. The company paid $250 a month with my office in Beirut where I will still stay and live, When I, went back the following day to sign the contract as promised, Mr. Tabbara said he was very sorry as the position was filled by another person who is more qualified than me! I found out later the position, was indeed offered to an Agricultural engineer who was a Christian Palestinian! Of course, I was devastated at the bad news and now I must seek another avenue to find a job.

I was very disappointed that I did not get the job, yet that did not surprise me at all, as I knew that Sunni Moslems in Lebanon, have a chummy and cozy alliance with the Maronite Christians who ruled the country. This un-written alliance dictated that among other things, all good paying jobs are, reserved in the following order: to Lebanese Christians, Lebanese Sunni Moslems, and Palestinian Christians, but not to Palestinian Moslems or Lebanese Shi'a! To understand this complex and discrim-inatory behavior against Palestinian and Shia Moslems, one to go back to 1943. In

December 1943 when Lebanon gained independence from France, the French left Lebanon with an un-written constitution that stipulated the President of the republic must be a Christian Maronite, the Prime Minister must be a Sunni Moslem and the Speaker of the House must be a Shi'a Moslem. The power was in the hands of the Christians and their surrogate, the Sunni Moslems. Menial types of jobs such as trash collection, street cleaning and other low-level jobs were, left to the Lebanese Shi'a! Since Palestinians were more educated than the Lebanese Shi'a, they would not accept these menial jobs even if offered to them!

It was clear that the reason I did not get the job with *American Cyanamid* is because of my national origin and my religious affiliation. Two strikes that determine the future of the individual, like me, in Lebanon!

I landed a job managing a small chicken farm, owned by a Palestinian, for a meager monthly salary of $100. The chicken farm was about fifty miles south of Beirut, which meant I had to spend the nights at the farm and had the weekends off to go to Beirut to spend time with my family and visit my fiancé. My job at the chicken farm was not what I dreamed of, as it did not provide any a means or hopes of establishing a family. I resigned my position three months later with no prospects for a new job. I was attempting to go to Kuwait which was considered and thought of, at the time, as the site of the gold rush in the Middle East.

IDENTITY WITH THE SHI'AS IN SOUTH LEBANON

I FELT IDENTITY WITH THE LEBANESE SHI'A MORE THAN I DID WITH their Sunni counterparts. The Lebanese Shi'a, who like me, were denied the basics of life required by a human being. Two differences separate us Palestinians from the Lebanese Shi'a:

1.   The Shi'a are citizens of Lebanon and us Palestinians are not

2.   In general, Palestinians are more educated than the Shi'as were

Lebanese Shi'a villages were completely cut off from mainstream and from any recognition of identity and help that should be, provided by the central government in Beirut. They were, completely abandoned as if they did not belong. There were no roads, no running water, no electricity or any other means of decent living in the Shi'a villages. There was one elementary school in the village of Tair Harfa where we lived after having been, forced out of Palestine. The pupils sat on the floor and the teacher whose profession was shoe repairs, sat on a chair in the back of the room and did his job repairing shoes while the class was in session. He had a long stick with which he would hit any of the pupils who was not reading the antiquated book provided to the school by the central government in Beirut. It was apathetic.

One of the most disturbing observations was, the lack of general knowledge the people in south Lebanon had. They were completely, shut off the rest of the world and did not even know what was going on except that the sun rises in the morning and sets in the evening. This observation of, ignorance among the population, was clearly apparent to me when I witnessed the reaction of the village people upon seeing a Palestinian riding his bicycle. They started to guess what that strange looking thing is. They came out with the conclusion that this may be a 'donkey without a soul'. That this new means of carriage is a lifeless donkey!

One other, incident that drew my attention again, was when some friends from South Lebanon visited my in-laws who lived in a suburb of Beirut, on a warm summer day. Upon seeing the electric fan swirling around and pushing air forward in all directions, one of the visitors asked as to what that gadget was. When my father-in-law told her it is, an electric fan used to push air around when it oscillates. One of the women was shocked and in amazement said, this is magic. Why there is no flame to coming out of it upon turning it on?

THE UNPLEASANT WORK EXPERIENCE IN KUWAIT

HAVING FAILED TO LAND A DECENT JOB IN BEIRUT, I HAD TO SEEK A job anywhere in the Middle East. I had to consider, perhaps going to Kuwait might be my ultimate dream. Kuwait was the dream that we all university graduates had. That dream was to go to Kuwait, as that country was the place to find a job and make some money. The problem was, Palestinians, unlike other Arabs were required to have a visa as a legal document to enter Kuwait. I secured a visa through a friend, but had no job offer from any company. Dr. Fouad Sarrouf, the provost of the *American University of Beirut*, gave me a letter of recommendation that he addressed to his former student, Mr. Tala'at al-Ghosain asking his help to secure a job for me. Mr. al-Ghosain held a very important position in the Kuwaiti government. It is worthwhile mentioning that Provost Sarrouf and Mr. al-Ghosain are both of Palestinian extraction.

Earlier and before enrolling a student at *AUB*, I became a member of the Arab Nationalist Movement. It became apparent to me, that it is not what you know, but rather it is Who You Know to land a job. Because of my acquaintance with one of the leaders of the Arab Nationalist Movement in Beirut, I was able to secure a letter of recommendation from one of the top leaders in the movement. This person had a close relationship with one of the leaders of the Arab Nationalist Movement in Kuwait. Provost, Dr. Fouad Sarrouf's letter to Mr. Al-Ghosain, did not bear any fruit, as the latter did not offer any help for me to find a job. As a reward for his services to the rulers of Kuwait, Mr. Al-Ghosain was, granted the Kuwaiti citizenship and later was elevated to become the Kuwaiti Ambassador to the United States.

One observation that caught my attention in Kuwait was Palestinians, in general, do not help each other like, other ethnic and minority groups do. Most of the Palestinians working in Kuwait came from the West Bank of the Jordan River that was under Jordanian sovereignty at that time. They did not share identity with us of the 1948 group of Palestinian refugees who moved to Syria and to Lebanon. I knocked every door of those Palestinians who held high positions with the hope of helping me find a job, but none of them offered any help.

After several meetings with one of the Kuwaiti members of the Arab Nationalist Movement who was part owner of a dairy farm, I landed the job as General Manager of the *Kuwait Dairy Company*. The company owned a farm that included three hundred and fifty dairy cows, a pasteurization plant, three hundred acres of arable land and 75 employees all of whom were Palestinians from the West Bank.

The Kuwaitis are very shrewd and greedy businesspeople. They make their fortunes by employing expatriates, at very low salaries and providing them with subhuman living conditions. As the manager of the *Kuwait Dairy Company* I was, provided with a furnished, air-conditioned studio apartment, at the farm and with a car. The other employees, 10-12 of them lived in little rooms that had no air conditioning and no bathrooms. I pleaded with the owners of the company to at least, install air conditioning units in the workers rooms as the temperatures in the rooms touched 140 degrees, but to no avail. This was a case of inhumane treatment of fellow Arab 'brothers', whose living conditions were no different than those at the barn where the cows were kept.

When I took over management of the dairy company, I set out my priorities in an effort, to improve the situation at the farm. The first one was, to eradicate the swarms of flies that infested the barn. It was hardly possible to see the way around, in the barn, because of the heavy fly infestation. I ordered pesticides from the Swiss company, Ciba Geigy and after a week of treatment, all the flies were gone!

The second priority was to cultivate the land and plant alfalfa to feed the cows. Prior to that locally produced alfalfa at the farm, alfalfa was, brought in from Iraq at a hefty price, as there was no other source of alfalfa in Kuwait.

The third priority was to plant 'Ethyl' trees all around the farm to act as windbreakers to shield the cows and people from the flying sand when sandstorms occurred.

All three priorities were, successfully met. Things started to look good at the farm.

The fourth priority was to improve the economic condition of the company and to stop the flow of red ink. Within six months of my tenure, as general manager of the company, not only milk production has increased, and the fly infestation reduced to a minimum, the company made a small profit after years of losses.

On a hot summer day, the guard came to my office and told me a man at the gate who does not speak Arabic wants to see you. I went out to the gate and met the man, who introduced himself as Mr. Vernon Cassin. He said he was the representative of an American corporation known as the *Earl Bunting Company*. I welcomed him in and we both had a pleasant meeting. At our meeting, he had several questions about the operations, marketing and income of the farm. He wanted to go into the barn to see the cows and to see the pasteurization plant. He wanted to have an idea as how the operation goes. I had no objection to, his request getting into the barn and to, see the Pasteurization plant. Before he left, he invited me to have lunch with him a couple of days later. I accepted his invitation and while we were having lunch, he had more questions about the company as to who the owners were, what they do, what the budget of the company is in general, about the farm and how much money there is in the company's bank account. Having asked such questions, I became suspicious as to what his motives were. When I, later reported the incident to, Mr. al-Homaizi, my Kuwait boss and aired my suspicions as to this American's intentions, the boss said, do not worry about it!

During lunch I said, well now Mr. Cassin, since I have answered all your questions, I do have only one question for you: What does your company, the *Earl Bunting Company* do? Mr. Cassin responded by saying, his company manufactures dried foods that are intended for sale in the domestic as well as in the international markets. We have an office, in Beirut and I encourage you to come visit our office to show you samples of our products. I said, I will be happy, to visit your office in Beirut. When I visited him at his office, in October 1962, he had another invitation waiting for me to have my fiancé and I join him and his wife for Thanksgiving dinner at their apartment. We accepted the invitation and had a wonderful time with the Cassin family.

Both Laila, my fiancé, and Mrs. Cassin met and chatted throughout the evening. During our dinner, I told Mr. Cassin that I was, accepted to the University of California at Berkeley and we shall be leaving for the United States in a couple of months after we get married. He was very surprised yet was encouraging and congratulated me for my acceptance to one of the top universities in the United States. That was the last time Mr. Cassin and I had any communications with each other.

Now as a married couple, we left Lebanon in February 1963, for the United

States. To my own astonishment, about thirty years later, Mr. Vernon Cassin's name popped up in the news. His name was all over national and international news that he was, identified as the chief CIA Operative, covering the Middle Eastern area throughout the 1960s! His tenure with the CIA was, at the same time t he and I had met in Kuwait in June of 1962. After Mr. Cassin's exposure as being the chief CIA operative in the Middle East, I now realized that the *Earl Bunting Company* that Mr. Cassin was representing in the Middle East was nothing but a front for the CIA.

Looking back at my tenure in Kuwait and the visit by Mr. Vernon Cassin to the *Kuwait Dairy Company* I was managing, left me with the suspicion of Mr. Cassin's intentions. It may have been entirely possible that Mr. Cassin was interested in recruiting me to become an agent of the CIA. This suspicion became apparent to me when I recounted our meetings in Kuwait and in Beirut. Why did he invite me to lunch while I was in Kuwait and then invite me to visit his office in Beirut and later invite my fiancé and me to have Thanksgiving dinner at their apartment in Beirut? Am I that important of a person to get his attention? I suspect Mr. Cassin was trying to learn more about me and to dig deeper into my psychology and social behavior to see if I fit the profile of an agent of the CIA! Should this have been his intention, the plan Mr. Cassin had for me, thankfully did not bear any fruit.

Of course, the objective of Mr. Cassin's visit to the farm was to collect as much information as possible about the economic, financial and organizational capability of the *Kuwait Dairy Company*. This amounts to nothing less than economic espionage as being one of the job descriptions of the agents of the CIA. What kind of a world and an unpredictable one we live in!

On another summer day while managing *the Kuwait Dairy Company*, the guard came to me to tell me that a visitor who does not speak Arabic wanted to see you. I told the guard to let the visitor in and bring him to my office. The visitor introduced himself as Mr. Gazda, as the representative of a company from Lichtenstein. He said, he had met with Mr. Yacoub al-Homaizi, before and got his permission to come and visit the farm. He wanted me to show him around the farm and insisted on going into the barn to see the cows. Of course, I had neither, an idea as to who this person is nor what his objective of visiting the farm was. A week later, Mr. Gazda came in with Mr. Yacoub al-Homaizi, who was one of the owners of the company and who, also was my immediate boss. The three of us, Mr. al-Homaizi, Mr. Gazda and myself went into the barn. Mr. Gazda while ignoring me completely told Mr. al-Homaizi that he wanted to take a picture of each cow. He will then send the pictures to his office in Lichtenstein for evaluation and for recommendations as to what each cow needs in the way of feed! I voiced my objection to Mr. al-Homaizi about Mr. Gazda's suggestion, by saying it is absurd to have photos of each of the 350 cows to send to Lichtenstein for evaluation and recommendation of individual feeding regimen. Mr. al-Homaizi did not consider my objection and brushed it off as a non-starter. He went along with Mr. Gazda's request and I had no choice but to follow the instructions of my boss. The following day the three hundred and fifty cows were paraded one at a time, outside the barn and the 'expert', Mr. Gazda, took pictures of each, and every one of the cows.

A month later, another 'expert' from Lichtenstein, Professor Dr. Korinek, came in. This time, the expert came in to consult on the agricultural aspect of the company and to advise as to how to grow alfalfa and other vegetables.

Contrary to the United States, the title of professor is, highly revered and the position is highly respected in Europe and in the Middle East. Because of this distinction, I introduce myself as Dr. Isa, in the United States, because the title doctor implies a high social status as it is perceived that doctors make lots of money, and as Professor Isa everywhere else. Now after the arrival of Dr. Professor Dr. Korinek to the farm, he checked the alfalfa field and the 'ethyl' trees, that I had planted around the farm. He was astonished to see how good these things at the farm are and nodded with approval. He said with a grin, you have done a good job Mr. Abdallah!

Professor Dr, Korinek, as assumed, must be up to date on the latest technological advances in his field of Agriculture. He came in with the latest Lichtenstein technologically advanced piece of equipment, the sickle what else? This was, not only demeaning, but was an insult to my intelligence as I thought he might have brought in a technologically advanced modern piece of equipment. He tried to show me how to harvest the alfalfa with his magical instrument, the sickle of course! That was the 'latest technology' of harvesting alfalfa 'invented' by the Lichtenstein scientists and recommended for use by the Kuwaitis. The sickle used for harvesting alfalfa was the latest technological advances of the twentieth century according to the Lichtenstein scientists and introduced to Kuwait by Dr. Professor Korinek! What a great consultation and advice that was!

Mr. Gazda was a very shrewd and convincing man. To impress the Kuwaitis, he wore the Arab robe and head gear to look like he was one of them. To my amazement, as I always thought the Kuwaitis are very shrewd businesspeople, Mr. Gazda outsmarted the Kuwaitis by convincing them that they should pay his Lichtenstein Company 22,000.00 Kuwaiti Dinars (US75000), as a down payment for their consultative services. The same amount was to be paid monthly, to the Lichtenstein consultants, for the life of the three-year contract. The 3-year contract was renewable for at least two additional terms. Of course, as the general manager of the company, I neither was, consulted nor was I told anything about this arrangement with the

Lichtenstein Company! Even if I were consulted, any input I may have will be trashed as a nonstarter. This is the way in which the Kuwaitis treat their fellow Arab employees.

People in the Middle East, in general, and wrongly so, believe that products imported from the West are of a much better quality and are superior to those produced locally even though the local products may be of a better quality! There goes the saying "everything western is superior".

The West, through many decades and centuries of occupation and coloniza-tion of the Middle East, has succeeded in brainwashing and skewing the mentality of the people, especially the Arabs, that everything western is better than anything Middle Eastern. This kind of brain washing led to a screwed-up way of thinking by the Middle Eastern people. This was not limited to consumables and other products but also was, carried over to include human beings too. Westerners are the 'experts' and are the leaders in everything they do. They have better judgment than those of the Middle Eastern people! This skewed mentality was, confirmed to me beyond any doubt during my employment with the Kuwaitis and the experience I had with the experts from Lichtenstein.

All I had improved the conditions at the farm after taking over its management, by improving productivity and efficiency as well as stopping the flow of red ink and moving it into profitability, I was never recognized by the Kuwaiti employers despite all such achievements. I never was, appreciated nor was I ever rewarded. The improve-ments, I introduced were never acknowledged nor was I, ever been thanked for the good things I have done at that company. The farm was losing money every year since its inception. It made a profit within one year after I took over management. This small profit was the first in its ten-year history. The reason my achievements were not recognized by the Kuwaiti owners was because I happen to be one of them and not a westerner, meaning I am a Middle Eastern Arab and according to their way of thinking, I am assumed to be mentally inferior to the western 'experts' like those from Lichtenstein!

The owners of the *Kuwait Dairy Company* imported the 350 cows from Denmark. They ordered 350 cows and only one bull to, service these cows! The cows and the bull were air lifted from Denmark to Kuwait! I pleaded with my immediate boss Mr. Yacoub al-Homaizi, to authorize the importation of at least three more bulls. He thought he knew better than I did, and his answer was always, we do not need more than one bull as the one bull we have is, enough to service the 350 cows! I thought for a moment whether I should ask him if he could service 350 women, but I refrained from asking him as it may be offensive for him. As a result, of his refusal to order the purchase of more bulls and the inability of the bull to mount the cows, I had to resort to artificial insemination of the 350 cows!

The 'expert' company from Lichtenstein pocketed close to three million dollars from the Kuwaitis for doing nothing over and above what I had done at the farm. This is what I call, the "stupid and ignorance-based extortion", resulting from the blind trust of the so-called 'Experts' from Lichtenstein by the Kuwaitis!

The Kuwaitis portray themselves as a superior stock when it comes to ex-patriates. They look down at the foreign workers who happen to be of brown or dark skin, Arab or non-Arab. They, like other Arabs, look up to the blue-eyed and blond-haired Johnny. They expect and demand the ex-patriate people of color workers to be subservient to them. This was clear to me when one of the other owners of the *Kuwait Dairy Company,* was planning a trip to Lebanon. He kept telling me about his trip and repeatedly specifying the day and time of the flight from Kuwait to Beirut. He never told me outright, but his intentions were, very clear to me. He wanted to feel important by, having me come to the airport and bid him a good trip wish. I brushed all his insinuations aside and never fulfilled his wish!

My fiancé was working at the *Kuwait Oil Company* hospital in Ahmadi, a town that was 30 miles from where my job was. I did go to see her about three times a week. On other evenings, I would meet my friends in a café to have coffee and smoke *Hukka.* Of course, the Kuwaitis expected to have me at the farm 24/7, with no time off! That amounted to nothing less than slavery they would not dare demand it from a westerner.

Social life in Kuwait was non-existent outside the home other than the coffee houses, where men and sometimes families, would assemble and spend the evenings together. Some of the coffee houses had restaurants where people could have a meal in addition to spending time socializing.

The city of Ahmadi where the *Kuwait Oil Company* is head quartered has two clubs: One club, the al-*Hubara Club,* was for the senior staff employees only, nobody except the senior employees and their guests is, allowed into the premises. The other club was for the junior staff employees. Both clubs had swimming pools and other amenities. As there were no clubs or other recreational centers in Kuwait City, where I was the only place to socialize with friends was in the coffee houses.

The Kuwait Oil Company's senior staff employees had access to al-*Hubara Club* which in addition to having a swimming pool, had a concession stand. Every Thursday evening, a game of Tombola (bingo) was, played for about two hours then followed by dancing and swimming. To get into al-*Hubara* club, employees had to show their ID cards indicating that they are senior staff employees of the *Kuwait Oil Company.* Guests were, allowed in only when they accompany their senior staff hosts.

Since my fiancé was working in the medical department of the *Kuwait Oil Company* hospital and was a member of the senior staff she was, allowed to have guests accompany her to the club facilities and take part in any of the club's activities. I was, always allowed into the club as her guest.

Life in Kuwait, for me, was boring. Living at the farm with no recreational facilities or people to socialize with left a void that was, filled only by me driving ten miles every evening to meet friends at the coffee houses or to drive twenty plus miles to see my fiancé.

Even driving, from the farm to the city, to meet friends had nothing to enjoy looking at. No trees, no shrubs or any greeneries could be seen other than the desert swats covering the area from all directions.

Occasionally however, some animals and reptiles appear roaming the area.

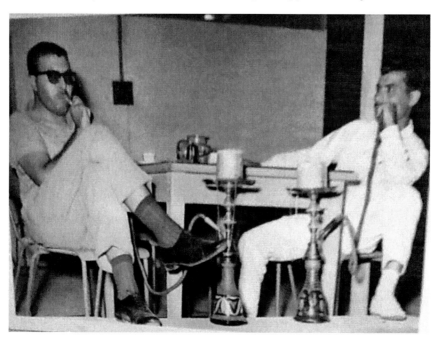

**(Socializing with one of my friends and former classmate at *AUB*
in the café' in Kuwait)**

I spent a total of twenty months in Kuwait and never liked the climate nor the working conditions. It is very hot and very humid in the summer months. The summers and falls of the year, had sandstorms that blanketed the whole area. The sandstorms could last for weeks at a time. These sand storms coupled with high humidity, almost 100% and the high temperatures of 120-130 degrees in shade, caused lots of health issues to people and animals. They cause lots of damage to property especially to automobile windshields. Because of the thickness of these sandstorms, it becomes extremely difficult to see, beyond five feet and navigation while driving becomes extremely difficult and dangerous.

Several people have died because of the high humidity and high temperature combo due to the loss of electrolytes and to heat strokes. For protection, however, people were encouraged to carry salt tablets for use when working outdoors.

More importantly however, the Kuwaitis were very snobbish and never treated us, ex-patriates as equals, but rather they looked at us as if we are their servants and slaves. I was not that desperate, but too proud to accept this kind of humiliation from anybody, especially from my fellow Arab `brothers`.

I hated working in Kuwait and felt there was no possibility for me to be able to establish and support a family based on the income I was earning in Kuwait. As ex-patriates, there was no guarantee for continuity for a long time on any job in the country. Working in Kuwait was temporary with no sense of continuity or permanence. Expatriates are prone to be terminated and expelled from the country at a moment's notice depending on the mood of the employer who always holds the upper hand. There are no job guarantees, no pension plans or after service compensation offered to us expatriates. I was searching and trying to find a way out of this dead end and decided to further my education. I wanted to come to the United States for higher education. I applied to graduate schools of several universities including *Yale University, Pennsylvania State university, Ohio State University* and the *University of California at Berkeley*.

The first response I received came from *Ohio State University* telling me that my application was, rejected because of my 'poor grades'! Of course, I was, devastated by the rejection news from Ohio State. The second response came from the *Pennsylvania State University* saying they did not offer a graduate degree in the field of study I wanted to pursue. Then I got two letters of acceptance to graduate school: one from *Yale University* and the other one from the *University of California at Berkeley!*

Ohio State University does not compare to and does not have the academic standing and prestige of either *Yale University* or of the *University of California at Berkeley*. Both, of these universities are, more prestigious and of a higher caliber *than Ohio State University* and one, *Yale University* is an Ivy League university and *Ohio State* is not! There was no room for me to lament the rejection by *Ohio State University* as I was, accepted by two of the topnotch American Universities

Of course, I had no idea at the time, as to which university I should choose to enroll in, as I did not know anything about the climate and living conditions either in California or in Connecticut.

An American employee of the oil company, Mr. Richards, a Texan who worked at the *Kuwait Oil company* where my fiancé was working in the medical department at the time, recommended *University of California at Berkeley*. The climate in California, he said, is very similar to that of Lebanon. *Yale* is in the State of Connecticut in the East coast of the United States where the winters are rough as it snows a lot and the climate is very cold!

Based on Mr. Richard's suggestion, I discarded the acceptance letter from *Yale University* and chose to go to *the University of California at Berkeley*. Now that I, am armed with two acceptances to graduate school in the United States, I felt I have the upper hand in deciding my future. Now, I can speak and act with confidence especially when talking to my Kuwaiti bosses. Acceptance to enroll at *Yale University* and the *University of California at Berkeley* gave me a very big psychological boost that did help me get out of the misery of living and working in Kuwait. It also helped me stand up to my Kuwaiti bosses and talk to them as an equal and not as a subservient.

Few days later, I was talking to my immediate boss at the *Kuwait Dairy Company*, Mr. Yacoub al-Homaizi, about things in general at the company. Suddenly he said, "You Palestinians, Syrians and Lebanese come here to Kuwait to take our money". To me, this was not only demeaning, but was very insulting. It was the straw that broke the camel's back. I said, "No sir, we come here to your Kuwait to help you out and improve your way of life. We Palestinians, Syrians and Lebanese built your countries, in the Gulf region, and moved you from living in tents in the desert and driving camels, into big concrete buildings and palaces and now you drive motor vehicles. We organized your governments, your police and your armed forces. Of course, we received minimal wages for our services, but were never appreciated by, your government. The few dinars you gave me for my hard work at your *Kuwait Dairy Company* are not worth the effort I put in to move your company from a losing streak into a profitable one. I beg you sir, please do not forget that we come here to enjoy your Kuwaiti summers with temperatures of 125-130 degrees F in shade and almost 100 percent humidity. Of course, I wish to also remind you sir to, please do not ever forget your 'wonderful' sandstorms too. Please keep your money and I am resigning my position as of this moment. As I saw a surprised look on his face, he said, "No! No! Abdallah this is not what I meant, and I do not want you to resign". I said, sorry Yacoub, calling him by his first name rather than using the word uncle or sir, whether you meant it or not, my resignation is, final and I will be leaving your lovely Kuwait in a week's time".

The snobbish attitude of Kuwaitis, I observed, was unbearable. They looked down on expatriate employees and treated them as servants and not employees with dignity. Mr. al-Homaizi was supposed to be one of the leaders of the Arab nationalist movement in Kuwait who strongly believed in Arab unity and paramount in that ideology is, the liberation of Palestine and of helping their Palestinian brothers! These are the fake slogans and attitudes with which the Gulf people, in general and some Kuwaitis in particular, try to impress other Arabs. It is far from being true as far as the way the Kuwaitis and other Arabs look at and treat their Palestinian brothers.

It is well documented that the Palestinians are the ones who helped these Arab countries, especially the Kuwaitis and other Gulf Arabs build a modern society. The Palestinians built and organized many of their governments and brought them into the twentieth century. They provided the Palestinian cause and the Palestinian people nothing more than lip service. More rhetoric and less substance, no rewards and no appreciation or recognition for what the Palestinians have done to these Gulf Arab countries!

Arab countries, except Syria and Iraq, looked at Palestinians as if they are alien people and are a threat to their survival. They did everything, within their power, to thwart Palestinian social and economic development. Lebanon, the country I love as I was, raised in Beirut, does not treat Palestinians as equal to the Lebanese. There are over fifty careers and professions, on the books, enforced by the government of Lebanon are off limits to Palestinians! The only means for survival for a Palestinians in Lebanon was to find a job in the Gulf region and send money back to Lebanon to support their families, or to start a business in Lebanon. The latter was sometimes, not possible, as seed money for the business may not be available. The other requirement by the government of Lebanon, as is the case with most of the other Arab countries, for a Palestinian to start a business in the country, he or she must have a Lebanese sponsor or a partner who must be part of the business! The business must, be registered as a legal entity under the name of the Lebanese sponsor or partner, but not under the Palestinian's name!

Several businesses that were established by Palestinians in Lebanon, were either destroyed or marginalized by the Lebanese government. Case in point was *Intra Bank*. *Intra Bank* was, established by Mr. Yusef Baidas, a Palestinian who was forced to come to Lebanon after the Palestinian catastrophe of 1948. The bank had thrived and expanded its activities beyond Lebanon. *Intra Bank* established branches all over the Middle East, Europe and in the city of New York. It has been said that the success of *Intra Bank* did not sit well with the Foreign Minister of Lebanon who had problems with the founder of the bank, Mr. Beidas. Allegations and false accusations about the bank and its founder resulted in declaring bankruptcy in 1966, by *Intra Bank*. Sadly, I lost money in the bankruptcy of *Intra bank*. Mr. Baidas was, forced to flee the country and re-settle in Brazil! Is not this the best way to treat your Palestinian Arab brother?

Again, mistreatment and mistrust of Palestinians was almost a daily occurrence. There was an incident, in my neighborhood in Beirut in which a thief tried to rob a house. While to trying to run away he was, spotted by the owners of the house. In the process of running away, the thief lost one of his shoes. One of the neighbors said, this thief is Palestinian. I asked him, as to how could he tell the thief is Palestinian? He replied by saying from his shoe. Can you not tell!

PLANS TO FURTHER MY EDUCATION IN THE UNITED STATES

WHILE WORKING IN KUWAIT, I PURCHASED A SPORTS CAR, AUSTIN Healy Sprite, as a gift for my fiancé for her birthday. After resigning my position with the *Kuwait Dairy Company*, I booked the car on an airline freighter for transport from Kuwait to Beirut. I left Kuwait the middle of October 1962. The car was, delivered at the Beirut International Airport a week later.

While I am now in Beirut and my fiancé was still in Kuwait, I was very busy trying to finalize the arrangements for our wedding the following December after which we were to leave for the United States. We planned our wedding to take place on Saturday December 15, 1962. We had all the invitations sent out about a week before the set wedding date. Marriage documents must first be, authorized and subsequently legalized, by the government, indicating the legitimate union between husband and wife prior to the wedding ceremonies. In order, for the documents to be formalized and legalized, they should be approved and signed by a Lebanese Moslem religious judge who is authorized to do so by the government. The documents are then, sent to the chief of the Lebanese Islamic High court, *Qadhi,* for the required signatures to take effect. We requested the High Islamic Court to allow a Moslem Palestinian *Qadhi* (judge), the one we chose to prepare the marriage documents.

Prior to the approval of our request by the High Islamic Court it must be approved first, by the Lebanese Central Committee overseeing Palestinian refugees in Lebanon. Upon receipt of the approval from the Central Committee, the Lebanese *Qadhi* then signs the documents presented to him by the Palestinian *Qadhi* (Religious judge authorized by the higher Islamic court to perform the marriage proceedings).

That was an ordeal to say the least. When I went to the Lebanese Islamic Court Office, to fetch the authorization, two guards in civilian clothes were standing at the door of the chief's office. They asked me as to why did I come there for and what did I want. I replied by saying, I need the written authorization, from his Excellency the Lebanese *Qadhi* permitting the Palestinian cleric we chose to formalize our marriage documents. One of the two men told me to come back in a couple of weeks. I said it is impossible, as we already have set the wedding date next Saturday, a week from today. He then opened with a big smile on his face and said, the boss smokes Kent cigarettes. I asked him as to who the boss is. He said, it is the head of the Central Committee smokes Kent cigarettes. Then I asked him, as to what brand of cigarettes does he himself smoke? He replied by saying Kent cigarettes too. I said no problem, I will get a carton of Kent cigarettes for you and I will get another carton, of Kent cigarettes for the boss. He said, great! Go get the cigarettes and the authorization paper will be waiting for you. I said, I am talking to you as man-to-man and you must trust me, as I am a man of my word. Please give me that authorization paper and I will go and get the cigarettes right away. He went to see the boss and came back with the authorization paper ten minutes later. After having the authorization in my hand, I started yelling and screaming at the guards, saying you want bribes to do your jobs, shame on you! Luckily, the Minister of the Interior at the time, Mr. Kamal Junblatt was in his office next door. After hearing the yelling and loud noise, he came out of his office to find out what was the yelling all about. I said, Your Excellency, please tell me if it is a crime to get married? He said, of course not! Then I told him the story that these people wanted a bribe of Kent cigarettes, one carton for this guard and another carton for his boss, for them to hand me the authorization paper to get married.

This was the requirement, to get permission to get married imposed by the Lebanese government on Palestinians! Mr. Kamal Junblatt was, one of the rare breeds of politicians in Lebanon. He was one of the most respected Lebanese, politician of the twentieth century. Well, Mr. Junblatt was very angry and ordered the two employees either fired or transferred to other areas of government.

Middle of November 1962, Laila left Kuwait and came to Beirut. Lebanon had new street traffic lights installed in the cities. Three new laws, which I was, not aware of were passed: one that introduced traffic lights, another law which was passed against honking the horns of cars in the evenings especially in the center of the city and a third law, that the number of passengers in the car should not exceed the number specified by the car manufacturer. Laila and I wanted to go to downtown Beirut to enjoy the evening in the downtown area. The downtown area is always lively and bustling with people. Two of her sisters wanted to join us. The car was, registered as a two-seater, meaning it should, by law, have only the driver and one passenger and no other passengers riding in the car. While driving in central Beirut in a beautiful evening and without knowing the new laws, I crossed the red light first and honked my horn. The officer directing traffic was standing on the sidewalk looking for offenders. He spotted me as I broke the three traffic laws. He ordered me to stop said, "I am going to give you three big fat traffic citations. I, asked why is that? He said, "because you have broken three traffic laws: one for crossing the red light, one for honking your horn and the third for having two extra passengers in a two-seater car"!

As he was preparing to write the citations, I pleaded with the officer to have mercy on me! I asked him if he were married or engaged, he answered by saying no to both of my question. Then I said well, this is my situation: I am engaged to this young woman. Her parents would not allow her to be with me alone without having a watchful eye.

The watching eye, in this case, is her two sisters who are riding with us in the car. Not only she and I could not, disobey her parents' orders, but because I wanted very badly to be with my fiancé, the woman I love, to enjoy the beautiful evening together.

He looked at me, with a sad smile and said:" Go, May God help you". He never wrote the citations. This cop, indeed, had a soft heart! The action of this cop exemplifies the general attitude of the people in Beirut, which I call 'the city of love'!

Well, we consummated the wedding plans and became husband and wife on December 15, 1962. It is customary that wedding invitations be sent to invitees, a month prior to the wedding ceremony with an RSVP request.

Some invitations were, sent to relatives and friends who lived in other places outside Lebanon. Of course, they were not expected to, attend our wedding, but that was the gesture intended to circumvent their potential negative criticism should we have not invited them.

Other invitations went out for relatives and friends in Beirut and in other parts of Lebanon. As expected, none of the invitees who lived outside of Lebanon ever sent an RSVP notice indicating their inability to join us in the wedding festivities but sent their good wishes. Some who lived in distant parts in Lebanon did sent their RSVPs saying they will not be, able to attend, but wished us a happy wedding and prosperous life thereafter.

One invitee who never sent an RSVP or came to the wedding attracted my attention. This was my cousin, Darwish, who lived in Beirut. I had hand- delivered the invitation to him to attend our wedding ceremonies a month prior to the date of the wedding.

(Our wedding picture was taken on December 20, 1962, five days after our wedding)

Cousin Darwish never sent an RSVP or came to the wedding. When I asked him, later, as to why he did not show up at the wedding ceremonies, he said, 'because you failed to come to pick me up'. It was not hard to imagine how screwed-up this man's way of thinking is. According to him, I should have driven across the city of Beirut, on my wedding night to pick him up so that he honors me by attending my wedding ceremonies! How absurd and ignorant this person is. Well, when he got married a couple of years earlier, he did not even extend an invitation for me to attend.

Cousin Darwish never graduated from high school. I had helped him out by calling on my friend and colleague in the Arab Nationalist Movement, Mr. Ahmad (Abu Maher) al-Yamani who was the principal of a Saudi-sponsored and supported school for Palestinian students in a suburb of Beirut. I asked his help in giving me a letter, on the school stationary, stating that cousin Darwish had successfully completed the course work for the high school diploma. I, again hand-delivered the letter to Darwish. With that letter, he was able to find a job in a local school, but of course, there was never a thank you nor a show of gratitude for my help from cousin Darwish.

Darwish had never thanked me or showed any appreciation for my efforts to help him out. He never was grateful or thankful for my going out of my way to help him find a job. This cousin must have been either jealous of me or he may have a mental problem that was expressed in his behavior. It may have been due to deep-seated hatred and jealousy that he harbored towards me. Unfortunately, I found out later, that he was an alcoholic and many a time his behavior was, messed up and he did not know what he was saying or what he was doing. His addiction to alcohol may have had an impact on his ability to make decisions or to respond in a responsible manner.

In the summer of 1971 when my family and I visited Lebanon. Darwish's older brother, Adel asked me to help Darwish come to the United States. I said it, is next to impossible to sponsor him, as the United States is a country of laws. The law stipulates that as an American citizen I can sponsor my parents, siblings and children only. Since Darwish does not belong to any of these categories, I cannot sponsor him. Further, I am not a citizen yet and will be one in a few years. However, I could help your half-brother Adnan who is educated and Darwish is not, to come and work with me in my laboratory. Adel responded in a very crude way and said, Adnan does not need your help as he can go to the United States on his own! I said, well I hope he could.

Well, cousin Darwish was able to come to visit the United States, through an invitation by a Palestinian American, he had met in Beirut, and who had secured a visitor's visa for him. This person was an employee of the Iraqi embassy in Washington DC. He helped Darwish find a job as a night guard at the embassy.

Having not known the rules and regulations of the United States that prohibit people holding visitor's visas from being offered a job in the country, Darwish was offered the job as a night guard at the Iraqi embassy.

Few months passed after he got the job at the embassy, a massive fire engulfed the building and destroyed everything. Upon investigation of the cause of the fire, the investigators found out that Darwish was an illegal alien and ordered him deported back to Lebanon.

It is not very difficult to speculate as to what had caused the fire at the embassy. Whether it was due to his drinking problem that lead to the fire or to anything else that ultimately led to his deportation from the United States is unclear to me. Few months after his deportation, Darwish passed on. Whether the cause of death was due to the grief caused by the deportation or alcoholism is an unknown. It could possibly be either the grief which is complicated by alcoholism or a combination of both that led to his death at a young age.

While in Beirut, cousin Adnan invited my family and me for lunch at his condominium. At the time, his mother-in-law who happens to be his maternal aunt was, also visiting with them. When he introduced me to her as my cousin, Dr. Abdallah, is visiting from the United States, she immediately broke into crying. To try to understand the reasons behind her crying one must understand the background. Her husband and her son are both doctors and while we were in Palestine, this same woman when she visited her sister, uncle Mohamad's wife, took my sister Fatima to do servant work for them in the city where they lived. This was the same woman, who denied me the pleasure of accompanying my sister and her in riding the bus to the city when I was a child. Now this orphan boy is a doctor, just like her husband and son, did not sit well with her. This orphan boy, whose sister was our servant, should not have the same status and title as those of her husband and her son! This behavior is, a reflection of the tribal way of thinking of those illiterate and poorly educated people.

EXPERIENCED CORRUPTION FIRSTHAND BEFORE LEAVING LEBANON TO THE UNITED STATES

TO BE ABLE TO LEAVE LEBANON, MY WIFE AND I NEEDED TO HAVE security clearances by the police department of the Beirut precinct. They found out that Laila had sixty-four unpaid parking violations. Traffic citations must be paid off prior to issuing the security clearance. Wow! What do I do now? I had a friend, who was a big shot in the police department. I called him, gave him all the details and pleaded with him for help. The following morning, he called me back and said, all is clear and all the traffic violations, your wife has, have been cancelled. Now you can legally leave the country. Whoever says that corruption is bad?

We planned our honeymoon to coincide with the trip to the United States. I had booked our trip on the honeymooners, cruise that was supposed to leave Beirut and doc for few days in several African and Spanish ports with its destination to Naples, Italy where we will board another cruise ship to New York City.

The cruise plans did not work out as intended because of the Lebanese government regulations and intimidation of Palestinians. In order, for my wife to accompany me and leave the country and according to the Lebanese government, her name must appear, as my legal wife, on my travel document! By the time her name was, added which was two weeks later, the Honeymooners cruise boat we booked our trip on has already left the Beirut docs!

Having missed the boat, so to speak, we flew into Rome on an Air France flight. The flight was quite scary as the Mystere jetliner jumped up and down upon hitting air pockets. We felt the plane was about to crash as it sank tens of feet at a time and then jumped up again. We stayed for two weeks at a pension (motel) in Rome and made sure to go site seeing to see all the historical places in the city. I told my wife we should go to see the famous fountain, the title of an American Movie that I saw in Beirut in 1954. In that movie, Frank Sinatra sang that beautiful song 'Three Coins in a Fountain.

To have a hot water shower at the pension, we had to pay extra for hot water over and above the pension nightly rate! After two weeks stay in Rome, we took a flight to Naples, Italy. The flight from Rome to Naples was even much scarier than the one we took from Beirut to Rome. Fire was coming out of one of the plane engines and the engine was burning red hot. I felt the plane was burning and was about to crash, but luckily, we made it safely to the airport. We stayed in Naples for a week and then boarded the *Queen Fredrica* cruise ship to New York City as our destination.

The *Queen Fredrica* cruise ship named after the last Greek queen whose dynasty was, toppled by a coup in the latter part of the 1960s. This trip by the 'Queen', from Naples to New York was its last as it was headed into retirement. The Mediterranean Sea was very violent and very angry during the month of February. The boat had to conquer the huge waves. The boat oscillated up and down according to the height of the waves. Furniture, on the deck kept sliding forward and backward as the boat moved forward while fighting the waves of the angry Mediterranean. Several people on the boat got seasick, but my wife and I were, spared the seasickness because we opted to spend most of the time outside on the deck sniffing fresh air.

The boat made a short stopover in Halifax, Canada for few hours. The passengers were, allowed to disembark for an hour at the port. It was, so cold that I questioned, as to how people survive under these extremely cold and harsh weather condition. It was the coldest feeling we ever had encountered in our life.

There were five Lebanese and two Palestinian students, including myself who boarded *Queen Fredrica*, at the Naples docs, heading to the United States. One of the

Lebanese students, Sabah, had a good voice and loved to sing. The hostess on the boat, requested me to organize a group to sing Lebanese songs to entertain other passengers. She called it 'The Abdallah M. Isa Troupe of Lebanese singers"!

Of course, I had nothing to contribute to the singing of the group other than asking them, please let us show the audience, our cultural heritage. Sabah, the Lebanese student who had the good voice was very enthusiastic and willing to sing. He got the most applause from the audience after finishing singing his Lebanese lyrics.

The hostess at the cruise ship announced to the audience, that the Abdallah M. Isa Troup of Singers have done a marvelous job entertaining the passengers on the ship, so please let us give them a big hand in appreciation of their efforts.

The audience went in an uproar as the hostess, handed us a gift as a reward for what we had done entertaining the people on the boat,

(This is the picture of the group of Lebanese and Palestinian students that came from Lebanon who boarded the *Queen Fredrica* in Naples, Italy to New York City. In the Front row from left is myself and my wife's picture is third from left)

My plans to enroll at the *University of California at Berkeley* in the spring Semester of 1963 was with the intention of being able to find a job and work during the summer months. According to the United States laws, foreign students are not, permitted to work during their first semester in the United States, but can work after spending one full semester at school.

After docking in New York, my wife and I were debating as to whether we should take the plane to San Francisco bus to Berkeley, California, or take the train directly to Berkeley. We asked around and were, told it is preferable, to take the train, as we can see more of the country. Flying however, we would not be able to see anything. The flight from New York City to San Francisco takes six hours while the trip by the train takes about four days. Although riding the train was more expensive than flying, we opted to take the train because we wanted to see as much of country as we could before heading back home to Beirut when I finish my schooling! Well, the route the train took did not offer us any means of 'seeing the country', as it was through mountainous and barren lands!

A family friend in Beirut whose son was a student in Chicago asked me to see his son and gave me a letter or to mail the letter to his son after arriving at the United States should I be unable to see his son. Since we took the train, from New York City to Berkeley and the train had a stopover for few hours in Chicago, I called my friend's son and told him that I have a letter that his father gave me to hand to him. Adel came to meet us, at the train station and we spent a couple of hours together updating him, on information on Beirut in general and on his father.

We had to change trains in Chicago where everything, even the tracks were covered with snow. After leaving Chicago, the train made another stop in Laramie, Wyoming where there was even more snow on the ground than was in Chicago. It took four days for the train to arrive at the Berkeley station.

Upon arrival at Berkeley, we were met by a group of American women, who were *University of California* faculty wives that waited at the station to welcome us as foreign students to the *University of California*. The women were very pleasant and helpful. They loaded our luggage into their vehicles and drove us to the campus office where foreign students were welcomed. We were, provided with information and directions as to where we were supposed to go. All in all, it was a very pleasant welcoming experience.

(Laila and I with a Palestinian student, after arriving in Chicago on February 23, 1963. We had to change trains coming from New York City and heading to Berkeley, California)

The acceptance letter from the *University of California* stated that 'housing is available'. Because we did not understand what the word 'available' meant and we assumed housing will be provided upon our arrival. Of course, that was not the case! The school suggested a nearby hotel. We reserved a room with a double bed. When we went to sleep, the bed was so small and not wider than a twin bed and neither one of us had a single wink of sleep. In the morning, I complained to the manager who then moved us to another room with twin beds. We realized later that this 'hotel' is not really a hotel, but an assisted living facility. On a Sunday afternoon, a young woman brought her father to this 'hotel' and told him to get in. He broke my heart when he said to his daughter, I do not want to be here, please take me back home. She insisted that it was better for him to stay there. When he started crying and pleading with his daughter to take him back home, I could not help it, but I started crying too! It was very sad to be a witness to such an emotionally filled negative interaction between father and daughter. I put myself in that old man's shoes and prayed to God that my daughter will never treat me in the same manner this woman treated her father.

MY EXPERIENCES AT THE UNIVERSITY OF CALIFORNIA AT THE BERKELEY CAMPUS

THE FOLLOWING MORNING, AFTER ARRIVAL, I WENT TO SEE MY GRAD-uate school advisor, Dr. Jacob Fong. He was a very gracious and a very re-assuring man. He said, we accept only the top ten percent of foreign students at our university. That statement gave me a great feeling of confidence that I must be one, of the top ten percent of international students applying to the *University of California at Berkeley*. My wife, who accompanied me to the meeting asked, as to how long will it take until my husband earns his doctorate. Dr. Fong responded by saying, seven to ten years or longer. My wife was shocked and said, we should go to England instead and you will get your degree in three years' time! She was partial to England as she spent five years of her life in London. I said no, I do not want to go to England or any other country. I want to have an American education and I want to earn an American degree.

Having been, accepted to graduate school in a foreign land and being a stateless person with no government to provide financial support, I was in a scary and fright-ening situation. I had to rely on my own savings because that was the only source of support I have in the way of defraying the cost of my education and to take care of our living expenses. I had to rely on my savings to pay my tuition fees, books and other supplies and to support a wife. The tuition fees for foreign students at the time were $275/semester. The only potential source of income that perhaps could help my financial situation would possibly be a scholarship from the university. The only route for me to qualify for such a scholarship was to prove myself and earn good grades. A scary feeling engulfed me all along that caused me to have sleepless nights, as I was terrified of the possibility of failure. 'Imagined' financial problems crept into my mind, as to how can I support a wife, pay my tuition fees and other expenses with no income prospects appearing in the horizon. Had I come to the United States as a single person, life could have been much easier, as should need arise, I could sleep on the sidewalk, but with a wife, this was not an option.

Two weeks after arrival at Berkeley I needed and had a haircut. Few days later, while getting ready to go to school, I felt a flat hairless spot on the left side of my head. I asked the wife to see what that hairless area was. She said it looks you are starting to lose your hair! I said, well, already I have been married for only a few months and it is too early to start losing my hair! The doctor at the campus infirmary diagnosed that smooth and hairless area as a ringworm. I jumped with horror when he mentioned the ringworm and said I never had any worms in my life. He assured me that the ringworm is a fungus that is contagious and is acquired and passed to others by contact. The ringworm infection was, traced back to the barbershop!

Because of my ringworm infection and its source was traced back to be the barbershop, a law was instituted and passed in the country, that all barbers, hairdressers and other outfits that deal with people's hair must have their instruments sanitized before moving from one customer to the other. It was my first contribution to society!

I enrolled in a required six-credit hour course, Pathogenic Bacteriology taught by Dr. Sanford Elberg, who I later found out him to, be the dean of the graduate school at *the University of California at Berkeley.* I thought, at the time, and naively so, that if I do well in his course, I might impress him, and he may be able to grant me a scholarship. When professor Elberg asked questions in the class and in an effort, to impress him, I always raised my hand to provide an answer to his question. He may have become tired of me answering questions and said, you have answered many of my questions Mr. Isa, let me give other students the chance to answer the questions. That statement of his, gave me the wrong impression that he may be impressed with me and might think I am a good student!

I called his office requesting an appointment to see the dean. I was, given a slot of time that is three days away to meet with the dean. During that meeting, the dean kept asking me personal and political questions and the meeting went on as the interviewer (the dean) asking the interviewee (me) questions and wanting answers in return:

Dean Elberg:	Why do you want to see me and for what purpose?
Me:	I want to ask your help for a scholarship, sir. I have no Government to support me and I am relying on my limited savings to cover my tuition fees and other expenses

Dean Elberg: Where are you from?

Me:	Although my folder, with all the information he needed to know about me is in front of him. I responded by saying I am from Palestine sir
Dean Elberg:	Where is that?
Me:	Palestine is geographically located to the south of Lebanon, South West of Syria, West of Trans Jordan and East of the Mediterranean Sea, sir
Dean Elberg:	This country is Israel
Me:	No sir, it is Palestine

Dean Elberg:	What will you do if, and when you receive your doctorate?
Me:	I will go back home, sir
Dean Elberg:	But where is home?
Me:	Since my home country of Palestine is still occupied by the Zionists, I will go back to Lebanon, stay there until my country of Palestine is liberated and is completely free from Zionist occupation
Dean Elberg:	What will you do in Lebanon?
Me:	I will try to find a job and if I cannot find one in my specialty, I will work in the refugee camps teaching Palestinian kids.
	Upon mentioning teaching Palestinian kids, he became agitated, blushed with anger, banged on the table and said, IsaI do not have any money for you
Me:	Thank you sir for your time and headed to the exit door
Dear Elberg:	Isa, Isa, come back. I want you to transfer from here and go to study at the *Hebrew University* to earn the Ph.D. degree from the *Hebrew University in Jerusalem*. I will, make sure of your acceptance *and* will guarantee you a scholarship and, also guarantee you have housing in Jerusalem. In addition,

I will provide airfares for you and for your wife, and make sure you be granted the Israeli citizenship within a couple of years

Me: No sir, I have come here to have an American education and to earn an American degree. Further, we are in a state of war with them, and left to the door.

Dean Elberg: Isa, Isa, come back, come back. He handed me a piece of paper on which he wrote, Professor A. L. Lasky at the *Hebrew*

University and said, "I will be calling professor Lasky tonight and will alert him to expect a letter from you indicating your willingness and interest in enrolling in the graduate school at the *Hebrew University in Jerusalem*".

Me: No sir, thank you for your time and left the room

After having these discussions with dean Elberg and his insistence that I quit the *University of California at Berkeley* and transfer to the *Hebrew University in Jerusalem*, I started to have serious questions as to his motives and about his loyalty. Is he really an American and dean of the Graduate School at an elite American University, *the University of California at Berkeley,* or is he an employee of the *Hebrew University in*

Jerusalem? Is he a representative of the State of Israel? Where does he stand as far as his loyalty is concerned? Is he loyal to his country of birth, the United States or to his perceived adopted country of Israel?

I felt dean Elberg might be setting up a trap for me to accept his offer so that he can use my acceptance to go study in Israel for propaganda and publicity purposes. Is this how Zionists behave and act as being loyal to a foreign country and not to their own country of birth? I started to wonder whether Zionists have their loyalty placed on Israel and not on their native countries, including the United States. I sincerely hoped that this was not the case with dean Elberg. I knew had I accepted his offer to enroll at the *Hebrew University in Jerusalem,* he will use me for propaganda purposes, as an example of Palestinians willing to renounce their right of return, to Palestine, and are willing to recognize and live under Israeli rule. This was the trap that he may have set up for me. However, I realized it very early and decided to go against his recommendation.

Of course, I did not get a scholarship from his office either! I had to enroll in his course, Pathogenic Bacteriology, as it was required to complete the prescribed courses for the Ph.D. degree. I had to work extra hard to do well in his course. Well, I earned (was given) the grade of 'C' in this six-credit hour course taught by dean Elberg! Whether he took it as a revenge against me by assigning the "C" grade or perhaps a confirmation that I am of a "C" grade quality student is open for serious debate.

EARLY IMPRESSIONS OF THE UNITED STATES

ONE OF THE FIRST OBSERVATIONS THAT ATTRACTED MY ATTENTION after arriving in the United States was the scene of women driving buses and big trucks or working as day laborers. I thought these jobs are the domain of men and now women appear to be engaged in them. When I inquired about it, I was told in America, men and women are equal and they can engage in the same kind of jobs if they so desire!

Few months after my wife and I arrived at Berkeley a classmate of mine, Miss Jane Cornelius asked me as to where did I come from. I said, my wife and I are Palestinians and live in Lebanon. She said, "My parents worked in the Middle East where my father was an employee of the US Department of Agriculture (USDA). They would love to meet you and your wife".

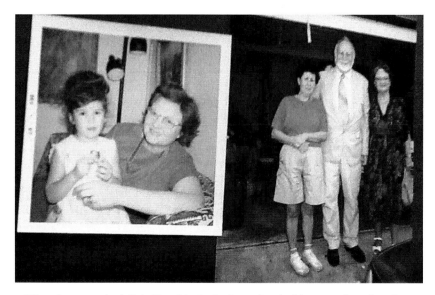

(The photo on the left is Mrs. Marjorie Cornelius holding our first daughter Reem (Kim). Photo on the right is that of Dr. Don Cornelius, Mrs. Marjorie Cornelius and my wife upon visiting them in Orlando, Florida, twenty years later)

We met Dr. Don and Mrs. Marjorie Cornelius at their home and immediately became very close friends. They had become our "adopted" American family. They had three daughters and after we had our first daughter, Reem (Kim). Don and Marjorie loved her so much and treated her as though she was their own grandchild. Of course, I was happy with our daughter, yet would have been happier if the first child were a boy! Don told me, girls bring boys home! I did not understand what that meant until our daughters got married. I then realized what Don meant, by having daughters bring boys home, meaning bring husbands home. He was absolutely, right!

I saw a 'For Sale' sign placed on the windshield of a 1961 Ford Fairlane car for $950. I tried to negotiate, 'bargain' the price with the owner, but he was adamant that the price of $950 is final, take it or leave it. Of course, I decided to take it and purchased the car!

While going to school at *the University of California at Berkeley, Vera*, one of my classmates, a Hungarian-American said to me, "Since you have a car, could you please help me move out from my apartment by loading my belongings into your car and drive me to my new apartment?" I said, of course, I will be more than happy to help you out and I did. I did not know, until later that after helping her move out, she told me that she was married and was unhappy in her marriage. That was the reason she wanted to move out. She also told me she was seeking divorce from her American husband. I was shocked to hear that and immediately thought of the possible consequences of me helping her moving out and in the process breaking her marriage. I said to her, having known earlier what you are telling me now that you are married and seeking divorce, I would have apologized for not being able to help you move out. Looking back at this incident, I realized how careless and dumb I have been. I may have put myself in a very serious and dangerous situation should her husband come home and see me loading her stuff into my car!

My wife graduated with a Registered Nursing degree from London, England. Mrs. Marjorie Cornelius, our adopted American family, asked my wife to accompany her to a friend's wedding. At the wedding, there was the director of Nursing of a neighborhood hospital. Mrs. Cornelius introduced my wife, as a registered nurse to the director of Nursing at that hospital. The Nursing director said we need nurses at our hospital and offered my wife a job on the spot to work at the hospital.

When the wife told me about the offer to work, I immediately told her she cannot work, because of the type of visa she has coming into the country. Before you can work, we need to find out from the Immigration office whether you can or cannot work. I came to the United States on an F-1 (student) visa, whereas my wife's visa was F-2 (companion to the student) visa.

For us to obey and respect the laws and regulations of the United States and not to engage in any illegal activities, my wife and I went to the Immigration and Naturalization Service office in San Francisco, to request permission for her to work at the hospital as a registered nurse.

The officer at the front desk, and after I explained the situation to him said, "It is between you and the hospital and should the hospital need your wife's services and offer her a job, it is perfectly legal". We thought we got the green light for my wife to work at the hospital. A week later, we received a letter from the immigration office, ordering us to leave the country within twenty-four hours! I was frightened from the order to leave the country and went to the Foreign Student Advisor's office on campus. I met with Mr. Smith, the assistant to the director of the Foreign Students Advisor. I explained to him the situation that led to us receiving the deportation letter. When I showed him the letter we received from the Immigration and Naturalization Service office, he felt bad about the situation and promised me that he will contact the Immigration office in San Francisco and try to do the best he could to resolve the problem with the Immigration office. It appeared that Mr. Smith was able to convince the Immigration Office to rescind the deportation order, as we received a phone call from the Immigration office advising us that the decision for our deportation was, rescinded and we will get a confirmation by mail. The confirmation letter came two days later.

University of California at Berkeley had a sizeable number of Arab students, most of whom were Egyptian. They all were sent and were supported by their government. I was the only Palestinian in the group. The Egyptian students were quite sympathetic to the question of Palestine. They followed the policy of their government under President Gamal Abdel Nasser who placed the liberation of Palestine as his top priority. The Arab Students Association was, established few years back at the Berkeley campus and was, recognized by the university as a legitimate student organization on campus. When the date for elections for the different positions of the Association were, announced I decided to run for the Association's Secretary. Consequently, I was elected as Secretary of the Association of Arab students on campus. The faculty advisor to the Arab Student Association on campus was Professor Linshowski, mentioned to us that Americans, as opposed to Arabs, do use their family names, while the Arabs do not. I was amazed at that statement, but after giving it a thought, I found out it to be a very true statement. As in many Arab countries especially in the Gulf region, they refer to so and so, son of so and so, is son of so and so., meaning they refer to the name of the father, the grandfather and may go as far back as to the great grandfather. They do not refer to, nor use the family name!

This is not the case in countries of Greater Syria: present day Syria, Iraq, Lebanon, Palestine and Jordan. In these countries, use of the family name is the rule.

Our mission, at the Arab Students Association, was to explain the Arab cause to the American Public and to promote a closer relationship between the American people and the Arab people. This mission succeeded to a limited degree, but in general, it was a failure. We, at the Arab Students Association misunderstood the deep-seated commitment of Americans to Israel. I did my work trying to find the roots of such unshakeable commitment Americans hold towards Israel, the disliking of the Arabs and the guilt feeling, resulting from the Nazis atrocities against the Jews, the Christian west has towards the Jews. In addition are other factors, contributed to the support of Israel:

a. The feeling of guilt due to the suffering of the Jews on the hands of the Christian Nazis

b. The declaration of "Judaism is the root of Christianity" was an outcome of the ecumenical council held in the early 1960s.

c. Declaration that the Romans, not the Jews, are the ones who crucified Jesus Christ, thus absolving the Jews from such horrendous atrocity that was committed against Jesus Christ. This is in direct conflict with what Moslems believe. According to the Holy Qur'an, Jesus was not crucified, but raised to Heaven to be shielded from suffering on the cross. Indeed, according to the Holy Qur'an, there indeed was a crucifixion that took place, oweverHhowever, the person who was crucified was not Jesus Christ, but was a Jesus look-alike who died on the cross. This is a matter of faith that could not be proven or disproven

d. The belief, among Christians especially the evangelists, the existence of the State of Israel is the fulfillment of the Prophecy of the coming of Jesus Christ. Moslems also believe that Jesus Christ will come and will rule the world. He will spread goodwill among all people and apply justice to all during his reign

e. The mainstream media, in the United States, whether in the audio, visual or in the printed area, plays a very important role in disseminating the information. Many a time the information that is fed to the information technology outfits are fabricated 'facts' and are fake news. These myths of anti-Arab and anti-Moslem myths have become, engraved in the minds and in the psyches of the west, in general and in the United States in particular. Hollywood and the evangelists played a major role in spreading these anti-Arab and anti-Moslem myths.

f. The early Crusades organized by the Pope and waged against Islam, have never ended. The Crusades we have now are the 'new and improved' versions of the original old Crusades. We all remember George W. Bush's statements that invasion of Iraq was the Crusade of the twentieth century! There is a misconception, based on ignorance in the west, that every Arab is a Moslem. This is farther from the truth, as Christians are an integral part of the Arab population. Christian Arabs are an important segment of the fabric of the Middle East. With the current atmosphere of Islamophobia in the west and the allegations leading to Islamophobia are the outcome of fake news promoted by individuals and organizations whose intent is to create a Christian/Moslem divide.

It is unfortunate that several Christian families opted to leave the Middle East and immigrate to the West. They are encouraged by, the Church and by other Christian outfits, to create the new reality of a Christian West and a Moslem East. In my opinion, departure of Christians from the Middle East to the West, regardless of the reason, had a negative impact on the makeup of the Middle Eastern society. The Middle East, the Cradle of Christianity, leaving only small Christian presence had left the area with negative economic and social outcomes.

(Photo of the Arab Students Association members at the University of California at Berkeley. It was, taken in front of Sproul Hall, the Administration building, on campus. I am pictured holding our first daughter Reem (Kim), first from right. My wife, Laila's picture is third from right.)

The Arab Students Association's platform was to explain the Arab position in regards, to the Palestine question to the American public, in addition to holding social and scientific events to which American students were invited.

On the academic and social arenas, I went to class wearing a suit and a tie as that was the way we were dressing up at the *American University of Beirut*. A female classmate, Miss Sherry said, 'Cool it Abdallah'! Of course, I did not understand what she meant by 'cool it', then she explained by saying relax, as coming to class, you do not need to wear suits, but wear casual clothes. I said, this is the way we went to college back home wearing suits, starched shirts, ties and polished shoes. Why would I not wear a suit and the rest of the garb going to school? She replied by saying, we Americans like to be free even in the way we dress up. Knowing well enough that students, in general, have limited financial means, thus we tend to wear what is appropriate yet affordable clothes. That is why we wear casual clothes.

(This is the attire consisting of suit, tie and the rest we, used to wear while attending the *American University of Beirut*)

Going back as to what Dean Elberg was asking me to transfer to the *Hebrew University* I must admit, after long hours of soul searching, I realized that I may have been brainwashed about the liberation of Palestine from Jewish rule! It was too late to remedy the damage I have done to my career by being anti-Zionist and anti-Israel at the *University of California at Berkeley* as many of the professors were Jewish and some, including Dean Elberg were staunch Zionists. Of course, they did not favor having me around on campus. They never said so directly, but the outcome was the same by their indirect action of intimidation and manipulation of my grades.

After completing the first semester, after arriving at Berkeley I was, permitted, by law, to work should I want to. By the advent of the summer of 1963, my finances started to dwindle, and I needed a job badly. The Placement center on campus had an opening at the local Humane Society. I went for the interview and met with the person in charge of the animals. The manager in charge told me that the interview is not between her and me, but between the animals and me. I asked her as to how that is and how can I, be interviewed by the animals? She said, should the dogs start barking and the cats start meowing upon seeing you it means that they did not like you. That means you have failed the interview, as the animals did not feel comfortable with you being around them. Should that happen, it means you will not get the job. The moment she and I left her office and went to see the animals, hell broke loose, and every dog started barking and every cat started meowing loudly upon seeing me. Well, she told me politely sorry sir, you cannot have the job. It is because you are not welcomed by the animals. It was so sad I lost the job even before it was offered,

There was another part time job opening at the Landscaping department on campus. The Landscaping contract was, consummated between the University grounds department and an Italian-American company. I had an interview with Tony, the president of the Landscaping Company and told him I had a degree in Agriculture from the American University of Beirut. He was impressed with my qualifications and immediately offered me the job. The position I was offered did neither require a university degree nor any experience to do the work. It was a weeding job, which required pulling the weeds from the flowerbeds. I was paid $3.50 an hour on a 20-hour weekly schedule. That was a great pay at the time considering the minimum wage was $0.69/hour. After working at that job for two months, I offered my resignation, against Tony's will. Tony, manager of the landscape company, tried his best to convince me and entice me to stay on the job by offering me a raise of an extra dollar per hour. I insisted on resigning and told him, I have come to the United States to learn, graduate with a degree and not to work as a day laborer pulling weeds from the flowerbeds. I will start looking for another job in an area related to my education in my department, if possible, as that will help me in my intended educational pursuit.

I found a job as a dishwasher in the laboratory in my department. The dishwashing job paid a little more than minimum wage. The dishwashing job paid me $0.99 an hour. This was a step down from the $3.50/hour, which was less than one third of what I was making as a day laborer! I worked so many overtime hours that I was averaging about $400 a month!

At this time, we have qualified to live in student housing. We moved to a one-bedroom apartment with a fully equipped kitchen at a monthly rent of $29 with all utilities paid. We stayed at that apartment for six months after which we qualified for a two-bedroom apartment when we had our first child. The university housing office offered us the two-bedroom apartment at monthly rent of $45! That apartment was located on the second floor with a large balcony on which we would sit, have our coffee and watch the traffic moving by.

Because, I was a good student I was promoted from a dishwasher to a teaching assistant in the department! With this assistantship. I was granted a waiver of tuition fees and a stipend of $275/month. This was a bonanza for me and proved to me that I must have a good head on my shoulder, and I am a good student regardless of what others think. Now I was making 'good money' and having a car, it allowed the wife and me to go sightseeing to the different parts of the State of California. The 1961 *Ford Fairlane* car, which I called it the tank, because it was as big as, looked very much like and drove like a tank, but was quite handy to facilitate our sightseeing trips.

The following Fall Semester, I enrolled in another course that was required by the department. The Virology course that was required and taught by Dr. Jacob Fong, Chairman of the department and my graduate student advisor. I did well in the course and I felt I earned the grade of "A" in that course after taking the final examination. To my big surprise, my grade in the course was a "B". Dr. Fong did not correct the papers himself but had a laboratory technician, who I found later to be Jewish, do the correcting. She graded my paper and gave me a score of 86% as she recorded (-14 points) on my paper. She had set her scale as follows: A=86.5-100, B=82.0-86.0 and so on. According to her scoring, I earned the grade of "B" in the course!

The examination papers are usually kept in the department office. They were available for the students to look at if they wish, and to see if there were any discrepancies in correcting individual papers. When I checked my paper, and counted the minuses, as corrected by that technician, I found that I had a total of (-12.50 points) and not (-14 points) as the technician counted. That meant that according to the technician's corrections my score would be 87.5 and not 86. This newly found correction entitled me to have a grade of "A". She was wrong adding the minuses, whether her 'mistake 'in counting the minuses was intentional or not was not clear to me. My score would have been, according to her grading system, 87.50. This score qualifies me for the grade of "A". I pleaded with Dr. Fong, to please go over my paper, but he refused. I said, "thank you sir for everything and goodbye. I am leaving this university. This is, not an American University, but appears to be a Zionist university. I am going to the newspaper to tell them the whole story how, as a foreign Palestinian student at the university, I was treated by the Zionist faculty in the department.

Dr. Fong was alarmed and did not want this bad publicity, should the proceedings of my meeting with the newspaper be published, as it may hit him directly since my complaint includes the Virology course he was supposed to have taught. He then decided to check my final examination paper. After going through the paper, he counted the minuses and came to the same conclusion I came with that the score should be 87.5 and not 86. Further, I pointed out to him that some of the questions, the technician marked wrong, were indeed correct. According to Dr. Fong's corrections, the score on my final examination paper was 94. Of course, I was very happy at the new score and asked him to have my grade changed from "B" to an "A". He said, I am not sure the Registrar will honor the change of grade request. I said to please write the letter requesting the grade change and I will hand deliver it to the Registrar and see what happens.

When I took the letter to the registrar's office the receptionist asked as to how is, my last name pronounced. I said, my last name is pronounced as EEsa. She smiled and said Oh, we have the same name! I asked if her name were Isa, she said no, but my name is Isabel and my friends call me Isa! I laughed and said, who knows we may be distantly related!

Indeed, this is the only change of grade from "B" to "A" that appears in my transcripts.

I was perplexed as to why Americans, especially women as they smile when they come across other people. Do the women really mean it when they smile or is it a fake smile? Does their smile suggest that they may like the other person? It took me a while to realize, that it is an inherent trait Americans have and is part of their character.

Shopping for groceries was a pleasure, yet a little scary at times as we had to convert Lebanese money into US dollars. The dollar, at the time, was equivalent to three Lebanese pounds meaning what we paid in dollars was indeed three times the value in Lebanese money. That had a negative psychological impact on us when we multiplied what we paid in dollars by a factor of 3. The fear that engulfed me was, whether the Lebanese money we brought with us, is enough to sustain our life until I can find a job.

I was quite intimidated and agitated when, the cashier at the Co-Op grocery store, asked me if we have food in our country. I said of course, we have food in our country and pulled the cucumber that we just purchased and said, let me tell you young lady, you do see this cucumber, we do not eat that. We use it as feed for our animals!

Life at Berkeley, aside from the university, was very pleasant. The city of Berkeley has a great location as it sits at the base of beautiful hills and is only 12 miles from San Francisco across the Bay Bridge. After arriving at Berkeley, the university had invited all foreign students to a dance in the ballroom of the Student Union building. The group that performed at the dance was the legendary Peter, Paul and Mary that played music and sang throughout the evening.

As newlyweds and right after arriving at Berkeley, we used to go sightseeing in San Francisco as we were trying to discover the places of entertainment and fine restaurants. We wanted to see as much as we can in California and in the United States before we go back home after I graduate.

One night we decided to go dancing at the Fairmont Hotel in San Francisco. We met the legendary Tony Bennet, who was a rising star at the time and sang the legendary song '*I left my heart in San Francisco*' in the Tonga room of the hotel. I am not sure if he had sung that song before, but I am more inclined to believe that this may have been the first time he had ever sang that beautiful song!

When the Beatles came to the United States, we again drove from Berkeley to the San Francisco airport to witness their arrival and subsequent concert they held. It was, a crazy scene as huge numbers of teenagers were screaming and yelling, trying to push through police barricades to get a closer glimpse of the Beatles.

The 1960s were the decade of social revolutions in the United States campuses. The *University of California Berkeley campus* was the locus of these revolutions. I was in the middle of the Free Speech movement on campus when. President Clark Kerr of the *University of California* nine-campus system and whose office is at the Berkeley campus, summoned the student body of twenty-seven thousand (eighteen thousand males and nine thousand females) students to, the Greek Theater. Female students were in great demand at the time as the male to female ratio was 2:1. The females did enjoy being sought after by men as they could be selective as to who they would date.

While the president was talking to us, telling us that the university's mission is to deliver an education and we students are the recipients of such an education from a great university. The educational experience at Berkeley is, intended to improve your intellectual capabilities and to improve your economic situation and open new doors for a successful career, the president said. One of the rebellious students named Mario Savio, jumped to the podium, grabbed the microphone from President Kerr's hand, and shouted "Do Not Listen to This Liar". There was an uproar and the students left the theater yelling and throwing barbs and profanities at the university administration.

One of my teaching assistants in the department who was a member of the ultra-conservative John Birch Society, insisted that I go out and stop those rebellious (thugs) students and order them to come to class. He asked me to demand they detach themselves from the revolution. I said, wait a minute sir, I am a foreign student and had neither a say nor an influence with these revolutionaries. Should I take any part in any of these activities, I guarantee you, I will be put on the first flight out of the country. I think you yourself should go and do what you have just asked me to do!

In addition to the Free Speech Movement, another social revolution that took place on campus, the Sexual Freedom Revolution. I was, stopped by a group of women who had a table outside the student union building. One of these women asked if I would like to join their league. I asked her for more details about the league and what does it takes to be a member. She said, our league is called the Sexual Freedom League with the following by-laws:

1. If a woman sees a man walking by and she desires him, she should get him. I said, I agree

2.   If a man sees a woman and desires her, he should get her. I said, I agree too. She then said, since you agree with our league's terms for joining, will you now join?

I said, thank you for the invitation and for the information, but regretfully I am not able to join. She said, why not? I said, I happen to be a married man and I am faithful to my wife. Her response was shocking when she said, go away stupid, you do not know what you are missing!

After few weeks of turmoil on campus, things started to cool down and students started to come to class and resume their studies. My teaching assistantship in the department was in full swing. I was teaching laboratories in Microbiology and Immunology to majors and non-major undergraduate students,

Unfortunately, Dr. Fong became sick with cancer and later died in the hospital and a new department head took over. Dr. Wofsy was now the new department head. One of his first acts as head of the department, was to remove my name from the list of teaching assistants. I was not sure whether my name was the only one deleted from the list of teaching assistants or other assistants' names were also deleted. Removal my name from the list of teaching assistants felt like the whole world fell over my head as now I will have to pay tuition fees and will lose the lifesaving $275 monthly stipend. I had one faculty member in the department, Dr. Benjamin Papermaster, Ben, as we used to call him is came to my rescue. He was very understanding of my situation and was true to his personal tradition of being compassionate and fair. He was not only fair, but also a man of principle. He felt, those in power should not punish students who disagree with their political stand.

Ben was very disappointed in seeing my name removed from the list of teaching assistants. Ben took it upon himself to do the best he could, to have my name re-instated in the teaching assistants list. He met with Dr. Wofsy for over an hour, arguing on my behalf and defending my position. Because of Dr. Papermaster's efforts, I was re-instated as a teaching assistant in the department. Now I am back as a legitimate teaching assistant with all benefits restored to what they were during the time of the late Dr. Fong and prior to Dr. Wofsy's taking over the chairmanship of the department!

I was determined to complete all the course work prior to my doctoral qualifying exam. I needed to complete the bacterial physiology course, another 6-credit hour course to satisfy all the requirements. I enrolled in the required bacterial physiology course that taught by Dr. Michael Doudoroff, a Russian Jewish and Zionist professor in the department.

Although I did well in the course, my final grade was a "C". When I asked Dr. Doudoroff as to why my grade was a "C" and I expected an "A" as I knew I did very well in the course and exams. He responded by saying, because I do not like you! Well, he had just come back after spending his sabbatical leave at the *Hebrew University in Jerusalem*. He must have been brainwashed and loaded with hate of Palestinians during his stay in Jerusalem!

This was and still is the plan of the Zionists to delegitimize and deny the existence of the Palestinians by any means possible. One should never forget Golda Me'ier's (the Israeli prime minister) statement: 'Where are the Palestinians, she looked around and said there are no Palestinians that I can see'!

Dr. Moshe Shiloh, Professor of Microbiology at the *Hebrew University in Jerusalem,* was on sabbatical leave from his university and spent one year at Berkeley. Dr. Shiloh covered the courses that Dr. Doudoroff taught when he was on sabbatical leave. It was an exchange of professors spending sabbatical leaves at the *University of California at Berkeley and the Hebrew University in Jerusalem.* Dr. Shiloh and his wife visited us, in our apartment and he and I had different political views regarding the Israeli/Palestinian question. Professor Shiloh and I discussed, rather argued, politics until 2:00 AM. He was a very fine and pleasant man who I could add his name to the list of my friends.

Continuing my studies at Berkeley, hit a low tone and I have become frustrated and disgusted with the attitudes of some of the faculty members and some of the employees in the department.

That did it, after spending two years at Berkeley, I felt I am, being singled out as the 'enemy of Israel' and, as such, I am unwanted in the department and at the *University of California Berkeley* campus. I must pay the price of being politically incorrect according to the Zionist faculty! Continuing my studies at the *University of California at the Berkeley* campus has reached a dead end. Because it had become very stressful due to discrimination against me for being opposed to Israel and for my grade manipulation by the Israel-loving faculty and staff sympathizers. I was not certain I be able to earn my doctorate from the *University of California at the Berkeley* campus. I opted to move on and leave the *University of California at Berkeley.*

I applied to and was immediately accepted, by the *University of California Medical Center at San Francisco.* The courses I had completed and passed at Berkeley were, accepted to be equivalent to those taught at the Medical Center's department of Microbiology. Looking back at my decision, I am more than ever convinced, that my move to the medical center in San Francisco was not only sound, but also led to a potentially better future.

The University of California Medical Center (UCSF)r in San Francisco offered a combined MD/Ph.D. degree program, which Berkeley did not offer. That was, a plus for me as a new horizon, will help me attain a better career.

As a student at the *University of California* at the Berkeley campus, I witnessed firsthand the social revolutions that took place on campus that had an impact, and a change, of the social norms of the country. Following the Free Speech Movement and the Sexual Freedom Movement that erupted at Berkeley, led to the formation of the Hippie Movement, an offshoot organization that came into being months later. The Hippie Movement took residence in the Height-Ashbury district of San Francisco. Haight-Ashbury became not only the national headquarters of the Hippie movement, but also it became the Mecca for runaway kids of all ages and from different parts of the country who moved in and joined the movement.

We lived in the Medical Center housing complex, a couple of blocks away from the Haight-Ashbury area. Going to school, I had to go through the Haight-Ashbury district. It was very beautiful at the beginning as most of the Hippies were intellectuals or claiming to be intellectual. They were unhappy with the status quo and wanted a change in society. They were trying to bring change and to have an impact on the social environment in the country. However, the peacefulness and the intellectual atmosphere exhibited by the Hippie movement changed course within few months and the Haight-Ashbury district became crime center USA. Criminals took over the Hippie movement that resulted in at least one murder every night at the Haight-Ashbury area.

Social revolutions in the country became a daily occurrence. Opposition to the war in Vietnam was at its height. Demonstrations against the war sprang out throughout the country. Placards with slogans such as 'make love not war' displayed all over the place. Of course, as usual, politicians employed these demonstrations to their advantage, Hubert H. Humphry, the democratic nominee for president in 1968, took advantage of the discontent in the country. He embraced the anti-war movement hoping that he would impress the public with anti-war rhetoric about the war in Vietnam and joined the anti-war movement with the hope to, be elected as the next president of the United States. The atmosphere in the country was very volatile and nobody could predict what would be coming next.

To make life in San Francisco more complicated, personal security was at stake. The Black Panthers were marching with their loaded guns on Lincoln Way, a main thorough way in San Francisco. It was a scary environment in which I did not wish to have our children be exposed to.

To graduate with the medical (MD) doctor degree required the passing of basic science courses (two years) and clinical sciences and training (two years). Students earn a medical doctor's (MD) degree. After receiving the MD degree, the new doctors, at the time, were required to enroll in an internship and later residency programs at institutions offering the specified program they want to train in. By the end of the internship program, some of these doctors, head to specialization in one of the different medical specialties available to them.

To graduate with the Ph.D. degree, on the other hand, is more rigorous with five different components that must be satisfied and completed successfully:

1.   Completion of all courses prescribed for the program

2.   Passing a qualifying written examination

3.   Passing a foreign language scientific article (German, French or Russian) translation

4.   Passing a qualifying oral examination

5.   Completion of original research, writing the dissertation and publishing their research findings in peer reviewed journals.

After passing the written examination and the foreign language test, the committee chair sets a date for the Oral examination by the assembled five-member committee.

To graduate with both the Ph.D. and the MD degrees in the combined degree program, students will have to spend one extra year over the four-year MD degree prescribed course of study to cover other required courses and to do research.

The committee for my Ph.D. degree consisted of five professors, three of whom chosen by the head of the department of Microbiology and Immunology and two members to be recommended by be. It was an ecumenical committee where in addition to the head of the department of Microbiology and Immunology, Dr. Ernest Jawetz, who nominated Drs. Leon Levintow as committee chair and Dr. William D. Linscott, along with himself to be members of the departmental committee. The faculty members recommended by the student must be approved by, both the head of the department and by the chair of the committee. I requested both Dr. John Najarian, professor of Surgery at the Medical Center, as I was interested in organ and tissue transplantation and Dr. Benjamin Papermaster, Professor of Immunology at the *University of California* at the Berkeley campus. Both Drs. Najarian and Paperpaster were approved by the Chairman of the department and by the qualifying committee chair, as members in my Qualifying examination committee.

Three of the professors, Dr. Ernest Jawetz, (department head) Dr. Leon Levintow, (Chairman of the Qualifying Committee) and Dr. Benjamin Papermaster were Jewish. Dr. William D. Linscott, professor Microbiology was a Mormon, Dr. John Najarian, professor of surgery, an Armenian Orthodox Christian and of course me as a Moslem. That mix created a new ecumenical council represented by the three divine faiths

The written examination consisted of questions submitted by each member of the committee. The questions are to be, related to the field of expertise of each of the committee members and that are relevant to the student's field of study. A quiet room and a pot of coffee were, provided to the student taking the examination. I wrote, non-stop, for eight hours. There was one comment, 'passing but not outstanding' posted by Dr. Linscott on my answer sheet! After having passed the written part of the examination, I was moved to the second phase of the qualifying oral examination. All graduate students working towards the Ph.D. degree were required to pass a test by translating a scientific paper published in a foreign language (French, German or Russian) into English. I chose an article published in German and translated it into English.

My oral Examination coincided with the six-day Middle East war of 1967. Dr. Jawetz, was very kind and considerate as he let it be known to the faculty that the outcome of the 1967 war was having a very negative impact upon Mr. Isa, to please refrain from mentioning or discussing anything about the war in Mr. Isa's presence. The outcome of that war had a tremendously depressing impact on me. My fear of failure combined with the outcome of the war, caused me to have sleepless nights caused and become mentally and emotionally drained, and physically fatigued due to the lack of sleep.

During the qualifying oral examination with the five members in the committee, they took their turn in asking me questions. Dr. Najarian started first with ridiculous questions. His first question was on which animal was the first skin transplant done and by whom. After answering both questions correctly, he added another one as to which side of the rabbit was the transplant done! He kept grilling me for thirty minutes with questions that were unrelated to my field of study. Dr. Papermaster interrupted him and told him point plank, John, I do not think you know what you are asking for and I do not think you know how to ask the question. The questions you are asking are irrelevant to the Ph.D. program. The chair of the committee, Dr. Levintow asked me to leave the room as the arguments between the two professors became heated and loud.

Fifteen minutes later and after Dr. Najarian had left the room, I was asked to come back to resume my questioning with the remaining four members of the committee who were ready to grill me further. I have become very anxious and had the feeling of failure that took over me was when I became completely numb, could not even think. I was frightened with the thought that kept swirling in my head that I might have to return home to Beirut empty handed with no degree to show for. I was, grilled for an additional hour and a half after which the chair of the committee asked me to leave the room. A long scary, depressing and anxious fifteen minutes wait that felt like a year, took them to deliberate among themselves and arrive at a consensus whether I pass or fail. The wait ended when Dr. Levintow, chair of the committee, came out with a big grin on his face, shook my hand and said, "Congratulations Dr. Isa" you have made it. Wow! What a relief that was! Now, I have started to regain all the confidence I have lost., my fears and the feeling of not being up to the challenge have, completely sublimed.

I felt Dr. Najarian may have been planning on failing me and I sincerely wanted to find out what his motive for failing me was. I found out through the grapevine and from people who knew his background that his father emigrated from Lebanon before he was born. I then became suspicious that Mr. Najarian senior may have had a bad experience in Lebanon, which he instilled in his son to have him get even with Lebanon through failing me!

This was only a suspicion with no hard facts to support it on my part.

With all the problems, I have encountered at the *University of California at Berkeley,* yet none were encountered at the *University of California San Francisco Medical Center* campus. Most of these problems I had at Berkeley were political in nature. Being opposed to Israel did not sit well with the Zionist faculty at the Berkeley campus. It would have been a great honor to graduate with the Ph.D. degree from Berkeley as it was the one and only school with the highest number of Nobel Prize winners in the United States, if not in the whole world. There were twenty-seven Nobel Prize Laureates on campus. To graduate as a doctor I managed to survive, against all odds, and ultimately, I earned the title of Dr. Abdallah M. Isa!

While visiting the Berkeley campus in my way to see my former professor, Dr. Ben Papermaster, I crossed path with Dean Elberg in the hallway. He said, Hi Mr. Isa. I responded by saying it is Dr. Isa that says Hi to you, sir.

Most of the problems I faced at Berkeley were not necessarily because of the way the professors treated me, but rather, many a time, were of my own doing. The indoctrination, instilled in us as young Arab nationalists, that it is our duty and obligation to do anything and everything we possibly can, to help achieve the liberation of Palestine from the Zionist state of Israel. My obligation in that regard was to explain to, the American public the injustices brought upon us Palestinians, by the establishment of the state of Israel. I failed to understand the huge Zionist influence in the United States, whether be it at the level of the university, the printed media or the visual and audio media and in many cases, the individuals. I then realized that everything has a price and that one is accountable as to what he/she says or what he/she does! The price I paid for being anti-Israel, whether in the form of insecurity or sometimes threats of failure, was very hard to endure.

The dean of the medical and graduate school called me, as I was the only Arabic-speaking student at the *University of California Medical Center campus.* He asked me to translate a letter he had received from a student from the Middle East. The letter written in Arabic contained very pleasant and complementary adjectives addressed to the dean. The writer of the letter detailed his 'requests' in a manner that I felt were demands rather than requests.

The student demanded the dean provide him with the following:

1.   Acceptance to medical school

2.   A fully furnished apartment with no rent to pay

3.   A car and vouchers to pay for gasoline

4.   Scholarship that will defray the cost of tuition fees and living expenses

5.   Written guarantee he will graduate in four years

When I read the letter, I could not stop laughing and to the dean's astonishment, he asked me as to what was making me laugh so hard. I translated the letter with all the demands the student had wanted him to grant. After translating the letter into English, the dean asked me as to what and how he should respond to that letter. I said since this person wrote to you in Arabic it suggests to me that he neither reads nor writes in or speak English. You could write the letter, in English, and I will translate it into Arabic, and mail him both the English and the hand-written Arabic translation. The dean agreed, and I have no idea what had transpired since.

As there were several other foreign students on campus, the Foreign Student Advisor requested a meeting with the foreign students including myself, to come to her office. One the questions she asked, was as to how, could she improve communications between her office and the foreign student body on campus. I said, the word foreign has a negative connotation and makes us feel aliens and not necessarily very welcome. How about deleting the word 'foreign' and replacing it with the word 'International', thus your office will be called 'Office of the International Students Advisor'. I believe 'International Students' has a more positive and welcoming description, although it still means foreign. She liked the idea and immediately ordered the name on her office and on her office stationary, was changed from 'Foreign Student Advisor's Office' to "International Student Advisor's office". A week later, I got a letter from her thanking me for the suggestion of the name change and told me that she made the recommendation to the department of Education and to the department of State in Washington, DC to replace the word Foreign to International. This was one other positive contribution I, made to the University and to the Department of Education of the United States.

Having instituted the term "International" in place of "Foreign" students was the second positive contribution that I have made to society ever since I came to the United States!

While attending school at the Medical Center, the Dental School at the university had appointed a Mormon dean. As a result, almost all, of the dental school students were, of the Mormon faith. There were four Mormon families living in the same building we were living in.

One late afternoon and while I was babysitting our children, I heard a knock at the door. It was one of our Mormon neighbors. After opening the door, she asked if she could come in. I said of course, please do come in. She asked if she could sit down. I said of course, please sit down. With a serious look on her face, she said I want to discuss something important with you. I must admit, I was a little worried that one of our two girls may have done something wrong to have our neighbor come to complain. After all, it was not a complaint, but rather she was seeking help and advice. I asked her, as to what she would like to drink. She asked as to what I have in the way of drinks. I said we have coffee, coke, tea, Scotch, Bourbon, Tequila and other alcoholic drinks. Which drink would you prefer? She said no to any of the drinks I suggested. Then she requested juice, but if juice is not available then water will do.

She then said, Mormons do not drink alcohol or any drinks that contain stimulants like caffeine. After she opened, up she started talking and said, I want your advice and suggestions: "I am looking for a wife for my husband. He is young and deserves to have a younger wife", I asked her if she were mentally O.K? Are you serious? She said yes, I am serious, and I am fine with it. She responded by the affirmative that she was serious about finding a younger wife for her husband. My next question to her was, as to what would happen to her should her husband acquire a younger new wife? She said, I will still be there, and will be the one who runs the show in the household! Admittedly, I became a little suspicious of her motives, as it might be a set up! Why would she come to see me when she knew my wife was at work and not at home? Why from all neighbors, she chose to confide in me about her personal life? I said to her I, cannot see how a woman wanting her husband to have another wife and both living under the same roof. It is illegal in the United States, is it not? She said yes, it is illegal, but he does not have to advertise or have his marriage legalized. Nobody will know about it except him, his new wife and myself. I said I wish I could advise you, but please hold the discussion until my wife comes home. She may see things differently than me and may have better suggestions for you or may become influenced by your request to look for a new wife for me! As you know women, in general, do understand other women better than men would. This couple already had three children and the wife was in her eighth month of pregnancy with the fourth child. The husband was a student at the dental school and after school he, comes home and does nothing in the way of helping his pregnant wife who was working as a Public Health nurse with the children or any house chores. He would lay down on the couch to watch television until dinner is ready and it is time for him to eat!

For the Ph.D. degree, my research project was on Chlamydia. The organism that causes Trachoma, a chronic eye infection that was prevalent in the Middle East (the old world) and is a sexually transmitted disease in the United States (the new world). I spent long hours working in the laboratory, seven days a week and would go home late at night, trying to finish the project as soon as I could. I wanted to finish as soon as possible, to allow me to be able to find a job to support my family of four. I communicated with my mentor, the Chairman of the department on a weekly basis, updating him on the progress of the research project. He was always happy and supportive of my work. He was impressed with the progress and approved the research findings. We, he and I, published a couple of papers in the Journal of Immunology where we reported the results stemming from my research.

I told him that the project that I was set forth to pursue is complete and I have spent one and half years to complete it. The findings are, novel and I am ready to write my dissertation. I am looking for his support and approval, as I am anxious to graduate and find a job to support my family. His response was, we normally expect the student to spend three to four years to complete the research before graduating. I said, is it the time one spends in the residency program to complete the research or it is the quality of the work and the results obtained from of the research? He was stunned by what I said and reluctantly signed the paperwork. I wrote my dissertation and moved on.

Traditionally, it is through the help of the faculty advisor and mentor who oversees the research project to guide and help the graduates to land a decent job by contacting his/her colleagues at other institutions. I felt my advisor, Dr. Ernest Jawetz, an immigrant from Austria, and as my mentor and the Chairman of the department, did not show any interest in helping me find a job. He did not recommend me to any university or helped me in trying to find a job anywhere in the country. After all, I am a permanent resident of the United States and not a native-born American!

It gives me great pleasure and pride that President Ronald Reagan, who was governor of the State of California at the time and later president of the United States, signed all my degrees. The governor of the state signs the degrees earned by students in public institutions in his state. Since the University of California is a public institution, then the governor signs all degrees granted by the university.

After graduating from the *University of California* and because of my inherent interest in Trachoma, I decided to spend one extra year as a clinical Postdoctoral fellow at the Proctor Foundation of the *University of California at San Francisco*. This foundation dealt primarily with eye diseases and disorders. One of the areas of studies, at the foundation, was research on chlamydial infections, including but not limited to Trachoma. Since my plans were to return to the Middle East where infections due to Trachoma were rampant in that part of the world, I wanted to gain as much expertise as I could in the clinical aspects and management of the disease, as well as in research trying to find a cure for it.

The director of Proctor Foundation, Dr. Phil Thygeson, was retiring and prior to his retirement, he recommended his assistant, to head the foundation. I was given a hint that with the new administration at the foundation, a position will be lined up for me.

Because the foundation's programs dealt with eye diseases and syndromes, it was under the jurisdiction of the Ophthalmology department of the University and any decisions related to the foundation will have to be sanctioned by the chairman of the Ophthalmology department. When the nomination of Dr. Thygeson's replacement was discussed, the chair of the Ophthalmology department vetoed the appointment to have Dr. Thygeson's assistant to head the Proctor Foundation

(This was the day I graduated from *the University of California Medical center* in San Francisco with me wearing the official Doctor's Regalia. This was the day when people started calling me, Dr. Abdallah)

UNSUCCESSFUL PLANS TO MOVE BACK TO THE MIDDLE EAST

I WANTED TO GO BACK TO THE MIDDLE EAST. ONE OF THE MAJOR reasons that had an impact on my decision to find a way to move back to the Middle

East was our middle, four-year old, daughter Randa's complaint. She broke my heart when she complained to me as to why does not her grandma come to see me as Terry's (our neighbor's son) grandma comes to see him all the time? I told her, your grandma lives too far away in Lebanon and for her to come see you as often as terry's grandma does is very difficult. However, I promise you that your grandmother will come from Lebanon to see you or you will go to Lebanon to see her. Few months later her grandma came over to visit and a year later, we all went to Lebanon as I have promised our daughter we will do.

A glimmer of hope in the direction of moving back to the Middle East appeared in the horizon when the medical school at the University of Jordan offered me a faculty position at a salary of $400 a month. That was a good start in my search for a way to move back to the Middle East, however a major problem that potentially thwarted the move came up: I had just purchased a new car that I wanted to ship to Jordan. Should I decide to bring my car to Jordan, I was told it will cost over $4000 in customs duties. Shipping charges from San Francisco to Aqaba, Jordan by sea, and from Aqaba to Amman by truck would cost an additional $1500. This meant the cost of customs duties and shipping of the car amounted to $5500. This cost is far over my annual salary of $4800. I will have no money left to support a family of five for the whole year and I will be $700 in the red! This offer was not adequate as it was not economically feasible. To my pleasant surprise, the University of Jordan withdrew the offer when they found out that I am a Palestinian and not a Jordanian citizen! Long live Arab solidarity!

Being a stateless person, with no country to be claimed by, is essentially like a wild animal that belongs to the wilderness. For most Palestinian Moslems, it was next to impossible to acquire the Lebanese citizenship because finances. Those Palestinian Moslems with deep pockets could obtain the citizenship. It was much easier for Palestinian Christians to acquire the Lebanese citizenship. I could not be, naturalized in Lebanon because it was not only costly, and I did not have the funds to pay for it, but also because of my birthplace and religious affiliation.

Palestinian Christians, on the other hand, got the Lebanese citizenship with no problem as the Christian rulers of Lebanon helped their Palestinian Christian brothers by granting them citizenship. The un-written rule that was left by the French colonial-ists was to maintain a Christian majority in Lebanon. The government of Lebanon issued Palestinian refugees a travel document, in lieu of a passport, to facilitate travel outside of Lebanon.

After graduating from the *University of California Medical Center in San Francisco* in 1968, and as a Stateless person with no country to belong to, I wanted to acquire a citizenship of any country that is willing to accept me and grant me the honor of belonging. I had to seek citizenship, because I hold the status of 'stateless' with no state to claim me as one of its subjects. The only option I had to pursue was that of Jordan as many Palestinians were granted the Jordanian citizenship. I naively thought with the qualifications I have, it would be possible to be granted that citizenship. Mr. Abdul Hamid Sharaf, a relative of king Hussain knew me well as he was one of my mentors in the Arab Nationalist Movement at the *American University of Beirut*.

Mr. Sharaf was, appointed as the Jordanian ambassador to the United Nations and later was elevated to become the prime minister of Jordan. At the time Mr. Sharaf was the Jordanian ambassador to the United Nations, I wrote him a letter and addressed it to his office at the United Nations in New York City. In my letter, I introduced myself, told him of my qualifications and reminded him of our relationship as members of the Arab Nationalist Movement while students at *the American University of Beirut*. I requested his help in acquiring the Jordanian citizenship. In my letter, I reminded him as to who I am and our affiliation with the Arab Nationalist Movement when he and I used to deliver lectures to small groups about the issue of Palestine. I was also keen on reminding him that he was my mentor in the Movement during our tenure as students at the *American University of Beirut*. Mr. Sharaf never bothered to respond to my letter directly, however he instructed Mr. Sultan Lutfy, the Jordanian consul general in New York City, to write to me. In his letter, Mr. Lutfy said, **Dear Dr. Abdallah M. Isa "We regret to inform you that we cannot offer you the Jordanian citizenship at this time"**. That did it, as it was the end of my ambition and desire to go back to the Middle East.

One of the burning reasons for my desire to move back to the Middle East was, I wanted our children to grow up in our culture and for them to enjoy the love and attention, which I did not have, of their maternal grandparents who I had great admiration, respect and love for.

By now, I have given up on the Arab countries and resigned myself to the fact that the Middle East neither wants me, my potential contributions, nor was I fit to be there.

AMBITIONS THROUGHOUT THE YEARS I HAVE SET AND WORKED HARD TO ACHIEVE

1. Graduate from High School-Achieved
2. Getting a college education-Achieved
3. Get a job in my field of study after receiving my BS degree-Achieved

4. Marrying the woman, Laila, I loved-Achieved

5. Have children, raise them properly and get them educated-Achieved

6. Against all odds, becoming a doctor and a scientist-Achieved

7. Attempts to move back to the Middle East-Dismal failure

8. Working in Academia in a Medical school environment that included a hospital and doing clinical and basic medical research-Achieved

9. Live long enough to have our daughters, graduate from college, get married and have grandchildren-Achieved

10. Having a country, the United States, that would grant me citizenship-Achieved

One of the major ambitions I had, in addition to becoming a doctor and a scientist, I wanted our children to be born in a country that claims them as its own citizens. I did not wish for them to be stateless as their mother and father are. Had they been born in the Middle East, regardless of the country in which they are born, they will always be Palestinian refugees, and they will be stateless. Our three daughters were born in the greatest country on earth- United States of America. Reem (Kim) was born at Berkeley, Randa was born at San Francisco and Deena, though conceived in San Francisco, was born in Nashville, Tennessee. Unlike my wife and me, our children are bona fide American citizens as the United States is their country of birth.

Failing to land a position or a citizenship that would eventually facilitate my move back to the Middle East, was indeed a blessing in-disguise that I did not realize at the time. Things always happen for a reason. In this case, it was a very good reason. It was not meant for me to go back to the Middle East, but rather to ultimately become a citizen of the greatest country on earth. Thank you, America, for honoring my wife and me, by granting us the honor of American citizenship and passports.

BECOMING A PERMANENT RESIDENT OF THE UNITED STATES

THE FOLLOWING MORNING AFTER RECEIVING CONSUL LUTFY'S letter, and after abandoning the burning desire to move back to the Middle East, I decided to go to the United States Immigration and Naturalization Service office in

San Francisco to apply for immigration. The officer at the desk was very helpful and pleasant. He gave me an application and said, you should fill the application out and mail it back to us. I filled the application out and hand-delivered it the following day.

The same officer, who gave me the application form a day earlier, received my filled-out application. He read the information I provided and said, you will hear from us in due time. That 'due time' was very short, as a week later, I received a letter in the mail asking me to come for interview. The letter specified the date, time and place of the interview. The interview took a little over two hours. After the completion of the interview the officer said, "We need your and your wife's expertise" and you will hear from us in a few days. A week later, the "Green Card", for me and for my wife came in the mail along with my Selective Service Classification of 5A. It took only two weeks to become a legal immigrant to the United States. It took only two weeks to have our status of 'stateless' with no country to belong to be trashed forever and to have a new designation of 'Permanent Residents' of the United States of America! How about that! Our children did not need to have immigration status as they were born in the United State and are bona fide legitimate American citizens.

That Permanent Residency status which confirms the legal status, is the Green Card. It qualifies the holder of the Green Card to become a United States citizen after completing five years of living in the United States. The Green Card holder has all the rights and obligations as any other citizen including, of course paying taxes, with one exception of not voting in local and in national elections. Had my wife been an American citizen, then I would have qualified for the citizenship in three years. The same would be the case for my wife, should I have been an American citizen before marrying her.

While training in the clinical aspects of eye diseases in general and

With special attention Trachoma at the Proctor Foundation, Dr. Nadeem Haddad of the *American University of Beirut,* asked my supervisor as to when will Abdallah be ready to join his team at the *American University of Beirut.* My supervisor told him, most probably Dr. Isa will be ready in six months. Dr. Haddad followed the university rules in requesting an application form the Personnel department of the *American university of Beirut* sent to me as a first step in the employment process. As regulations go, the American University Personnel department complied with Dr. Haddad's request and sent me the employment application form to fill out and mail it back to Beirut.

In that application, there were explicit requirements in which the applicant must indicate his/her religious affiliation and their place of birth. Upon reading these two requirements a funny feeling crept into my spine that being Palestinian-born and of the Moslem faith would lead to the rejection of my application. With these two strikes against me, my application will never be acceptable. Confirmation of these fears came, in writing, from the *American University of Beirut* Personnel office telling me: "No Position is Available"! It appeared at this time that the jinx of the dual strikes, Palestinian and Moslem kept pace with me wherever I went. Five years later, I was, contacted by the dean of the Medical School at *AUB* requesting that I meet him in Chicago to discuss the possibility of me joining the faculty of the Medical School in Beirut. The Chairman of the department at the *American University of Beirut* wrote me back telling me that the dean was impressed with my qualifications and the job at *AUB* is a tossup between me and another candidate. Three weeks later, I got the news from the Personnel department, "No position is available". At the same time, I got a letter from the Chairman of the department telling me that the dean had offered the position to the other candidate, a Christian, who later declined the offer. When the position was offered to me again and after it was declined by the other candidate, I told the dean to look for another candidate, as I am not interested in his position!

A third time around when the position for the Chairmanship of the department of Microbiology and Immunology at the Medical School of the *American University of Beirut,* was open, I was asked to apply for that position. My application was again, rejected and the position was offered to another microbiologist whose resume did not compare with mine. He had no experience as a faculty member in a medical school and hospital environment and the number of his publications was about one fiftieth of mine, yet he was offered the position. Well he was a Christian Lebanese and I am a Moslem Palestinian! It appears that my Palestinian identity and my religious affiliation are still alive and well and may not suit the *American University of Beirut.* As usual, *AUB* keeps bombarding me with letters asking for money to help in their general and scholarship funds.

AUB policy of recruitment changes with the political atmosphere in the Middle East, in general and in Lebanon in particular. Armenians were the top priorities after World War I. With the influx of Palestinians after the1948 Catastrophe, both Moslems and Christians alike were, the choice for recruitment. After the 1975 civil war in Lebanon and the rise in the number of educated Shi'a, they became the candidates of choice for recruitment.

At the time of training in ophthalmic diseases at the Proctor Foundation of the *University of California Medical Center in San Francisco (UCSF)* campus, I met a Russian ophthalmologist who came from the Soviet Union for a short visit. While talking to him, I said, there is so much in common between the Russians and us Arabs. He got very agitated and angry. With a loud voice, jumped and almost hit me. He said, no we have nothing in common with you Arabs. I then realized that nobody holds any respect or love for the Arabs, not even the Soviets who were supposed to have been staunch supporters and allies of the Arab countries!

MOVING TO NASHVILLE, TENNESSEE

I HAD MADE MY MIND UP THAT I WANTED TO WORK IN AND DO BASIC and clinical research in academia, especially in a medical school and hospital environment. Because of my work on Trachoma, Dr. Roger Nichols of the *Harvard School of Public Health* asked me to come for an interview and give a talk about my *Trachoma* findings, in Boston. The Harvard position required that I spend six months in Boston and six months in Saudi Arabia as Harvard had a contract with the government of Saudi Arabia to diagnose and treat patients with *Trachoma,* as well as doing clinical research on the infection. *Trachoma,* a communicable disease that inflicts the eyes and if undetected and treated early, could ultimately lead to blindness. Trachoma was rampant in many parts of the Middle East including Saudi Arabia. The offer from *Harvard* did not appeal to me because of the terms that required me to spend six months of the year in Saudi Arabia away from my family. Because the offer was not palatable, I declined that offer and started looking for another position in the United States. Within few weeks of my decision to decline the Harvard offer, I was approached by a minority medical school in Nashville, Tennessee to join the ranks of its faculty. I was more inclined to accept that position as I was sympathetic to and felt an obligation to help disadvantaged people achieve their goals anyway I could! I felt identity with people of color who, like myself, are subjected to discrimination. I joined the minority Medical School faculty in July 1969.

We left San Francisco and drove from California to Nashville, a 2500-mile trip in one week. We would drive 400 miles a day and spend the night at a hotel. One of the wonders of the world lays in the state of Arizona. We drove from San Francisco south to Arizona to see the Grand Canyon, then north to Utah and then to Denver, Colorado. At the hotel swimming pool in Utah, one of the kids at the pool was calling the name Kim. Our daughter Reem answered the call. She told us, as of now my name will be Kim! She changed her name because she wanted to fit in with her peers with an American name and not with a foreign one!

TALE OF TWO CULTURES

MY WIFE AND I CAME FROM A CULTURE THAT IS QUITE DIFFERENT from the American one. We accepted any person, regardless of their name, looks, religious affiliation, accent or national origin. Here comes our first daughter who changed her name because she may have felt, a foreign name is not acceptable to her peers. She decided to change her name from Reem to Kim. That same daughter, although she never admitted it, but it was quite apparent from her behavior that she would rather prefer American parents, than having foreign-born parents. She preferred her mother, who has a lighter skin color than mine and not me to take her to school. Whenever this daughter and I went for a walk and upon seeing someone who knows her and happens to be walking by, she would leave me and go to the other side of the street. I thought she did not want others to know that she is associated with me, because I look foreign, with a foreign name and a 'funny' accent! Admittedly, I was very hurt, not only because she changed her name, but also by my feeling of rejection by my own daughter! I have always been proud of my heritage and wanted to instill this pride into our daughters. Of course, my desire was out of question with our first daughter who did not show any interest in the Arab culture. The middle daughter, Randa, was quite different from her older sibling. She, at the time, could not pronounce the word Arabian and instead she would say 'I am a radio' instead of saying I am Arabian! With time, children change their outlook towards their parents and become more accepting of their parents' ethnic background. As time went on our daughters Kim and Randa have become more secure and more accepting of the foreign origin of their father.

IMPORTANCE OF A SECOND OR MORE OPINIONS IN MEDICAL SITUATIONS

FEW MONTHS AFTER ARRIVING IN NASHVILLE, I STARTED HAVING A very intense pain in my Jaws. The pain was more pronounced and more intense when I had my coffee. One evening after having an after dinner, coffee the pain was so intense and intolerable that made me feel that the end is near. I sat with my wife and our three daughters on the porch and told them that I probably may have cancer. I want you all to be prepared for my departure from this world. I reminded the wife of what our assets were and told her to take care of herself and of our three daughters.

In the morning, I checked with my doctor who recommended that I have X-rays of my head to determine what is causing the pain. The Chairman of our Radiology department took no less than sixty-five X-ray images of different positions of my head. He sent the X-ray images to my doctor who in turn will evaluate the X-rays and inform me of the diagnosis. My doctor called me at nine o'clock, on a Sunday morning, and with a not so assuring voice said, I do not want your legs to shake, but you should come to my office immediately. Of course, his tone of voice and the urgency he had for me to come to his office on a Sunday morning suggested a very serious condition may be in place. It re-affirmed at least, in my own mind, of the thought that I must have cancer.

Upon meeting with my doctor on that Sunday morning, he showed me the X-ray images and pointed to a dark spot in one of the X-ray images of my head. He said this is a very suspicious spot and we must think seriously about starting radiation and chemotherapy. I said, but the spot in the X-ray image appears to be on the other side of my jaws and away from where the pain emanates from. Is it possible that the dark spot that we see, may be an artefact in the X-ray film? He said, it is possible, but to eliminate that possibility, we need to have more X-rays images taken. Indeed, after several X-ray images, the 'dark spot' disappeared completely and as a result, the possibility of cancer was trashed for now!

I then went to the dean of our Dental school requesting his help in evaluating my teeth, with special attention to the teeth that have gold crowns. Several X-ray images and no problem found because X-rays do not penetrate gold! Then one of our dental students, present at the time, suggested that since X-rays do not penetrate gold, perhaps we should drill into the gold crowns covering the molar teeth. The dean agreed and upon starting the drilling process, the burr went through the tooth so fast with no resistance. That suggested the tooth is completely gone and must be, extracted! It was a great relief as the pain was gone and no evidence of cancer, and now I am awarded a new lease on life!

ESTABLISHMENT OF A
CLINICAL CANCER RESEARCH LABORATORY

OUR MEDICAL SCHOOL OFFERED ME THE FREEDOM OF DOING research in any area of my own choosing. Because *Trachoma* was, essentially non-existent in the United States and pursing such a line of research requires access to clinical specimens, grant money to support the work and because there were no *Trachoma* patients at our hospital or any other hospital in town, it was difficult to get clinical specimens to pursue that line of research. I decided to drop the *Trachoma* research altogether and turned my attention into the area of cancer research. Clinical specimens were readily available from our hospital as we had patients inflicted with different kinds of cancer. In addition to my teaching load and hospital obligations, clinical research was my top priority. To pursue research in cancer, specialized equipment needed 'to be purchased. Several funding agencies were approached to fund such purchases. The first agencies that responded to my requests for funding were Fight for Sight and Research Corporation, which funded the purchase of a Zeiss fluorescence microscope and the United States National Institutes of Health (NIH), funded the purchase of a high speed, refrigerated centrifuge. The purchase of laminar flow hoods, for the use in cell culture, the Fraction Collector for the separation of cell fractions, obtained by sonic disruption of cancer cells and for the isolation of antibodies from the blood of cancer patients were all funded by NIH.

With the abundant availability of clinical specimens and funding, research on cancer was going quite smoothly. In addition to research on clinical specimens, another experimental cancer research project was established. This project involved the use of mice that were, inoculated into the peritoneal cavity, with a germ cell carcinoma. In addition to the research projects, I supervised the research of three Ph.D. students in my laboratory. I was averaging three to four scientific papers a year. The papers were, published in peer-reviewed journals. Notable among these scientific journals were the journal of Immunology, the Transplantation journal and the journal of Cancer Research.

(Sitting by the Zeiss Fluorescence microscope and contemplating the identity
the cancer cells I have seen. I have sought the expertise of the faculty of our
pathology department for help identifying the cell types)

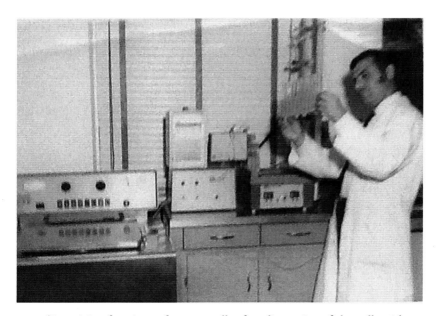

(Examining fractions of cancer cells after disruption of the cells with
ultrasonic waves)

Racism and bigotry are still alive and well in the United States. Laws, in the books, prohibiting racism and discrimination based on color, religion or national origin are important, but what is more important however, is not what is in the books, but rather what is in the hearts of people. Feelings of racism and discrimination that are in the heart appear to supersede those laws and regulations printed in the books! All of us, must weigh in what we say in public before we say it as we must be politically correct otherwise, a lawsuit may follow. Neither Blacks nor Whites are innocent of racism. Blacks are more vocal about it than Whites are. One of the white neighbors who befriended my wife used to come and visit our house almost every day, when she found out that I worked at a minority institution, not only she stopped visiting us, but would not even say hello to me if we ever cross paths at a store, a restaurant or somewhere else!

The move to Nashville from San Francisco was a cultural shock, to say the least. San Francisco is a lively and cosmopolitan metropolis while Nashville was nothing more than a little provincial town. Driving the main thorough- way, West End Avenue in Nashville, we could see only ads for Minnie Pearl southern fried chicken and Eddie Arnold southern fried chicken joints. There was one Spanish restaurant, La Vizcaya, which disappeared from existence two month after we landed in the town.

One major reason that influenced my decision to move to Nashville was, the social problems engulfing California and specifically the Bay area and the city of San Francisco. We lived in the University of California Medical Center student housing that was two blocks off the Haight-Ashbury district. This area of the city had become the headquarters of the Hippie movement and a mecca for run-away kids. It was wonderful at the beginning, because most of the Hippies were intellectuals who did not like the status quo in the country. They had great ambitions for social change. Within few months however, the Haight-Ashbury district, changed hands from the peaceful Hippies to the hard-core criminals. The district has become crime center USA, as there was at least one murder every night. To amplify my decision, to leave San Francisco, was the horrific scene of the Black Panthers marching in the streets with their loaded guns! I did not want our children to, live in a place and be exposed to danger, in a potentially dangerous environment.

Nashville has a confusing infrastructure. City planning for an old city did not compare with that of San Francisco where most of the streets in the city are laid in parallel to each other. It is next to impossible to find an address in Nashville when looking for the parallel street as a starting point. Further, it was difficult to find an address as store numbers do not appear on the storefront or for that matter, on the street signs. However, there were some exceptions as very few stores, in any one area that do have the street number on their doors. Although this does not compare with San Francisco, it however, reminds me so much of Beirut. To find an address in

Nashville, our best bet was to stop at a gas station and ask for directions to the address we are looking for. Gas stations, at the time, used to have maps of the city and the attendants were happy to help. Now this option has sublimed as gas stations have mini markets managed by temporary workers who have no idea where the streets are. This problem has been resolved, in part, as we have the Global Positioning System (GPS) that guide us to our intended destination.

A funny incident happened to us about a week after arriving in Nashville. We purchased our house to which we have not moved into yet. The house was in the suburban hills on the west side of the city. We drove to the area wanting to see the house, drove around and around, in circles, for two hours and got nowhere. We did not have any information about the house or the house number, other than the name of the street on which the house sits. Luckily, while driving around a police car crossed path with us. I honked my horn at the police car and the officer came to our rescue. I said, sorry to bother you sir, but we purchased a house in this neighborhood and cannot find it. It looks like we may have lost the house! He sarcastically asked, did you really lose the house? I said we sure did. After we gave him the street name, he said I, can show where the street is but cannot help you locate the house on the street as you have no house number! He asked us to follow him and he showed us where street was! Fortunately, there was the "SOLD" sign still sitting in the front yard of the house. The sign that said 'SOLD' in the front yard confirmed to us that the house with that "SOLD" sign is indeed the house we had purchased!

Driving in the streets of Nashville is a nightmare! There are too many traffic lights that were not and still are not synchronized. Traffic lights change at every block, which may be only few yards from the previous one. By contrast, traffic lights in San Francisco were, all synchronized. There was no problem at having to stop at the red light every few yards as the case is in Nashville.

MR. 'CLARK GABLE' IS VISITING NASHVILLE AND IS DINING AT OUR 'TAIL OF THE FOX" RESTAURANT

IS THIS TRUE? THE WAITRESS SERVING US WAS SHOCKED TO SEE ME AT the restaurant and went back to tell management "Mr. Clark Gable is here and we should all go to his table and welcome him". The whole crew, management, waiters and cooks of the restaurant came to the table and said,' Good evening Mr. Gable' and welcome to our restaurant. Of course, I played the game and pretended that I really was Clark Gable. One of the waitreses asked if I would prefer to go to the manager's office and have a drink on the house or you would rather stay at this table and the manager comes to you? I said, "Frankly my dear I don't give a damn". She yelled loudly saying, it is him, it is him, it is Clark Gable. I love your statement, the one you said in 'Gone with the Wind' movie, 'Frankly my dear, I don't give a damn'. I nodded with approval then said, what makes you think that I am Clark Gable? She said, your well-groomed hair style, glittery black hair and your Douglas mustache make you look like an exact copy of Mr. Gable. I thanked her and the rest of the employees at the restaurant and said, well I will take it as a complement. My Clark Gable look-alike look was, because I was using Bryll Cream, at the time, to give a glitter to my dark black hair!

Clark Gable, my favorite actor, was one of the most famous Hollywood stars. He was the legendary icon of Hollywood from the 1930s until his death in November 1, 1960. Mr. Gable was the leading man in several Hollywood movies, including 'Gone with the Wind' and 'Mogambo' among others. 'Gone With the Wind' is the movie in which he said his famous statement " Frankly My Dear, I don't Give a Damn". When I mentioned this legendary statement, the the waitrewss yelled louldly, it is him, it is him. It is Clark Gable! The guests at the restaurant, that evening, came to our table to greet the Hollywood supertstar! One of the customers shed some doubts about the authentacity of this 'fake Clark Gable' as not being the real Clark Gable who was a little taller! Yet another customer insisted that this is the real Clark Gable, who I met in Los Angeles three years earlier!

(Photo of my wife and me, the "fake Clark Gable", at Tail of the Fox restaurant in Nashville)

I used to think and believe that the Hollywood movie stars we saw in American movies, to be superhuman beings and do not belong to our cadre of people. My view was, turned upside down when I saw Cary Grant in Boston and Doris Day in San Francisco. They both looked like anyone of us terrestrial people. Later and through-out the years, I have had the pleasure of meeting, in person, several other movie stars including Johnny Mathis, Shirley MacLaine, Yul Brenner, Jerry Lewis, Neil Sedaka and of course, Tony Bennet. After all, I reckoned, no super humans exist on the place we call earth, but regular people with different gifts and talents.

Unlike Europe and San Francisco where the Downtown area is the most vibrant part of town bustling with people and activities, the downtown area in Nashville was essentially empty, as no people could be seen in the evenings except for some home-less individuals. It was scary as crime was rampant in that part of the town.

Tennessee's location, in the south of the United States suggests, it to be considered a South Eastern State. Up to the early 1960s, people of the northern states used to look down on the people of the southern states and described them as backward, poorly educated and with a funny accent. Thanks to the role of television and improved economic environments in the country that helped change that negative attitude. Since Tennessee is part of and is in the middle of the Bible Belt and as might be expected there are more churches per capita than any other place in the country and perhaps in the world. The first question southern people ask of outsiders is to which church you belong to? Several people asked us, as to which church we belonged and go to. Our response was always, we neither go nor do belong to any church. A southerner asked me the question: Which church do we go to or belong to and upon my response, he opened his eyes wide and said how dare you, not go to church? I told him we are Moslem and we neither belong to nor do we go to any church. That immediately made him believe that we may be a good catch and he should work hard at convincing us to convert to Christianity and to join their Baptist church. He said, after joining their church, we would be able to see the light that will pave our path to Heaven! I said, sorry but we are Moslem and have no intention of converting to Christianity or to any other religion or joining your church. Please do not waste your time on us. We will not abandon our faith and join yours or for that matter, to any other religion.

A week later and on a Sunday morning, this same man came with his wife, knocked at our door and demanded that my wife and I accompany them to church. I told him to please do not bother us and you can go to church and enjoy the sermon. This person was quite adamant and persistent in his demand that we go to church with them. I got so intimidated to the point that forced me to show him to the door. Even with that, he would not budge. I had to throw him and his wife out of our house. I have not seen their faces again!

Tennesseans are pleasant and welcoming people. Women in our neighborhood, organized a welcoming party for my wife with coffee and cake and offered her the opportunity to meet woman in the neighborhood.

The neighbors had another party for us when we became US citizens. They made us feel very much as a part of the community by welcoming us and by them saying 'you are now like us and are ones of us' that gave us a great sense of belonging to the community.

Things in the country have gone in the opposite direction, especially after Donald Trump was elected president of the Unite States, Well, I did vote for Trump, not because I liked him or liked his agenda, but simply because I had a dislike to Hilary Clinton. I normally judge politicians I vote for with respect to their stand on the Palestinian question. Well of course, with Trump's Middle East agenda and his very strong commitment to Israel, I felt that my vote for him was a wasted one.

Barak Obama, who I had voted twice for, did not do what he said he would do, regarding the Middle East and particularly to the Palestinian question. His actions were contrary to the promises he gave at Cairo University when he visited Egypt. Now before leaving office and to help Hilary Clinton in her 2016 presidential bid, his administration provided Israel with 38 billion dollars of our taxpayer money as a gift. It was intended to have Jewish and Christian right money and votes pour into the Clinton campaign.

With the presidential win by Mr. Trump, I among others was hopeful that he would have an even-handed approach to the Palestinian question. He instead, showed his true colors of being more of a Zionist than the Zionists themselves. He not only is 100% pro-Israel but is100% anti-Palestinian. He projected himself as the Christian liberator of the Jewish people at the expense of the oppressed Palestinians.

Mr. Trump's actions of moving the United States embassy from Tel Aviv to Jerusalem is a de-facto recognition of Jerusalem as the eternal capital of the Israeli State. His action in this regard is contrary to the United States government policy as the status of Jerusalem is concerned. Further, he recognized Israeli control of the Syrian Golan Heights. The latest action taken by the Trump administration, in the words that came out from secretary of state, Mike Pompeo's mouth that Israeli settlements, in the West Bank, are not in contradiction of international law, thus they are not illegal! What a farce! All these statements, and actions by the Trump administration, are intended to appease the Christian right and neocons to support Trumps campaign for a second term, come November 2020.

Mr. Trump, in addition to cancelling $200 million of the $500 million the United States offers the Palestinian Authority, he is trying to close any avenue that helps the Palestinians, by doing his best to close the United Nations Relief and Works Agency (UNRWA) that supports Palestinian refugees.

Looking deeper into Mr. Trump's chaotic actions and saying something today and saying or doing the opposite tomorrow, gives the impression that either he or his advisors are amateurish when it comes to foreign policy, or perhaps they are learning by trial and error.

Mr. Trump has embraced the Christian right (the neocons) agenda implementing the Evangelists principles when it comes to religious ethnicity. His ban on people from six Moslem countries, from entering the United States, proves he is subservient to the evangelical group to which his Vice president Pence belongs.

His love for Israel and doing his utmost to support it, stems from those evangelical doctrines that say Jesus Christ will come when the state of Israel is in existence. Well, Moslems also believe, Jesus Christ will come at the end of the world and clean the mess we are in.

While Republicans, in general are Christian and hold conservative views on world affairs among other things, Jews on the other hand are more liberal in their views. Love of Republicans for Israel seems to suggest that conservative Christians and Liberal Jews appear to be strange bed fellows as both share in the love and support of Israel.

Is this love and support of Israel by Republicans true and genuine because of the coming of Jesus Christ or they may have another hidden agenda? Is it conceivable that the hidden agenda the Republicans hold relates to encouraging Jews to leave or forcing them to leave the Christian West to the country they call Israel? Should we ever 'forget the Nazis were right wingers as the Republicans claim to be? Wasn't Hitler's agenda and hate of the Jews a rightwing agenda? Doesn't the love the rightwing Republicans hold for Israel suggest that since the Jews have their own country, they should live in it and not in the Christian West? Of course, nobody dares to openly mumble a dislike or hate of the Jews, as they will be immediately accused of being anti-Semitic, a title that is a passport to character assassination. As recent as November 2019, the Pastor of the Flowing Streams Church of Christ, in Florida, the 'reverend' Rick Wiles defied the odds and came out in the open accusing the Jews of trying to take over the United States. In his far right, TruNews website, 'reverend' Wiles said, "There will be a Purge when Jews take over our country, they will kill millions of Christians'. These accusations of the Jewish conspiracy to take over the United States, by a rightwing pastor, were in response to the Donald Trump Impeachment proceedings, led by the United States Congressional Judiciary Committee Chair, Mr. Adam Schiff, who is Jewish. Does the purge 'reverend' Wiles is referring to echo the purge Palestinians went through when the Jews took over Palestine? Attacks on Jews and Jewish establishments are on the rise in the United States and in western Europe. The love for Israel, and hate of the Jews, stems from the Christian West's desire to get rid of the Jews and send them off to live in Israel. This is a spell for the Jews in the West and a bonanza for Israel. Of course, it also is, a bad omen for the Palestinians as support of Israel by the West will never stop!

Do these emerging historical facts of the rightwing and neocon hatred of the Jews and love for Israel not give credence in support of what I suggested that Israel is a Clearing House for the Jews as the Western conservatives want? Does anyone entertain the validity of this hidden agenda? Only time will tell.

Now considering that the Christian West's beloved Israel is in existence and Jews are encouraged to immigrate to it, thus making it a 'Clearing House' for the Jews brings three possibilities come to mind:

1. How long will Israel survive, considering it is surrounded by over a half billion potential enemies? Will the Christian West come to the rescue should a war break out ending with the defeat of Israel?

2. On the other hand, should Israel be defeated in the war, will such a defeat bring the 'Final Solution' to the Jewish problem as Hitler wanted?

3. Should Israel win the war and prevail, what would its relationship with the Christian West be? I believe, a Moslem/Jewish alliance will emerge with the intention of standing up to the Christian West, who both allege as the 'Infidels'!

Having been a United States Citizen for almost fifty years, I never was harassed or told to go to the home where I came from. Unfortunately, things have changed after Mr. Trump was, elected president of the United States.

Phone harassments are a daily occurrence. Callers call from phone numbers from almost all area codes in the country. The phone rings and nobody answers. Thanks to the caller ID that records the caller's number and sometimes along with the caller's name. I tried to call these people back, the response is "the number you are calling is not in service" or "the number you have called is not in existence"! One of the callers said, "Hello grandpa", when I ask for his name he would hang up. I have blocked scores, close to 200, of these harassing phone numbers. Yet another caller, who happened to be in Tennessee, somehow got hold of my cell number. When I answered the call, no response from the other end. When I called the number back, this person denied he called me! The same number that called my cell number, another time, was a woman. When she denied that she had called my number, I reminded her that the caller ID does not tell lies and it is she who is the liar! It seems there exists a well-coordinated national campaign by some groups, whose function is to harass people of different names and ethnicity. Thank you, president Trump, for your great efforts in paving the way for the potential of hate crimes against your fellow Americans.

MISTAKEN IDENTIFY OF OMAR AL-SHARIF

YEARS AFTER THE WAITRESSES AND STAFF AT *TAIL OF THE FOX* RESTAU-rant in Nashville, saw 'Clark Gable' at the restaurant, and while attending the wedding of a friend's son, a woman at the wedding was yelling loudly, Omar, Omar, ran to me and gave me a bear hug. She said, I am honored to meet you, Mr. Omar el-Sharif in person! I loved you when I saw you the first time in the movies "Lawrence of Arabia" with Peter O'toole and in "Funny Girl" with Barbara Streisand. Well, as I grew older with a few gray strands of hair appearing in my head, my looks must have morphed from those of Clark Gable into the image of Omar al-Sharif! This new Omar al-Sharif image, as seen by this lady, reminded me of when as a teenager, a friend of my sister's told her, your brother's looks favor those of Omar al-Sharif.

SCIENTIFIC ACHIEVEMENTS

IN THE MEANTIME, WHILE AS A FACULTY MEMBER AT THE MEDICAL school I was, elected to membership in several elite scientific societies, including but not limited to, The American Association of Immunologists (AAI), the Transplantation Society (TS), the European Dialysis and Transplant Association (EDTA), the American Society for Microbiology (ASM) and the Lebanese Immunological Society (LIS) among others.

It is customary, among scientists, to present their research findings at different institutions and at different scientific meetings. In the summer of 1971. I was, invited to participate in, and report on my research findings, on cancer at the University College in London and at the European Dialysis and Transplant Association Congress held in East Berlin.

In addition, I presented my work on cancer at the International Congress of Immunology in Paris, the Institute of Cancer research in Chicago, the Institute of Clinical Immunology in Bern Switzerland, the Ministry of Health of Iraq, in Baghdad and the European Institute of Experimental Immunology, University of Zurich, Switzerland.

Success may lead to problems along the way. My publications record, averaging 3-4 scientific papers a year, election to membership in elite scientific societies and other scientific achievements, prompted the dean of our medical school, Dr. Ralph Cazort, to announce at the monthly meeting of the faculty of the medical school by saying, "Dr. Abdallah M. Isa, is the most prolific writer at our medical school". This announcement, by the dean during the faculty meeting, did not sit well with some of my black colleagues because I am a non-Minority individual, foreign-born with a different name, different religious faith and of course, a different accent. The announcement by the dean created a feeling of jealousy and sometimes hatred and rejection of me by these individuals. In fact, some even spread false and negative rumors with the intent of damaging my reputation.

Having lived for six years in California, we have established some roots and would pay visits to San Francisco and the Bay area at least once a year. The visits to California were in a sense intended to re-charge our batteries! Upon our visits to California, and in addition to calling on old friends, I went to my alma mater, the *University of California Medical Center (UCSF) at San Francisco,* to pay visits to some of my former professors. When I stopped by my former mentor, Dr. Jawetz's office to say hello, I was surprised at his cool reception and more so, when he said, 'I understand you are becoming a well-travelled scientist'. I said, what do you mean? Then he reminded me of the International meeting at Harvard Medical School where he and I were, invited to present our research findings on Chlamydia. He further mentioned my presentations on cancer research work in East Berlin and in other places. The look on his face and the tone of his voice gave me the impression that he was not only surprised and never expected that I am, capable of attaining such scientific status. I started to speculate as to what his motive really was. Is it jealousy or he was trying to re-affirm that I am his junior and have a long way to achieve and attain his scientific standing. I said, it is true but keep in mind that credit belongs to you, as you were my mentor who trained me to become the scientist I am. You had prepared me to reach the scientific level I am at now and I thank you for all your help!

I stopped by to see Dr. Speck, another former professor in the department who was good at telling stories. One of the stories he told was about an AIDS patient who came for treatment at the hospital and who admitted, to have acquired the HIV virus through the shooting of drugs. To treat this patient by intravenous injection, none of his veins was adequate except of the one in his genital area!

A third professor that I stopped by to see was Dr. Carlyn Halde who taught us Mycology and Mycotic diseases. Unlike Dr. Jawetz, Dr. Halde was very pleasant, complementary and proud of my scientific achievements. She came by to visit, in Nashville, a couple of years later where we sat and reminisced about the good old days when I was, a student at the *University of California Medical Center in San Francisco.*

On a second trip to San Francisco, I avoided visiting Dr. Jawetz, but headed straight to Dr. Speck's office. I was saddened and shocked when the secretary told me that Dr. Speck had passed on a month earlier!

From San Francisco, my wife and I traveled east, across the Bay Bridge to the *University of California Berkeley* campus. I went to see my former mentor in the department of Microbiology and Immunology, Dr. Ben Papermaster, who I have developed a sense of friendship with him and considered him to be a good friend and confidante. We chatted for a couple hours and he was complementary and expressed his pride in me for my scientific and academic achievements.

After my meeting with Dr. Papermaster, my wife and I strolled through the Berkeley campus looking for any familiar faces that we may recall. We spotted one of the former friends, an Egyptian student, who had been at the university for at least ten years. I asked him if he had received his doctorate yet, his response was a muted, not yet!

(Laila and I took a picture right under the Sather gate on the *University of California* Berkeley campus)

SCIENTIFIC PRESENTATION IN A COMMUNIST COUNTRY

I WAS INVITED TO PRESENT MY WORK ON CANCER AT THE EUROPEAN Dialysis and Transplant Association Congress that was scheduled to take place in East Berlin in the summer of 1971. I did not have the American passport at the time, as I have not been a citizen yet. I had to use my travel document issued by the government of Lebanon for Palestinian refugees to apply for a travel document from the United States government. To allow me to re-enter the United States, after visiting a communist country, I was issued "a white passport", a travel document issued by the government of the United States to facilitate travels of permanent residents to and from the country. I flew from Rome to West Berlin and from there crossed to East Berlin through the Brandenburg gate.

East Berlin, a beautiful city that still showed the ruins and destruction caused to its infrastructure during World War II. It is ruled by the communists. It was a very scary police state. Food at the hotel was plentiful and very cheap according to our standard in the United States. A three-course dinner with a band playing music cost only $2. Of course, very few East Germans could afford eating out, as their income was very meager. There was a resident Texan, who claimed to be a well-heeled communist in East Germany. He was sent to welcome us and tell us about the great things one enjoys living under a communist regime!

There was no way to avoid feeling the pressures imposed by the communist regime on its people. A waiter at the restaurant would ask me several times during dinner, if I have any dollars. I always said no I do not. He was very persistent in asking if I have dollars every evening at dinner. His annoying persistence forced me to threaten him by going to the authorities and said to him, should you continue bothering me by asking me if I have dollars, I will call the police. Who knows, this waiter could be one of those several undercover agents of the East German Stassi.

PROBLEMS ENCOUNTERED WITH THE AUTHORITIES AT THE ROME AIRPORT

THE PLAN WAS, FOR THE WHOLE FAMILY, TO FLY FROM NASHVILLE TO New York to Rome where the family and I would split. The plan was that the family take connecting flight to Beirut and I board a flight to Berlin. We booked our flights on Alitalia airlines from New York JFK airport to Rome and on Middle East airlines from Rome to Beirut for the family and on Alitalia flight from Rome to West Berlin for me. The Alitalia plane was, delayed for seven hours at JFK airport in New York which meant my family and I already have missed our connecting flights from Rome. Since my wife and I were not American citizens yet, we could use the travel document issued to us by the Lebanese government to travel internationally. Our three daughters had American passports, as they were bona fide American citizens by the fact they were born in the United States. The Italian Security at the Rome airport said, the girls can go to the city, but my wife and I will have to spend the night at the airport to catch our connecting flights the following day. There was, a problem of communications as neither any of the Italian security agents at the airport spoke any English, nor my wife or I spoke any Italian. Our youngest daughter was only a year and a half old at the time.

I asked the Police chief, at the airport, as to how will he allow separation of a very young baby from her mother? Is this the Italian system of family and human tradition? These, back and forth, arguments went on for at least three hours. I said, sir since Alitalia airlines is the Italian government flagship and Alitalia flight was delayed for seven hours before leaving New York City and as a result, of this delay, we missed our connecting flights. It is not our fault, but rather it is that of Alitalia's. He accepted my explanation, and offered us a night stay, at no charge, at one of Rome's hotels with food and taxicab from and to the airport paid for by Alitalia airlines.

The following morning, my wife and children boarded the Middle East airlines flight to Beirut and I boarded an Alitalia flight from Rome to West Berlin. At the airport, in West Berlin, I was issued a visa to enter West Germany that allowed me to cross from West Berlin to East Berlin through the Brandenburg gate.

The meeting of the Congress of the European Dialysis and Transplant Association (EDTA) started the following day after arriving in East Berlin. The organizers of the congress did a great job trying to make the meeting a success. The East Germans went the extra mile to make the European and one 'American' guest, feel at ease! They welcomed us in open arms and planned entertainment programs to entertain us every evening until the congress was over. At the hotel, a large portrait of Angela Davis, was hanging on the wall behind the Reception desk, and a pad and pen placed on the desk asking visitors to sign the petition to "Free Angela Davis"!

(Photo of me presenting my work on cancer at the EDTA Congress in
East Berlin in 1971. All participants and attendees at the congress, except for
one American, were Europeans)

A week later, when the meeting of the European Dialysis and Transplant
Association congress in East Berlin was over, I tried to cross the border to West
Berlin and head to the airport to catch a flight to Frankfurt and from there to catch a
flight to Beirut to reunite with my wife and children. Standing in line for clearance by
security to leave, and when my turn came, I handed my travel document to the official.
He yelled in a loud and stern voice (the German way), HALT! He ordered me back
to the waiting room. I inquired as to what the problem was and as to why I cannot

leave. I was, told that my stay on West German soil has expired over a week ago, thus I am not allowed to re-enter West Germany. I was, told my visa was granted for only nine hours to stay in West Germany. What can I do? They said I, can either go back to East Berlin and board the *Interflug*, the East German airline, or take a flight from West Berlin to any other country in Europe. The *Interflug* airline, they said, flies only to Baghdad once a week and on Thursdays only. That will be three days from now, or you can take a flight to London or Paris from West Berlin, but you cannot land in any place in West Germany. Of course, as far as I was concerned, neither taking the *Interflug* nor taking any flight from Berlin to another European city was an option. After five hours of back and forth negotiating and arguing with the West German authorities, yet the problem was not resolved. I requested and obtained a meeting with the chief of security at the airport. I explained to him the situation and the dilemma I am in. I told him, I neither speak nor read German to find out that my visa to stay on West German soil was only for nine hours. Because I was issued a visa on my travel document that was issued by the government of Lebanon and was also provided with the "white passport", a travel document that permits re-entry to the United States after vising a communist country, I suggested that he grant me a visa on the "white passport' as a way out of the dilemma. He felt very sorry for me and said, I could pay five German marks, the fees for the new visa, and I can board a flight from West Berlin to Frankfurt. I said I, will be more than happy to pay the visa fees and I thank you for allowing me to legally 'enter' the country.

My trip to East Germany through West Germany, coincided with the unfortunate airplane hijacking, phenomenon of the early 1970s. The fact that I had a travel document stating that I am a Palestinian raised a red flag, and rightly so, with the German authorities. Of course, they could have denied me admission into the country altogether, but the 'white' passport that was issued to Permanent residents, by the United States Immigration and Naturalization Service, helped me obtain a German visa on my Lebanese-issued travel document. The 'white passport' saved my neck and gave the German authorities reason not to suspect me of being a terrorist or deny me a visa to enter their country.

Well, after spending one week in East Berlin I flew to Frankfurt and from there went on my last leg by boarding Middle East airlines flight to Beirut to reconnect with my wife and children.

European countries, unlike in the United States, have convenient facilities at International Airports. Passengers can have a shower and freshen up prior to boarding flights to their intended destinations. When I paid the fees to have a shower, the attending women at the Frankfurt airport asked me, in a crude and stern way, as to what my nationality is. I said, American. She said no you are not American. She believed me only after I pulled my 'white passport'. After that, she changed her tone of voice and asked if I needed to go to the Red district where husbands drive their wives to work as prostitutes! I said thanks for the suggestion, but I am not interested.

After arriving at the Beirut International Airport and going through security, the officer asked me as to how long I have been away. I said eight years. He looked at me with disgust, and scorned me with a shameful look and said, you stay away for eight years without visiting your country? Shame on you! This officer gave me a new shot in the arm and gave me the feeling of belonging to Lebanon, a feeling I never had before.

A couple of days later, I went to run some errands, and someone yelled by calling my name. I looked around and it was my cousin Suleiman. He was sitting with the other cousin Darwish at the coffee shop as they were waiting for Darwish's older brother, Adel, to be done with his haircut.

Adel asked me to help bring Darwish to the United States. I said, I am sorry I cannot do that, as the United States laws are very clear in this regard. Further. I am not a citizen yet. Even if I were a citizen, I cannot sponsor him because the law specifies that only immediate family members (parents, grandparents, sisters, brothers, children and even foster children), can be sponsored by an American citizen to come to and live in the United States. However, I possibly can bring your half-brother Adnan, as he has a university degree and he could possibly work with me in my laboratory at the medical school. Darwish did not even have a high school diploma! So, how can I bring him over?

Adel was very upset with my response and immediately said, Adnan does not need your help, he can go the United States on his own! I said that is fine, we will wait and see. Three years later, I received a card from cousin Darwish with a Washington DC address. I immediately called him to find out where he is and what he is doing and if he needed any help. He said I do not need your help! I have come to the United States for a visit. I got a visitor's visa through a Palestinian man who I met in Beirut. This person works at the Iraqi embassy in Washington, DC. He promised to help me find a job at the embassy. Indeed, he got a job as a night guard at the Iraqi embassy that provided him with a salary, living quarters, health and other benefits. This was the job he had never dreamed of having before!

Well, that is good news I said! Apparently, he liked the United States and wanted to stay and live here. He kept demanding that I sponsor him for the United States citizenship. I said that is impossible. How can I? For me to sponsor you, I must comply with the rules and laws of the United States government. The law states that an American citizen can sponsor a brother, a sister, a father, a mother, a son or daughter. Since you do not belong to any one of these categories, even if I try to sponsor you my application of sponsorship will be rejected,

Few months after he arrived in the United States and working as a night guard at the embassy, a fire broke out engulfing the whole embassy building. After the fire was put out, an investigation as to the cause of the fire followed. The investigators found out Darwish, the night guard at the embassy, was an illegal alien with no authentic papers to support his stay in the country. Based on the results of the investigation he was ordered to leave the country and was deported back to Lebanon. When I saw Darwish, in Lebanon few years later, he told me he was planning to come to the United States to kidnap his son and bring him back to Lebanon. I tried to dissuade him that his outlandish scheme is doomed to failure. I said he better abandon his plans for the simple reason the United States is not Lebanon and it is next to impossible for him to enter the country especially after he had been deported. Further, it is in the best interest of your son to stay in the country of his birth rather than him coming to Lebanon and live a miserable life as a refugee.

ACQUIRING CITIZENSHIP OF THE UNITED STATES

IN JUNE 1973, I RECEIVED A LETTER FROM THE UNITED STATES Immigration and Naturalization Service, specifying the date and time of my interview for the citizenship. This interview was five years after I became a permanent resident of the United States. Prior to my interview, two of my colleagues, one black and one Jewish were interviewed first. The interviewer was a white male in his mid to late fifties. He had a receding forehead and wore half-frame glasses and had several questions to ask me:

Interviewer:	Are you married
Me:	Yes sir
Interviewer:	Which colleges did you go to?
Me:	American University of Beirut, University of California at Berkeley and the University of California Medical Center in San Francisco
Interviewer:	Do you have any children? If so, how many
Me:	Yes sir, we have three daughters
Interviewer:	Are you or have you ever been a communist?
Me:	No sir

Interviewer:	Do you drink alcohol?
Me:	Socially, sir
Interviewer:	Should a war break out between the United States and your Country, will you ever bear arms against the United States of America?
Me:	I laughed loudly and said, I have no country sir, if I have a country and I do not, I will say with absolute confidence that I will never bear arms to fight the United States. I could see and feel he was happy with my answers, as he was smiling throughout the interview.
	Additional to his smiles I noticed he, also has an Intrinsic, sense of humor he had exhibited throughout the interview.
	His demeanor gave me the sense of confidence that he, not only liked my answers, but also liked me as a person.
	Now that I have realized he is, blessed with a sense of Humor, I started to have the feeling of easiness towards his questions.
	He then moved to ask his last question:
Interviewer:	With a big and shy smile on his face asked: Do you cheat on your wife?
Me:	Occasionally sir (with a big smile on my face) suggesting I was kidding and what I said not to be true
Interviewer:	Now, he dropped his half-frame glasses down his nose and said, "Don't we all"? Then very big and reassuring smiles appeared on both of our faces were, followed by a loud laugh.

Apparently, the interview went well as we got a letter, a month later, advising us of a meeting with the federal judge to receive our Naturalization papers. This is the difference between the sound thinking by, Americans as opposed to the skewed and screwed up way of thinking by the governments in the Middle East, The Middle Eastern governments, think the Palestinians, especially the educated ones, are a problem that has the potential of being a threat to their regimes and their own survival. What a shame!

THE OIL BOOM OF THE 1970S AND THE UNFORTUNATE EXPERIENCE WITH THE STATE OF TENNESSEE GOVERNMENT

DURING THE OIL BOOM IN THE MIDDLE EAST IN THE MID 1970'S AND the burning desire of American business to join in, I was appointed by the Governor of the State of Tennessee, Mr. Ray Blanton, as his personal consultant for the Middle East in 1975. At the same time, the executive vice president at our institution, Dr. Ralph Hines, jumped in and asked me to help establish a link between our medical school, other medical schools and ministries of Health in the Middle East.

During one of my trips to Baghdad I, called on some of my old Iraqi friends who were classmates at *AUB*, to reminisce on our good old days in college. One of the friends asked me as to what my travel plans were. I said I am leaving Baghdad in a few days to go to Kuwait. He then asked me if I would hand deliver a letter to his friend, the former Minister of Education of Kuwait. I said I, will be more than happy to do that for you after I arrive in Kuwait in about three days.

When I met the former Minister of Education at his home, he asked me as to what I would like to drink. I said a soft drink if available, otherwise I will have a glass of water. He said, no, no, come with me and we both went to his bar. His bar was, well stocked with top brands of scotch, bourbon, vodka and other fancy alcoholic beverages.

He tried to convince me that I should move to Kuwait and work as a professor at the *Kuwait University School of Medicine*. He made plans for me to meet with the dean of the medical school, a Singapore-born Kuwaiti, who in turn invited me to dinner at one of the fancy restaurants in the city. Well, since alcohol was supposed to be 'illegal' to be sold and prohibited from consumption by Moslems in the country, Christians, on the other hand were permitted to purchase a limited number of bottles of liquor per month from only one designated and government approved supplier.

The medical school dean brought his bottle of scotch in a brown bag to the restaurant and hid it under the table. He then asked, for a mixer to mix with the scotch as a make-believe it is a soft drink and not an alcoholic drink!

While in Kuwait, I paid a visit to the minister of Health of Kuwait, Dr. Abdel Rahman al-Awadi, who I met earlier and developed friendly relationship with him in Geneva, Switzerland during the World Health Organization meeting. He was my first choice to establish a possible link between his Ministry and our medical school. Negotiations went on for over a year then Dr. al-Awadi sent a delegation of "experts" from his Ministry to come to Nashville and check out our facilities at the medical school. Apparently, their report to the Minister was favorable and based on that report, he agreed to send Kuwaiti students to learn English first and then to enroll in our school of Medicine. Indeed, seventeen Kuwaiti students came to Nashville and enrolled in the English class.

At that time, we did not have telephones in our offices except for one installed in the departmental office. Should we receive any calls, the secretary would alert us, by coming to our office, telling us to come to the department office to answer the phone call! Dr. Ralph Hines, the executive vice president at our institution, saw an opportunity in my ability to negotiate with the minister of Health of Kuwait for a long-term agreement between our school of Medicine and his Ministry of Health. He had a black telephone receiver installed in my office and a telephone line with permission to place long distance and international calls. That "black box", as I used to call it, which was installed in my office, created more problems and heightened the jealousy with some of my colleagues, especially the black ones. Some of the faculty started to complain and spread damaging rumors and false innuendos about Dr. Isa and his close relationship with the school's administration.

Dr. Ralph Hines, the executive vice president at our institution, was a very ambitious administrator. He wanted Kuwait to pay our Medical school sixty million dollars for training Kuwaiti students in Medicine and Dentistry. He asked me to negotiate with Dr. Abdul Rahman al-Awadi, the Minister of Health of Kuwait, for the sixty million dollars deal. Dr. Al-Awadi thought sixty million dollars was too steep a sum to pay. He, however, kept the door open for further negotiations in our future meetings.

As a consultant to the governor of the State of Tennessee and now as a member of the Tennessee trade delegation, and prior to embarking on the Tennessee trade mission to the Middle East, I sought the help of my friend, Dr. Clovis Maksoud to, identify a company or a group in Lebanon that has good experience in international trade. Dr. Maksoud recommended a Lebanese company headed by Mr. Ibrahim el-Hibri. I contacted Mr. el-Hibri by phone and discussed with him the possibility of identifying business people and outfits in the Middle East that can become business partners with businesses in the State of Tennessee. Mr. el-Hibri got excited about the offer and the new opportunity. He organized a Lebanese delegation who came to Nashville. To impress the governor, Mr. el-Hibri brought in eight people who he had flown into Nashville, as representatives of his company, from different parts of the world! The show was quite impressive. The governor arranged for a Tennessee business delegation to be headed by his commissioner of Economic and Community Development, Mr. Tom Benson and his assistant Miss Pat Burns. Now as a bona fide and recognized consultant to the governor of the State of Tennessee, I was asked to accompany the Tennessee Business delegation to travel to different countries in the Middle East. Our itinerary included visits to Egypt, Lebanon, Qatar, the United Arab Emirates, Iraq and Iran. To my surprise, Saudi Arabia was not included in the list of countries for our delegation to visit.

Upon landing in Beirut, we were driven to the Excelsior hotel to check in and rest after a long flight from the United States. The following day we were welcomed by Mr. Ibrahim el-Hibri, head of the Lebanese group and a couple more members of his company.

(My photograph with Mr. Ray Blanton, Governor of the
State of Tennessee, after appointing me as his personal Consultant
for the Middle East)

(Photo of the Lebanese delegation with the governor of the State of Tennessee. From left: Mr. Tom Benson, Commissioner of the Tennessee Department of Community and Economic Development, third from left is me, fifth from left, Governor Blanton. sixth, Dr. Clovis Maksoud, seventh, Mr. Ibrahim el-Hibri in a white suit, Head of the delegation of the Lebanese group)

A day after the arrival of the Tennessee business delegation in Beirut, I had a meeting with Mr. el-Hibri to discuss the next steps for the delegation to take and to provide me with the schedules we should follow while visiting the different countries. I requested the list of the officials in each of the different countries we are to meet with so that I could share the information with our Tennessee business delegation. It was my responsibility to update the Tennessee business delegation and to keep them informed on the plans and to provide them with the names and titles of each official to meet Mr. el-Hibri was stalling in providing any information, but instead his office in Beirut, arranged a social outing for the Tennessee Delegation to the *Casino du Liban* (Casino of Lebanon). The outing to the Casino was another means to impress the Tennessee delegation by the Lebanese company.

At the meeting I held, in Beirut, with Mr. el-Hibri, I felt he was not forthcoming in giving me any information or details as to the programs or the schedules they have prepared for the Tennessee delegation to follow. His demeanor was different from the one he showed me in our previous conversations and at an earlier meeting in Beirut.

(Photo of the Tennessee Business Delegation at the *Casino du Liban* {Casino of Lebanon}. Seated from left is Commissioner Benson and his assistant, Miss Pat Burns on the right with me sitting next to her)

I speculated Mr. Tom Benson, the Commissioner of the Tennessee Economic and Community Development Department who headed the Business delegation and who I had great respect and admiration for, may have asked Mr. el-Hibri, not to deal with Dr. Isa and to have him marginalized. The commissioner may have had other plans. The commissioner may have wanted to have his department reap the credit accrued for any business consummated with the Middle East. These were only speculations on my part with no hard evidence to support their validity. My marginalization, by Mr. el-Hibri was realized and confirmed at our meetings with Syrian and Kuwaiti contacts. The Syrian and Kuwaiti contacts not only did not acknowledge my presence, but completely ignored me as a member of the visiting delegation. My marginalization was further confirmed after coming back from our extended Middle East trip to Nashville, as I was completely left in the dark as to what is going on.

Back in Nashville, the Lebanese delegation had several meetings and parties with their Tennessee counterpart with none of which was I, invited to participate in. I felt I was completely out of the picture and was no longer a member of the Tennessee delegation.

Ignored by both the Tennessee and the Lebanese groups, I was watching the events unfolding on the sideline. Since never was I asked to join any of the meetings or take part in any activities or parties, confirmed that I was completely marginalized and left out of any activity. I wrote a letter to the governor to bring him up-to-date on our activities and lodged a complaint about the marginalization and treatment. In my letter of complaint to the governor,

The governor never responded to my complaint, but I got the message when I crashed a party that the Tennessee and Lebanese groups were having at the Hyatt Regency hotel. When the commissioner spotted me in the lobby, he said, how dare you complain to the governor? I asked him as to how did he know that I complained to the governor since I did not copy you on the letter? He responded by saying that the governor was upset with the behavior of his department. I said, you know it was I, who initiated the whole thing for the establishment of the Tennessee Trade Delegation in the first place. I was the one who convinced Governor Ray Blanton about the importance and feasibility of trying to secure business for the state. He then requested my help to have the State of Tennessee do business in the Middle East and appointed me as his special consultant for the Middle East. Here is my card showing "special consultant to the governor" sir, as a proof of my appointment.

Of course, I was kept in the dark as to what was happening as far as the business collaboration between the State of Tennessee and the Lebanese group. To my big surprise and bewilderment, something must have gone terribly wrong when the collaborative agreement between the Tennessee and the Lebanese groups fell through and now was destined for suspension.

Two weeks later, it became clear to me that serious disagreements must have occurred, and problems arose between the Lebanese group and their Tennessee hosts. A fight had erupted between the two groups with accusations flying in both directions. Now each party went its own way and the whole ordeal was over. The Tennessee business delegation did not sign a single contract with any Middle Eastern government or business group.

The cost of travel and entertaining the Lebanese delegation was high. The whole affair was a poorly executed adventure with no business transactions to show for.

Disagreements and fighting between the two groups ended the relationship that led to a divorce, so to speak, between the Tennessee government and the Lebanese business delegation. It cost the Tennessee taxpayers hundreds of thousands of dollars, spent to finance such a delegation to travel to different countries in the Middle East and to entertain the Lebanese delegation in Nashville. Of course, there was also a tremendous cost to the Lebanese delegation due to travel and other expenses, as they landed no business from Tennessee. They had to go home empty handed. That was, the end of the Tennessee-Middle East business ambitions that our governor had envisioned!

What was more amazing and quite surprising, was both parties, the Tennessee and the Lebanese group started to befriend me again after their breakup. Both parties wanted my advice and direction for securing business in the Middle East and in the United States. My response to both groups was to get lost and find you another consultant you can mess up with in the future!

After the breakup between the Tennessee government and the Lebanese group, Commissioner Benson and I became close friends and shared our common interests as to how to go about reaching these interests. Commissioner Benson suggested that I join and become an employee of the Tennessee Economic and Community department. I was saddened to hear that Commissioner Benson passed on recently in 2019.

BUSINESS ADVENTURE WITH PFIZER MEDICAL SYSTEMS

AT THE TIME OF THE VIBRANT BUSINESS ACTIVITIES IN THE MIDDLE East I was, granted the distribution rights for the Pfizer Medical Systems for several countries in the Middle East. The crown jewel of Pfizer Medical systems was the ACTA Scanner, a head and whole body, tomographic scanner. Doing business, by a foreign company in the Middle East requires the appointment of a local agent who will be recognized, by the government as the sole representative of the foreign company.

I had appointed 'The Scientific Office' as our agent in Syria and another in Lebanon and tried to appoint another agent in Saudi Arabia. The Saudi office manager demanded 25% of the sale price of the ACTA Scanner to be paid in advance of any sales: 10% for him and 15% to bribe government (ministry of health) officials who will then recommend the purchase of such equipment for the different hospitals in the country. I said, I have no objection to providing you with 10% commission, but will not honor the 15% bribe funds, as it is illegal in the United States. The penalty for bribes is tens of thousands of dollars and up to ten years in jail. I am neither ready to pay penalties nor willing to face jail terms. That resulted in the loss of potential orders from Saudi Arabia.

The Syrian agent made, arrangements for me to speak to the medical staff of the Ministry of Health and to show them what the ACTA scanner can do in diagnosing cancers and other medical conditions.

The group was impressed with the presentation and I got the impression that the purchase of at least five ACTA scanners will follow within a matter of weeks. I realized later that this was a false impression when I found out that our appointed agent in Syria and his partners, went behind my back and contacted Pfizer Medical

Systems, asking for representation in Syria! They were, rebuffed by Pfizer and were told Dr. Abdallah M. Isa is the only recognized, Pfizer Medical Systems, representative for Syria and any discussion for the purchase of the ACTA scanner should come through Dr. Isa and nobody else.

The Syrians then opted to contact the Pfizer Medical Systems competitor, Nuclear Ohio, for a representation deal in Syria and of course, they failed again as Nuclear Ohio has a well-established representative in Syria.

The Lebanese agent, Mr. Breidi, was the only reliable Middle Eastern agent. He brought a potential buyer for the ACTA scanner, Dr. Tomeh, with him to the United States and the three of us went to the Pfizer Medical Systems manufacturing facility. Dr. Tomeh was 'impressed' with the operation, but I did not feel he was serious about purchasing the equipment. At the end of the meeting Dr. Tomeh, wanted to fly from New York to Paris on the Concorde. The cost of one-way ticket, at the time, was $1500. He asked me to pay for his trip and unfortunately, I did agree as I gave him the benefit of the doubt and paid $1500 for his flight to Paris on the Concorde! Well Dr. Tomeh, in my opinion, was never serious to purchase the equipment, but wanted a free trip to the United States paid for by the Breidi group and a free trip to Paris on the Concorde paid by me!

A month later, Pfizer Medical systems, after finding out that Nuclear Ohio is a formidable competitor that cannot be beaten, abandoned the manufacture of the ACTA Scanner and the Pfizer division folded!

POLITICS AT OUR INSTITUTION LED TO THE TERMINATION OF THE AGREEMENT WITH THE KUWAIT MINISTRY OF HEALTH

NOW THAT I HAVE SECURED A SOLID RELATIONSHIP BETWEEN OUR medical school and the Ministry of Health of Kuwait with seventeen Kuwaiti students are on our campus, talk of establishing an International center at the school came to the surface. Dr. Charles W. Johnson, who always had claimed that, Dr. Isa is my "right hand", told me that he already had identified the person he has in mind and who he wishes to appoint as the director of the newly established International Center. The person he wanted to appoint as the director of the International Center was not, affiliated with our school. He was an employee of a failed travel agency. I felt betrayed by

Dr. Johnson too as I was betrayed earlier by the State of Tennessee and by the Syrian agent. I told him after all the hard work I had done to secure this relationship and you tell me the new center will be headed by an outsider who has no knowledge of Medicine or International business. This is a betrayal of my efforts. I was neither consulted nor asked for any input as to the makeup of the International Center or to the qualifications of its new director. I expressed my dismay and disappointment to Dr. Johnson and told him "the deal is off" and I am out.

I called on my friend, the Minister of Health of Kuwait, and told him that I no longer will be taking part in any further discussions, as I have resigned my position as promotor of the collaboration between our medical school and his Ministry of Health. His response was disappointment and indicated that his agreeing with the collaborative activities, in the first place, was because of my assurances, to him, of the feasibility of such a collaboration. The point I was driving at during our negotiations with the Kuwaitis was, the collaboration, will no doubt benefit Kuwait in having its citizens earn a medical degree from an American institution. After telling him of my decision to abandon my role as a promotor of the collaborative effort between our medical school and his Ministry of Health, he said the agreement between our Ministry of Health and your medical school as of now is annulled and the seventeen Kuwaiti students will be brought home. That signaled the end of the collaboration between my institution and the Ministry of Health of Kuwait. All the Kuwaiti students were pulled out of Nashville and sent back to Kuwait. Having been, stabbed in the back twice before and betrayed once by the Tennessee government and again my own institution, raised some questions, in my mind, that one should be extremely careful dealing with others. However, I was the only winner in both instances: my institution on one hand and the state of Tennessee on the other, since neither activity had any economic impact on me. Neither cost me a single penny but was quite costly for the other two parties.

The back stabbing, by the Tennessee department of Economic and Community Development, the Lebanese delegation, the Syrian representative and now by Dr. Charles W. Johnson that I have been exposed to, convinced me that trust is a far-fetched and elusive goal to be realized!

On the positive side, Tennesseans are a welcoming people. They welcomed us, as new neighbors with open arms. When we got our United States citizenship, the neighbors had a party for us and said, you are now like us and are members of our American family!

Because of my contributions to the State of Tennessee and to the city of Nashville, the mayor of Nashville/Davidson County, Mr. Richard Fulton bestowed upon me the honor of "Honorary Citizen of Metropolitan Nashville", an honor that I will cherish.

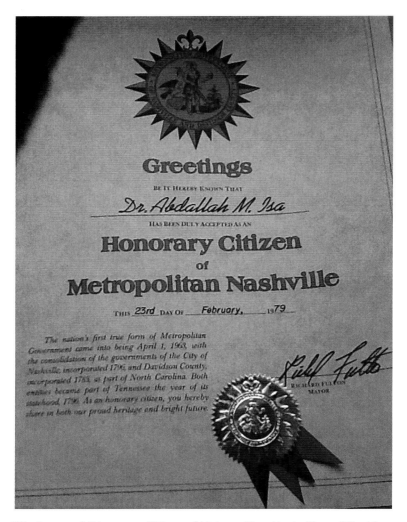

(The honor of "Honorary Citizen of Metropolitan Nashville and Davidson County" bestowed upon me by Mayor Richard Fulton on February 23rd, 1979)

COMPARISON BETWEEN SAN FRANCISCO AND NASHVILLE

MOVING FROM SAN FRANCISCO WITH A POPULATION OF 750,000 INHABitants in 1969 to the city of Nashville, a provincial town with a population of 175,000 people was, different from life in a city as opposed to much smaller one was indeed a letdown.

West End Avenue, a major thorough way in the city, had two foreign restaurants: one Italian and one Spanish. 'Eddie Arnold country fried chicken' and 'Minnie Pearl country fried chicken' were the most dominant food chains in the city. Nashville has grown to a fully-fledged city with a population over half a million people under the leadership of the late mayor Beverley Briley. Mayor Briley's leadership was instrumental in uniting the surrounding municipalities into one named Metropolitan Nashville/ Davidson County. Because of its reputation as the center of country music, Nashville has become the Mecca not only for music aspirants, but also for tourists from across the country to come to listen and to watch country music shows with their vibrant country music. Three interstates, I-24, I-40 and I-65 pass through the city connecting several parts of the country: North to South and West to East. It has a great location.

A huge contrast of the city exists between the time when we moved into the city and the way it is now. Some changes were good, yet others were not so good. In July 1969, I could count the number of cars and trucks on Interstate 40 on one hand. Now, the city chokes with traffic jams at any time of day! The traffic problems in the city reminds me of those in Atlanta. This comparison led some people to say that Nashville is becoming little Atlanta.

My medical school, in Nashville, hosted a national medical meeting in 1976. Several renowned speakers with expertise in different areas of medicine were invited to participate in that meeting. My responsibility was to organize the section of Immunology as it relates to cancer and infectious diseases.

One of the exhibitors at the meeting sent a message to me, after my presentation, requesting a meeting. I thought he may, have wanted to ask questions about the content of my presentation or anything else relating to the meeting. He said, I wish to draw a caricature picture of you, should you grant me that privilege. I said go for it! He was, done drawing my image in less than 5 minutes! What a talented caricaturist this man is!

(Abdallah, as seen in the eyes of the caricaturist)

OFFER TO RELOCATE TO IRAQ

THE DECADE OF THE 1970S, WHICH I CALLED THE 'ARAB OIL DECADE'
was a wakeup call for the Arab governments, especially those whose economies
depended on oil exports. As the price of oil skyrocketed, some of the Arab countries
realized the urgent need for having highly educated and trained technocrats to join

their labor force. They targeted the United States and Western Europe as the potential suppliers of these highly educated Cadres.

Iraq under president Saddam Hussain opened its doors for any Arab holding, graduate and higher scientific degrees to move to Iraq to work in their field of expertise with the government promising them a lot of land to build a house, an interest-free loan for building the house and within a year they will acquire the Iraqi citizenship. Further, the government of Iraq instructed its embassies in the United States and in Europe to organize trips for children of Arab immigrants to visit Iraq at the expense of the Iraqi government. Two of our daughters who took part in one of these trips, described the visits as very pleasant and worthwhile. Upon arriving in Baghdad, those 'Arab' kids were given pocket money, were shown around the country and were told, Iraq is your country and asked them to consider moving back to Iraq.

MY VISITS TO THE UNIVERSITY OF BAGHDAD AND TO ALMUSTANSIRYAH UNIVERSITY

WHILE SERVING AS A CONSULTANT TO THE GOVERNOR OF THE STATE of Tennessee and a member of the Tennessee Trade Delegation, I visited the Baghdad University medical school and met with the Dean, Dr. Al Mu'alla and met with the president of the al-Mustansiryah University, Dr. Sultan Al-Shawi. The purpose of those meetings was to explore the possibility of collaboration between their medical schools and our medical school. The responses from both, the president and the dean were lukewarm. Instead, they both asked me to join the faculty of the medical schools in Baghdad instead.

The government of Iraq, in 1978 invited the Arab American Medical Association (AAMA) of which I am a member, to hold its first medical congress in Baghdad under the auspices of the Iraqi Ministry of Health. Dr. Riyad Ibrahim el-Hajj Hussain, the Minister of Health of the Republic of Iraq, who holds both the Ph.D and MD degrees, asked me along with another Palestinian-American colleague to run a course in Clinical Immunology at his Ministry of Health in Baghdad. Three other colleagues from different American institutions, Dr. Zeineh and myself ran the two-week course in June of 1979. Doctors, laboratory directors, technicians and staff from Iraq and from different parts of the Middle East came to Baghdad to enroll in the two-week course.

As a follow-up to our Clinical Immunology course we held in Baghdad in 1979, Dr. Riyad, the Minister of Health of Iraq invited me in the summer of 1981 to visit the Ministry of Health. At our meeting, Dr. Riyad asked me to move to Iraq with an offer to establish and run a Clinical Immunology and cancer Research Center at the Ministry of Health in Baghdad. On the professional level, his offer included an area in the Ministry to be dedicated solely for the Research Center, a Telex machine to be placed in my office that I can use to order any equipment and supplies I needed from anywhere in the world. Technical personnel, in different areas of medicine at the Ministry will be available for the proposed center.

On the personal level, his offer included a fully furnished four-bedroom condominium, a car and a driver, American-style school for our daughters, at no cost to us, first class annual round-trip air tickets for the family and of course a hefty salary.

I did thank the Minister for his faith in me and in my abilities but declined the offer. He was quite surprised at my refusal to accept the offer and asked me why I would not accept his offer. I said, Your Excellency, you are acting and talking on behalf of a government and I am acting and talking on my own behalf of one individual. Let me be perfectly honest and candid with Your Excellency: As you perfectly know, Iraq is a police state with informants scattered all over the place. Should there be any person or group of persons to ever say or spread a false rumor that I mumbled derogatory statements or anything negative about Iraq, the Baath party or about President Saddam Hussain what will happen to me? I know I will be decapitated. This is the reason I respectfully decline the offer. Regretfully I must say that I will be unable to accept your offer to move to Baghdad however, I am willing and ready to help you and your Ministry, in any way feasible, from my position in the United States. Dr. Riyad then recognized my unwillingness to move to Baghdad but accepted my offer to help from my position in the United States. About three weeks after my return from Baghdad, I received a telephone call from the Iraqi embassy in Washington DC. The caller informed me that they have a package and they needed to have my mailing address to send it. They said, I should expect a package from the embassy within a couple of days, as the package to be sent by FedEx.

Upon receiving the package three days later and when I opened the Manella envelope, there was another sealed Manella envelope inside it. Upon opening the second envelope, yet there was a third sealed envelope. In that envelope was, the letter from the Minister of Health of Iraq signed by Dr. Riyad and addressed to the Iraqi Minister of Foreign

Affairs, in Baghdad requesting the facilitation of my efforts in helping the Ministry of Health acquiring medical professionals to work at his Ministry of Health.

Reading the letter and paying special attention to its contents, I realized that the request by the Minister of Health of Iraq, had not only professional dimensions, but may also have legal ramifications. I had no concerns about the professional issues, but I had to consult with my attorney to make sure there is no liability either from the United States government or from the government of Iraq.

Attached is a photocopy of the letter from the Ministry of Health of Iraq, requesting my help in recruiting professionals, from the United States, that are needed by the Iraqi Ministry of Health. The letter sent from the Ministry of Health in Baghdad to the Ministry of Foreign Affairs in Baghdad who in turn sent it to the Iraqi Embassy in Washington. DC.

Since there were no diplomatic relations between the government of Iraq and the government of the United States. All activities, between the two countries were, done through the Iraqi Interests Section of the Indian Embassy in Washington DC.

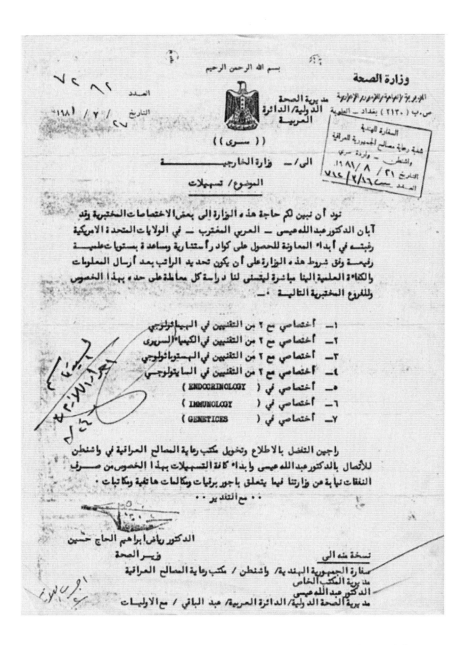

The letter was, written in Arabic and its translation into English is as follows:

"In the name of GOD, the Merciful

Ministry of Health

((CONFIDENTIAL))

Indian Embassy

Section of the Iraqi Interests of the Indian Embassy

Washington-came in as Confidential

Date 21/8/1981, # S16/3/712

International Health Directorate/the Arab Area

To: Ministry of Foreign Affairs

Subject: Facilitation

We wish to bring to your attention to the needs of this Ministry, to some Laboratory expertise which Dr. Abdallah Isa, the Arab immigrant to the United States of America who expressed his desire to cooperate, to obtain Consultative and helpful cadres with high scientific levels according to the terms and conditions of this Ministry regarding the salaries. After sending us the details and scientific achievements, so that we can evaluate case by case for the following Laboratory areas:

1. Two specialists and two technicians in Hematology

2. Two specialists and two technicians in Clinical Chemistry

3. Two specialists and two technicians in Histopathology

4. Two specialists in Endocrinology

5. Two specialists in Immunology

6. Two specialists in Genetics

We appreciate your looking into this request and authorizing the Iraqi Interests Section in Washington to contact Dr. Abdallah Isa and provide all facilities regarding this matter as to the cost, on behalf of our Ministry regarding any costs for cables, telephone calls and any correspondence

Kind regards,

Dr. Riyad Ibrahim Al-Hajj Hussain

Minister of Health

Cc: Embassy of the Indian Embassy/Washington/Office of Iraqi Interests

Office of the Directory Private Office

Dr. Abdallah Isa

Directorate of International Health/the Arab Department/Abd al-

Baki/ with all priorities"

To get the best cadres to join the Ministry of Health of Iraq, I requested and received permission from the Iraqi embassy in Washington DC to place advertisements in select medical and scientific journals.

More than two hundred applicants sent their resumes to me, which in turn I sent directly to Dr. Riyad Ibrahim al-Hajj Hussain, the Minister of Health in Baghdad. I included in my cover letter that I will neither act on nor will I choose any of the applicants, but it is the Minister of Health who will have the final say and make the decision, as to which candidate is acceptable and which is not.

Two months have passed without hearing a word from the Minister. At that time, the news broke out that Dr. Riyad was executed for the alleged crime that his Ministry imported defective and outdated drugs for use to treat the soldiers who were wounded during the eight-year long Iraq-Iran war! To me this was absurd and hard to believe. This was an incredible news, as I know how nationalistic the Minister was. Rumors floated around that President Saddam indicated during the cabinet meeting that the war with Iran is not going well. He asked the cabinet ministers if any one of the ministers has an idea as to how to end the war. Dr. Riyad raised his hand and said, my president, I have an idea and wish you would end this war, as it is not in the best interest of our people. President Saddam said, let you and I meet in private after the cabinet meeting. Of course, after the meeting between the two, Dr. Riyad was, found dead in the meeting room!

In retrospect, would I have been next in line for execution had I accepted Dr. Riyad's offer to move to Iraq? Only time could have provided the answer!

OFFER TO JOIN THE IMPERIAL MEDICAL CENTER OF IRAN AND MEETING MR. RICHARD HELMS, OUR CIA DIRECTOR

THE IRANIAN EMBASSY IN WASHINGTON INVITED ME TO COME AND meet with the president and with the dean of the newly established, *Imperial Medical Center of Iran*. I had meetings with the president, Dr. Samei'i and with the new dean of the medical school for about two hours. They went over the history of the establishment of such a medical center and that His Majesty, the Shah of Iran, has appointed his sister, princess Ashraf to head the center. The center as they explained to me, looked very impressive. Dr. Samei'i offered that I should join the faculty in Tehran. The offer included an excellent pay, fully furnished housing for the family and the children will go to the American School with all expenses paid by the center. Annual, First Class roundtrip tickets for the family to the United States and for me to attend three scientific meetings anywhere in the world every year!

At the reception which was held at the Iranian embassy were, the ambassador, Mr. Zahedi as well as Mr. Richard Helms, the CIA director and other dignitaries from the Washington DC area. Mr. Helms and ambassador Zahedi were mingling among and chatting with the invitees at the reception.

To my big surprise and astonishment, Mr. Helms was very persistent in encouraging me to accept the offer and go to Tehran. I promised Mr. Helms, ambassador Zahedi and Dr. Samei'i that I will consider the offer after thorough discussions with the family and will let them know of my decision in due time.

It does not take much speculation as to where Mr. Helms, our CIA director, was coming from. The CIA was running the show in Iran during the rule of the Shah. Was Mr. Helms interested and perhaps planning to recruit me as an agent of the CIA? He never said anything to that effect.

While visiting Tehran, as a consultant to the trade delegation of the State of Tennessee in 1975, I noticed American troops, tanks and United States Airforce Planes covering every inch of the grounds at the Mehrabad, now the Khomaini, International airport. Talking on the phone, in Teheran at that time, was very difficult to hear, as there were many interfering voices on the line. Telephones were bugged and communication, be it local or long distance, was essentially left to the discretion of the intelligence service to let it go through or not. The scene was typical of a police state and Iran, a police state it was!

The Shah of Iran acted as though he was the cop of the area. His role was not only to protect the western interests, but also to expand the influence of the 'Persian Empire' throughout the Middle East.

Imam Ayatullah Khomeini who was in exile in France was working underground to unseat the Shah. When rumors of an Iranian revolution headed by Imam Khomeini went on the air, they spread like fire in a stack of hay. The rumors frightened the neighboring countries who became scared to death of the potential of the spread of Shi'aism in the predominantly Sunni Moslem Middle East. For many years, Iraq had fought a Kurdish insurgency that was supported and armed by the Shah of Iran. Fear of the revolution was felt not only in Iran, but also throughout the Middle East. While in Baghdad in 1979, as an invitee of the Ministry of Health of Iraq, I witnessed the arrival of Empress Farah Deeba, the Shah's wife's first visit to Baghdad. Of course, that was her last visit to Iraq, as the Shah's regime was, toppled and he and his family had to flee the country. Farah Deeba's visit to Iraq was, intended as a preludeer visit was intended for mending relations between the two neighboring countries, and to build a coalition to face the tide of the Khomeini revolution. The way the thinking of the Middle Eastern countries goes, the Shah's Iran was the lesser of the two evils when compared to that of Imam al-Khomeini. They are willing to accept the Shah's rule and the potential of expansion of the Persian Empire, but not the Khomeini Revolution. They were, frightened by the Khomeini revolutionaries who will spread Shia'ism at the expense of the Sunni majority. Iraq was, the country obsessed with fighting the Khomeini phenomenon, as it was feared it may influence the Shi'te majority in the country to rebel against the Sunni dominated government.

Rumors of a revolution in Iran followed by the toppling of the Shah's regime were all over the place. Had I accepted the offer to join the *Imperial Medical Center of Iran,* it would have been a disaster for me and for my family. The Iranian embassy, before the revolution took hold, called me at least three times a day, wanting to know when I will be ready to move to Teheran and join the Faculty of the *Imperial Medical Center of Iran.* I was stalling all along giving excuses such as I am waiting for the sale of our house and for the children to finish their school year. I promised that upon the sale of the house and the children finishing the school year, I will immediately move to Teheran. Of course, I had neither the intention of selling the house nor even planning on moving to Iran.

When it became clear to me that Ayatollah Khomeini, while still in exile in France, has inspired the revolution that had reached its maturity in Iran and was on his way to Tehran, I decided to shelve the offer. I called the Iranian embassy in Washington and told them that I am declining the offer to join the *Imperial Medical*

Center of Iran. Thank you, Ayatollah Khomeini, for making the decision for me not to move to Iran. I did not wish my children and us to meet the same fate Americans met, resulting from the revolution, during the 1979 occupation of the United States Embassy in Teheran.

The Khomeini revolution appeared to be unstoppable and was moving forward with lightning speed. The sleeping cells were ready, at a moment's notice to rise and do the job they were assigned to do. The president of the *Imperial Medical Center of Iran* and Mr. Richard Helms, our CIA director, were dismayed and disappointed at my decision declining the offer and did their best to convince me to change my mind. Because of the ascension of Khomeini to the leadership of Iran, the Iran-Iraq war broke out and lasted for eight years with millions of dead on both sides of the conflict!

THE SWISS INSTITUTE OF CLINICAL IMMUNOLOGY EXPERIENCE

IN THE SUMMER OF 1974, I WAS ASKED TO TAKE PART IN RUNNING A United Nations World Health Organization (WHO)-sponsored Clinical Immunology course at the American University of Beirut Hospital. The course was headed by Dr. Fouad S. Farah, who had requested the help of several international scientists, including myself, to participate in teaching and supervising the course. Two of these, international scientists that I had a great admiration for were Drs. N.A. Mitchison of the University College in London and Dr. Alaine de Weck of the Clinical Institute of Immunology at the University of Bern in Switzerland. Dr. Mitchison invited me to spend a month in his Zoology department. I should mention that Dr. N. A. Mitchison earned his doctorate degree under the supervision of the late Sir Dr. Peter Medawar who was, awarded the Nobel Prize in Physiology and Medicine in the early 1960 for his work on transplantation immunology. He also was, knighted by the British Monarch and the title of Sir was, bestowed upon him.

The last time I saw and chatted with Sir Dr. Medawar, was in Dallas Texas at our annual meeting of the American Association of Immunologist in 1976. At that meeting, Sir Peter Medawar told me that he just had a stroke and because of the stroke, he has difficulty walking. Unfortunately, Sir Peter Medawar passed on few months later.

Dr. de Weck, invited me to spend my sabbatical year, as a visiting professor of Immunology, at his Institute of Clinical Immunology at the University of Bern. I combined the two visits by spending the month of August 1979 in Dr. Mitchison's department and after that spent one year at the Institute of Clinical Immunology in Bern, Switzerland. To fund the trip to London, during the month I spent in London, I received a fellowship from the Burroughs Welcome Fund. The School of Medicine, University of Bern, Switzerland provided me with a grant to cover my expenses as a visiting professor at the Institute of Clinical Immunology, which is an integral part of the School of Medicine, University of Bern in Switzerland. I used that, as my sabbatical leave from my medical school appointment in Nashville. It was one of the best decisions I had made not only because, it was a great learning experience, but it also was a wonderful social one.

The family and I drove from Nashville to New York, loaded our car on the boat for transport to England and flew to London. Two weeks later, I picked the car up from the Southampton docs. A week after that we drove from London to Dover, England and took the hovercraft to Calais, France and from there drove to Bern, Switzerland. It was a wonderful year as, in addition to having a great academic experience, the family and I were able to see Europe and different cultures first hand. In addition to driving all over Switzerland, we drove to Paris, to Milano and Florence in Italy and to Frankfurt, Germany as well as to many other destinations in Europe.

The natural beauty of Switzerland and its high mountains are beyond description. Well defined, hiking trails were everywhere. The Swiss, unlike us, cherish walking and hiking. They hike a lot and take pride in their country and its nature. They, however, were obsessed with security and were very apprehensive and worried about the Warsaw Pact Forces in Eastern Europe under the command of the Soviet Union. The Swiss army I was, told could deploy 600,000 troops overnight should the security situation demand!

While driving to the mountains and hiking, in the well-maintained and clearly marked directions in the trails, we had the opportunity to see a glacier for the first time ever. It was the one and only glacier that we have ever seen which is in the mountains of Switzerland.

(My photo holding the beautiful snow puppy someone must have made and left it behind close to the glacier where the ground was still covered with soft snow. Upon touching the glacier, it felt as though we are touching a solid rock)

While living in Bern, Switzerland, we went to Gstad, a beautiful suburb of the city where Julie Andrews, the famed actor and singer who played a leading role in the movie Sound of Music, owned a house there. My wife, our daughters and I walked through the knee-high snow and went to her house. After ringing the doorbell, a man answered the door and said Miss Andrews was not there. I said, we just saw her car coming in and she stepped out into the house. Please tell her that an American family wishes to have the honor of meeting her. She came out, with a big frown on her face and said what can I do for you? I said, we saw your movies and enjoyed listening to your beautiful voice, and we would be honored and love to have a picture with the International superstar named Julie Andrews. She mellowed a little bit, smiled and we had a beautiful picture of her with us.

It is amazing how we tend to take things for granted. Moving from one state to another in the United States does not require a passport or identification papers to show at the border. I learned that lesson when we drove from San Francisco, California to Nashville, Tennessee in the summer of 1969. We crossed the border from California to Arizona in our way to see the Grand Canyon. At the Arizona border with California, I stopped and had my travel document and driver's license ready. I showed the documents to the officer at the border. The officer looked at me with surprise and said, you do not need to show any documentation crossing from one state to another in the United States as you are still within the same country. It is, as if you are going from one city to another within the same state!

The route we took was, driving from San Francisco south to Arizona then north to Utah. After driving through Utah, we came into the State of Colorado. After Colorado, we entered the state of Kansas and then the state of Missouri. The states of Utah and Colorado are extremely beautiful. They are mountainous with gorgeous scenery. Coming down the mountains from Colorado to Kansas was the most boring drive I ever encountered. The state of Kansas is flat with no landmarks to see except lots of dust whirlpools coming from the dust storms. The dust was flying all over the place. The dust storms could pop up anytime during the day and cover the endless flat landscape. The route we took crossing from the state of Kansas and entering the state of Missouri, had another landscape of flat land. The landscape in the western part of Tennessee is not different from those of Kansas and Missouri. Again, no landmarks in western Missouri were visible until we came close to St. Louis where we saw the large Arch at the entrance of the town.

Things started to look a little better when we entered Middle Tennessee, where Nashville is located. There were no more boring flat landscapes, but beautiful green rolling hills covering the whole area.

At the borders of Tennessee, the sign said, "Welcome to the Three States of Tennessee". When I saw that sign, I said to myself, to which state of Tennessee are we supposed to go? Luckily, there was a road sign ahead that showed Nashville with an arrow pointing to its direction and its distance from the border. I realized then we were going in the right direction. I later found out that the "Three States of Tennessee" referred to the three regions of the state based on their geography. West Tennessee (Memphis) is flat, Middle Tennessee (Nashville) has rolling hills and East Tennessee (Knoxville) is mountainous.

The drive from California to Tennessee is about 2500 miles long. We would drive for 400 miles and stop to spend the night then resume our driving the following morning. On our way from San Francisco to Arizona, we stopped and spent the night in the town of Needles, a little town located in the desert area of Southern California. Temperatures were in the upper nineties and humidity was almost 100%. The combination of high temperature and high humidity is hazardous to health. Getting ready to leave the following morning, I found out our car was locked with the ignition and door keys sitting on the back seat of the car. When we were ready to leave Needles, there was no way to have the car unlocked as it was Sunday morning, and all shops were closed with no wrecker service available. It was very frustrating, as I wanted to drive early so that we reach our next stop before dark. Luckily, I found the trunk key in my pocket. I unlocked the trunk and found a big hole on the back of the trunk that touches the back of the car's backseat. Through that hole and with the help of a clothes hanger, I was able to retrieve the keys and we set out for the new 400-mile drive to our next destination.

During our stay in Switzerland, we planned to visit Milano, Italy to expose the children, to museums and other cultural places. We had to drive from Bern, Switzerland through the mountain passes to the Italian border. At the border crossing separating the two countries was a very big gate. The officer asked to see our passports. He did not speak any English, nor did we speak any Italian. He kept saying *Passaporto, Passaporto* and I responded by saying no *passaporto*. As I did assume and wrongly so, that we did not need a passport or documents to show for crossing from one state to the other as is the case in the United States. Well, Italy and Switzerland are two independent and different states and travel between the two countries requires a passport! After two hours of negotiations and getting nowhere, we were told by, a passerby who spoke English and Italian that we must have a passport to enter Italy. We had to drive back in the evening to spend the night in Bern and drive back to Italy the following morning. The drive back from the Italian border to Bern was very scary as the fog set in and it was difficult to see the windy roads high in the mountains. We picked our passports from Bern and drove back to Italy the following morning. Now with our passports in hand, the Italian border guard let us into Italy with a big smile on his face! We drove to Milano and went directly to the museums and to el-Duomo.

While driving in Milano with its narrow and winding streets and because our car had an American license plate with USA decal affixed on its rear end, a small Fiat, 'Topolino', car was following us and yelling, loudly, "Yankee Go Home", "Yankee Go Home". After fifteen minutes of driving in the narrow and winding streets and while the Italian car was still following us, I stopped, got out of the car, looked at the people in the 'Topolino' car chasing us and said, "Do I look like a Yankee to you"? They drove away with no more harassment! At the time, anti-American feelings were high in Europe and more so in Italy where the communists were thriving. After spending few days in Milano, we drove to the beautiful city of "Firenze"-Florence and checked out the museums and other place of interest.

The convenience of having our car in Europe was beyond description. In addition to visiting Milano and Florence in Italy, we would drive to France and spend the weekend in Paris, in Zurich, Switzerland, in Frankfort, Germany or Lugano in Italy and the Black Forest in southern Germany. We spent a weekend in Florence, Italy and enjoyed the beauty of this ancient city. While in the 'pension' where we spent the nights, we witnessed the interaction between an Italian mother and her daughter. The mother, who was managing the 'pension' and her daughter who lived with her mother in the same facility, helped her mother in running the pension. Every morning, the mother, who was healthy and with no sign of disability would sit on the chair and ask her daughter to get mama's socks and shoes and put them on her mother's feet! It was, we felt, a little demeaning to the daughter, as the mother should not have demanded her daughter's help for these chores! I asked the mother as to why she had her daughter put her socks and shoes on her feet, her reply was, it is a good way for the daughter to develop respect to the elderly!

The visit to Europe was a very important educational experience for our daughters. They were, exposed to and visited all historical sites and museums in Italy, France and Germany. In Paris we visited the Bastille, Notre Dame, the Eifel tower and of course, the Louvre where we saw the original Mona Lisa portrait firsthand.

My wife, Laila's uncle Dr. Nasrat Fadda, has a penthouse in the German town of Neunberg, a little town just east of Frankfort. We spent a couple of weeks with Dr. Nasrat Fadda and his wife Hilda. While in Germany, I had to go to a meeting in Paris and Laila and the girls stayed with Laila's uncle and his wife in Neunberg. I can boast that I had the great pleasure and honor to claim riding the historical and famed, the "*Orient Express*" train. I rode this train from Paris, France to Neuenberg, Germany. I have heard and read a lot about the *Orient Express* and now I am having the great pleasure of riding in it too. Wow, what a historical achievement that was!

The inspector on the *Orient Express* kept looking at me with a suspicious and scary look. He would go back and forth several times then at the end, he asked for my passport. He took the passport and I guessed he checked with the authorities in France and Germany to see if I were on the terrorists list. He handed the passport back to me and few minutes later came back and asked for the passport again. At the end, it appeared that he found out that I was not a terrorist after all, handed me the passport and no more questions asked.

One thing that attracted our attention in Europe, unlike in the United States, was that every little town has its own unique character with its distinct landmark. There were forts and monuments all over the place with lots of history behind each fort and each monument.

The Swiss have a great love for America and Americans and are very proud of their country. Neighbors offered to teach German to our daughters so that they can communicate with their friends. When we left Bern, Swiss girls, who befriended our daughter, Randa, lined up at the road crying loud and saying good bye, good bye Randa!

TURMOIL AT OUR INSTITUTION
IN NASHVILLE

IN THE MID 1970S, MY CAREER JUMPED TO HIGH LEVELS. MY SCIENTIFIC contributions, election to elite medical and scientific societies and the high number of scientific publications, made Dr. Ralph Cazort, the dean of our medical school, to announce to the medical faculty, during the medical school faculty meeting, that Dr. Abdallah M. Isa is the star of our medical school. Dr. Isa is the most prolific writer at our institution. Of course, this announcement by the dean did not fare well with some of my black faculty colleagues.

Coming back from Europe after my sabbatical leave, I felt some bad undercurrents were engulfing our institution. Activities and actions, by the board of Trustees of the institution suggested instability and discontinuity of all programs. That did not look right to me, as it pointed to potential problems that may take a long time to overcome.

In addition to the problems and the murky situation, at the institution had led to paralysis throughout the educational and clinical programs. These problems of inactivity and indecisiveness on the part of the interim administration led to complete paralysis of the total operation at the school. To add insult to injury, I developed rash and itchy blisters on the lower back of my head. I also developed raised glossy red spots on my nose. I used different shampoos including the so-called 'medicated' shampoos, but the blisters would not go away. I then consulted with the dermatologist at our hospital. He indicated, in his diagnosis report, that I have a genetic disease that flares up at a certain age and nothing can be done to cure this disease. He suggested, however, that to alleviate the symptom, I must follow his recommendations to stay away from the sun, should use heavy doses of sunscreen, wear long-sleeved shirts and wear a hat! I conformed to his recommendations except for wearing a hat. With all the recommendations that I have complied with the blisters and the red spots on my nose stayed on and would not go away. I became suspicious of the medical credibility of this dermatologist and decided to check out his credentials. I found out he was a bogus and neither trained as a dermatologist nor was he board-certified in Dermatology!

I consulted with another dermatologist when I visited Saudi Arabia. This dermatologist rejected the 'genetic disease' diagnosis by the previous dermatologist. His diagnosis was altogether different from the previous one. He asked me if I have an oily skin and I said yes, I do. He then concluded that I have a bacterium that thrives on oily skins and that is what he thought caused all the problems I have. He gave me samples of a lotion to wash the blisters and my face with. Of course, neither the blisters nor did the red spots on my nose go away.

Having given up on the so-called specialists in Dermatology, I decided to diagnose myself as the blisters and other symptoms did not occur or appear all the time. I decided to watch what I eat. I found out that the blisters flare up only when I include black peppers in my diet. I decided to abstain from using black peppers for few months. The blisters disappeared completely within the first week of my abstention of the use of black peppers! Six months later, I decided to check the validity of my diagnosis by adding black peppers to my diet and no blisters ever developed. It appeared that I must have developed an allergic reaction to black peppers and since the symptoms did not appear after I consume black peppers in my diet, it suggests that the allergic reaction I had developed is of the immediate type. I must have become allergic to black peppers due to a mutation in my genetic makeup that was, translated into ordering my immune system to respond, by projecting the allergic reaction to black peppers with the appearance of the blisters on the back of my head and the red spots on my nose. The fact that these blisters and red spots on my nose did not appear when using black peppers again after few months of abstention, I must have mutated back to normal as the allergic reaction disappeared completely.

COUP AT OUR INSTITUTION AND THE TERMINATION OF ALL ADMINISTRATORS

THE YEAR 1981 WAS THE YEAR WHEN A COUP TOOK PLACE AT OUR institution. The board of Trustees sacked the president, vice presidents, deans and all department heads including that of my department. The head of my department was, forced to resign and was, replaced by another colleague, Dr. Julius Jackson. Dr. Jackson was a junior faculty member who joined the department few years earlier. I felt the new department head was very jealous of my achievements as a non-minority and foreign individual who has shined, not only in the department but also in the medical school at large. He tried to do anything and everything within his power to intimidate me first and ultimately to get rid of me. It must have been quite frustrating for him, as he could not do that before, because he was not in a position of power to do anything about it.

Few years earlier, Dr. Charles W. Johnson, chairperson of the department of Microbiology, asked me to establish and head a new division of Immuno-Biology in the department. Dr. Thomas Shockley, the vice-chairman of the department at the time and who later succeeded Dr. Charles W. Johnson as department head after Johnson's appointment to the deanship of the School of Graduate Studies and Research. Dr. Shockley vetoed my appointment to head the anticipated and newly to be established division of Immuno-Biology. That created tension between Johnson and Shockley that was serious enough to lead to a break of a long personal and professional association between the two. Dr. Shockley's rationale for opposing my appointment as head of the anticipated Division of Immuno-biology was his fear that I may devote less time to the department and devote more time into developing the newly formed division of Immuno-Biology. He reasoned that it might lead to less productivity on my part in his department of Microbiology. Dr. Shockley's fears, were indeed well founded as I, was publishing an average of 3-4 scientific papers a year which was more than the total number of the 16 other faculty members in the department! With all the productivity I had, I neither was rewarded nor was I appreciated by the department. There goes the saying "if you are any good, you really are not that good"!

Dr. Charles W. Johnson, who always claimed that Dr. Isa is 'my right hand', is now the dean of the Graduate School and Research and the director of the Sickle Cell Disease Center. He confided in me that Dr. Julius Jackson, whose wife worked as a secretary at the Sickle Cell Disease Center, had threatened to "bust his (Johnson's) head" should he not leave his wife (Jackson's) alone. Mrs. Jackson, according to what Dr. Johnson told me, was taking confidential files from the center and passing them to her husband. When Dr. Johnson confronted her about the issue, she got mad and told her husband what had happened. The incident between Dr. Johnson and Mrs. Jackson escalated to the point that her husband, Dr. Julius Jackson, threatened to 'bust Dr. Johnson's head' should he not leave his wife alone! When Dr. Johnson confided in me and asked as to what I thought he should do. I told him since you are the dean you have the power and authority to fire him, if for nothing else, at least for his threats and for insubordination. I did then believe that Dr. Johnson was physically afraid of Dr. Jackson, as the latter was tall and very muscular and did not care about the consequences of his actions.

Dr. Jackson always came to work wearing sloppy attire of torn up jeans and torn tennis shoes. He would keep to himself, did not socialize with his colleagues in the department but stayed busy in his laboratory.

When the 1981 coup at the institution took place, it was clear that Dr. Charles W. Johnson, who at the time was the dean of the graduate school, had a hand in the coup. Dr. Shockley, head of the department All administrators at the institution except Dr. Johnson were sacked. of Microbiology was, removed and replaced by Dr. Julius

Jackson, upon the recommendation of Dr. Charles W. Johnson as the new department head. This was the reward the now powerful Dr. Johnson has bestowed upon Dr. Jackson who eight years earlier threatened to bust Johnson's head!

As of July 1, 1981, Dr. Jackson, as the newly appointed head of the department, got rid of his torn-up jeans and tennis shoes and started to wear designer suits with fancy neckties and polished shoes!

Ten days after Dr. Jackson became head of the department, and on July 10, 1981 when I was busy finalizing plans to go with the family to Europe for vacation at the end of the month, the departmental secretary called me and said, the chairperson (Dr. Jackson) wants to see you. I said O.K. I am on my way. Upon meeting with Dr. Jackson, he handed me an envelope with the letter stating: "I have been watching your performance over the years and want to advise you that, a year from the date of this letter, you will not have a position at this institution". I said wow, smiled, shook his hand and said, thank you so very much for making the decision for me. I have been contemplating leaving this place for some time and now I feel relieved of the pressures of trying to make the decision. I want to thank you again for helping me out in making the decision for me to leave this institution. The letter of termination from Dr. Jackson, did not impact on our plans to go Europe as the trip went on as scheduled.

Alliances, among individuals are not different from those among nations. Alliances shift, from friend to foe and from foe to friend. These shifts were clear in the collapse of the relationship between Dr. Charles W. Johnson and Dr. Thomas E. Shockley and later between Dr. Charles W. Johnson and Dr. Julius Jackson. These shifts followed the change in interests between these two individuals. When it comes to nations, we all know that the United States, a British colony, gaining independence after a grueling war between the two countries. After being staunch enemies, not only they are staunch allies, but the roles have been turned around and Britain is now a colony of the United States with American troops stationed in that country!

Another situation of shifting alliances is that of India and Israel. India, as a member of the non-aligned pact, comprising Egypt's Gamal Abdel Nasser, India's Nehru and Marshall Tito of Yugoslavia. India, was anti-Israel and a strong supporter of the Palestinians, is now a strong supporter of Israel, under Modi.

Racism in the United States is still alive and well. As a non-Black and a non-White foreign person, I was approached on several occasions, by both Black and White individuals who would confided in me to air their grievances and hatred of each other. While Blacks are more vocal in public about resentment of whites, the same does not appear to be the case with whites who appear to be subtle and discrete about it.

My experiences at minority institutions, led me to believe that Blacks in America, although were victims of discrimination, tend to classify and treat people of different racial and ethnic backgrounds in varying degrees of acceptance. The ethnic grouping, as to my observations have been confirmed by a Black colleague. He did tell me, 40 years earlier, that blacks look at different ethnic groups and classify them into different tiers based on their acceptance:

1. American blacks (African Americans) hold the number one position of acceptance.

2. The number two position is reserved for Whites regardless of their ethnicity, American or European

3. African blacks hold the third position

4. Non-black, non-white foreign ethnic groups (Asians) hold the fourth Position of acceptance and

5. Arab-Americans, especially those with the Moslem faith hold the fifth position.

When I told, my black colleague that several blacks, like him, who hate whites, why are they the preferred group after American blacks over any other ethnic group? With a big sigh on his part said, there is still a feeling, primarily among the older generation in the black community of the slave/master relationship, but it does not exist among the younger generation. This statement, by my black colleague, rang a bell with me too. Although I hated the Brits, as they were the cause of my becoming a refugee and a stateless person with no country to belong to, yet I have deep seated feeling of respect and a slight emotional attachment towards the Brits. I was, exposed to them during my formative years when they mandated my country of Palestine and looked at us, Palestinians, as their slaves! This may explain the master/slave relationship felt among the older generation of blacks in America.

Whites are not innocent of bigotry and racism either. We had a white neighbor who once told me that the United States accepts non-black immigrants like me, to dilute the influence of and to keep blacks as a minority population. I am not too sure of the validity of his outdated assertion.

Upon asking my White neighbor as to how do you classify different ethnic groups, in regard, to their acceptance and desirability as opposed to other ethnic groups? He responded as follows:

1. Whites come first

2. Europeans regardless of their country of origin come second

3. Asians and Middle Easterners third

4. African blacks fourth

5. Black Americans (African Americans) fifth

Well, thanks to the late Dr. Martin Luther King, who lost his life for standing up and fighting against bigotry and racial inequality. Because of Dr. King's efforts, anti-discrimination and anti-racial laws were passed and became the law of the land. Although these laws are in the books, discrimination and bigotry are still widespread. It is what is in the heart and not what is in the books that counts. Freedom of Speech is one of the most sacred icons in a democracy, yet one cannot use Free Speech to intimidate or degrade others. All of us have, to be careful as how to say anything in public or even in private to others. One should comply with Free Speech and never deviate from being 'politically correct'. As an addendum to what Dr. Martin Luther King did in helping African Americans gain their political rights and their acceptance as an integral part of the American weave, Barak Obama elevated their economic status. Television ads directed at African Americans, are all over the place. It is assumed they have the money, thus the advertiser, want a share of their wealth. Indeed, the improvement in their economic status can be seen in their driving late model cars and shopping in upscale stores. Thanks to both Dr. Kind and to president Obama for their roles in lifting the social and economic status of fellow Americans.

Dr. Jackson did not know the rules pertaining to employment, retention, promotion, tenure or termination at our institution. He never read the faculty handbook of the institution which specifically and explicitly says, hiring and firing of a faculty member lies in the legal authority vested in the dean only and no other person has the authority to fire or hire. They can make recommendations to the dean who in turn will or will not honor their recommendations.

This person was full of hatred, discrimination and racism. He believed, very strongly, in black power. I have always felt he may be an active member of the Black Panthers Party. He had his cronies, call my home at three in the morning to cuss me out and throw ugly profanities at me and at my family. His actions were not only racist, unethical but also outright unprofessional.

He felt he had the moral and professional responsibility of and the obligation to 'cleanse' the institution from those non-black faculty members. Black faculty, as he saw it, must be the ones to teach and interact with black students and to treat black patients. He did not trust any faculty member who is not black to do a good job. He was paranoid, thinking that non-black faculty members were nothing but a fifth column whose intentions were, and still are to the detriment of the minority institution. This is where ethnicity supersedes professionalism!

It appeared, at the time, there was a policy from the higher ups of the new administration to get rid of all non-black faculty members. Several other white

American faculty colleagues were terminated within few months of the life of the new administration!

Should the actions of the new administration regarding non-black faculty, be looked at as a genuinely professional or as a racist action? In my opinion, it does not have a speck of professionalism, but rather it is a behavior loaded with discrimination and outright racism.

Well, I waited until the beginning of June of 1982, eleven months after Jackson's letter of termination was handed to me to, confront him. I told him he should be more careful and not make rash decisions based on ignorance and racism. He should read and comprehend the rules and the by-laws of the faculty handbook at the institution regarding employment and termination. If he has difficulty understanding what the policies say, I will be more than happy to help him understand them. They are all contained in the faculty handbook. I pointed out the page numbers, which specify the rules on termination. I said to him, you have no authority to terminate me or anybody else for that matter, as you are neither the dean nor an authorized administrator at the institution! He was numb and did not say a word in response to what I said.

Dr. C. W. Johnson who was the only survivor of the purge by the new administration was, appointed as the acting dean of the Medical school. As dean, Dr. Charles W. Johnson, tried his best to convince me to move to another department. He said, since you have a joint appointment with the Ophthalmology department, you have the choice to be full time in that department or if you prefer, in the Pediatrics or in the Surgery department, you make the decision and I will endorse it. It is your choice as to which department you wish to be affiliated with. His offers did not appeal to me, as a matter of principle. Should I have accepted any of his offers, it will provide more confidence and more ammunition to Dr. Jackson and the like to act and arrive at more rash decisions that may affect other faculty members. I told Dr. Johnson, sorry sir, I would rather leave the institution altogether than succumb to Jackson's desire by leaving my department and joining another department at the institution. I declined his offer and decided to move on. The acting dean of the medical school had no choice but to comply with the rules, as stipulated in the faculty handbook. He had no choice but to grant me an extension of one extra year prior to my termination. Six months later a new dean of the medical school was, brought in.

While shopping at the mall I crossed path with Dr. Jackson who appeared to have reverted to his earlier days of wearing torn-up jeans and tennis shoes again. I asked, sarcastically, as to what had happened? Where are the designer suits, fancy ties and polished shoes you used to wear? His subdued response was, I am no longer the department head. I said you know my friend "what goes around comes around", smiled and left.

I found out later when he was out of town, he called his office and asked a student of his to check his mail. The student told him there was a letter from the newly appointed dean. He instructed the student to open the letter and read it to him. The letter said, "As of the date of this letter and because of your incompetence and of making rash decisions, you are to be relieved of your duties as department chairperson and also one year from the date of this letter, you will not have a position at this institution"! Wow! It sounded like, in the dean's letter to Dr. Jackson, the dean has borrowed the same language, Dr. Jackson had written to me a year and a half earlier!

About a week into the new extended year, I received a call from the Saudi Arabian Educational Office in Houston, Texas. The caller said, Dr. Tawfiq al-Tamimi, Dean of the Medical School at the King Faisal University in Al-Dammam, Saudi Arabia wants to talk to you should you be available. I said to, please put the Dean on. He asked me if I am interested in joining the faculty of the School of Medicine in Saudi Arabia. I said let me think about it. However, I need more information about the institution and more details about the terms of the offer. Dean al-Tamimi said we, will send you a packet with an invitation and airline tickets, to come to Houston, by FedEx, to meet with me and get all the details of the offer I have just made to you.

A week later, I met with dean al-Tamimi in Houston and he provided me with all the details of the offer. Housing, airline tickets, academic position at the medical school and the hospital and the salary were, discussed. All terms were acceptable to me, with one exception, the salary, which I felt was a little lower than what I am worth. I pointed out to the dean that the salary he offered was unacceptable. He then asked me to please do not turn the offer down yet and hold on for one week, I will be contacting the Minister of Higher Education and the Minister of Health in Saudi Arabia asking their approval to raise the offered salary. He called my home two days later and told me, both of their Excellencies, the Minister of Higher Education and the Minister of Health have agreed to double the salary that was offered to you! Please accept the offer and let me know as early as possible so that I can start the procedures for your coming to Saudi Arabia. In September 1983, I flew to Saudi Arabia and started my job as professor of Immunology and Infectious Diseases at the King Faisal College of Medicine.

INTERACTIONS WITH THE PALESTINE RED CRESCENT SOCIETY MEETINGS AND THEIR SEQUEL

THE 1980S WERE FULL OF SURPRISES FOR ME. IN ADDITION TO THE Saudi Arabian medical school offer, I also received a call from Dr. Fathi Arafat, who I had met earlier in Geneva Switzerland, during my Sabbatical year at the Institute of Clinical Immunology. Dr. Fathi Arafat, the brother of Mr. Yasir Arafat, head of the Palestine Liberation Organization (PLO) is, also the president and CEO of the Palestine Red Crescent Society (PRCS), headquartered in Beirut, Lebanon. We had briefly discussed the possibility of establishing a "Frozen Blood Center" at the Red Crescent headquarters in Beirut. In addition to managing and running the center, I offered to go into a joint venture with the Red Crescent and be a partner in the project. I will prepare the feasibility study with the infrastructure, equipment, employees etc. After completion of the study and receipt of a copy of the details of the turnkey project by Dr. Arafat, he sent me an invitation to visit Beirut, for a face to face meeting to discuss the full details of the joint venture.

While at the Red Crescent headquarters, a 'very important Latin American person' was visiting the Red Crescent Society in Beirut. Dr. Arafat asked me to join him to have a picture taken with his guest, who happens to be the 'very important visitor' from Latin America. I thanked Dr. Arafat for the invitation and declined the offer to join them in the photo session.

Of course, I had no idea who that 'very important visitor from Latin America' was until few weeks later, and after I came home to Nashville. I was reading *Time* magazine and the picture of this 'very important Latin American person' appeared in *Time* magazine. He was described, according to *Time,* as the most senior and notorious dedicated communist in Latin America. Wow! I could just imagine what would have happened had I taken a picture with this 'very important and notorious dedicated communist' from Latin America!

After leaving Beirut, on my way home to Nashville, I decided to break the trip and stop over to spend the night in Copenhagen, Denmark. I noticed, from a distance, a middle-aged bold man, wearing a tan raincoat was following me everywhere I went. Whether I went to the shopping mall, to the restaurant or to a café, there he was. I felt he was following me but could not determine his reasons for following me. Several thoughts came to mind: Is he a pimp who is trying to solicit foreigners and show them where the women clients are or may be, he is a member of the Danish Intelligence Service. If he were a pimp, well several questions popped up in mind, as to why he was selectively following me and not any of the several other foreigners at the mall. Therefore, very likely, he must be an agent of the intelligence department of the Danish government that was tipped off by another agent in Beirut. I stopped and asked him, as to what can I do for him and what did he want from me. I told him, I observed you following me wherever I went. He said, I want nothing from you, but I thought you might enjoy having a beer with me at my house and I would like for, you to meet my daughters. I told him, I am not interested in either proposition and I suggest you, to get lost and if you do not leave me alone, something unpleasant could happen to you! That did it as the man disappeared from my sight.

I then, firmly believed the Palestine Red Crescent Society's headquarters in Beirut, has more than its share of spies and undercover agents. It has informants, but to which organization or government these agents work for was an unknown to me, as I had no way to tell. The place, in addition to being corrupt, it has a very loose security apparatus. The administrators appear to have a trust in everybody that works there or visits the society's headquarters!

While waiting for my flight from Copenhagen to New York, I had a lot of lay time on my hand. I stopped by the Duty-Free shop at the Copenhagen international airport trying to purchase gifts for my children and for my wife. The sales person at the shop asked me as to where I was from. I said, United States. He said you Americans are crazy. I asked him, why is that? He said, you work like dogs and never enjoy life. You should live like us in Europe: we work for six hours a day from 8-12, go home for lunch and have a short siesta then come back to work for two more hours. Our evenings are, filled with parties and visits to our friends and other family members!

On the plane from Copenhagen to New York, two gentlemen seated behand me, were watching every move I make and listening to my conversations with others. I felt they were undercover agents that were sent to see if I act like a terrorist. These two individuals did not go through security at the airport, like other passengers, and disappeared upon landing at JFK airport.

Well after arriving at JFK my luggage was, thoroughly searched and the Customs agent found a plastic bag filled with a brown powder. The brown powder was a kilogram of 'Henna'. I had placed in the luggage. The officer searching my luggage asked as to what was in that bag. I said, jokingly, Hasheesh. He said hold on and let me call the specialist who knows about Hasheesh. The specialist came and after inspecting the bag said, I just came back from Lebanon where I was one of the investigators looking for any evidence of any Hasheesh being prepared for export to the outside world. He looked at me with a smile and said, the stuff you have is 'Henna' and not

Hasheesh. After leaving the Customs area, I was met by, a man who was accompanied by an Arabic speaking person at the gate. This man neither identified himself nor showed his badge. Since he did not identify himself so that I could tell as to which agency he belonged to, he started asking me if I had any Letters of Credit. I said no. Any watches. I said yes. I showed him, my wrist watch, which was given to me, by my wife seventeen years earlier. Then he asked if I have any gold. I said, of course I do. His eyes opened wide and said show me the gold. I opened my mouth and showed him the gold crowns on my inner teeth. He got mad and said, let us be serious! I said sir, I am very serious. You asked me the questions and I gave you my answers to all your questions. Could I be more serious than that? He left the gate and I went to board my connecting flight to Nashville. I suspected then, that this person was an agent of the Internal Revenue Service (IRS), since he asked me if I had any Letters of Credit, watches or gold or perhaps he may be an agent of the FBI. What I am sure of, however, was that a tip from some person, at the Palestine Crescent Society Headquarters in Beirut, must have transmitted to the government agency this person represents to question me, after arriving at JFK airport.

A week later, the FBI contacted my office and wanted to see when I would be available for the agent to come to my office and meet with me. I said I am available to meet with the agent any time that is convenient for him. The agent came to my office and questioned me for four hours every day. The agent kept asking as to why, did I go to Beirut in general and to the Palestine Red Crescent Society (PRCS), and what was the purpose of the visit. I told the agent my visit, was for discussions about the establishment of a joint venture between me and the Red Crescent Society for the establishment of a frozen blood facility. He asked as to who, did I have meetings with at the PRCS. I said the only contact I had was Dr. Fathi Arafat, who is the head of PRCS. Then he asked if I ever met Dr. Arafat's brother, Yasir, I said I never did. After questioning me for two weeks, I was cleared from any wrongs as they could not tie me to any security breaches. The agent never asked me, directly, about the "Very Important Latino "who was visiting the PRCS at the time I was there. Should the agent, have asked me about this Latino man, then, it would be obvious they knew all the details, as to who visits the PRCS and that will undoubtedly expose the FBI and perhaps the CIA that they may have undercover informants at the PRCS Headquarters in Beirut, and they know who visits and what is going on at that organization

This incident was reminiscent of another one I encountered in 1971. After spending a week in communist East Berlin, as a participant and speaker at the scientific sessions of the European Dialysis and Transplant Association (EDTA) Congress. A week after I returned, a woman, Mrs. J. Srouji, who I have known for years before, called my office and said she wanted to stop by and 'welcome' me home and know how my trip to a communist country went. I have never told her anything about my impending trip to East Berlin, as I have not seen that woman for at least fifteen years. Since I have not seen or talked to this woman for several years, so how did she know about my trip to a communist country? How did she know that I went to communist East Germany?

To my great surprise and deep disbelief, she told me that she is a communist and WE, Americans, should rise, have a revolution in this country and overthrow the United States government and by force, if necessary! I said, you must be kidding, are you not? You do not know how good and blessed you and I are to have been living in this country. You should go and just visit any country communist or otherwise in Europe or anywhere else in the world, for that matter, and see for yourself how they live. I just came back, after spending one week in communist East Germany and saw how people are treated and how they live. It is a police state and have no personal freedoms whatsoever. There were long lines of people trying to get their groceries, the streets were almost empty, as there were no cars and I have not seen a single smile on peoples' faces! There was a huge contrast between the people in East Berlin and those in West Berlin. The West Berliners were more cheerful, smiling and appear to be happy while those in East Berlin have a depressed look on their faces. If you are a communist, as you say you are, then perhaps you should leave this country and go live in the communist country of your choice. You are an adult and hopefully you know what you want in life. It is your choice to be a communist. I have never been and now I am not and will never be a communist. Please do not communicate with me anymore, as I have no interest in seeing your face again.

Mrs. J. Srouji used to invite foreigners, especially, Arabs to get-together meetings at her apartment. Why primarily Arabs, I was naive to think that the reason she invited only Arabs was perhaps due her ex-husband was a Palestinian Arab! Now putting these get-togethers and her latest admission that she is a communist, makes me suspicious of her intentions as being an undercover informant for the FBI, CIA or both or to any other intelligence agency!

While in East Berlin and while I was, fast asleep, and around two in the morning I was, awakened by a loud voice. The voice was that of the legendary Tennessean, Miss Lynn Anderson singing '*I Never Promised You a Rose Garden*'. I thought for a moment, am I dreaming or am I in my bed in Nashville? Looked around the room while I was, still half asleep, nothing in that room reminded me of my bedroom. Then I realized that I am somewhere else and that somewhere else, happens to be East Berlin. The nostalgic feeling of being home sublimed within ten minutes after I found out where I really was.

Getting out of East Berlin, after completing exit formalities and crossing into West Berlin was a nightmare. It took a very scary and long half hour. The East German authorities required our passports to be deposited in one cub hole with a black curtain and we had to wait until the processing of the passports is complete. After processing, the passports come out from another cub hole with a black curtain. No eye contact between the passport officer and the passport holder could occur as both were, separated by black curtains. It took thirty long and agonizing minutes before my passport came out with permission to leave. I had a very long and deep sigh of relief that I am free now. I was quite anxious and worried, that I may be, detained for any fabricated reason or crime. That will be, an important event to jail an American for a crime that never took place. I was very suspicious of the waiter, at the hotel restaurant that he may be an informant of the *Shashi* (the East German police). He was persistent in asking me for dollars. These evil thoughts kept hovering over my mind. Was he an undercover agent and if so, did he report me to the authorities? Apparently not!

It was a great relief to enter the American sector separating the Communist and American controlled sectors of Berlin. I asked the American officer to show me where it is safe for me to take pictures of the wall separating West and East Berlin. His response was quite reassuring when he said, you can stand anywhere you wish and take as many pictures as you want. You are now in the American sector and you are safe here.

The American University of Beirut Hospital invited me to participate in an international clinical immunology conference sponsored by the World Health Organization in 1974. Our daughter, Kim, accompanied me on my trip to Beirut. We went to the Kuwaiti embassy, in Beirut, to apply for visas to visit Kuwait. I wanted our daughter to meet her maternal aunt and her children who lived in Kuwait. The receptionist's, a Palestinian at the embassy, first question to me was about my nationality. I said Palestinian. He apologized saying I am very sorry, but the visa must come from Kuwait, as we are not authorized to issue visas to Palestinians at our embassy. I said, but it may take three months for the visa to be issued by the Kuwaiti authorities in Kuwait, and I have only three days. He apologized again and said I am very sorry. It is true the visa might take three months to come from Kuwait, but I cannot grant you a visa from our embassy in Beirut.

He then asked his second question as to the purpose of my trip to Kuwait, am I going to Kuwait to look for a job? I said, trust me sir, if they put the whole of Kuwait on a silver platter and offer it to me, I will refuse to accept it. No sir I am not going to look for a job in Kuwait. His last question was if I had any money. I said I am O.K. Now can I get the visa please. He again said I am sorry, but the visa must come from Kuwait. At that point, I pulled my American passport and asked him if I could get a visa on this passport. He said, Oh, hold on, hold on, please wait and let me ask the consul general. Within two minutes, the receptionist came back with the answer saying, the consul general will issue the visa and the visa will be ready in about thirty minutes. I asked the receptionist if there was a different person, other than me, who applied for the visa or it is the same person that happens to carry a different piece of paper (passport)? I said, tell your consul general that I am sorry I do not have thirty minutes to waste, waiting for his visa. If the visa is ready in ten minutes I will wait, otherwise please cancel my request. The visa was ready in less than ten minutes! I then wondered as to what has changed. I am still the same person whether I am holding the Palestinian travel document or the American passport. The only difference is that piece of paper!

LOSS OF FAITH IN DEALING WITH THE PALESTINE RED CRESCENT SOCIETY HEADQUARTERED IN BEIRUT

I SUSPECTED SPIES WERE ENTRENCHED AT THE HEADQUARTERS OF the Red Crescent Society in Beirut. This suspicion of spies at the Palestine Red Crescent Society's offices was, again confirmed, in my opinion by the incident at JFK airport and the FBI questioning me for two weeks after my return to Nashville.

My intention of partnering, with the Palestine Red Crescent Society in the establishment of a frozen blood facility in Beirut was, I thought and wrongly so, I am fulfilling my commitment in trying to render a little help to my people with the latest Blood Bank technology to move forward. Although I spent a week in Beirut trying to discuss the joint venture, Dr. Arafat and I met for no more than ten minutes discussing the Frozen Blood joint venture! I realized then that I have wasted my time and my money preparing the feasibility study with all the details of the proposal. At the end of our meeting, Dr. Arafat told me, that the Red Crescent Society pays its doctors a monthly salary of three thousand and five hundred Lebanese pounds (a thousand dollars at the time). I could not understand as to why he said that. He knows or should have known that I did not come to the PRCS to look for a job. I went there with the intention of establishing a joint venture in establishing a Frozen Blood facility. I told him, I did not come here to seek a job, but wanted to help you and your organization. Now I understand where you are coming from and ask you if you thought I came to apply for a job with the Red Crescent? Of course, not. I offered to put my own money into the joint venture in an effort on my part, was the least I thought, I could do to help my people. That signaled the end of the discussion of the joint venture and at least on my part dealing and communicating with the Red Crescent Society, under Dr. Fathi Arafat, in the future. The meeting ended with a handshake and a good-bye. In retrospect, I am pleased and thank God the joint venture did not materialize. Should that joint venture ever see the light, the outcome would have been my declaring bankruptcy due to, extortion and corruption or at the extreme, my murder. This happened more than once before to Palestinian Americans who went to the territories controlled by the Palestinian Authority to start a business with the intention of helping the people. They disappeared overnight without any trace of them was ever found!

Upon my return home to Nashville, I wrote Dr. Arafat a long letter expressing my disappointment and dismay, for the lack of interest on his part regarding the frozen blood project and for wasting Palestinian funds to pay for my travel expenses, as well as, the expenses I incurred preparing the proposal and going to Beirut to meet with him. I put my terms down should I be interested, and I am not, in applying for a job with the Red Crescent as he implied:

1. Monthly salary of $20,000 at a minimum paid in US$, not by Lebanese money

2. Fully furnished 3-bedroom, preferably 4-bedroom apartment

3. Car and driver for me

4. Schooling for our three daughters at the American Community School in Beirut

5. Five first class airline roundtrip tickets to the United states annually

6. One month paid vacation annually

Should these terms and conditions be palatable and acceptable to you and to the Palestine Red Crescent Society, you have my address and my phone number. I would not mind hearing from you.

It appeared that Dr. Arafat had an agenda of his own that was quite different from mine. I tried to help my people, by putting my own money and expertise into the joint venture, but Dr. Arafat thought, perhaps, he did not feel there is any personal financial gain for him out of the joint venture as it was, planned between the PRCS and myself. The project, its intended use and my ambition to help my people, went down the drain.

THE SAUDI MEDICAL SCHOOL EXPERIENCE AND THE PROBLEM OF EDUCATION OF OUR DAUGHTGERS IN SAUDI ARABIA

SINCE I STILL HAD ONE MORE YEAR TO GO AT MY INSTITUTION IN Nashville as dictated by Dr. Charles W. Johnson, interim medical school dean, I got a call from Dr. Tawfiq el-Tamimi, dean of the College of Medicine at the King Faisal University in Saudi Arabia. He asked me if I am interested in a professorship of Infectious Diseases and Immunology at their College of Medicine. I said thank you for the offer, however we have, to address several issues, prior to making my decision.

When I met with Dr. el-Tamimi in Houston, I found him to be very pleasant, humble and forthcoming. He had agreed, a week later, with all my conditions including salary, housing, benefits etc. My strong negotiating points with him were: I have a long history of teaching and researching in a medical school environment and I am bi-lingual, speaking both Arabic and English. I can teach the Saudi students in English and help them understand the material by talking to them in both Arabic and English.

His offer included a four-bedroom fully furnished condominium, a great salary (no taxes) and four first class roundtrip tickets to Nashville annually. The problem I had moving to Saudi Arabia, was the education of our daughters. The medical college was, located in al-Dammam, while the hospital and my living quarters were in al-Khobar, a ten-mile drive between the two locations. Our daughters, born and raised in the United States, would not fit in the local government schools. They could neither speak nor read Arabic as their mother tongue is English.

The only option left for me was to seek admission into the American School at the Arabian American Oil Company (ARAMCO) in al-Khobar. I called the school and spoke with the principal requesting admission for our three daughters into the American school. The principal of the school was very apologetic as she told me there were no vacancies available at the school. Suddenly, she asked me as to where did I come from, I said, Nashville, Tennessee. Now, I could imagine her having a big smile on her face when she said Oh well, I am a Tennessean too and I come from Knoxville, a city that is two hundred miles east of Nashville. Her tone of voice had changed dramatically when she said, I want you to know that three spots are, reserved for your daughters at the American school at ARAMCO. I was quite elated at the news and now I can move to Saudi Arabia with the family.

Because my wife is a registered nurse graduating from London, Dean el-Tamimi offered her a position at our hospital saying: Your wife would come with you in the morning and leave with you in the evening. He offered her a very attractive salary and said there was nothing for me to worry about, as rent and all utilities are, paid for by the University.

Securing schooling for our daughters was great news for me. However, the euphoria did not last long as the American school at ARAMCO was, closed by al-Mutawa'a, (the religious police) because the school was co-ed!

For that reason, I decided that moving the family to Saudi Arabia was out of question and was placed on the back burner. I joined the faculty of the medical school in Saudi Arabia while my family was still in Nashville,

My experience and certification in laboratory management led Dean el-Tamimi to request me to evaluate the medical laboratory services at our King Fahd Hospital. The Medical director of the hospital was Dr. T. Mustapha, an Egyptian with a degree in hospital management from the United States. All heads of departments and most staff members in the hospital were Egyptian. Some were good yet others, including the laboratory director who had poor qualifications were, not so good. I found out that the director lacked the knowledge and was not qualified to head a large university hospital laboratory. My evaluative report to the dean pointed out the positives and the negatives of the laboratory management and services. The report was hand-delivered to Dr. el-Tamimi, the dean of our medical school. Upon reading the report, the Dean found that many of the points I have raised in my report echoed the same concerns he had about the laboratory services at the hospital all along.

The Medical School has a rule stipulating all medical school faculty had to have hospital appointments as consultants. All appointments are, forwarded with recommendations from the department heads, for approval or disapprovals, to the medical director at the hospital. The medical director at the hospital will then deliver the names of approved faculty consultants to the dean of the medical school for the final endorsement. Appointments for all faculty members were approved except that of Dr. Abdallah M. Isa's, by the medical director, Dr. T. Mustapha. Dr. Mustapha's reason for denial of approval as provided in the denial document, "Dr. Isa is not qualified to be a consultant at our hospital"! An employee in the dean's office passed on to me, a copy of the list of approved faculty members and a copy of rejection of my appointment. The list of approvals had an attachment explaining why Dr. Isa's recommendation for appointment as consultant, was rejected. It is because Dr. Isa is not qualified to be on the hospital staff.

A German American Pathologist with a heavy accent, Dr. Boehme was, appointed as head of the Pathology department at the hospital with one additional responsibility, to oversee the medical laboratories. Dr. Boehme was a puppet of Dr. T. Mustapha and would do anything he asked him to do. Dr. Boehme was, instructed by Dr. T. Mustapha, to write the letter of rejection of Dr. Isa's appointment as consultant at the hospital. The letter signed by both Dr. T. Mustapha and Dr. Boehme was, delivered to the dean of the medical school for his action. In that letter they stated Dr. Isa is neither fit nor qualified to be a medical consultant at our hospital.

Dr. Y. el-Jindan, the Saudi administrator who was Dr. T. Mustapha's immediate supervisor at the hospital, called a meeting to discuss several issues relating to the hospital operations, including the 'new' faculty consultant appointments. Dr. el-Jindan, requested that I be at the meeting, as the topic of my rejection as consultant is in the will be discussed. When the discussions of the hospital laboratories came up and the question as to why Dr. Isa's appointment as consultant was rejected came up, Dr. T. Mustapha stood up and said Dr. Isa is not qualified to be a consultant at our hospital. When asked by Dr. el-Jindan as to the reason for the rejection, Dr. Mustapha was mum and never said a word. I stood up and told the committee that I am here today, wearing two different hats: One as the acting chair of the department and the other is for myself. I passed a copy of the letter of rejection of Dr. Isa's appointment as a consultant bearing the signatures of both Dr. T. Mustapha and Dr. Boehme, to each member of the committee. I apologized to the committee about wanting to leave the meeting as I was heading home to the United States. Dr. El-Jindan requested that I stick around for few more minutes. Upon questioning Dr. Taher Mustapha about the rejection of Dr. Isa's appointment, Dr. T. Mustapha jumped, raised his voice, and said Dr. Isa's report to the dean about the operations of the hospital laboratories was very negative and destructive! That was the reason for rejecting his appointment. Dr. Y. el-Jindan overruled both of Dr. Mustapha's and of Dr. Boehme's decisions, my appointment as a medical consultant at the hospital was, finally approved.

Upon my return from the United States, I was very surprised to find out that, mass terminations, including Drs. Mustapha and Boehme and the Egyptian Director of Laboratories have taken place at our King Fahd hospital. It should be, pointed out that being an Egyptian, Dr. T. Mustapha like, other Egyptians in positions of authority, appoint only Egyptians to fill vacant positions in areas they have control of!

The King Faisal School of Medicine had state of the art medical and research equipment that was imported primarily from the United States. While the medical equipment was, put into use at the hospital, the research equipment was kept in a huge room under lock and key. There was no research activity to speak of as the equipment in the locked-up room was off limits to any of us. Any ambition to do research, basic or clinical was thwarted by orders of the university administration!

Saudi Arabia had a contract with Harvard Medical School to have faculty members from Harvard come to Saudi Arabia to consult and lecture, on their specialties, to the faculty and students of the different medical schools in the kingdom. Dr.

John David, a Harvard professor of Immunology, who I knew before, came in to lecture to us on Immunology. His lecture sounded, at least to me, as though he was talking to high school or grammar school kids. He showed slides of old and irrelevant material. I stood up and said, John, please talk to us about the latest advances in Immunology instead of talking to us and showing us slides of antiquated and irrelevant information. The information you are presenting to us is at least one hundred years old. This is insulting to our intelligence!

To my great surprise and astonishment, the contract with Harvard medical school was, cancelled within few months of the incident that Dr. John David and I had. Whether my comments to Dr. John David, during his lecture might have had anything to do with the termination of the contract with Harvard or perhaps, there may have been other complainers like mine is unknown to me.

In the meantime, there was so much turmoil at my former institution in Nashville. Problems at the institution started to come up in the open in 1981 and became more complicated through 1984. The interim president and the crew he brought in, as a new group of professionals and as part of his new administration in 1981 were, all sacked. Another 'new' president and his team were, brought in in 1984. A sense of stability did set in at the institution. The newly appointed dean of the medical school that came with the new administration, contacted me and offered me the position of chairperson of my former department. I politely declined the offer, thanking him for his faith in me and in my abilities to lead the department, as I had other ambitions I wanted to pursue.

I spent a total of twenty months in Saudi Arabia, coming home every two months as the family was still in Nashville. The feeling of separation from the family and having our daughters grow up in my not being there for them had its toll, on me. I contacted Dr. el-Tamimi, dean of our medical school to inform him of my decision, for family reasons, to resign my positions at the medical school and at the hospital citing lack of schooling possibilities in the kingdom for our daughters. He was visibly upset and tried, for two weeks, to dissuade me, to abandon my decision of resignation. He even suggested that I could send our children to schools in Italy. I was infuriated at that suggestion and said to him: dean, are you telling me that my wife and I should be separated from our children by sending them to Italy while we are in Saudi Arabia? Is not family separation against our religion of Islam? How different would that be for them to go school in Italy or going to school in the United States and still live at home? He started to play on my emotions by saying this is your country and this is your medical school and your hospital, we want you here. When he realized that my decision to resign was, final he said, whenever you are ready to come back you could inform me by phone, telex or letter of your intention to return and your position will be held and waiting for you.

During my tenure in Saudi Arabia and prior to their adopting a system of payment of salaries by check, all salaries to employees were, paid in cash. We used to carry a large brown bag to collect our monthly salary in Saudi Riyals. Our salaries were net, as no deductions in the way of taxes, medical care, housing or utilities were made. The only expenses we incurred were for food and for gas for our cars. Gas, at the time was, 25c a gallon!

I did enjoy working at the medical school in Saudi Arabia, however, the feeling of being in an open-air jail never left me. Saudi Arabia is a secretive society and many decisions are made at the institution, without involving the faculty in the decision-making process. Our passports, as expatriates were, retained in the security office of the university. To travel outside the country, or for that matter, travel within the kingdom, it was not possible without first having a 'special permission' to do so. This 'special permission' had to come from the highest office at the university that must also have a prior approval from the security services at the institution!

One other thing that I observed while in Saudi Arabia that Saudi colleagues do not socialize and interact with non-Saudi faculty, especially Arab faculty. They would come to visit me at my condominium, but never was I invited into their homes. I inquired about this phenomenon from other expatriate colleagues who confirmed the same observation. I believed, then that the Saudi the government discourages intermingling and socializing of Saudis with other Arabs, as that may influence their way of thinking and open their minds as to what is going on outside their country.

The government of Saudi Arabia was holding back, as mandated by the Arab League, 5% of the monthly salary of every Palestinian working in the Kingdom. The funds deducted from the salaries will be transferred to, the Palestine Liberation Organization (PLO) office in Riyadh. The same rule was, implemented by all Arab countries because the decision was adopted by the Arab League to fund the PLO through the incomes of Palestinians working in the Arab countries.

I was told by the Bursar's office that, because I am Palestinian, 5% of my monthly salary will be deducted and sent to the PLO Office in Riyadh, Saudi Arabia. Of course, I did not agree with the deduction of the 5% of my salary as it won't go to help the Palestinian people, but rather it will be destined to benefit a few at the top of the organization. Corruption and misuse of the funds at that organization is a common day occurrence. I told them, I am Lebanese and not Palestinian. Please check my passport that is held by your security office at the university. It will show you that I was born in Lebanon and not in Palestine, thus I am Lebanese and exempt from the 5% deduction of my salary that would be, diverted to the PLO. When they found out that I am 'Lebanese-born' as my passport indicates, the rules did not apply to me, no deduction of 5% of my salary had ever taken place!

We, Palestinians have always boasted of having the highest percentage of university graduates, not only in the Middle East, but also in the world at large. This confirmation was, reported by *Newsweek* magazine in the early 1970s. Parents were telling their children that the only way to move forward was through education as there was nothing else for them to depend on other than their university degrees. This quest for education, by Palestinians, was the only route to pursue, in the hope of guaranteeing survival and perhaps lead to potential success in the world. This dream of going to school disappeared completely and its value vanished when *Fatah*, the major faction of the Palestine Liberation Organization (PLO), became so popular that led many of the Palestinian kids join its ranks instead of getting an education. As the power of the PLO reached new heights, it was now able to dictate its terms and conditions on the Arab governments. This was a serious strategic mistake, in my opinion, that was committed by, the PLO. It had turned the Arab governments, who were supporting its agenda to become haters and enemies of the PLO and of course, of the Palestinian people as a group!

The euphoria of the power of the PLO and the belief that Palestine is close to be liberated, has subsided because it has backfired. It had a negative impact on the attitude of young Palestinians regarding going to school and get an education. Going to school, requires discipline and commitment on the part of the student and on the ability of the parents to instill in them the importance of going to school and later to the university. Having lost that discipline and guidance, young Palestinians opted to take the easy way out and join the PLO militias rather than going to school. The level of education has plummeted to new lows and we ended up with an uneducated and to degree of illiterate generation. The way I look at it was a complete brain washing of the younger generation of Palestinians, by the PLO, that bearing arms in the quest for the liberation of Palestine was much more urgent and more important than pursuing an education.

I was disgusted, yet at the same time frightened, with the response of one of these militias who I met in a taxicab during my visit to Beirut. I asked him as to what he does as a member of the armed militia. He responded by telling me the story of a fellow militiaman who wanted to marry the girl he loved, except that the girl's father was opposed to the idea and refused to accept the man marrying his daughter. This militiaman said, and I repeat verbatim: 'we went to the girl's house, beat the hell out of her father, kidnapped the girl and delivered her to the militiaman who planned to marry her in the first place'.

I said to him that is wonderful and because of your dedication to the cause, you have achieved the first step into the liberation of Palestine. Because of your action, we will return to Palestine next year. Only and only, after you and your colleagues, prey on more innocent Palestinians as you did to the girl's father, Palestine will soon be liberated. What a shame to lose a generation of young Palestinians to ignorance and to potential crime!

The actions and behavior of some members, of the *Fatah* movement, blemished the image of the Liberation Movement, as not a liberation movement, but rather a bunch of hoodlums and thugs. These actions, as seen by the Lebanese population, had a negative impact, not only on the PLO itself, but also on the Palestinians as a whole. It reminded the Lebanese of the Black September debacle that took place in Jordan. At the time, Yasir Arafat, trying to project the PLO muscle by telling the Jordanian king, we Palestinians are the ones who had built your capital Amman, and now we are, capable of destroying it. Do you understand that? When the PLO was expelled from Jordan with a bloody nose, it moved its forces and established a base in Lebanon. The PLO gained acceptance by allying itself with the Lebanese Sunni Moslem population who had grievances against the Lebanese government of Lebanon ruled and over-whelmingly controlled by Lebanese Christians. The newly formed alliance between the PLO and the Sunni Moslem community brought the wrath of the conservative Christian population. They claimed and branded the PLO to be an occupying force and must be, dealt with as such. The alliance between the PLO and the Lebanese Sunni Moslems sowed the seeds for the second civil war that began in the summer of 1975.

The Tennessee Business delegation, which I had a hand in establishing and was a member of, landed at Beirut International Airport and drove directly to the Excelsior hotel in West Beirut. While sitting in the lobby of the hotel waiting for the Lebanese partners to come in, I saw one of the hotel employees picking a machine gun from the trunk of his car. He brought the machinegun to the hotel. When I asked him as to the purpose of having a machinegun in the hotel, he responded by saying, to fight the Palestinians who are trying to take over our country. Of course, I did not dare mention to him or to others at the hotel that I am of Palestinian extraction as the anti-Palestinian emotions were very high at that moment!

Few hours later, the civil war broke out, when a bus loaded with Palestinians coming back to Beirut from a wedding ceremony was, ambushed by the Phalange (Christian) militia in the town of Kahale, east of the city. That ambush killed scores of innocent Palestinian men, women and children that were riding the bus, singing and celebrating the wedding ceremonies.

Unfortunately, the 1975 civil war reminded me of the first one that took place in the late 1950s. The first civil war, which I witnessed firsthand, at the time, started in 1958. In both wars, the conflict turned sectarian with Christians killing Moslems and Moslems killing Christians based on their names and religious affiliation. At the height of the 1958 civil war, the Lebanese army split into two opposing factions: Christian and Moslem armies. What added to the cause of the split of the army was the deci-sion by the then President of the Republic, Mr. Camille Chamoun, to go against the constitution to, renew his 6-year term as president of the republic. Of course, things went out of hand in the country, as the government (no government) was unable to function and bring stability to the country.

After the end of the 1975 civil war, things started to calm down a little bit, but tensions remained as the grievances of the Sunni Moslems were not addressed or acknowledged by the other party. It did add more restrictions against the Palestinians living in the country.

The PLO, as a well-armed and very powerful organization, was still in control over the Moslem areas of West Beirut. When I was in Beirut in June of 1981 discussing the joint venture of establishing a frozen blood manufacturing facility with Dr. Fathi Arafat, head of the Palestine Red Crescent Society, I noticed armed Palestinians roaming the streets with their loaded guns and mountains of garbage scattered all over the neighborhoods. When I complained to Dr. Arafat about what I saw, his response: Dr. Abdallah, this is a revolution! I then said, had I been a Lebanese person, I would, hate Palestinians and would do anything in my power to get rid of them!

Well, things did not cool down in the country in the aftermath of the civil war. The Lebanese government still considering the PLO as an occupation force and must be fought and forced out of the country. Events started to seriously, turn against the PLO when Mr. Basheer Gemayyil, a member of the conservative Christian Phalange party was, elected the new president of the country. Having been unable to route the PLO and push it out of the country, he sought the help of the Israelis to do the dirty job. Ariel Sharon the Israeli Prime Minister, not wishing to lose the golden opportunity of routing the PLO forces, was more than happy and willing to help, as he was fighting the same enemy. Prime Minister Sharon's army invaded Lebanon and occupied Beirut in1982. It is, documented that the Israeli invasion of Lebanon took place upon the request of the Lebanese president, Mr. Basheer Gemayyil. In a shameful demonstration of welcoming the 'perceived' enemy, the Christian community in Lebanon, welcomed the Israeli army as liberators with roses and rice! Coordination between the Christian militia led by President Basheer Gemayyil and the Israeli army led to the atrocities that were committed against Palestinians in both the Sabra and Shatila refugee camps. Under the protection and eyes of the Israeli forces, the Christian militias ravaged the camps and committed those horrific atrocities for which hundreds of innocent Palestinian men, women and children were, massacred. It was a horrific massacre that amounted to war crimes committed by, the highest offices of the Lebanese and Israeli governments.

The Israeli invasion of Lebanon, at the request of the president of the country, caused the disruption of the PLO activities and the dismantling of its bases and presence in Lebanon. Under American protection, some of the PLO forces boarded ships with their guns, were sent to Tunisia and to Libya. Others were, sent to Yemen and others to 'too far places' away from the Israeli border. Dismantling of the PLO presence in Lebanon had a dual victory for both Lebanon as well as for Israel.

With the essential removal of the PLO threat to Israel, it has become clear that events leading to ending the PLO presence, in Jordan first and more recently in Lebanon, were the work of clandestine, secret discussions and planning, between Lebanon and some other Arab countries, on one side and with the Israelis and the Americans on the other side.

The dream Yasir Arafat was dreaming of, was his vision to build a national Palestinian identity. His dreams and ambitions of building such an identity were, smashed and destroyed by Israel and by the conspiring Arab governments.

Now, having achieved the goal of removal of any threat to Israel by the PLO or others from neighboring Arab countries, all efforts were directed at having a peace treaty between the Arabs and Israel. The first and foremost discussion that gained prominence was the signing of the "Oslo Accords" that were championed by Mahmoud Abbas in 1993.

The Oslo Accords champion, Mahmoud Abbas, is now head of the Palestinian Authority. He sold the idea to Yasir Arafat, who apparently accepted it at its face value. Those accords stipulated the extraction, from the PLO, the recognition of the existence of the Israeli state. I personally was, and still am opposed to these accords. My opposition stemmed from the facts, on the ground, that the Arabs in general and the Palestinians are no match to the Zionist lobbying and propaganda machine in selling the accords to the world. I am also opposed to these accords because they legitimized the existence of Israel as a state, thus resulting in the abrogation of our right of return that is now in a deep freeze. The accords, as envisioned by Mahmoud Abbas and blessed by Yasir Arafat backfired. They did not achieve any of the legitimate rights and aspirations of the Palestinian people and no peace treaty was, signed between the Zionists and the Palestinian people. The accords were a ploy employed by Israel and blessed by the United States to achieve more expansion on the ground, and acceptance, not only by the Arab states but also by the world as, a whole. Several countries that were sympathetic to the Palestinians and to their cause, have rushed to recognize Israel as a legitimate state and as a member of the world community, only after the PLO recognized the existence of Israel. Case-in-point here is that of India. India was a staunch supporter of the Palestinians and their rights never recognized Israel, but since the Palestine Liberation Organization (PLO) had recognized Israel so why would not India do the same? Now India did. In short, the Oslo Accords were the last nail in the coffin of Palestinian national identity and the aspirations Yasir Arafat was dreaming of and struggling to achieve.

Of course, as of this writing, no resolution of the Palestinian/Israeli problem has come to the surface. Instead Israel has become stronger and the Arabs in general and the Palestinians in particular, have become much weaker. Thanks to you Mr. Mahmoud Abbas. You have robbed our identity and destroyed our dream of return!

MY TENURE IN THE KINGDOM OF SAUDI ARABIA AND THE POLITICAL ENVIRONMENT IN THE COUNTRY

HAVING JOINED THE FACULTY OF THE SCHOOL OF MEDICINE OF THE King Faisal University in 1983, as a professor of Microbiology, Immunology and Infectious Diseases gave me the feeling of fulfilment of my potential contributions into the betterment of the Arab students. To my big surprise, it was more of an illusion than a reality.

Working in Saudi Arabia felt like working in a police state. And a police state it is! Once a week, I was, asked to visit the university hospital at another satellite campus to lecture to and consult with the doctors and medical staff. The hospital is in el-Ihsaa', a 50-mile drive from our King Fahd hospital in al-Khobar.

A car and driver were, provided for me for each weekly trip. The driver always 'complained' to me that his government of Saudi Arabia, particularly the intelligence service, keeps bugging him and pressuring him demanding that he works for them. He said he was confused and wanted to see if I have any suggestions to help him reach a sound decision, as to what he should do. We would leave in the morning of every Thursday and come back in the evening. Every time we went to visit that hospital, the driver 'complained' to me throughout our trip, that he was under pressure by the government to work for them.

After getting tired of hearing the same redundant complaint time and time again, I said, should my government ever ask me to work for I would never hesitate to accept. I will do exactly what my government wants me to do. If you still want my advice, I would say to you go for it and work for your government! The same discussion, asking for my opinion, went on for the whole semester. Of course, I knew where this driver was coming from. Although he works as a driver at the university but his main job, in my opinion, was to be an informant for the Saudi intelligence service. The driver was trying to pull my leg to say some negative things about Saudi Arabia in general and about the Royal family in particular! Had he succeeded in having me, open and criticize the government or the royal family, I am very sure I would be on the first flight out of the country if not sent to jail!

While in Saudi Arabia, our daughters came to visit with me and spend a month in Saudi Arabia. My wife flew into Saudi Arabia, a week later after she visited her family in Beirut. The security services at the airport would not let her out of the security office at the airport and into the city, or to allow her to, even talk to us.

Our daughters and I waited until about 1:00 AM hoping, my wife, will be allowed into the country. They would not let us come any closer to where she was and would not allow us to talk to her. I did my best to try to find out what the problem was. They said, although she does have a legitimate visa to enter the country, but because the stamp affixed to the visa page on her passport, was not embossed with the endorsement and confirmation as required! I tried to reason with them by saying it is not my wife's fault, but rather it is the fault of the Saudi embassy in Washington DC who issued the visa to have this discrepancy. They would not budge. I then asked to use their phone to call my friend and former classmate, Prince Faisal Ibn Abdel Aziz. The officer asked his boss who came out to question me about my relationship with Prince Faisal. He asked me as to how did I know the prince. I told him Faisal was my classmate at the University of California at Berkeley. He then made a phone call to his immediate supervisor and few minutes later my wife was, united with me and with our daughters!

My cousin Suleiman, who also worked and lived in Saudi Arabia, came to visit us and to meet my wife and our daughters. When I took him home about 1:00 AM, our youngest daughter, Deena wanted to come along. While driving my cousin home, I noticed a police car coming from the opposite direction.

I kept driving on the right side of the street, but the police car kept coming to the left side towards me. I got a little nervous and worried about having a head-on collision with the police car. I stopped and two of the cops came out and asked as to why am I driving on the wrong side on a one-way street? I said, oh, is this a one-way street? Did I miss seeing the one-way sign? Where is the one-way sign? Where I come from, there are always 'Do Not Enter or One Way' signs posted on the street. I do not see a 'Do Not Enter or One-Way sign' to tell me this is, the wrong way or it is one-way street. They asked for, and I delivered, my Saudi issued driver license. When they read the details on my Saudi driver license that showed my nationality, one of the officers asked me, are you American? I said yes, I am. He, with a big frown and surprised look on his face asked me again, why am I an American? I, said why not? This is the way it is, sir! They let me go without giving me a traffic citation! Whether because I am American, which is more likely, or because there was no one-way street sign is not clear to me. Had I not been a holder of an American passport with my Saudi driver's license indicating of what my nationality is other than American, more than likely, I would end up spending the night in jail. When it comes to traffic violations, minor or serious ones should they happen, such as an accident regardless who the perpetrator is, the blame and fault is always that of the expatriates as it is their fault and never is the fault of the Saudis.

Clandestine contraband alcohol was available all over the place in the Eastern Province where our medical school and hospital are located. Although alcohol sale or consumption is illegal in Saudi Arabia, it was available and sold by individuals in secret places in the area. However, the supply of such contraband alcohol dries up whenever the king and his entourage paid a visit to the area! I was, told the king and his company arrange for the purchase of all the alcohol available in the black market, not for its destruction, but rather for their own use!

Having difficulty securing schooling for our daughters in Saudi Arabia and not wishing for them to grow up in my absence, I offered my resignation from the faculty of the Medical School and from the hospital as well. Dean el-Tamimi was very upset about my decision to resign and tried over a two-week period to make me withdraw my resignation. I said, I am willing, to withdraw my resignation, only and only if I could be granted a leave of absence, otherwise my resignation still stands. He said, he will investigate my request for a leave of absence by discussing the issue with the Personnel department and with the higher-ups in the Ministries of Health and Higher Education. To his dismay, he found out there are no provisions in existence for a leave of absence at the university. The Ministry of Higher Education in Saudi Arabia does not allow permission of a leave of absence. He insisted that I should withdraw my resignation by saying this is your country and this is your university, we want you here. I said, Dean, I appreciate your confidence in me, but my family comes first and regretfully, I must resign so that I be there to see my daughters grow up and become adults where both parents are in the same household.

When the dean realized that I am very adamant and serious about my resignation, he then said, "Whenever your family situation is resolved and after your daughters go to college and you are still willing to come back, your position will always be there waiting for you. You could just write to me a letter or phone me to tell me that you are ready to come back. I will take care of all the formalities and will send you the airline tickets and supporting documents".

Upon leaving Saudi Arabia and while at the airport, trying to catch a flight out of the country something weird and unusual happened. Customs officials started inspecting my luggage and other passengers' luggage too. I thought customs agents, at airports, normally check out and inspect the luggage of passengers coming into the country and not those leaving it unless there is a problem. As the Saudi Customs agent inspected my and other peoples' luggage upon leaving the country, I wondered if they had any suspicion of us stealing a mattress, a window, a door, a car or other items of value that we were not supposed to have taken out of the country.

Coming home, at the end of my tenure in Saudi Arabia, was a combination of happiness and sadness. I was, of course, happy to be back with my family, yet I was sad for missing the many fine friends I had made during my twenty-month tenure in Saudi Arabia.

Leaving Saudi Arabia was timely for me. A year after leaving the country, as conditions of employment changed regarding the employment of expatriates. The kingdom instituted a new law of "Saudization" of employment with the intent of replacing expatriates with Saudis. In addition, the government slashed the salaries of expatiates by half to be in line with those of the Saudis. It is worth mentioning that salaries for Saudi employees were, much lower than, those provided to us, expatriate employees. With the "Saudization" law in effect, many of the perks such as housing and travel allowances that were accorded to expatriates and not to Saudi employees were, slashed to the point that working in Saudi Arabia has become no longer worthwhile. The expatriates were, given the choice of either leaving the country or accepting the new terms of employment. Several of my colleagues opted to leave, yet others decided to stay.

DONATION OF MONEY TO HELP EGYPTIAN WIDOWS AND ORPHANS OF WAR

UPON RESIGNING MY POSITION IN SAUDI ARABIA AND MY RETURN TO Nashville, while attending the Friday Noon Prayers at the Mosque, an Egyptian cleric came and gave the sermon to the congregation. At the end of the sermon, the blind cleric asked the congregation for help for Egyptian widows and orphans who lost their husbands and fathers in the 1973 Middle East war. His plea was very emotional and convincing. I wanted to do my civic duty to help by donating some money. I asked the cleric as to what name should the check be written to? He said, to me, "Shaikh Omar Abdel Rahman". I wrote him a check for $100 and wrote on the check "for Egyptian widows and orphans". Few months later, it was all over the news, that the blind Egyptian cleric, Shaikh Omar Abdel Rahman, was raising money, not for the Egyptian widows and orphans, but for the support of terrorists! He was, arrested and ordered to jail where he spent time until his death in February 2017. Had I donated cash to the cleric or wrote him a check without mentioning "to help the Egyptian widows and orphans", I am sure the FBI will be knocking at my door in the wee hours of the night as I may be a suspect of terrorism!

A month after my return from Saudi Arabia, a former colleague at the medical school, in Nashville, who is now dean at the other school in town, called to tell me a professorial position at his school is open and the position is mine should I be interested. My response was fine, but only as part time as I have other commitments and plans to pursue. I am in the process of establishing a Biotechnology company. He said, that is fine, please come by to review the terms of the contract and sign it if you agree.

Reviewing the terms and conditions of employment as provided by the department head, I found there was no mention of promotion or tenure. When I questioned the department head about these two important items prior to signing the contract, he was unable to provide an answer, but said he will check with the Human Services department and let me know as soon as possible. Well, the answer came with the affirmative that Promotion and Tenure provisions will apply after one year of employment. I have been a member of the faculty at this institution since August of 1985.

ESTABLISHMENT OF A BIOTECHNOLOGY MANUFACTURING FACILITY

STARTING THE BIOTECHNOLOGY MANUFACTURING FACILITY WAS NOT an easy feat. It required financial resources that will support the purchase of equipment, consumables, payment of the lease for rented structures and more importantly, to pay the salaries of employees and benefits which take the biggest chunk of the budget. Financial resources to support the operation could come from any of the many possible sources. Such sources include Venture Capitalists, partnerships, bank loans or personal funds. I did not wish to borrow money or have any partners in the enterprise but opted to use my own personal funds to finance the operation.

To have a successful enterprise and in addition to its funding, it demands commitment and perseverance as the road to success may not be easily arrived at. It took over two years for the first product in the form of a diagnostic test kit to be available for the market. Of course, these diagnostic test kits were designed and intended for use in hospitals, medical laboratories and in doctor's offices, but not intended for use by the public.

Building a customer base and introducing the products to market, required an aggressive advertising campaign in national and international medical and trade publications.

Amico Laboratories Inc., the Biotechnology Company, was established in August 1985 in Nashville, Tennessee. The charter of Amico Laboratories Inc. states, for the manufacture of state-of-the art diagnostic test kits and reagents intended for use in the diagnosis of infectious and autoimmune diseases. The focus of the company was the manufacture of diagnostic test kits and reagents to use in the diagnosis of autoimmune disorders and infectious diseases caused by bacterial, viral and protozoan agents. The company was registered with the State of Tennessee as a for profit organization. It was also registered with the US Food and Drug Administration (FDA), with the US department of Health and Human Services and with the Tennessee Department of Health. These registrations entitled the company to legally manufacture and distribute top-of-the line diagnostic test kits and reagents in the domestic as well as in the International markets.

To, legally place the products on the marketplace, the US Food and Drug Administration (FDA) must first approve the facility, including the premises, equipment and all the records pertaining to manufacturing on an annual basis. Compliance with Good Manufacturing Practices (GMP) and Medical Device Register (MDR) are top requirements by the FDA. In addition, FDA certifies the facility only, if it passes the annual inspection by FDA investigators. FDA must also approve every product placed on the market, not only in the United States, but also throughout the world. Every diagnostic test kit, the individual components of the kit, as well as the different reagents the company plans to market, are required by the FDA, to be registered prior to their introduction to the marketplace.

Upon his/her arrival to the facility the investigator checks the facility, the floors, the walls, heating and cooling equipment, the bathrooms and the equipment used in manufacturing and its maintenance records. After examining the physical structure and the equipment/she he moves to examine all the manufacturing records including those of labeling, R&D, shipping and most importantly the complaints file.

While reading the records he had requested, the inspector is writing notes as to his findings during which time the responsible person at the facility is, nervously waiting for any questions from the investigator!

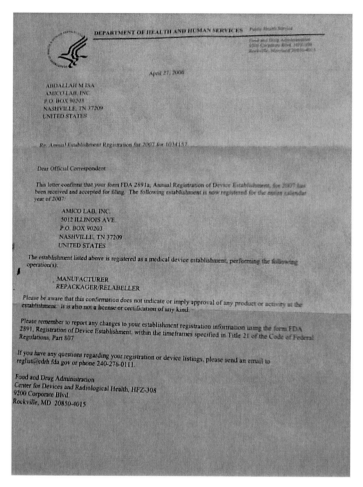

(Certificate from the United States Food and Drug Administration, FDA, issued
annually to Amico Laboratories Inc. to continue to legally manufacture and
distribute Biotechnology test products for Infectious Diseases and for
Autoimmune diagnosis)

The company produced over fifty different diagnostic test kits and over twenty
different reagents for sale in the domestic and international markets. All products
were designed and intended for use in the diagnosis of Infectious and Autoimmune
diseases with special attention paid to their safety and effectiveness. Several of the
products were, intended for the diagnosis of acute and of late stages of viral, bacterial
and protozoan diseases.

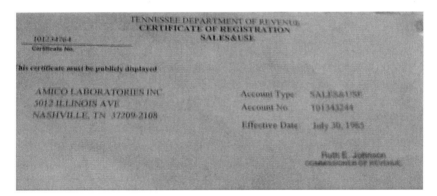

REGISTRATION NO.: 1034157
FOR: 2006

OWNER / OPERATOR NO.:   1034157

DEPARTMENT OF HEALTH AND HUMAN SERVICES
PUBLIC HEALTH SERVICE
FOOD AND DRUG ADMINISTRATION

**ANNUAL REGISTRATION OF
DEVICE ESTABLISHMENT**

NOTE: This form is authorized by Section 510 of the Food, Drug, and Cosmetic Act (21 U.S.C. 360). Failure to report this information is a violation of Section 301(p) of the Act (21 U.S.C. 331(p)). Persons who violate this provision may, if convicted, be subject to fine or imprisonment or both. The submission of any report that is false or misleading in any material respect is a violation of Section 301(q)(2) (21 U.S.C. 331(q)(2)) and may be a violation of 18 U.S.C. 1001.

REGISTERED ESTABLISHMENT

AMICO LAB, INC.
5012 ILLINOIS AVE.
P.O. BOX 90203
NASHVILLE, TN   37209

OWNER / OPERATOR

AMICO LAB, INC.
5012 ILLINOIS AVE.
P.O. BOX 90203
NASHVILLE, TN   37209

OFFICIAL CORRESPONDENT

MR. ABDALLAH M ISA
AMICO LAB, INC.
P.O. BOX 90203
NASHVILLE, TN   37209

ESTABLISHMENT TYPE   MANUFACTURER
REPACK/RELABEL

Detach Part 1 and Keep as Proof of Registration.
Complete and Return Part 2.
Detach and Refer to Part 3 for Specific Instructions.

Form FDA 2891a (5/02)   Part 1 - Keep for Your Records

Form Approved: OMB. No. 0910-0387
Expiration Date: March 31, 2005

(Certificate of Compliance by FDA annual renewal of the license to operate as a Manufacturer and Distributor of Medical Devices)

In addition to licensure by the US Food and Drug Administration (FDA) and the Tennessee Department of Health, the company was also certification by the State of Tennessee department of Revenue must be secured prior to operation.

TENNESSEE DEPARTMENT OF REVENUE
CERTIFICATE OF REGISTRATION
SALES&USE

101234764
Certificate No.

This certificate must be publicly displayed

AMICO LABORATORIES INC
5012 ILLINOIS AVE
NASHVILLE, TN 37209-2108

Account Type   SALES&USE
Account No.   101343244
Effective Date   July 30, 1985

Ruth E. Johnson
COMMISSIONER OF REVENUE

(License to manufacture and sell Biotechnology products in the State of Tennessee, the United States and the world at large. The license indicates that the manufacturing facility is a legitimate and legal entity)

In addition to manufacturing of diagnostic test kits and reagents, a clinical laboratory testing service was also established at Amico Laboratories Inc. Clinical specimens from patients with infectious and autoimmune diseases were analyzed and the results with recommendations were, reported to the attending physicians.

As a historical fact, the Clinical Laboratory Service at Amico Laboratories Inc. was, the first and only laboratory service in the state of Tennessee to provide confirmatory test results for the diagnosis of HIV/AIDS infection using in-house produced reagents.

The Biotechnology laboratory operation consisted of a well-equipped facility with state-of-the art equipment. Its main departments are:

1. Cell culture: in this area cells, especially cancer cells, ware grown *in vitro*, passaged and maintained. Many of the cell lines that are grown to be used for infecting them with different viruses and some bacteria, notably among those bacterial infections, the Chlamydia bacterium that are used in the preparation of the diagnostic test kits. The infected cell culture sheets are the source of the integral component of the test kits that are designed to diagnose viral or bacterial infections. Other cell culture sheets were used to prepare components of test kits that are intended for the diagnosis of autoimmune diseases.

2. The Centrifugation and Separation department is designed for the separation of the *in vitro* grown cells, from the culture supernatants, as well as, to isolate cell products that could have anti-cancer activity and possible therapeutic properties. Also, in this department, separation and purification of fluorescein and enzyme-labeled antibody conjugates are done and the final products used as components of the diagnostic test kits

3. Research and Development department. In this department, investigation of the effectiveness of the supernatants and their individual components, as to their activity against cancer cells and to ascertain the labeling of the antibodies with fluorescent dye (Fluorescein Iso-thiocyanate), enzymes (Horseradish Peroxidase) or Latex particles for use in the diagnostic test kits

4. Labeling and packaging department of complete test kits for shipment to the domestic and the international markets

5. Shipping department

6. Clinical laboratory Service department where clinical specimens are, analyzed and results reported to the patient's doctor. Many of the reagents used for diagnosis of disease were prepared in house, other reagents needed but not produced in-house were, ordered from other suppliers.

(The Amico Biotechnology Company Laboratory street sign at the entrance of the facility at 4820 Charlotte Avenue in Nashville, Tennessee)

(Research and development (R & D), in the area, of Enzyme Immunoassays depicting whole 96-well plates on the left with removable 8-well strips, The Elisa readers are used to read the Optical Density {color intensity} in the whole plate or in individual 8-well strips)

ELISA (Enzyme Linked Immunosorbent Assay) Readers are employed in R&D to test specimens and confirm results prior to inclusion into the final product.

The Elisa readers are also employed in the Clinical Testing department, to analyze clinical specimens from patients suspected of having bacterial or viral infections. Once confirmation of the test results is done, the test results are reported to the physician attending that patient. Records of the results along with then patient's name and the physician's name are to be maintained as required by the Tennessee Department of Health and the Health and Human Services of the United States government.

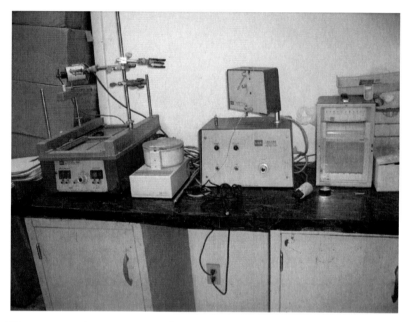

(Chromatographic separation of molecules from cell culture supernatants as well as from cells fractions obtained after disruption by ultrasonic waves)

The fraction collector is used to separate cell fractions after the cells have been sonicated fur further study. The Fraction collector is also used to separate different components of serum depending on the matrix for separation used. Some matrices use beads that physically separate components based on their molecular weight (Sephadex beads), yet others use ion-exchange matrices that allow the chemical binding of the serum component to the charged matrix. To avoid denaturation of the charged protein, specially formulated buffers are used to elute the product from the ion-exchange columns.

(Lyophilizer {Fereeze Dryer} is used to concentrate serum components, infectious agents grown in cell culture and cancer cell components obtained after ultrasonbic wave disurption to be stored for extended periods)

The lyophilizer (freeze dryer) employs the lyopholization process to concentrate cell components by freezing them and then pulling water from the frozen state by applying vacuum. It is the same lyophilization process employed in preparing instant coffee or instant tea. This process does not cause damage to the protein or to the infectiuous agent as their integrity is maintained.

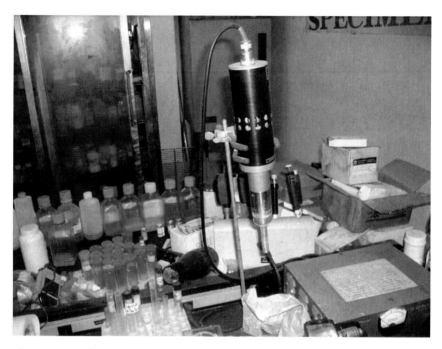

(Disruption of cells by ultrasonic waves {sonication} to gently break the cells and to isolate different fractions of cancer cells for further evaluation and studies)

In order, to isolate cell components from cancer cells, cells are treated with short pulses of ultrasonic waves to break them into small fragments and to also release the different components for further study. Caution must be exercised when sonicating a biological specimen to avoid damage to its chemical makeup and denature its activity.

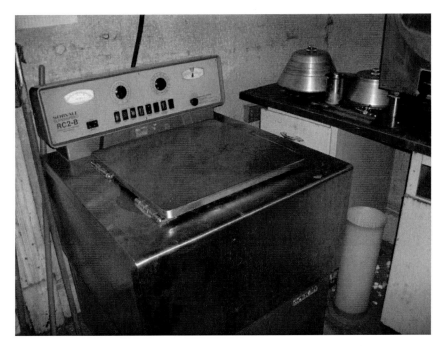

(Ultracentrifuge used for the concentration of cell products and to separate soluble components from the insoluble ones including cell fragments)

Refrigerated centrifuges with speeds of up to 20000 RPMs are used to concentrate the cells after harvesting from the cell culture apparatus.

Damage to the cells, during centrifugation, due to heat is, prevented when the temperature in the centrifuge is set at a temperature that is high enough to prevent freezing and low enough to avoid overheating and to maintain the integrity of the cells and their components.

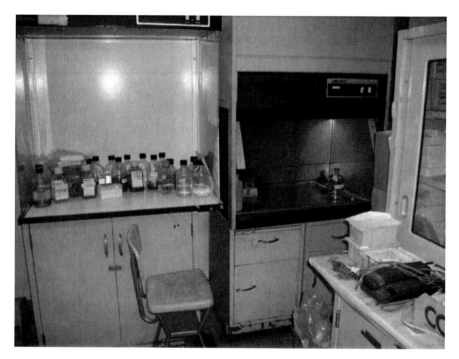

(Sterile hoods are used in cell culture to grow cell lines *in vitro* and for the infection of cell sheets with viruses and other infectious agents)

Working with cell culture requires sterile environments. Laminar flow hoods, especially those equipped with Ultraviolet light and exhausts are used, The challenge of having a successful cell culture is to prevent viral, bacterial and fungal contamination of the culture from happening, as these organisms are in the surrounding environment. The laminar flow hoods.are ideal for the *in vitro* culturing of cells.

(Two water distillation systems are used to double distill water for use in the preparation of cell culture media with supplements to provide nutrients for the cultured cells. The double distillation process removes bacterial, fungal and chemicals that could harm the cultured cells)

To promote growth of cells, powdered nutrients in buffer, are dissolved in double distilled water and sterilized by filtration to remove bacterial and fungal contaminants that could infect the culture and kill the cells. Sterilization of culture media is never done by autoclaving as many of the additives and supplements used to support the growth of cells are heat sensitive and can be destroyed, thus the only possible to sterilize the growth media is by filtration using filters of 0,2 uM pore size or less. Preparation of culture media and the addition of required supplements must be done in a sterile environment thus the use of laminar flow hoods for this purpose.

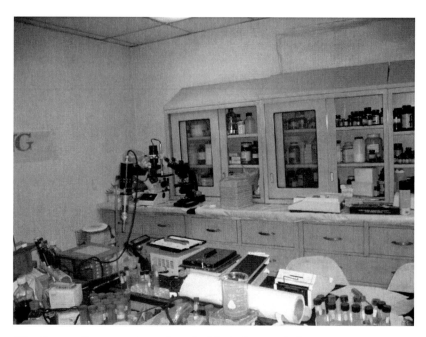

(The Preparation room is equipped with shakers and ultrasonic apparatus to break the cells. The shakers are used in Enzyme Immunoassay, Immunofluorescence and Latex Agglutination research for the preparation of the diagnostic test kits. Shaking of the Elisa plates leads to continuous contact between the immobilized antigen and the primary antibodies first and the labeled antibodies next),

(Roller apparatus used to enhance the *in vitro* growth of cancer cells and other cell lines. The apparatus is, placed in the CO_2 incubator with the roller bottles containing the cells and nutrients are partially closed. The rollers roll the bottles to provide continuous bathing of the cells with the liquid media containing nutrients and will allow them to stick to the glass surface to form a continuous sheet. After cell sheets are formed dislodging of such sheets from the glass surface is, achieved by the addition of the enzyme Trypsin. After the trypsinization step, a process to dislodge the cell sheet from the glass surface, the cells are washed and concentrated using sterile wash buffers and centrifuge tubes, by centrifugation for further investigations and uses. The roller apparatus is ideal to affect infection of cell sheets with viruses and bacterial agents).

All these processes are performed under strict aseptic and sterile conditions.

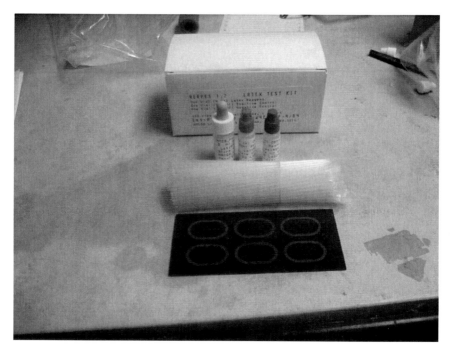

**(Finished Diagnostic Test Kits for Latex Agglutination
Assays is packaged and ready for shipment to customers.
The test kit includes all components needed to help in the
diagnosis of the disease)**

The Latex Agglutination diagnostic test kits are designed for the fast diagnosis of early (acute) and late (chronic) infections. Early infections indicate recent exposure to the infectious agent, while late infections indicate previous exposure to the infectious agent. Results of the test are obtained in five minutes for the diagnosis of acute and three minutes for the diagnosis of chronic infections.

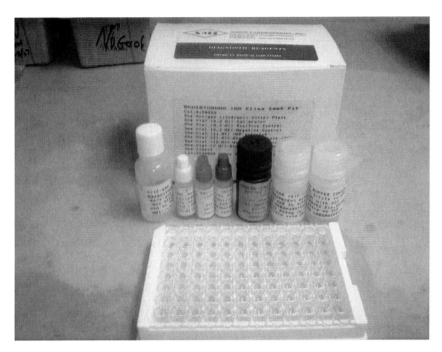

**(Complete Enzyme Immunoassay diagnostic test kit with its components for
the detection of early (IgM) antibodies due to acute infections caused by
organisms including parasitic, bacterial and viral agents in the patient's serum)**

Amico Laboratories Inc. offered test kits in three different formats for the diagnosis of disease using Antigen-Antibody interactions:

1. FITC (Fluorescein Iso-Thiocyanate) labeled primary and secondary antibody conjugates test kits that included Positive, Negative controls, FITC-labeled antibody conjugate, glass slides and product insert. Use of these kits requires the availability of a Fluorescence Microscope and a well-trained technician that can read and interpret test results.

2. Enzyme Immunoassay (EIA) test kits for the detection of IgM antibodies for early (acute infection) and IgG antibodies for late (chronic infection) in patient serum (plasma). The kits contained all the reagents for dilution and washing, positive and negative controls, Enzyme-labeled secondary antibodies, 96-well plate (12x8-well strips) coated with antigen and product insert. The enzyme Immunoassays (EIA) requires the use of an Immunoassay reader with the capability of having different wavelengths.

Test results, depending on whether the test is for early (IgM) or late (IgG) antibodies, will be available in 60-120 minutes

3. Latex Agglutination test kits intended for the diagnosis of early or late infections.

> The Latex Agglutination test kit includes positive, negative controls, latex particles labeled with antigen, a glass slide and product insert. This test assay provides the test results in 3-5 minutes, as opposed to the FITC and Enzyme Immunoassays (EIA) kits that require at least one hour to two hours to show results. Of course, the Latex Agglutination Assay is not as sensitive as the Enzyme Immunoassay (EIA) or the Immunofluorescence (IFA) Assay, but the short time it takes to get results is a plus.

The Latex Agglutination Assay is an old technology that was developed in the 1950s. It gained relevance later because it is fast as results are ready within a short period of time. It takes 3 minutes for the detection of IgG antibodies Indicating a previous exposure to the organism and 5 minutes for the detection of IgM early antibodies, which diagnose an acute infection.

Reading and interpretation, of the Latex Agglutination Assay results, neither requires sophisticated and expensive equipment nor highly- trained technicians, as the results are read and scored visually with the naked eye.

Our products gained acceptance in the United States, Europe and the Middle East. However, one of our distributors, in the Middle East, relayed to us that one of their customers stopped using some of our products because that customer thought they were, locally manufactured, thus they are assumed to be of inferior quality! He wanted the same products manufactured only in Europe or the United States!

In addition to being board-certified as a Medical Laboratory Director by the American Board of Bio-Analysis, I was licensed and certified as the Medical Director of the Clinical Laboratory Service at Amico Laboratories Inc. by the Department of Health of the State of Tennessee and by the Department of Health and Human Services of the United States.

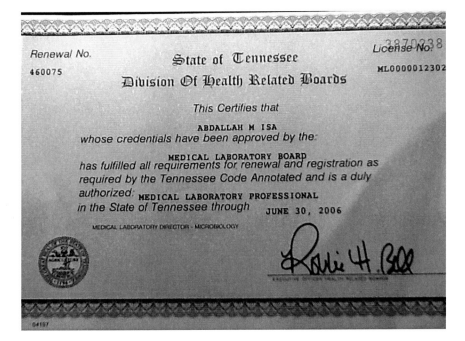

Renewal No.
460075

License No.

State of Tennessee
Division Of Health Related Boards

This Certifies that

ABDALLAH M ISA
whose credentials have been approved by the:

MEDICAL LABORATORY BOARD
has fulfilled all requirements for renewal and registration as
required by the Tennessee Code Annotated and is a duly
authorized: MEDICAL LABORATORY PROFESSIONAL
in the State of Tennessee through   JUNE 30, 2006

MEDICAL LABORATORY DIRECTOR - MICROBIOLOGY

(Photo showing the annual renewal of my certification as a Medical laboratory Professional by the Department of Health of the State of Tennessee)

One of my doctor friends in town asked me to help him confirm the diagnosis of one of his patients. He suspected the patient to have Syphilis. He planned to send the patient to me. I told him not need to send the patient to me however, he could send me a vial of blood from that patient. Upon testing the patient's blood, the results confirmed that this patient is reactive to Syphilis. Syphilis is one of these communicable diseases that is required, by law, to be reported to the Department of Health. Our Clinical Laboratory Service communicated the results of the patient's blood test, in writing to the physician attending that patient. The doctor. in turn, reported the results to the department of Health of the State of Tennessee.

A couple of weeks after the diagnosis, I received a call from the Tennessee Department of Health asking as to whether that patient is sexually active or not. I said, I have no idea, we have not seen the patient, but let me find out from the patient's attending physician and will let you know. This patient's doctor told me that his patient is an eighty-three old woman and he did not know if she were sexually active or not. I called the Department of Health and relayed the message as to the sex and age of the patient. I said, this patient is an eighty-three old female, you make that determination whether this woman is sexually active or not!

of the facility. It is a very serious matter and compliance with FDA regulations should be taken very seriously to avoid penalties or criminal convictions. The industry complained about the clandestine unannounced visits by the FDA inspectors as that amounted to no less than a police state affair. FDA bowed to pressure from the industry and changed its system by providing a week's notice of the visit by its investigator. The complaints by the industry of FDA's clandestine operations bore fruit as investigators refrained from popping up at will, at the doors of the facility. FDA started alerting the facilities of the date and time the investigator's visit a week in advance of his/her visit to investigate the facility. The date and time scheduled for the investigators to come depended primarily on the availability of FDA personnel who will do the investigation. Facility investigations could last for a minimum of four hours to complete or, in some cases, it may take weeks to complete, based on the findings of the investigator. The investigator thoroughly examines the physical structure of the facility, equipment, equipment maintenance schedules and records including, manufacturing records as well as all other documents including complaints file, production protocols, record keeping and shipping records. Any deviations from the Master Device Register (MDR) if detected by the investigator, may suggest deviation of or any non-compliance with any of the processes applied in the manufacturing protocols, would raise a red flag. Attention the investigator pays is to find out if any area is compromised and of other areas of non-compliance be it in manufacturing or with the FDA Regulations and the laws of the United States. Having an inspection by the FDA is not a laughing matter. The investigators always have the upper hand and one has, to be knowledgeable about every aspect of the operation, to show the inspector that he/she knows the ins and outs of the operation. The meeting with the investigator is very stressful, to say the least, as it may lead to passing of the investigation or in a worst case, scenario closure and possible criminal persecution would follow.

For over twenty-five years in business, our facility passed the FDA investigations with no problems and no Form 483 ever issued against our facility. An FDA investigator, who had some political motives, came to investigate our facility. He questioned me for a week, beginning at 8:00 in the morning until noon. He had erroneously written in his report that I should be persecuted for shipping 'unapproved' investigational (for research use only) devices to an overseas client. He stated that it was a deviation from FDA's regulations and therefore opened the door for a possible criminal indictment. His report led the FDA to issue Form 483 against our company.

Form 483 is a declaration of non-compliance that is issued by FDA to companies showing deviations or deficiencies in any of the FDA Rules and Regulations. Upon FDA inspection, the investigator looks carefully into the physical facility, equipment, record keeping, manufacturing protocols and most importantly, the Complaints File. FDA is keen to see if any complaints were dodged against the manufacturer or about any of the products sold in the domestic or international markets. Should there be any complaints, the FDA demands to know what has been done, and show the proof in remedying the problem related to that complaint is arrived at.

Under FDA regulations, shipping devices for 'Investigational Use' is allowable and does not need to have FDA approval. This investigator who wrote the report that lead to the issuance of Form 483 against our company, failed to mention, in his report, that the shipped devices were intended for investigational use only and not for diagnostic use, as it was clearly indicated on the labels of the devices, the product inserts as well as in the shipping documents. I felt very strongly at the time, that his allegations were short on the truth, but long on misrepresentation and perhaps biases. His allegations were political in nature as he and I happen to be on opposing sides of the Palestinian/Israeli question.

After receiving Form 483, I called and requested a meeting with the Regional FDA Director located in Nashville. Armed with the FDA book on Rules and Regulations as well with Form 483 and upon meeting with the regional director, in the presence of the 'infamous' investigator, I showed them the printed rules in the FDA's "Good Manufacturing Practices" publication. I pointed out, to the Director, that this Jewish investigator is, biased against me because I am Palestinian. Our government prohibits discrimination based, among other things, on religious or national origin! The inspector said in his report that because my facility, Amico Laboratories Inc. and I are not, in compliance with FDA rules and regulations, criminal action could be pursued against the facility and against the president of that facility.

The regional Director, after reading the FDA Rules said, "You and your facility are fine, and you are in compliance with our rules and regulations". At that point, I said, FDA should be more vigilant and instructive in training its investigators. I requested and received written confirmation, of our compliance with FDA rules and regulations. The confirmation letter was signed by the Regional Director of the FDA. I was very concerned and questioned our laws of non-discrimination that are in the books. Here is a federal employee who is supposed to honor, obey and implement these federal laws, was the one who broke the non-discrimination laws based on national origin!

A few months later, this same investigator came in to inspect our facility. He checked all the records dating back from his previous investigation. He indicated to me that he planned to have me prosecuted and have our facility closed. I was very irritated at his statement and told him that his allegations and the issuance of Form 483 based on his recommendation earlier were related to his personal bias against me because I am Palestinian, and he is Jewish. The political disagreements between this investigator and me should not have any implications that would lead to his biased actions. I told him, you are a federal employee and should not use your personal and political stances and biases to interfere with your job. You should comply with the rules and laws of the United States. You, and not me, should be prosecuted for breaking the federal rules and regulations. He must have repented and refrained from issuing or mumbling any negative reports or statements about me or about our facility. His report of the latest and most recent investigation was very complementary. Our facility and I passed his inspection with, flying colors. What a change of heart on the part this investigator has taken place!

COLLEGE EDUCATION OF OUR DAUGHTERS

MY WIFE AND I HAD DIFFERENT OPINIONS AS FAR AS THE EDUCATION of our daughters was concerned. She wanted them to work part time to support themselves and to pay tuition fees (the American way), for their college education. My opinion was quite the opposite. I wanted them to go to college without having to worry about expenses. I will take care of all their college expenses. The daughters, I said, did not choose to come to this world, but it was our choice to have them, thus it is imperative that we take care of them and of their needs. We are responsible for their well-being as well as for their education.

It so happened we had two daughters, Kim and Randa in college at the same time. The colleges were in different cities in Tennessee: The University of Tennessee in Knoxville and Middle Tennessee state University in Murfreesboro. When Kim graduated from the University of Tennessee in Knoxville, we still had Randa and now Deena at different colleges located at different towns at the same time!

I told our daughters I will provide each of them with a car, a checking account, pay their tuition fees, supplies, daily expenses and apartment rents provided they would comply with my three requirements:

1. Focus on their schooling and earn good grades

2. Graduate on time

3. Not to abuse the checking account

Well, apparently, they heeded my advice and complied with my requirements. They earned good grades and did not abuse their checking accounts. It was a great financial relief and a blessing when the three of them graduated from college and professional schools. None of the three daughters had to spend extra time at school because of deficiencies or for missing other requirements before graduation. The three of them graduated right on time.

As a family man who has come from a society that has deep roots relating to the importance of the extended family, I wanted the three daughters to live close by, in my neighborhood, but not farther from the town where I live.

Independence and making a living have their own price. Our daughter Kim moved to Florida where her job was and ultimately moved to Atlanta where she now lives.

Our daughters Randa and Deena stayed in Nashville, but ultimately Deena, after she got married, moved to Naples, Florida.

THE BLESSINGS OF HAVING OUR DAUGHTERS GET MARRIED

HAVING NO SONS, BUT ONLY DAUGHTERS AND LIKE ANY OTHER parent, I was anxious to see our daughters get married and establish their own families.

Admittedly, I was a little selfish in that regard, because I had a burning desire to have grandchildren and see them grow while I am still around. Well, the three daughters did get married in the order they were born. Kim got married first to Izzat (Izo) Hodzic, a fine young man that was born in Sarajevo. Bosnia who had immigrated to the United States. Kim and Izo with their two children, Deena Summer and Amar Harrison live in Roswell, a suburb of Atlanta.

Two of our daughter Kim and Deena who do not live in Nashville, but live in different states, was very disappointing to me. This is not what I have always desired as Kim lives in Atlanta. Georgia and Deena, lives in Naples, Florida. Randa was the only one who chose to live in Nashville to be close to her parents.

Atlanta being a four-hour drive from Nashville, is not that of a big deal as we can go see Kim and her family or they come to see us more often than seeing Deena and her family, as Naples is a two-hour flight from Nashville.

However, we communicate by phone almost on, a daily basis.

**(Photo of family members with our daughter, Kim on her wedding night.
Clockwise from left: Randa {Kim's sister},
Laila {Kim's mother}, Kim {the bride), me and our daughter
Deena {Kim's sister})**

Few years later our daughter Randa got married to Rodney Reep and both live in Nashville

(Clockwise from left: Myself, our daughter Deena {Randa's sister}, my wife
Laila {Randa's mother}, Randa {the bride}, Rodney {the groom}, our daughter
Kim {Randa's sister} with flower girl Deena Summer {Kim's daughter}, Izo
holding Amar Harrison {Kim's husband holding his son Harrison}
at Randa's wedding)

A year later after Randa's wedding, our youngest daughter, Deena got married to
Mahesh Krishna. The three sons-in-law are family oriented and are heavily involved in
rearing and taking care of their children, a characteristic that their father-in-law has.

(Our daughter Deena on her wedding night)

Like any other parent, I was happy to see our three daughters get married and establish their own families. As a grandfather, I was elated that our three daughters blessed me with two grandchildren each. A feeling of fulfilment and happiness that is quite difficult to describe.

(This is the photo of the Abdallah M. and Laila F. Isa's tribe: Seated on the couch from left to right: Halle Isabella {Randa's daughter} on my right. Myself, Deena Summer {Kim's daughter} holding Cameron Lucas {Deena's son} on my left. My wife, Laila holding Lilli Ryann {Randa's daughter}. Sitting on the floor from left to right: Amar Harrison {Kim's son} and Kaden Nicolas {Deena's son})

COMMUNICATIONS WITH THE ISRAELI PRIME MINISTER'S OFFICE

THOUGHTS OF MY DISCUSSIONS AND PERHAPS, DISAGREEMENTS I HAD with Dr. Sanford Elberg, dean of the Graduate School at *University of California at Berkeley* came back to me that he may have been right. Perhaps I should have listened to him and transferred to study at the *Hebrew University in Jerusalem* to earn my doctorate degree! I wrote a letter to Mr. Ehud Barak, Prime Minister of Israel on July 28, 2000, requesting his permission, for me and for my family, to move back to live in Israel. In my letter, I mentioned my family and I are well to do, highly educated and will never be a burden on the state. However, I am also requesting that I have my properties, which were confiscated by the state, be returned to me as I am the rightful owner of these properties.

Prime Minister's Bureau

נושא מדיניות חוץ במשרד ראש הממשלה
Foreign Policy Department

03 October 2000
ד' תשרי תשס"א

Dr. Abdallah Mohamad Isa
AMICO LABORATORIES INC
American Medical Industries
POB 90205
5012 Illinois Avenue
Nashville, TN 37209, USA

Dear Dr. Isa,

On behalf of Prime Minister Ehud Barak, thank you for your letter of July 28, 2000.

We have forwarded this matter to the relevant authorities, and will inform you as soon as we have a reply.

Sincerely yours,

Danny Ayalon
Deputy Foreign Policy Adviser
To the Prime Minister

02-5611842 :פקס 02-6705437 :טל 91919 ירושלים, הקריה, 3 קפלן רח'

3 Kaplan St. Hakirya, Jerusalem 91919, Israel, Tel: 972-2-6705437 Fax: 972-2-5611842

(Acknowledgement of receipt of my letter to the prime minister of Israel signed by Mr. Danny Ayalon, Deputy Foreign Policy Advisor to the Prime Minister)

Text of the letter from the Prime Minister's office:

"Prime Minister's Bureau

        Foreign Policy Department

                03 October 2000

Dr. Abdallah Mohamad Isa

AMICO LABORATORIES INC.

American Medical Industries

POB 90203

5012 Illinois Avenue

Nashville, TN 37209, USA

Dear Dr. Isa

On behalf of Prime Minister Ehud Barak, thank you for your letter of July 28, 2000.

We have forwarded this letter to the relevant authorities, and will inform you, as soon as we have a reply.

          Sincerely yours,

          Danny Ayalon

          Deputy Foreign Advisor

          To the Prime Minister

02-561-1842 02-670-5437 91919

3 Kaplan St. 91919, Haxirya, Jerusalem, Israel. = Fax: 972-2-5611842"

I received a response from Mr. Barak's office dated October 3, 2000 telling me that my request, had already been forwarded to the relevant authorities for evaluation and possible action. That letter from the Prime Minister's office was music to my ears. I felt good about the response and thought I may be able to see my birth country and regain ownership of my properties before I die!

The euphoria I had, completely sublimed upon receiving another letter dated November 19, 2000. The Prime Minister's office letter specified, beyond any doubt that my request, is rejected because the claim of "the Right of Return" (of Palestinians) is not and will not, be recognized by the State of Israel! The bad news contained in the rejection letter had a very negative impact on me. I have now realized that seeing my homeland and my properties, in Palestine, may be an illusion and may never materialize during my lifetime. The decision, by the Israeli government, to deny my request to return was devastating to me. In my letter of July 28 ,2000 I was keen to indicate that my family and I are very well to do and will never become a burden on the state. I also indicated further, that our willingness to live under Israeli rule and we will obey all Israeli laws, pay our taxes and be responsible citizens of the state. So why was my request of return denied?

Although I knew beforehand, the Israelis will never allow us Palestinians to return, yet I wanted to make sure that my thinking is not out of line, as far as the current Israeli thinking regarding the Palestinian issue is concerned. My letter to the Prime Minister was, intended to either confirm or refute my thoughts and willingness to return. It was, intended to find out, what their current thinking about the return of Palestinians to their homes and to their land is, as the right of return dictates.

Looking back at Dr. Elberg's, dean of the graduate school at the *University of California at Berkeley,* suggestion in 1963, that I should go and study at the *Hebrew University in Jerusalem* instead of the *University of California at Berkeley*, may have had some merit. Should Dr. Elberg be still alive now and make the same recommendation to me, will I comply and move to Jerusalem? Absolutely, not! Should it be a secular I will never recognize the existence of Israel as a Jewish state. A State with Jews, Christians and Moslems living together in peace, I will have a more positive attitude and incentive to decide to move back.

Will the United States use its influence over the Israeli leaders to force a fair resolution of the conflict with both Jews and Palestinian Moslems and Christians, live together in a peaceful environment? Unlikely, as Jewish influence and money are too powerful tools to cause a change in United States policy. With the Trump administration, the foreign policy regarding the Middle East, is essentially run by Ben Netanyahu, the Israeli prime minister. His influence to steer the white House policies in favor of Israel is through Jared Kushner, a devout Orthodox Jew and whose family is a staunch supporter of Israel. He is, in charge of the administration's policy on the Middle East. As Trump's son-in-law and senior advisor, Mr. Kushner convinced Trump to move the United States embassy from Tel Aviv to Jerusalem and paved the way to have the Syrian Golan Heights annexed to Israel. Mr. Kushner's next moves will be to force the annexation of the West Bank to Israel and the establishment of greater Israel to include areas between the Euphrates and the Nile Rivers. His plans for the Middle East are not only supported by the White House, but also by the so-called moderate Arab governments. They are divided, too weak to counter Jewish influence as their leaders are obsessed with clinging to power and depend on the west to maintain the status quo. They have more urgent issues to deal with, that is to fight each other. They are mentally occupied and would do nothing against their mental occupiers, the Zionists and the West.

Letter received from Prime Minister Ehud Barak's office, dated November 19, 2000, denying me the right to return to occupied Palestine)

Text of the letter of November 19, 2000, from the office of the Prime Minister:

"Prime Minister's Bureau

19 November 2000

Dr. Abdallah Mohamad Isa

AMICO LABORATORIES INC.

American Medical Industries

POB 90203, 5012 Illinois Avenue Nashville, TN 37209, USA

Dear Dr. Isa.

We refer to your letter of July 28, and our reply of October 3, 2000

The government of Israel aims to achieve a Permanent Status Agreement, for the resolution of the Israeli-Palestinian conflict. The subject of the refugees will be, discussed in this framework of the Permanent Status Agreement. However, while Israel acknowledges the plight of the Palestinian refugees and the need for a comprehensive permanent solution thereto, it does not recognize the Palestinian claim for a right of return to Israeli territories. This is Israel's overall, indiscriminate policy in regards, to all Palestinian refugees.

We join you with the hope that peace will eventually prevail between Israel and the Palestinians.

With best wishes,

Sincerely yours,

Gilead Sher

Prime Minister's

Bureau Chief

& Policy Coordinator

02-6705555 91919

3 Kaplan St. .Haxirya Jerusalem, 91919, Israel

Tel: 972-2-6705555"

ACADEMIA AND ITS OBLIGATIONS

WORKING IN ACADEMIA IS A PRIVILEGE THAT PROVIDES A FORUM TO express and exchange ideas and to interact with students, other faculty members and the academic community at large. Yet it carries the burden on the part of the professor to be able to reach and communicate with the students. Many challenges lie in his/her ability to make students understand the concept and build on it. The other challenge the professor has, in the classroom, is to have a dialogue between him/her and the students and to be open to answer questions from the floor regardless of their relevance, even while the professor is lecturing. In my experience, I found some students are genuinely interested in learning while others would not care less about putting an effort and yet others with the attitude' I dare you to teach me if you can'.

The I-phone, generation of students created a new cadre of people whose main interest is playing games on the I phone rather than coming to class or even pay attention while in class! I have noticed the change in students' commitment to learning after the introduction of the new technology. This generation, in my opinion, is a bad omen for the country, as it will end up having a society led by a bunch of ignorant and un-educated group of leaders.

Being a privilege. Academia also provides security for the faculty in the form of tenure. To gain tenure at academic institutions, the candidate must first be approved by a series of steps beginning with the departmental committee on tenure, then by the dean and finally by the vice president for Academic Affairs who in turn makes the recommendation to the president of the institution.

When time for my tenure came up, although my application was approved by the departmental committee on tenure and by the dean, yet it was denied by Dr. A. Washington, the then Vice President for Academic Affairs. This person was brought in as Vice President for Academic Affairs few months earlier. He was a racist and said it openly that did not wish to, and shall not, have any non-minority faculty members at our university!

When I asked Vice President Washington for an explanation as to why he denied my application for tenure, his response of "no reason" was shocking! I said, there ought to be a reason for your action and I need to know that reason. He then said, I could appeal his decision. I said, I sure will. Upon appeal, his decision of denial of my application for tenure was reaffirmed. When I questioned him again, he suggested that I should go and look at my file that is, kept in his office.

Upon looking into my file, I found:

1.   Neither of the copies of two of my recent publications that were hand delivered to him a couple of months earlier were in my file

2.   Two copies of a letter from Dr. T. Johnson, department head, addressed to Dr. A. Washington, the VP for Academic affairs were in my file. In that letter, Dr. Johnson stated, "He was amazed at the decision of the departmental committee to recommend Isa for tenure as his teaching performance is not good enough to qualify him for tenure, thus I recommend that Isa be denied tenure. He further added that a student broke down in tears when she was told Dr. Isa's class will be split into two sections, as there are too many students in his class. She said, according to Johnson, Oh No, I want to be in Dr. Isa's class because I want to get my 'A' in his course. He further stated that all students in Dr. Isa's courses receive 'A's as their final grades! Therefore, Dr. Isa's application for tenure must be denied"!

3.   When I read that communication, I snatched one of the two copies of Johnson's letter to A. Washington. That was a clandestine and conspiratorial communication between the department head and the VP for Academic Affairs as neither of the copies bore a cc: to me!

4.   Upon arriving on campus, Dr. Johnson showed his racist colors by assigning the graduate courses I was teaching to, a non-qualified person, removed my name from the Graduate faculty and dropped my name from summer teaching!

The new VP for Academic Affairs, Dr. A. Washington, is the one who brought in his friend, Dr. T. Johnson to head our department when he joined the institution seven months earlier.

This VP thought he was powerful and is above the law. He felt he has the power of running the institution according to his own ideals and ambitions. Both Washington and Johnson have been in their positions only seven months before my application for tenure was submitted. Neither of them had enough time to judge my performance before reaching their decision of tenure denial.

During the regular monthly cabinet meeting, the president of the university called for, an argument erupted between the president (the late Dr. Otis Floyd) and this vice president for Academic Affairs (Dr. A. Washington). The latter told the president, at the meeting, when it comes to this institution, stay out of it and I will take care of it!

The president was furious and told him, you, S.O.B, tell me to stay out of this institution, did you forget that I am the president and I am your immediate boss?

Dr. Washington lacked the social skills of communication with others. He brought all his problems upon himself, because he lacked the ability to deal with people in a professional manner. He got himself involved in another serious fight with Dr. A. Bankhead, a Business School professor at our institution. Professor Bankhead told Washington, you S.O.B do not belong at this institution. That was, the straw that broke the camel's back. Washington's inability to communicate professionally with his superiors and colleagues led to his demise. He was fired from his position as VP for Academic Affairs and replaced by Dr. Bankhead. After confirmation of Dr. Bankhead's appointment, he asked me as to the status of my tenure application. I said. Dr. Washington denied my application for tenure twice citing no reason for his denials. He then asked me to provide him with all the correspondence I have had with Dr. Washington.

The new Vice President for Academic Affairs, Dr. Bankhead, wrote a letter to Dr. Hefner, the president of the institution regarding the problems I had with Dr. Washington. In his letter to the president, Dr. Bankhead stated that Dr. Washington, neither understood the rules for tenure nor has the tact or mental capability to how to deal with people in a professional manner. In his letter to the president, Dr. Bankhead was very critical of the ex-Vice president and implied bias and racism on the part of Dr. Washington against Dr. Isa. Two weeks later and upon Dr. Bankhead's recommendation to the president who in turn endorsed it and sent the recommendation for tenure to the Board of Trustees of the university requesting their approval of my tenure. My application for tenure was approved with no regard to the efforts of Drs. Johnson and Washington to have my tenure denied!

While in the hallway talking to a student, Dr. Washington passed by and said, Hi Dr. Isa. I responded, sarcastically, by saying Hi and asked, what is your name, sir? Have I met you before?

Few months later and after I was awarded tenure, Dr. Johnson complained about the many 'F' grades students get in my courses. I then reminded him of his letter to Washington saying that all students get 'A's in Isa's classes. What has changed? You have turned hundred eighty degrees from all students earning 'A' grades in my courses to earning many having 'F's. What is going on? Have you come to your senses?" What a change in his attitude that was!

PLEADING WITH GOD AND HIS MESSAGES TO ME

I HAVE PLEADED WITH GOD BY ASKING HIM TO PROTECT MY FAMILY and to bestow upon us peace and security. As a reward, I believe, God sent me the following messages:

One night in 1995 and while I was asleep in a room with my head facing a bare wall, I had a dream in which a picture frame appeared on the bare wall facing me. In that framed picture was the portrait of a man wearing a turban

The man, in the portrait, called me by name and said" Abdullah"! I answered by saying, yes. He said, keep on doing your prayers as scheduled, keep on paying Alms and help poor people. I said I sure will, then I asked him as to who he was. He said (Angel) Gabriel. I said O.K. I will follow your orders and will do what you have just asked me to do. I woke up, opened my eyes and looked around and at the wall, I could see no picture frame and no portrait of the man with the turban. There was nothing on that bare wall! Was that an affirmation that I must continue engaging in my religious, humanitarian and civic duties and a blessing by communicating with the Angel Gabriel or it is just a dream? It is very hard to tell. I hope it is the former.

FAREWELL TO THE TWENTIETH CENTURY AND WELCOME TO THE TWENTY-FIRST

AFTER LIVING IN THE HOUSE, WE HAD PURCHASED IN 1969, AND LIVED in it for thirty-two years, I have developed an organic attachment to that house and to the area where the house sits. My emotional attachment was because our three daughters were raised in that house which sits on top of a hill with the superb environmental setting of the area. The house sat on, a one-acre plus lot of land in a cul-de-sac with no through traffic going in either direction. No traffic, no noise except that of the singing of birds. Deer, rabbits and raccoons were frequent visitors to our backyard. Occasionally, different kinds of snakes pass through, some are venomous, yet others are not.

1. A driving range owned by the famous Hill family of Nashville that was three miles away from our house, was subdivided into ninety-nine building lots in 1995. The wife saw the opportunity of purchasing a lot with the intention of building a house on that lot. Her strategy for convincing me to purchase the lot was two-fold: One that she would love to build a house that reminded her of her childhood home back in Palestine. The other was, as we are getting older, we need to live in an area that is physically closer to the hospital.

Although her arguments had merit, yet I was not convinced that we should purchase a lot with the intent of building a house on it. I did not wish to move farther away from our current house and its beautiful setting.

At the end, the wife succeeded, and I purchased a lot and sat on it for seven years before we decided to build on it. Of course, the wife had her wish fulfilled and we moved into the new house in May of 2002.

(Our house that was built in 2002 to satisfy my wife's desire to have a house that reminded her of her childhood home in Palestine)

2. Sadly, my sister Fatima who was like a mother to me, did not see the house so that she be happy and proud of her brother's achievements and his improved social status. She passed on few months before building of the house was completed. She passed on, after a short illness in Murfreesboro, TN, a town that is 30 miles south of Nashville. Her passing was devastating to me, as she was my idol and I was very attached to her. It took several years for me to recover from the shock of her passing.

She played the role of not only my sister, but also that of a mother to me. She watched me grow from a little boy, a teenager and then an adult. She was the nurturer of my well-being and was the guiding force that pushed me to get an education and to get to where I am now. She deserves all the credit for raising her brother to become a good and responsible citizen he is.

3. On December 2, 2016, my other sister, Amina passed on, in Lebanon. On the evening of her death, which I did not know about, I had a dream. In that dream I went to Paradise (Heaven) and saw how beautiful and gorgeous the nature in Heaven really is. While there, I started questioning as to where are the beautiful homes and palaces that we were promised and believed in upon, our death and ascension to Heaven? Where are those great things that God, the Almighty, has promised us? I do not see any in the Heavens I have just visited! All, of a sudden, our youngest daughter, Deena came out in the form of a beautiful little blue bird. Few minutes later, the beautiful little blue bird dived down from Heaven to earth! I could neither, pay attention, nor understand why the little blue bird left Heavens and dived to earth or what that dream meant, except at about 12:30 AM, on December 2, 2016, I was awakened by a phone call from my nephew, Mohamad, telling me that his mother (my sister Amina) has ascended to Heaven a short time earlier!

I firmly believe that my dream of going to Heaven on December 2, 2016 was another important message from God, that some person who I love may be on his/her way to Heaven. That dream may have occurred at the same time of my sister's passing in the morning of that day. As to our daughter (the beautiful little blue bird) descending from Heaven to earth, perhaps it was to hand carry, my sister to Heaven! Considering the eight-our difference between Nashville and Lebanon in which Nashville time is eight hours behind Lebanon. Is it possible my dream had happened the moment of my sister's passing? My inability at interpreting dreams and in my simplistic way of thinking, I am more inclined to believe that the dream was an important message directed to me. That message was alerting me that a very dear person, to me, may have already passed or is on the verge of passing. That dear person, my sister, who was in route to Heaven to meet her Creator, her parents and her two other sisters.

The following night after my sister Amina's passing, I had yet another dream. In this second dream, I was told I should read the following two chapters in the Holy Qur'an:

a. Prophet Yusuf's (Joseph) chapter and

b. Al-Zummar chapter.

I woke up at 4:30 AM after the dream, did my abolition, and read the two chapters of the Holy Qur'an as ordered in the dream and prayed the Dawn prayers.

There were other developments, some were good, yet others were not so good during the first decade of the twenty first century. At the end of 2007, and after lengthy rounds of negotiations that lasted for over a year, Amico Laboratories Inc., was acquired by another company. Now Amico Laboratories Inc. is no longer an independent entity but is now a division of the larger conglomerate parent company. The CEO of the parent company insisted that I retain the title of President of the newly added division.

UNWARRANTED HOSPITALIZATION AFTER COLECTOMY

COLONOSCOPY IS RECOMMENDED FOR PEOPLE OVER FIFTY YEARS OF age to be done every five years, unless suspicious polyps are, detected. The time intervals for the upcoming colonoscopies, may vary from two to three-year intervals, should polyps, be discovered. Few months later, after the 5-year of my last colonoscopy had passed, the doctor detected few polyps in my colon. He determined that the polyps appear to be benign. He snipped all the polyps off and sent them to the laboratory for evaluation. Laboratory examination of the polyps confirmed that they were benign and not cancerous. Although the polyps were benign in nature, the doctor recommended colon surgery, as a safety measure, to avoid having colon cancer. He recommended surgical removal of the portions of my colon that had the polyps.

I was not asked as to which hospital I prefer to, be sent to. I was assigned to Baptist hospital where the colon surgery was to be performed. After spending 24 hours at the hospital, the operation took place at eight in the morning and lasted for two hours. Indeed, the surgeon removed eight inches (20 centimeters) of my colon. After the excised portion of my colon was examined, it was confirmed that there was no evidence of cancer in the excised colon specimen! This was the confirmation of the benign nature of the polyps that were observed in and subsequently removed from my colon, prior to the surgery. That raised some questions, in my mind, as to whether the surgery was, at all warranted in the first place!

The hospital stay after Colectomy is normally 3-5 days. In my situation, it was a 23-day hospital stay! The surgeon said, your intestines are still asleep and undergoing Ileus after the surgery. Pain medication, anesthesia and other interventions after colon surgery may lead to Ileus, causing the intestines to go to sleep. The surgeon wanted to make sure the Ileus my intestines are experiencing are not caused by an obstruction. Several CAT scans were taken of my abdomen after the surgery, and none of the scans showed any sign of obstruction. The surgeon, apparently not believing the CAT scan results said, should your intestines not wake up by Thursday, I will have to open you up again to check for any obstruction, on Friday, because I am going on vacation!

Well, he opened me up, again on Friday morning, finding no obstruction he then sewed up within few minutes! Since the surgeon was on vacation, his associate would come every morning to check on me. He would spend about three minutes and say and record, everything is fine! The associate doctor never checked anything and never asked me any questions. On the third day of his visit, I got furious and said what the hell are you talking about? What do you mean everything is fine? Nothing is fine sir! Do you think I have come from the street or from a cattle barn to be treated the way I am being treated? I want you to know sir, I may be more educated than you and I may have graduated from universities that are much more prestigious than the ones you have been to.

The following morning, when that same doctor came to my room to check on me said, 'I am honored to be your doctor, Dr. Isa'! I said, Oh yeah, only after the fact. Is it not?

It was not a very pleasant experience at that hospital. Although I was in a private room, service in the hospital had a lot to be desired. The bathroom faucets were leaking, and bugs were flying all over the room. Nurses and supervisors did not give me the impression of being professional regarding care of the patients. It would take them a long time before they responded to my calls. The only persons who showed professionalism, at that hospital, were the nurse assistants and nurse technicians.

Suddenly I felt very cold and shivering as if I was laid, in the nude, in a -85- degree F freezer. The shivering was so intense that the bed frame was jumping up and down in tandem with my shaking. It was determined by laboratory analysis of my blood that the shivering was due to septicemia (infection involving the blood stream). In trying to determine the type of organism, and its portal of entry into my blood stream, it was essential to trace the source of the infection. Entry of the organism into my blood stream as I speculated, may have been through the Intravenous (IV) fluid from the reservoir, through the tubing and finally through the needle. It is inconceivable to believe the infection to have originated from the fluid, tubing or needle, as they all are supposed to have been sterilized prior to introduction into the vein of the patient. The other possibility of how the organism was introduced into the blood stream may have been due to leakage of fecal matter during surgery. However, that possibility was eliminated too and any other point of entry of the organism had to be identified. I found out that the area around the point where the needle pierced my skin to deliver the IV solution, was swollen and indurated. This suggested, very strongly, that the point of entry of the organism into my blood stream was indeed at the site where the needle pierced my skin. Having eliminated the intravenous fluid, tubing or needle or fecal matter leaks after surgery were eliminated as the source of the organism causing septicemia, it pointed out to the possibility that whoever installed the IV apparatus on me was the source of the bacteria. It further, suggested that the infection is not related to, the surgical procedure, because the infection occurred two weeks after the surgery and not a week or less after the operation.

In an effort, to determine the identity of the organism that caused the infection, laboratory analysis of my blood confirmed the infection was caused by E. coli. This organism is an inhabitant of the human intestines and does not live on the skin. Millions upon millions of this organism are shed with the fecal matter upon visiting the bathroom. After analyzing these facts as to the identity of the organism and considering the laboratory results, my speculation as to the IV solution, its tubing and needle were invalidated. I conclusion that the person who introduced the IV solution into my vain is the only possible culprit. He or she, having not washed their hands thoroughly after visiting the bathroom and came directly to introduce the needle into my vein were the cause of my septicemia and shivering! What a miserable hospital stay that was!

Needless, to say the longer the patient stays in the hospital, the more money the hospital adds to the bill. My hospital bill exceeded $100,000, which was over and above that of the surgeon's fees. It is not too difficult to imagine what would happen should the patient be unable to cover the cost of hospitalization.

A month after I was released from the hospital, I received another bill for an additional charge of $17,000.00. When I questioned this bill, I was told it was to help defray the cost, to the hospital, other patients who were unable to pay their hospital bills. Essentially, I was asked to reimburse the hospital for charges and subsidize other patients who could not afford or who refused to pay their bills!

It is so unfortunate that medical care in our country has become a privilege and not a right. Because of the trend engulfing the country, 'for-profit-hospitals' are springing all over the place and the 'not-for-profit' hospitals, are folding. The obvious result is medical care is becoming a luxury and out of reach to the bulk of the population. Rich Americans have no problem securing quality medical care as they can afford to pay all expenses. Poor American on the other hand get their medical care at no charge, through the federal program, Medicaid. The Middle class is the one that suffers the most as its members may not qualify for medical care through Medicaid and may have difficulty paying for the expensive medical care!

All medical, dental services follow a code regarding pricing of products and devices. These codes are designated by the American Medical Association (AMA), the Boards of Medical Specialties (BMS) and by the American Dental Association (ADA). The healthcare professional applies these codes regardless of the time it takes, or the technology used to perform the procedures. Now, in addition to the Medical and Dental codes, other services follow the same coding system. Case in point is, a mechanic who I asked to install hood struts on my car. He gave me a labor cost estimate of $65.00 to, install the struts. When I questioned the cost, he said the code says it takes an hour to install. I installed the struts myself in less than ten minutes! This is no less than a system of extortion the public deals with.

It is my understanding the for-profit hospitals originated in my hometown of Nashville when Hospital Corporation of America (HCA) was established by Dr. Thomas Frist Sr. in 1968. In that year, Dr. Thomas Frist Sr., Dr. Thomas Frist Jr. and Jack Massey opened the first for-profit hospital (Park View hospital) in Nashville H. Published reports indicate HCA to currently control over 170 hospitals and close to 100 surgery centers. The idea was copied by several other companies and for-profit hospitals sprung across the country like a spring garden, followed by the demise of not-for profit hospitals.

Unlike Europe and Canada where medical care is handled through a system of socialized medicine where governments control pricing and availability of service to their citizens, medical care in the United States is a business. Although it is supposed to be regulated by the government, as dictated by Congress, yet the healthcare provider has the final say when it comes to pricing.

Although pricing of medical and dental procedures, follows codes instituted by the medical and dental associations and the codes implemented by the insurance companies, many a time there are hidden costs the healthcare providers charge over and above what the insurance company publishes. Medical facilities, doctors and hospitals are, reimbursed according to the code for the service that the insurance company sets for any procedure or treatment protocol. What the insurance company pays these facilities is rarely what the cost really is and always is less than the bill specifies. The balance must be paid by the patient, of course. There are always out-of- pocket expenses that the patient must dole out to the healthcare provider. Many an instance such excessive charges have led to the declaration of bankruptcy by patients and their families as the charges are far beyond their financial capabilities.

Although there is a provision for patients to lodge complaints against doctors or against the healthcare provider by the patient to, the insurance company, yet the patient rarely ever wins the case. It appears, as though there exists a symbiotic relationship between the healthcare providers and the insurance company. They both need each other to keep the system working and the patient is the one that pays the price for such symbiotic relationship. Should the patient choose to go to a medical provider that is not a member in the 'in-network' group the out of pocket cost may at least be double the amount that is charged by the 'in network' group.

Should a patient who did not get satisfactory resolution of his complaint from the insurance company, go further to complain to the State department of Finance and Insurance that regulates the business of insurance and finance in the state government, the outcome of the complaint is no different than that he/she receives from the insurance company!

I had cataract surgery done by one of the 'in-network' ophthalmic surgeons that was short on success. The surgery was, never done right. I had to go back to his office almost on, a daily basis to correct my vision. Every time I went to his office I was, asked to pay $45 fee for a specialist copay. I refused to pay and complained to the insurance company several times. I said should a mechanic do a job on my car and the problem that was fixed still exists, the mechanic will correct the problem without having to pay him for the fix. The insurance company always had its\r skewed explanation that had no bearing on the substance of the complaint. I followed my complaint to the insurance company, by a complaint to the State of Tennessee department that regulates medical specialties and insurance companies. Their response was not different from that of the insurance company! I wrote the State agency back, telling them their department does not only does not care about the consumer, but its main purpose is to protect the insurance companies and the service providers, because they pay more in taxes than I do! What a shame!

This ophthalmic 'specialist' had to redo the cataract operation again. This second time around, he used a laser to remove the remnants of the cataracts left over from the previous operation! When I asked him as to why did he not use the laser in the first place, he was mum and never said a word! The response of the insurance company about my complaint left me with the thought that there indeed exists a collusion between the insurance companies and the healthcare providers. It is a shame 'to say the least that it is at the expense of the public.

Because of the symbiotic relationship between insurance companies and healthcare providers and because of the absence of oversight in healthcare cost, the national bill for healthcare keeps rising above the acceptable level of inflation. Insurance companies need the services of healthcare providers to do the work and the healthcare providers welcome working with the insurance companies as they are assured of prompt payment of the charges they bill the patient. An illustration of this cozy relationship between insurance companies and healthcare providers is illustrated in the following story:

A person I know went to the doctor for a regular checkup. The doctor recommended an echogram to check the condition of his heart, Heart tissue was found to be normal and the heart was functioning properly.

The bill for the doctor's visit and the echogram was as follows:

Doctor's bill for seeing the patient	$ 260.00
Cardiologist bill for reading the echogram:	$ 844.00
	————
Total bill	$1104.00
The insurance company paid the healthcare provider:	-$1032.00
The balance paid by the patient:	$ 72.00

which is in addition to the copay the patient pays upfront!

There were many taboos in certain sectors of the economy regarding advertising. One of these taboos was attorneys who were not supposed to advertise in the print, audio and visual media, but now their advertisements appear in newspapers, magazines, posters on busses, and on the highways as well as on radio and television offering the services and contact information.

The Pharmaceutical Industry, hospitals, medical facilities and doctors' offices as well as dentists also joined the foray of advertising. Of course, advertising, in addition to exposing the advertised products and services to the public, it also offers a platform for consumers to choose the product or service they need. Yet advertising is costly and to maintain the margin of profit, companies raise the prices on their products and services to compensate for the advertising cost. This cost is in turn passed on to the consumer which explains the exponential rise in the cost of healthcare and other services,

The government, the advertisers and the providers are the winners. The consumer is the loser in this case. Federal and state governments benefit by increased tax revenues from three sources: from the advertisers, from companies that buy advertisements for their products and services, as well as the consumers who pay a sales tax on the products they purchase. To compensate for the cost of advertising, companies add extra charges to their products and services in the way of fees or price hikes.

Having the for-profit hospitals trend been so successful, it was then followed by the establishment of medical groups. These were, formed as independent providers or as part of a hospital or a medical school. Non-hospital and non-medical school affiliated groups were also established. Companies employing doctors, nurse practitioners, nurses and physician assistants to service the need of the community were, established across the country. These new trends in healthcare led to the demise of the solo medical practice to render it as obsolete and is no longer a viable option.

Hospitals and medical groups have a list of codes that specify the cost of the procedure or service and the copay the patient must pay upfront.

In order not to be left behind dentists, followed suit by applying the medical business model and established their own codes as dictated by the American Dental Association (ADA). New for profit, dental companies, employing dentists, dental hygienists and dental assistants were, established nationally through a franchise system of business.

As a result, of the 'commercialized' medical and dental services, the price of health care in the country, has skyrocketed and has become out of reach of the average American.

Our legislative body, the Congress and Senate, whose members we send to Washington to represent us and we are supposed to trust their opinions and respect their decisions in instituting laws to protect the public, has a lot to be desired.

Although members of Congress write laws and rules, many a time these laws and rules are not in the best interest of the general American public. These laws and rules are drawn in support of the lobbyists' agendas. The lobbyists are the ones who have the upper hand in the hallways of the United States House and Senate. The lobbyists are, armed with money and they are ready to dish it out to any member of congress who is willing to support their intended agenda.

The people we elect and send to Washington DC to represent us, have become subservient to the lobbyists and beg them for money to support their re-election campaigns. Many a time, the lobbyist's agenda is the one that prevails and will have the upper hand regardless of its potential impact on the interest of the general population.

It is a known fact that there are more than twenty registered lobbyists for each member of Congress! This translates to 435 congressmen and 100 senators when multiplied by the number of lobbyists, ends up with a staggering number of 10700 lobbyists whose jobs are to influence decisions by people in position of power! These lobbyists use their money to 'bribe' a member of congress to block or to support regulations that agree with or is, in conflict with their agenda. As money is the most valuable commodity, I am compelled to propose a change in the slogan on our currency **'In God We Trust'** to be deleted and be appropriately replaced by the **'In the Dollar We Trust'**.

I had a discussion with a woman 'friend' who I thought was educated about Trump's decision to move the United States embassy from Tel Aviv to Jerusalem. The discussion turned to an unpleasant confrontation when she said, but Congress voted to have the United States embassy moved from Tel Aviv to Jerusalem. I must admit I got furious at the suggestion that our Congress passed a law claiming Jerusalem as the eternal capital of the State of Israel. At that point, I said, does Congress own Jerusalem and who gives a damn about what Congress says or does. Congress, as you know, is a tool that is moved around by money swaggers known as lobbyists. I reminded my friend of the power of the American Israel Public Affairs Committee (AIPAC) in swaying congressional votes to support its agenda. AIPAC is a staunch supporter of Israel and its agenda. Look around, do you see any anti-Israel resolution in congress? Do you see, in the mainstream printed media, on the radio or on television anything in support of the Palestinians or their cause? Of course, not! All the reporting that we hear or see is pro-Israel propaganda. AIPAC uses its money wisely. It knows where to invest its money with the highest return. That investment having the highest return is the United States Congress and the other media outfits. To put it bluntly, my friend, Congress is for sale and whoever pays the right price gets all the goodies. There is no more conscious when it comes to re-election campaigns. Conscious as far as Congress is concerned has been dead ever since the Republic was established!

PLANS TO TRAVEL INTERNATIONALLY TO SEE THE WORLD WITH BOSNIA THE FIRST COUNTRY TO VISIT

THE SUMMER OF 2016 WAS THE BEGINNING OF OUR INTERNATIONAL travel. The first trip was planned to go to Bosnia with our daughter Kim, her Bosnian-born husband, Izzat Hodzic and their two children, Deena summer and Amar Harrison. Kim and Izzet purchased a beautiful condominium in Sarajevo and wanted us to see it. Our Flight started in Atlanta and headed first to Istanbul, Turkey. Istanbul is a great modern city with beautiful arcades and bustling shopping malls. Because of its location as a bridge between Asia and Europe, Eastern and Western cultures meet face to face.

After leaving Istanbul, we landed in the great city of Sarajevo. This city hosted the Winter Olympics games before the civil war fragmented the country of Yugoslavia into mini states: Serbia, Croatia and Bosnia-Herzegovina and Monte Negro. That break up led to fierce fighting in Bosnia Herzegovina between the Orthodox Christian Serbs and Catholic Croats coalition against the Moslem Bosnians. The atrocities committed by the Serbs and the Croats against the Bosnian Moslems were not limited to raping of women, but included routing of young men, detaining them starving them to become skeletons of skin and bone. Ethnic cleansing and the massacre of over 8000 Moslem men and boys in Srebrenica and the discovery of mass graves, proves beyond any doubt, the Serbs and the Croats committed war crimes amounting to genocide against the Bosnian Moslems.

After the breakup of Yugoslavia and the eventual independence of Bosnia and the pain caused by the atrocities committed against them, I did not detect any animosity by the Bosnian people against the Serbs or the Croats. Bosnians are very pleasant, peaceful and friendly group of people. Very few of them speak English. The only way we could communicate with the local population was through an interpreter, our son-in-law.

We travelled throughout Bosnia, a beautiful country, crossed the borders to Croatia, Serbia and other neighboring countries. Luckily, we had access to a car as our son-in-law had a car that he had kept in the parking area under the condominium, which he used to drive us around the country and to the neighboring countries.

Shopping for groceries in Sarajevo, is primarily through small Mom and Pop stores. One of the things I observed in Bosnia and in Croatia, was merchants will not accept US dollars to pay for groceries or any other product or service. They will accept only the Euro and the Mark. This Mark is not the German Mark. It is the local currency that is shared between these post breakup countries of the old Yugoslavia. Thus, the only way we could purchase goods from the store was, to pay them in Euros or in Marks. To have access to these two currencies, we had to go to the bank and exchange our dollars to the currencies that are acceptable to do any transaction. The reason merchants do not accept US dollars, they say, is because the exchange rate of these currencies against the dollar, vary from day to day. There are always long lines waiting to, change money at the banks as there are no other money exchanges in the form of kiosks are available in these countries.

I was keen on comparing the infrastructures in these countries to ours as they relate to their maintenance. To my pleasant surprise, and considering that these countries are poor, I could not see a single pothole in the city streets or on the highways. Unlike our roads and highways, their roads are in perfect condition.

Contrary, at least to my own belief, which I have known throughout the years, seas and oceans always have rolling waves, the opposite was the case in the Adriatic Sea which is peaceful with no waves, high or low, could be seen. The surface of water looked exactly as smooth as that of a swimming pool when it is free from swimmers.

It was a pleasure to have seen the summer home, in Bosnia, of the late Marshall Tito, President of the Socialist Republic of Yugoslavia. The home lies on top of a hill overlooking a large swath of carefully manicured lot of land. Marshall Tito, I am told used to come and spend few days at a time at this home.

The countries we visited in this part of the world have beautiful topography settings with high mountains and deep ravines. I was greatly surprised when I discovered that I have become acrophobic with a severe fear of heights, especially when looking down at the deep ravines. When going up the mountains and looking down at the deep ravines, I became dizzy and had the feeling that I am falling off into the ravine. At that point, I came down the mountain crawling to avoid falling off into the deep ravines below. It was a very scary feeling to say the least!

Travelling to different parts of Bosnia was a pleasure as the scenery was breath taking. From Sarajevo, we drove to the national park, the Bosnian rain forest at Sutjeska. From there we ended up in Gacko, where our son-in-law's mother was born

After leaving Bosnia, we drove to Croatia to see the beautiful country with high mountains, deep ravines and pleasant people. We spent few days in Croatia where we visited the capital of Dubrovnik and visited its old heavily fortified castle. On the way back to Bosnia we spent few days in Zatun, a small town, close to Dubrovnik where I noticed, Carob trees, Fig trees, Pomegranate trees, a scene that was reminiscent of what I was used to seeing back in Lebanon and in Palestine.

One other thing that attracted my attention in Croatia was that people appear to be homogeneous in regard, to their ethnicity. They appear to be racially pure as they all are white European and are very, very tall. I felt very much like a midget compared to the Croats!

The Croats and the Bosnians have a great love for ice cream. Stands of ice cream vendors pop up every hundred yards or so in the cities and their ice cream is, not only delicious, but is very cheap compared to what we pay for in the United States. A two-scoop cone of ice cream cost about 50 cents

Coming back from Croatia to Sarajevo, we spent some time with Shadi Fadda, Laila's cousin's son. Shadi was preparing for his Ph.D. degree at the International University of Sarajevo. The International University was established in Bosnia, by Turkey as a higher education venue to Bosnian students.

The trip to that part of the world was very pleasant and informative. We had witnessed how people in different countries and different cultures have a life style that is decidedly different from ours in the United States.

Gypsies were all over the place. They are the human birds who cross borders and enter countries without having to apply for a visa. They swarm the streets, restaurants and coffee houses, begging for money. The sad thing about these people is, they train their children in the art of begging. They send them out to beg from people eating at restaurants or sitting in the Café, while keeping a watchful eye on them few feet away. While having lunch in an open-air restaurant, we were approached by a little girl who I could estimate her to be around seven years or age. She came to ask for money. I offered her food, but she refused and wanted only money. What a shame for a wasted generation!

OUR VISIT TO CHINA

IN A CONTINUING EFFORT TO SATISFY OUR DESIRE TO SEE THE WORLD, my wife and I decided to take a trip to Mainland China. The trip was organized by, a Chinese group located in Toronto, Canada. I got the information about the trip by email from the Chinese group. Arrangements for the trip were very swift with no problems and within two weeks, we landed in Beijing. We flew from Nashville to Chicago on April 17, 2018, on United Airlines and after a short stop in Chicago, we boarded another United Airlines flight to Beijing, arriving on April 18, 2018. The international flight from Chicago to Beijing took thirteen non-stop hours. It was a tiring trip as the time difference of thirteen hours between Chicago time and that of Beijing time, where the latter was thirteen hours ahead of that of Chicago.

Upon landing in Beijing, we were welcomed by a representative of the Chinese company that made the arrangements for the trip. The representative took us to the Great Wall hotel named after the Great Wall of China, which we learned later that it was the Sheraton hotel. The hotel is, described as a 5-star hotel. Indeed, it is a five/star hotel, as evidenced by its excellent service and comfortable accommodation.

At the hotel we were, introduced to members of another American group coming from different parts of the United States who took the same trip.

The following day, an optional program at $75/person was scheduled to visit the "Forbidden City", the formal seat of Emperors through the Ming and Qing dynasties.

At the Forbidden City, were museums depicting the history of China, but most importantly for me, was Chairman Mao Tse Dong's Mausoleum located at one end of the Forbidden City and at the other end was his portrait hanging on the wall. I have always been fascinated and admired Mao's achievements. With a small rag tag army, he was able liberate his country from European, Japanese and other foreign occupiers.

These achievements are great by any measure. Of course, prior to Mao's coming, China was under occupation by foreign powers. It was a very poor country and with time, especially after the liberation and through hard work and perseverance, the country was moved from medieval times into the twentieth century. China with 1.4 billion inhabitants, not only was denied membership in the United Nations and a seat in the Security Council of the United Nations, because it was not even recognized by the United States as a legitimate country! Reason, being a communist regime dictates that the United States will not recognize or deal with. Communist china was described as a rogue state thus it should not be recognized. The isolation of and subsequent acceptance of China as a legitimate country, by the United States, ended after Richard Nixon's visit to China in 1974. Nixon's visit to China began the process of recognition by the United States, and ultimately China won a permanent seat in the Security Council of the United Nations.

Again, everything has a price. Prior to the admission of China to the United Nations and gaining a seat as on the Security Council, the other country, other than the United States that had a veto power was, the Soviet Union. The Soviet Union has always voted against the wishes of the United States and now there are two of them: Russia and China who have veto power against United States. This is the price the United States had to pay for supporting the admission, to and subsequent gaining of a permanent seat on, the Security Council by China at the United Nations.

Should the United State ever regret recognizing China as a legitimate player in the world scene, unlikely. China, after the United States, sits on the second largest economy in the world. It is becoming a military superpower with the ability to threaten American and Western supremacies anywhere in the world.

(My photo under the eyes of Mao's portrait in the Forbidden City. My sad look was because I could not see a portrait of Zheu En Li, China's foreign Minister under Mao. I was always fascinated with Zheu's and Mao's names which, to me, sounded as romantic as those in the old fairy tales.)

The Forbidden City was built and completed in the year 1420. It was home for 24 emperors during the Ming dynasty (1368-1644) and the Qing dynasty (1644-1911). In addition to the Forbidden City as the seat of the former emperors throughout the Chinese Ming and Qing dynasties, it houses several outfits that describe in detail the history of China from centuries back to the present day. It was fascinating and quite informative. In the Forbidden City, lies the Tiananmen Square, site of the 1989 rebellion for democratic change that was brutally crushed by the army.

The Palaces in the Forbidden City are an architectural marvel. They are well maintained and display the glory of the Chinese Ming and Qing dynasties.

After exploring the palaces and other architectural designs in the Forbidden City, we proceeded to the National Palace Museum. At the museum, we saw how the Chinese used to perform their chores in their traditional ways at those times.

The Forbidden City was bustling with tourists from many parts of the world and from local Chinese. The buildings with their traditional beautiful Chinese architecture are well maintained. The grounds are also kept clean and well maintained. Not a single plastic bottle, paper cup or any kind of trash was seen on the grounds. Thanks to the several trash and recycling bins strategically installed every so many yards.

The Chinese are keen on keeping their environments clean. We saw a man on a dingy clearing the lake by, picking weeds and any other items that may have been thrown into the lake.

Several Chinese, in Beijing, wore masks covering their mouths and noses, apparently as a protectant against smug and other air pollutants afflicting the city. Indeed, the atmosphere in the city was quite hazy. I asked our guide whether the haze we see is due to pollution, he said No! It is due to the pollen from the flowering plants and trees!

I was quite surprised to see road signs posted in Chinese and in English. Also, at many an outlet, were signs in English as can be seen in the list of charges levied for entering the museum.

young & children	27.5	The children between 120cm(ir (Special half price boats and i
	Free	The children under 6 years old((The free island tickets).
Aged	45	The old between 60 to 69 years (Special half price island ticke
	35	70 years of age or older. (The free island tickets).
Special people	35	The servicemen, the disabled, th (The free island tickets).

Youngsters should present Valid ID card or stud available for youngsters from Hong Kong, Macao and Hong Kong and Macau Residents" or student I.D.)

(List of charges levied at visitors going into the National Palace Museum, in English, is meant for non-Chinese speaking tourists)

(This photo was, taken with some members of our American group, two Indian American brothers who are doctors, from Chicago and Detroit with their spouses, with us prior to us going into the National Palace Museum.)

At the Museum were statues of people preparing the grains for their own use and for the use of their, animals.

(This was how goods and products were, carried from
one place to another)

(A worker transporting sacs of grain for storage or for processing in old China, using an old-fashioned wheelbarrow)

(A worker, in old China is trying to separate grain from chaff by sieving it using a large circular sieve)

(Mixing flour in a large bowl in preparation for baking it into bread in the old tradition in China. Note that two men are needed one to add the water to the flour and the other one to continue mixing the flour and water to prepare the daugh.)

Unlike today, family sizes were much larger with a larger number of family members Because family planning was, at the time, not heard of with more mouths to feed and bread being the main staple, large quantities of bread were prepared. To maintain freshness and because there were no proper storage facilities to maintam freshness, bread was prepared on a daily basis.

(Chinese woman feeding wood to the wood stove to heat their living quarters and to bake the bread on top of the stove).

Wooden stoves were the only source of heat for heating the home, cooking, heating water for bathing and for washing clothes. On top of wood stove, a sheet metal is placed to bake bread. The multi- purpose fireplace, in addition to having multiple uses, it is safer than having an open hearth. Wooden stoves, throughout the Asian countries, were also the site where family members would assemble and socialize in the evenings. Public places, where people used to meet, were also heated in the winter months by such wooden stoves.

**(The Chinese take pride in their bronze sculptures such as this portrait
of an old Chinese man with his kitchen utensils, exhibited at the
National Palace Museum.)**

A very large number of impressive Bronze sculptures and portraits describing life in and activities in old China and the importance of its culture, are exhibited throughout the National Museum. These sculptures and portraits depict the rich history of an ancient culture.

(Picture of Smiling Buddha at the National Palace Museum. To earn his blessings according to Chinese tradition, one must rub his forehead and going down to rub his stomach)

One should not forget that Buddhism is the leading religion in old and modern-day China, yet religion is officially banned by law, by the communist regime. Religious activities may be practiced in secret in homes and in private settings.

(These are statues of three Chinese leaders in old China. What was striking, to me, is the statue of the man in the middle happens to have been a Moslem Chinese leader)

After visiting the museum, we proceeded to the Imperial Palace and the Imperial Garden to enjoy the fine architecture of the palace and its beautiful gardens.

The following day, our American group was taken to the Tonrentag, the Chinese Medicine Institute. This Institute was established for, the purpose of producing and providing of medicines for the royal pharmacy at the imperial palace for 188 years. At the Institute, which is still in existence, we were briefed by 'experts' on the efficacy, safety and effectiveness of Chinese Herbal Medicine in treating all the diseases and syndromes known to man!

The session started with a thirty-minute pep talk and a slide show, by the expert who spoke fluent English, a rare commodity in China. At the end of his talk, a group of 'nurses', each carrying a bucket of lukewarm water for each member of our group, came in. We were, asked to take our shoes off and dip our feet in the water for about thirty minutes.

During the dipping process, another 'expert, on Chinese Herbal Medicine came in to talk to us about the importance and effectiveness of Chinese Medicine through-out the centuries. He recommended we all must adopt the use of such medicine, as it is safe and effective. Because of its herbal nature with no side effects such as those that could develop upon the use of chemically derived medications marketed by pharmaceutical companies and used by the people in the western countries.

At the end of the second pep talk and while we had our feet still dipped in the water bucket, another group of 'super experts' referred to as the "professors" came in. They wore white gowns, but without stethoscopes or blood pressure gadgets to examine each one of us to come up with a diagnosis.

The "professor" who examined me, held my left hand at the wrist and turned the hand left and right, and back and forth for about three minutes. He recognized the problem I am suffering from. He diagnosed me with a little smile on his face, that I am suffering from partial ischemia. Because he did not speak English, his diagnosis was communicated to me, not verbally but visually by showing me a card he pulled from his white gown upper left pocket. Since he did not speak any English, the diagnosis was in the form of a picture, in color, that showed I have partial blockage in my arteries. The blockage in my arteries is depicted as a yellow streak in the picture. That meant the blockage, will result in not having enough blood pumped out from my heart. I must be treated immediately otherwise I may end up having a stroke or a heart attack, as explained to me by an interpreter. His recommendation for treatment and a cure, was the purchase of a small glass vial filled with some liquid that I should use. The vial contained the herbal medicine I must use for at least three months. The 'professor' did not tell me how to use this medication whether I should take it orally or rub it on my skin! He did not tell me how it works either. According to his prescription. I needed a three-month supply of the medication at $150/month, to treat my problem and have a proper supply of blood pumped by my heart! To get the medicine, I was, asked to pay $450 upfront to cover my treatment for three months!

VISIT TO THE GREAT WALL OF CHINA

THE GREAT WALL (JUYONGGUAN), IS A SERIES OF WALLS AND FORTIFIcations extended to about 4000 miles, were built to protect the territory from foreign invasions. The best-preserved and maintained part of the wall is a 3700-mile marvel originally planned by Emperor Qin Shi Huang during the third century B.C. Conception of building of the Wall, by this emperor was because of his fear the country may be, invaded from the north due to incursions by the barbarian nomads.

This section of the wall stretches over the mountain and is open for visitors who wish to climb the steps between the two sides of the wall. I have always wanted to see the great Wall and attempt to climb it.

At the foot of the Great Wall there was, a sign in English, instructing the climbers, what to do and what to avoid when climbing the steps between the two sides of the wall. It was a very informative piece of information that helped avoid any potential mishaps. Surprisingly, no Ambulance cars were seen in the neighborhood to take care of the injured in case that happens!

The in-English sign appears to be intended for international visitors that swarm the Great Wall from the four corners the world to see and possibly climb the steps of the Great Wall. There was, no Chinese language signs warning people of the potential hazards, as there were no Chinese visitors I could see. I met some tourists from Germany, England, Malaysia and other nationalities at the entrance of the Great Wall.

No signs, in Chinese could be seen anywhere, at the Great Wall or in its vicinity. I wondered, perhaps it is assumed that only foreigners and not the Chinese who visit the wall.

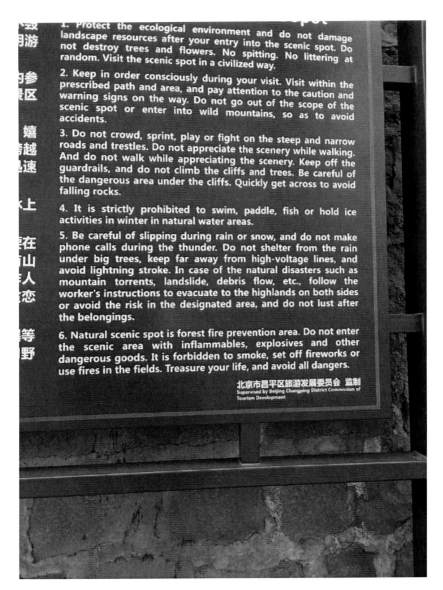

1. Protect the ecological environment and do not damage landscape resources after your entry into the scenic spot. Do not destroy trees and flowers. No spitting. No littering at random. Visit the scenic spot in a civilized way.

2. Keep in order consciously during your visit. Visit within the prescribed path and area, and pay attention to the caution and warning signs on the way. Do not go out of the scope of the scenic spot or enter into wild mountains, so as to avoid accidents.

3. Do not crowd, sprint, play or fight on the steep and narrow roads and trestles. Do not appreciate the scenery while walking. And do not walk while appreciating the scenery. Keep off the guardrails, and do not climb the cliffs and trees. Be careful of the dangerous area under the cliffs. Quickly get across to avoid falling rocks.

4. It is strictly prohibited to swim, paddle, fish or hold ice activities in winter in natural water areas.

5. Be careful of slipping during rain or snow, and do not make phone calls during the thunder. Do not shelter from the rain under big trees, keep far away from high-voltage lines, and avoid lightning stroke. In case of the natural disasters such as mountain torrents, landslide, debris flow, etc., follow the worker's instructions to evacuate to the highlands on both sides or avoid the risk in the designated area, and do not lust after the belongings.

6. Natural scenic spot is forest fire prevention area. Do not enter the scenic area with inflammables, explosives and other dangerous goods. It is forbidden to smoke, set off fireworks or use fires in the fields. Treasure your life, and avoid all dangers.

北京市昌平区旅游发展委员会 监制
Supervised by Beijing Changping District Commission of Tourism Development

(Sign in English, at the entrance to the Great Wall, advising people as to what to do and what to avoid while climbing the Wall)

(Photo of the winding section of the Great Wall of China with vivid and bright colored surroundings. The Great Wall is clean and well maintained. It is a great and pleasant marvel to look at)

I was quite surprised to learn that very few Chinese speak English or any other foreign language. It is very possible, as China is becoming a major player on the world scene, that introduction of, and encouragement to, learn foreign language languages should be a priority. English should be required to be taught in schools because China is becoming a major business behemoth that requires English as it is the universal language in business.

A pleasant Chinese Buddhist monk in his traditional garb was among the visitors to the Great Wall. I tried to talk to him, but he did not speak English. We communicated by sign language instead.

(This picture is of the Buddhist monk, in his colorful garb,
we met at the bottom of the Great Wall. This monk was one of the few climbers,
who made it to the top of the mountain where he planted a flag)

My wife and I climbed up the Wall only for a short distance. The climbing was a little difficult and hectic as it was steep with uneven width and height of the steps. Should one be not careful going up or coming down the steps without paying attention to their steps, they may fall down the steep steps with the potential of injury.

Following our descent from the Great Wall, I saw a very fascinating Chinese man wearing western clothes and a hat. What attracted my attention to him was his goatee. He did look like the classical Chinese leaders with their long goatees. This man did not appear to be well to do but gave me the impression that he is a poor and may be unemployed, or he may be a retired worker. Nonetheless, he was a very pleasant and cooperative person. Of course, he did not speak any English and I did not speak any Chinese, yet we could communicate with body language.

Although he was sitting on the concrete bench at the entrance of the Great Wall, he stood up when I saluted him and immediately pulled his hand to shake mine. This is the typical Eastern tradition of respect by standing up to greet people regardless of their age or prior knowledge of them. This tradition is, still practiced by people all over Asian and Middle Eastern countries.

**(This fascinating Chinese man with the traditional Chinese goatee attracted my
attention as he was sitting at the bottom of the Great Wall.)**

This Chinese man was very pleasant and did not mind me touching his goatee. He
spoke no English. He smiled and laughed loudly when I started massaging his goatee.
Climbing part of the Great Wall requires lots of energy and a sustained stamina, which
neither my wife nor I could muster the energy needed to climb the steep areas of the
wall. We opted to terminate the climb after a relatively short distance.

The next stop was to go to the 2008 Olympics Campus where the famous Beijing
National Stadium, also referred to as the Bird's Nest, and the Water tube sits.

(This photo is of the "Bird's Nest' that was constructed at the 2008 Olympics Center. Construction of the structure took only four months to complete.)

On the grounds of the Olympics Campus stand impressive statues of Chinese competitors that took part in the 2008 Olympics games that were held in the city. The statues give the impression of their pride in their country's participation and achievements at the Olympics games.

(Statues of proud Chinese Olympiads exhibited at the entrance of the 2008 Olympics Campus.)

After leaving the Olympics Campus, we went to the Cloisonne Jade factory. This Jade factory is claimed to be the largest in Asia. At the exhibit, we witnessed the skilled artisans working the intricate purification and processing of Jade and working it into marketable finished product.

Leaving Beijing, our group was bussed to Suzhou, sometimes referred to as the Venice of the Orient for its exquisite canals, bridges, pagodas and beautiful gardens.

A tour to the Temple of Heaven, an architectural masterpiece of the time was breathtaking. It took over fifty years (1406-1460 AD) to build. Its intended use by the Ming and Qing dynasties, was to perform ceremonies honoring the god of harvests. Then we visited the beautiful Lingering Garden, a private garden with 500 years of history. From the Lingering Garden, we went to the largest silk factory in China, the Suzhou Silk Factory. At the factory, we listened to a long talk about the history of silk throughout the centuries. The talk was, accompanied by a slide show beginning with the Silkworm munching on Mulberry leaves up to the end of its life cycle.

The silkworm life cycle takes about 8-10 weeks from the egg to the final step in the form of a moth. The metamorphosis time to complete the process depends the proper temperature and humidity conditions. Eggs hatch in 10-25 days after being laid by, the female moth. The newly formed hatchlings become larvae, which ultimately develop into worms in 20-32 days. After that the worm morphs into Pupas in 10-14 days and then to a moth in 5-10 days. Thus, in the span of 20-33 days the silkworm, starts forming a cocoon, a process that may take up to 48 hours. The cocoon the worm makes is made of long filaments of silk that could be a kilometer in length. Morphing into a moth while inside the cocoon may take 10-14 days. Upon their release from the cocoon, male moths become very active and scramble around spending their time looking for a female to mate. After mating, each female will lay between 300 and 500 fertile eggs before it dies. The eggs start the life cycle of the silkworm that tends to perpetuate the species.

While at the silk factory, we were shown the different stages the silkworm undergoes from eggs, to larvae, to pupas, to cocoons and finally to the moth stage. In general, silkworm moths do not fly, but move around looking for a mate, as their intended job of fertilizing the eggs takes place. After the laying the fertile eggs by the female, her life is over as it succumbs to death. To my surprise, before the moths die, they are boiled and consumed as a food staple!

The woman at the Silk Factory explained, in detail, as to how the silk filaments are pulled from the cocoons. The cocoons are cut open to remove the moth inside and the silk filaments are pulled out gently then sent the manufacturing facility where the filaments are woven into sheets. The silk filaments are processed and weaved into bedspreads and other garments. It is fascinating to learn about the process, throughout the centuries, in which the silkworm is used as a source of silk filaments that are weaved into clothing, bed sheets, pillowcases, bedspreads and other household silk products.

(Photo of cocoons floating in a water trough that are ready to be processed, to pull the silk filaments.)

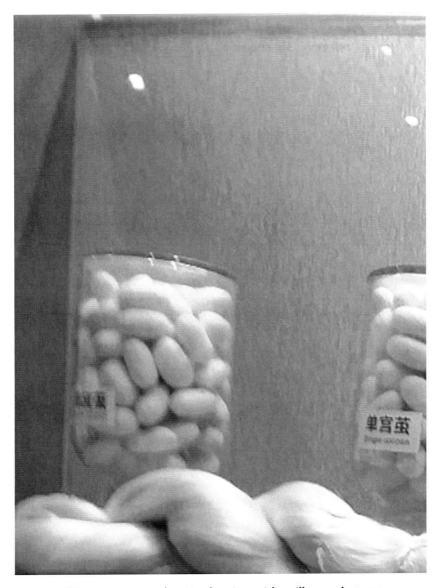

(Silkworm cocoons kept in glass jars with a silk yarn that was
obtained from the cocoons.)

(Demonstration of how newly harvested silk filaments are
being prepared for weaving.)

(Demonstration of the final product (Bed sheets) made
from silk filaments.)

(A finished product of a colorful silk bedspread that was made available for us tourists to purchase at the low factory prices!)

Whether it is the jade factory, the jewelery factories, silk factories and even general merchandise markets, one outstanding trait that cannot be missed is that sale prices are never those advertized on the tags. The prices are open for negotiation (bargaining). Should the customer be interested in buying the item and he/she knows how to bargain, and the seller willing to sell it at the price the customer offers, the sold sign appears on the item. Sale prices could see a drop in the order of 80 % of the advertised price.

Shopping malls in China, do not compare with what we are used to seeing in the United States. Chinese shopping malls, we visited can be described not as malls, but rather as baazars. The merchandise offered for sale is rarely boxed. It is kept loose and placed on the floors or hung on the walls of the shop.

The next stop was after a 4-hour bus ride from Beijing to Hangzhou, a culturally viable city with the beautiful West Lake and famous historical culdtural sites. The city lies between two high mountain ridges with the cool feeling of a summer resort. What was fascinating, to us, in that part of the country is, the tea plantations covering vast areas all over and around the city, especfially in the mountainous regions. This was the first time we saw tea plants, as we have never had seen prior to our visit to Hangzhou.

The roads in China whether in the city or on the highway are very clean, well maintained with no potholes. Highways, on both sides of the road as well as in the median are, lined with evergreen trees and flowering plants including roses. The flowering plants and roses give the roads a continuous pleasant view as the pots are replaced every so often, to maintain a beautiful look on the highways.

(Both sides of the highway and the median are, lined with trees and flowering plants that give the roads a pleasant look)

Wherever one goes in China, the scene of multiple story high rise buildings is everywhere. A construction boom engulfing China is evidenced by the presence of multiple cranes rising within any one block of the city. The high-rise buildings are primarily condominiums built for sale to the well-to-do clients.

Additionally, traffic appears to be moving smoothly and traffic jams were not observed during our visit. Traffic congestion problems are remedied by the construction of multi layered overpasses throughout the cities.

(Because of my fascination with the tea plants *Camellia sinensis*, which I have never seen before, I decided to have our picture taken at the foothill of a Tea plantation on the hillside in Hangzhou. Tea plants, in the plantations, are planted in well designed and well aintained terraces to avoid erosion when the rain hits the area)

The famed Mr. Li whose statue stands in the center of Hangzhou, is revered by the Chinese as being the encyclopedia on tea, its origins and its uses.

He was the only expert on tea who wrote a book about tea with reference to the different types of tea and their grades as regards to their health benefits.

(The statue of the famed Mr. Li, the Chinese author of the book about tea and its benefits, Mr. Li's statue erected in the city center of Hangzhou in appreciation of the knowledge he dissiminated about the health benefits of drinking tea. He explained, in his book, the different grades of tea (Green, and Black tea as to their health benefits)

Of course, the trip to Hangzhou was intended to appreciate its renowned importance of its tea plantations was very valuable and met our expectations. We visited the No.1 tea plantation in the area where we were given a detailed discussion about tea and its different grades. Green tea for one, we were told, consists of newly formed young shoots which are picked right after they appear on the tea plant. Black tea on the other hand and other types of tea are prepared from the older leaves whose color may be brown or purple. These older leaves are picked, cut and exposed to the sun to undergo fermentation. After the fermentauion process is over, the cut tea leaves are dried, processed and sent out for export.

During the discussionm we were offered a taste of the acclaimed and well-known 'Dragon Well Tea'. This tea is described to being the best known Green Tea, not only in China but also around the world!

(A tray of Green tea that was recently harvested, was brought in to show to us during the discussion.)

Needless to say, after the lecture and the discussion about tea that ensued, workers came in with different size containers filled with Green tea. We were all provided with cups of green tea, with the hope that we may like it and utimately purchase the product. The prices offered were those of factory prices which are much lower than those in the supermatkets. Some of us, uncluding myself, opted to purchase a can of the Green tea to bring home!

American companies can be seen all over the place in China. While in Zanghou, there was Starbucks Café in a Chinese Pagoda-styled structure.

.(Our picture in front of the Starbucks Café in Hangshou)

Our next stop, after leaving Hangzhou, was Shanghai. It was a 2-hour flight from Hangzhou to Shanghai. While in the waiting room at the airport, waiting to board the flight to Shanghai, I was surprised to see a sign, in English only, saying "The Military has Priority". The fact that there was no sign in Chiness suggested, to me, that this sign is directed towards the non-Chinese international visitors. It also is intended to impress the tourists of the importance of the Military, the Chinese government places on. This was the only indication of militarism I noticed throughout our stay in China.

After arriving in Shanghai we were bussed from the Shanghai International airport to the Marriott Delta Class hotel. Through my travels and stays in hotels in the United States, Europe and the Middle East, I could not remember seeing a hotel, including those of the Marriott hotels in the United States, that is as grand as this hotel is. This hotel looks grand not only on the outside, but more so in the inside too. It looked very royal in regard to its architecture and the amenities it offers. One of the amazing observations I had noticed at this hotel was its technologically advanced toilets. They open up the moment the bathroom door is opened and automatically flush without any handles, which they don't have, being touched! The hotel furnishings, whether in the lobby or in the rooms are indeed ornate. When we inquired about the room rates the concierge said the hotel charges 700 yuans/night. Considering the official exchange rate between the US$ and the Chinese yuan of 6 yuans to the dollar, that translates to roughly $117. That is very cheap when compared to hotel room rates in the United States. I know, for a fact, that room rates in my hometown of Nashville, Tennessee range from $275-$450/night!

The high hotel rates/night that were adopted in Nashville is due to the large influx of visitors and the city has become the mecca of country music lovers and those aspiring to become musicians.

(This is the entrance to the Lobby of the Marriott Delta
Class hotel in Shanghai)

(Photo of my wife in one corner of the lobby of the hotel
with its fancy décor)

SHOPPING IN SHANGHAI

AFTER AN OVERNIGHT REST AT THE HOTEL, OUR AMERICAN GROUP was bussed to the main shopping area in the city. Unlike stores in the malls in the United States, shops in shopping areas in China, are much smaller and are more or less specialized as to the products they sell. Shoes are sold only in shoe stores, clothings only in clothings stores, food outlets are only in make-shift fast food outfits.

Again advertised prices on items as seen on the sales tags are intended for people who lack the ability and knowhow to bargain. This is typical of the situation in America and in other western countries where shoppers pay the prices advertised on the price tag as these advertized prices are final. Price tags are also placed on the items in China, but these advertised prices are never final as they are open for negotiation and bargaining.

My wife and I having been raised in an area of the world where the price tags on items in the stores are meaningless and open for negotiation, The prices are not final, but open for negotiations and bargaining to reach a price acceptable to both the buyer and the seller.

Some of our American members of the group purchased clothings, electronics and luggage items. They paid the prices posted on the price tag. My wife wanted to purchase a woolen shaal whose price tag was 480 Yuans ($80.00). We bargained with the sales lady and got that shaal for 75 yuan ($12.50)! The Chinese are very shrewed business people and have a long stamina when they want to sell a product.

As there is a surplus of men over women in China, estimated to be over thirty five million eligible men over the number of eligible women, women are in great demand. Women have become a very sought-after commodoty. As a a result they have become spoilt, selective and demanding as to who they will marry. With this newly acquired and enhanced self confidence, they can opt to choose a man to marry only if he is very well to do and have deep pockets. Does this mean that love is compromised and the woman's choice of money over love will prevail? Well, not necessarily as women can choose the man to love preferably the one who is financially stable. Women are quite choosy as to who their future husbands will be. In the words of one of our female tour guides,"My future husband will have to be a millionaire, otherwise I won't marry him"! They play the game real well and their number one requirement in a husband, he must be well to do and can afford to purchase a three million dollar condominium! Is there room for love here? It has always been known that love conquers all barriers including those of economics. Will a Chinese girl marry the love of her life should he be of limited means? I should have asked this question while in China, but I did not.

One other thing that attracted my attention in China is, the importance of the number 8. The Chinese are obsessed with number 8 as they believe that the number 8 is the lucky number that will bring them good luck. They try to acqauire it and have it in their car license plates. Those who can afford it and who wish to have more good luck acquiring the number 8, they can purchase license plates with as many number 8s as they wish and fit on the license plate.

TRAVEL TO NEIGHBORING COUNTRIES

HAVING TRAVELED TO, AND MANY A TIME SPENT TIME IN, SEVERAL countires of the world including those in the Middle East including Syria, Iraq, Jordan, Saudi Arabia, Kiwait, Qatar, the United Arab Emdirates, Morocco, Lebanon, Turkey as well as England, Germany, Italy, France Switzerland in Europe, Croatia, Bosnia, and of course China and several states and cities in the United States, it was decided to visit couuntries closer to home.

In July 2019 my wife and I decided to visit Mexico. We flew from Nashville to Atlanta to connect with our daughter Kim and her family and from Atlanta, we all flew to Cancun, Mexico. From Cancun we were driven a fifty kilometer stretch to the *Playa del Carmen (*Carmen Beach*)* to go to the *Paradesus*(Paradise*) del Carment* Resort. The settings of the resort were out of this world. The resort borders the Carribean sea on the gulf on one side and the town of *Playa del Carmen* on the other.

(Photo of me, as the modern day Sphinx, sitting on a bench depicting the the
***Paradisus* (Paradise) *in Playa del Carmen resort* in Mexico)**

Food was exotic and plentiful with several casual buffet resturants and other resturants requiring formal attire. Bars are scattered all over the place. The bar at the edge of the pool, was the busiest of them all. Swimmers congrogate at the edge of the pool to order their favorite drinks while still standing in the pool. Since drinks are free, drinking binges by some guests lasted for hours at a time.

We decided to go shopping in the town and to my great and pleasant surprise, was a tall and handome native American (Red Indian) wearing his traditional garb, standing in the middle of the street. I approached him and we chatted for a while. He asked me as to where did I come from, I said the United States, but originally from *Palestina* (Palestine). Upon hearing the word *Palestina*, he gave me a very tight bear hig and said, my grand mother told me so much about *Palestina* and the palestinian people. She was saddened to see the fate of the Palestinians, their expulsion from their homes and the suffering they had and still are enduring. You (Palestinians) and us (Native Americans) are in the same sinking boat: Our country is occupied by the Europeans which they call the United States, and your country is occupied by the Jews they call Israel.

I have to admit, I did not expect *Fredrico* to know anything about Palestine or about the Palestinians, yet he proved to be well informaed on these issues!

(Photo with *Fredrico*, the Native American in *Playa del Carmen-Mexico*)

CHANGE IS A PERMANENT PHENOMENON. IT NEVER UNDERGOES CHANGE AND WHILE IT STAYS CONSTANT, EVERYTHING ELSE IS DESTINED TO CHANGE

SOCIETIES ARE MADE UP OF PEOPLE WHO THROUGHOUT HISTORY introduced changes and modification to the character of society in trying to influence the behavior and outlook of their people. The purpose of such changes in behavior stems from the need for a change from the *status quo,* being political, economic or military. Many a time, the three areas interconnect with the purpose of achieving the desired end.

On the political/military fronts, several instances where lies, deceit and greed led to wars that ended with the defeat and occupation of weaker countries and some of them divided to make them easier to rule:

1. British occupation of India and its subsequent breakup into two countries, present day India and Pakistan. Occupation of Palestine, Iraq, Trans Jordan and Egypt and of Australia as a depository for British criminals

2. French occupation of Algeria lasting for 132 years and claiming it to be a French province. Occupation of Lebanon and Syria

3. White European occupation of South Africa to become the Apartheid state of the twentieth century and, also occupation of parts of Indonesia

4. Belgian occupation of the Congo and claiming it to be the Belgian Congo

5. Spanish occupation of a large swath of Latin America

6. Portuguese occupation of Brazil and Macau in China

7. European occupation of North America-The Unites States

8. Jewish occupation of Palestine

Charles Darwin was absolutely correct when he coined the term 'Survival of the Fittest', yet he missed adding the word POWERFUL so that his statement, should read: **Survival of the Fittest and the Powerful'.**

It is documented the late Martin Luther King Jr. made great strides towards the improvement of life and the well-being of blacks and other people of color in the

United States. African Americans are, now recognized and accepted as an integral and important segment of the American fabric. Barak Obama's presidency, thankfully, elevated the economic stature of African Americans to a new level. Evidence of such improvement is realized and can be observed in their spending ability as driving late model cars and shopping in upscale stores.

The gain in the recognition of African Americans as important members of the American weave, the independence of South Africa from White rule and the abolition of the Apartheid state, gave me the false hope that the world's conscious has awakened in the way of sympathy with the oppressed people of the world. I thought the time has come for the world to recognize the injustices the Palestinians have suffered and endured under Jewish rule. I had hoped such awakening of the world conscious might bear fruit by forcing the independence of Palestine from Zionist occupation. I felt a change of heart, by the world powers, is around the corner. It has not happened yet, but I am confident it will come sooner than later.

'SIGNS OF THE TIME'

ON THE ECONOMIC FRONT, WE HAVE WITNESSED CHANGES DUE TO 'Signs of the Time'. These changes resulted from fierce competition, mismanagement, mergers or unseen disasters led to the demise of such icons that ruled the market place including, but not limited to

1. Transworld World Airlines (TWA)

2. Pan American Airways (PANAM, later PAA)

3. Eastern Airlines

4. Braniff Airlines

5. Sears Roebuck chain of stores

6. Eastman Kodak, the icon of cameras and photography films

7. K-Mart

The first two airlines ruled skies of the world, by flying passengers to the four corners of the earth. The latter two were significant players in the American skies. Sears Roebuck and K-Mart which was acquired by Sears Roebuck, were the largest chains of stores covering the 50 states of the union. They were the icons whose light has dimmed.

Another 'Sign of the Time' is the introduction of the Internet and its use as a marketing tool. The Online-marketing tools led to the emergence of economic giants like Amazon, Walmart and the like. Although the Online marketers have, lowered the cost of products to consumers, yet their lower prices had negative impacts on smaller retailers, as many of them have been forced to close shop or declare bankruptcy.

The introduction of Smart televisions had another added benefit to consumers. The smart TV added a new dimension into viewing programs, podcasts, news and movies emanating from any place on earth.

The explosion in the Information Technology (IT) sector helped connect countries of the world with the speed of light. Introduction of the 'Smart Phone' with many of its apps has become so popular that, on average, households may own one or more of such cell phone lines.

Having a Credit Cards used to be a luxury. I applied to several Credit Card vendors during the 1970s to have a credit card. Except for one, American Express, all refused to issue me a card. Many of the denying companies claimed my income was not up to their expectations to be eligible to own their card! For the past thirty years, however, I have been bombarded by at least three requests a month from Credit Card issuing companies to accept their card. The ball is in my court now and it is me and not them who is refusing their offers!

Like anything else, everything has a price. The popularity of the smart phone, among the younger generation, appears to lead to the emergence of a society that may become ruled and governed, in the future, by a bunch of illiterate leaders. The Smart phone, although a convenient means of communication, is pushing people away from each other, as no face-to-face interaction takes place between the caller and the called. Such phone users are not required to use their brains anymore, the smart phone does all the thinking for them!

In yesteryears, women enjoyed men's complements directed at them, but now these complements have become a curse and may put the male 'perpetrator' in big trouble. Whether we like it or not, the fact remains that women rule the world. Accusations of sexual assaults, unwanted sexual approaches or an unsolicited complement that had may have happened thirty years earlier, have now come to the surface and the accused perpetrator is, subjected to character assassination and possible legal action and jail time.

Money is the central part of such sexual harassment accusations, especially when the accused happens to be a high-profile person or a person with deep pockets full of money. Well, Mr. Harvey Weinstein is the latest person to be accused of sexual abuse, misconduct and harassment. This is not to deny that such sexual harassments and assaults may have taken place or to minimize their impact on the victim but why were they not reported at the time they happened? To answer the question, one needs to look further into the changes taking place in society. It is all related to money. Our society has become overly individualistic and selfish. The abundance of hungry lawyers who are willing to file a lawsuit on behalf of the plaintiff have overwhelmed the country's dockets and rendered the justice system overflowing with lawsuits.

On the political front, enemies become friends and friends become foes when it suits their purpose. Case in point is the British/American relationship. The United States was a British colony and after a grueling and brutal war between the two countries and the defeat of the Brits, the United States became a free and independent country, now the United States and Britain are the staunchest of allies with American troops stationed in Britain, suggesting that Britain is now a colony of the United States!

The installation of high intensity halogen lamps on late model automobiles emitting high intensity beams of light, has caused many problems to drivers. As these lamps produce more intense bright light, the brightness of the high beams tends to blind the drivers coming in from the opposite direction. The blinding effect becomes more acute under stormy and rainy conditions. The combination of falling rain and high beam makes it very difficult for drivers at the receiving end. The difficulty of seeing the markings on the road due to this combination of rain and the high beams leads to accidents with the possibility of loss of life. As a friendly gesture I, have tried several times to alert drivers coming from the opposite direction and who have their high beams on, to switch to low beam, by me alternating switching between low and high beams. Some drivers get the message and showed courtesy by switching the headlights from high to low beams, yet many do not. The 'don't' drivers almost invariably happen to be drivers of pickup trucks. My observations, through the years, with many of these 'don't' drivers led me to describe them as the people of the 'pickup cult'. Vast numbers of this cult have no courtesy towards other drivers and have no respect for the rules of the road. They cut on other drivers in a split second, causing a very dangerous situation with the potential of serious accidents.

We tend to value animals, especially dogs, over human beings. Dog owners walk them twice a day, snow, rain or shine. Should the dog owners be unable to walk the dogs twice a day as scheduled, they hire 'dog-walkers' to do the job for them. I have yet to see people walking with children twice a day! Dogs are the favorite pet in the American and western cultures. They are cherished and looked upon as valued members of the family. Dogs are fed, groomed and medically well taken care of. Practically speaking, no hungry dogs can be seen roaming the streets or sleeping under the bridge. People, on the other hand, do not hold the same privilege dogs have. As opposed to dogs, many kids go to bed hungry and swarms of homeless people roam the streets and sleep under the bridge!

Dogs do not shoot and kill any of their kind, but people do! We have become a violent society with shooting and killing incidents in schools, in worship places and other places where people congregate or on the highways due to road rage are daily occurrence! Is it not high time for us 'people' to learn from dogs to how to become more compassionate towards each other and become more peaceful and more respectful of human life? Is it not high time we must look at ourselves and decide as to whether we want to live in a civilized society that respects human life or in a society that lives under the rules of the jungle? We should make that decision fast before it is too late.

Having lived in the country since 1963, I have witnessed the erosion, if not the altogether disappearance, of the great American values. The great family and social American values we used to have are no longer there. The decade of the 1960s was the beginning of such an erosion. Families are disintegrating, the divorce rate is running faster than the rate of marriage. Marriage rate is in decline because many of the social taboos we used to have are now lifted and have become the norm. Young people now live together. It is becoming a given that boyfriends and girlfriends share the same bedroom and premarital sex is the norm. Why should they get married? They cherish their freedom and independence. People in a live-in relationship, have the benefit of a spouse but not the responsibility of a married couple.

It is not uncommon these days to see women of all ages, but more so among the younger generation, wearing more 'stylish' and yet quite revealing clothes. Such stylish garments show half of their bosoms and the short and loose skirts hanging around the upper thighs are short enough to show their underwear!

It appears, as though people are getting crazier by the hour. Children are bringing guns to school and bullying other kids who they do not like. Killing of innocent people in schools, the workplace or places of worship where people congregate is almost a daily occurrence. Even the police, who are supposed to protect the public, are themselves being targeted by gun-toting criminals. Drivers whether on the highway or on city streets are also being killed because of road rages. All these evil activities may be related to the way our children are raised. They are told, beginning at a very young age, they can do anything they want! Well, the price we are paying for such crimes nowadays, stems from such freedom to do what they want. Is it not time we wake up before animal instincts overwhelm us and take over our ability to reason and be rational?

LIFE EVENTS REVOLVE AROUND SELFISH NEEDS AND SELF INTEREST

GOVERNMENTS IN GENERAL AND THOSE ELECTED BY THE PEOPLE ARE supposed to act in the best interest of the electorate just like parents looking after the wellbeing of their own children. Politicians elected to govern are selected, by the people, with the anticipation that these politicians meet the needs and aspirations of the people that elected them, meaning it is a two-way street. It is not different from the manner individuals act. Let us take the employer/employee situation: An employer offers a job to an employee, only when the employer is convinced the employee has the potential of meeting the needs of the business as set by the employer.

When it comes to friendship between individuals, it is not any different from that of the employer/employee situation. It is a symbiotic relationship. Friends tend to rely on each other, and use each other, to satisfy emotional and psychological needs when discussing an issue, either one or both may have. Two opinions may be better than one.

In the case of LOVE, again it involves satisfying the selfish needs of either one or of both. In addition to physical attraction between the two which happens at first, emotional attachment between the two individuals follows next. The emotional attachment reaches its height when either one or both parties to the love affair, become anxious and have dreams, as to when will they again meet and see the one they love. The emotional interaction between the two lovers is not different from that of the politician and the electorate or that of the employer/employee situation. Love between two individuals entails satisfying the emotional and ultimately the sexual needs of either or of both parties in the love affair.